HISTORIC PHOTOS OF
RALEIGH-DURHAM

TEXT AND CAPTIONS BY
DUSTY WESCOTT AND KENNETH PETERS

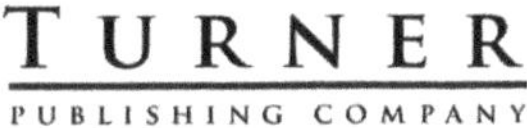

In this rooftop view of Trinity College, ca. 1904-6, one can see Craven Memorial Auditorium, the Library, Alspaugh Dormitory, and Crowell Science Building. Erwin Mills and Ninth Street are in the background.

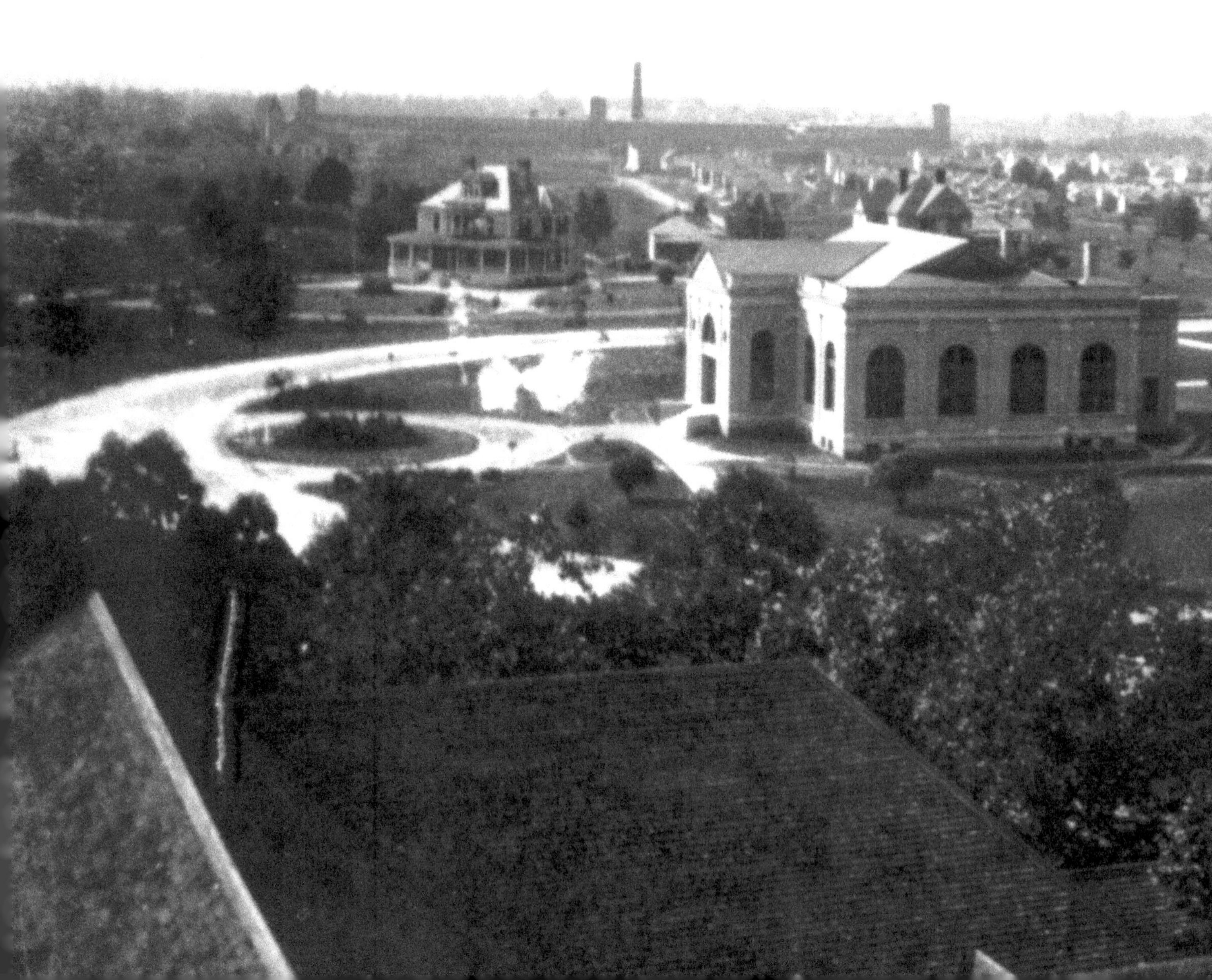

HISTORIC PHOTOS OF
RALEIGH-DURHAM

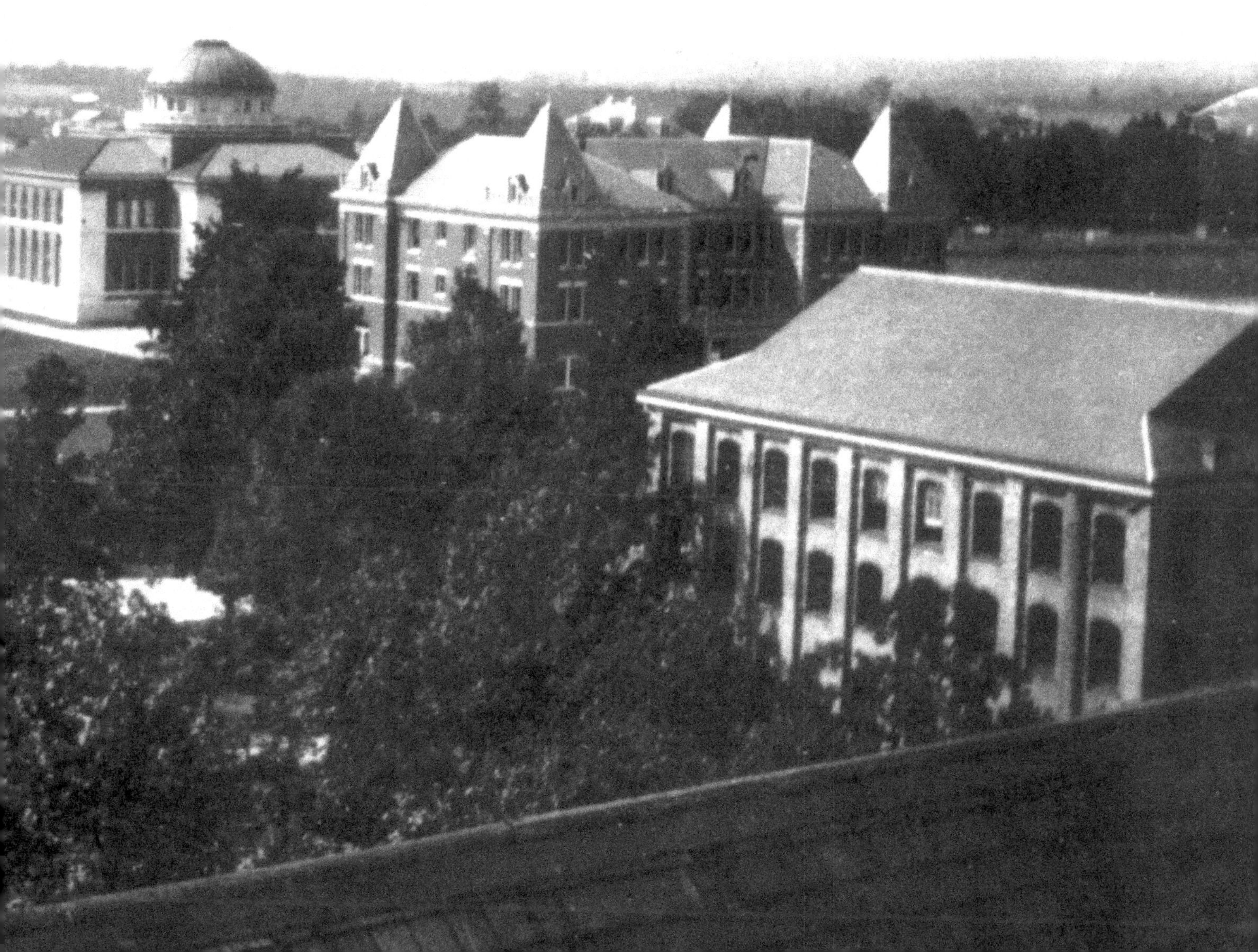

Turner Publishing Company
www.turnerpublishing.com

Historic Photos of Raleigh-Durham

Library of Congress Control Number: 2007923665

ISBN-13: 978-1-59652-338-8
ISBN-10: 1-59652-338-7

Printed in the United States of America

ISBN 978-1-68336-952-3 (hc)

Contents

Two Raleigh trolley cars pass each other in this undated photograph.

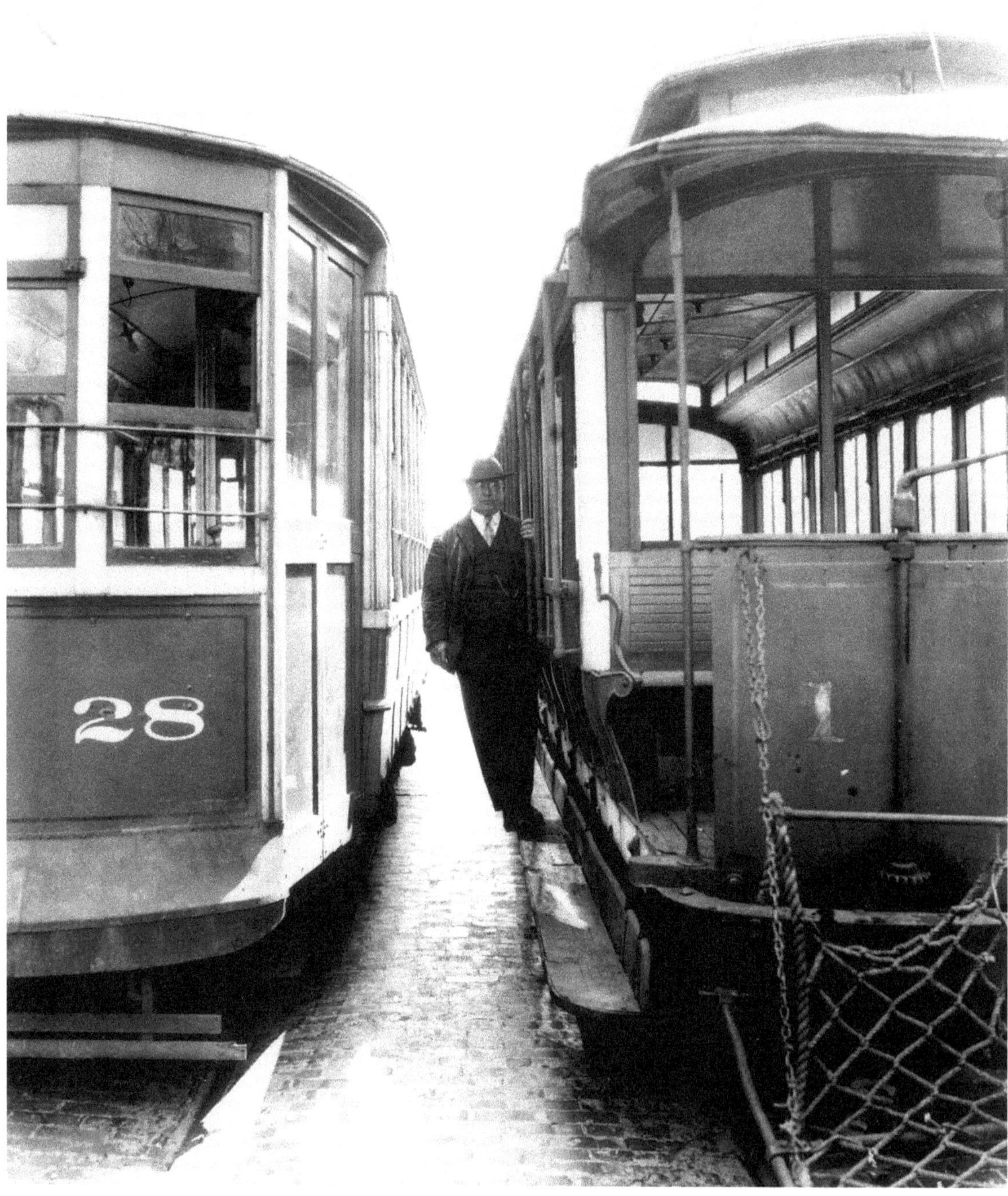

ACKNOWLEDGMENTS

This volume, *Historic Photos of Raleigh-Durham,* is the result of the cooperation and efforts of many individuals and organizations. It is with great thanks that we acknowledge in particular the valuable contribution of the Durham County Library's Durham Historic Photographic Archives, North Carolina State Archives, and the Library of Congress.

Preface

Raleigh-Durham has thousands of historic photographs that reside in archives, both locally and nationally. This book began with the observation that, while those photographs are of great interest to many, they are not easily accessible. During a time when Raleigh-Durham is looking ahead and evaluating its future course, many people are asking, How do we treat the past? These decisions affect every aspect of the city—architecture, public spaces, commerce, infrastructure—and these, in turn, affect the way that people live their lives. This book seeks to provide easy access to a valuable, objective look into the history of Raleigh-Durham.

The power of photographs is that they are less subjective than words in their treatment of history. Although the photographer can make decisions regarding subject matter and how to capture and present it, photographs do not provide the breadth of interpretation that text does. For this reason, they offer an original, untainted perspective that allows the viewer to interpret and observe.

This project represents countless hours of review and research. The researchers and writer have reviewed thousands of photographs in numerous archives. We greatly appreciate the generous assistance of those listed in the acknowledgments of this work, without whom this project could not have been completed.

The goal in publishing this work is to provide broader access to this set of extraordinary photographs which seek to inspire, provide perspective, and evoke insight that might assist people who are responsible for determining Raleigh-Durham's future. In addition, the book seeks to preserve the past with adequate respect and reverence.

With the exception of touching up imperfections caused by the damage of time and cropping where necessary, no other changes have been made. The focus and clarity of many images is limited to the technology and the ability of the photographer at the time they were taken.

The work is divided into eras. Beginning with some of the earliest known photographs of Raleigh-Durham, the first section records photographs from before the Civil War through the late nineteenth century. The second section spans the early years of the twentieth century through the World War I era. Section 3 moves to the twenties and thirties. The last section covers the World War II era up to recent times.

In each of these sections we have made an effort to capture various aspects of life through our selection of photographs. People, commerce, transportation, infrastructure, religious institutions, and educational institutions have been included to provide a broad perspective.

We encourage readers to reflect as they go walking in Raleigh-Durham, strolling through the city, its parks, and its neighborhoods. It is the publisher's hope that in utilizing this work, longtime residents will learn something new and that new residents will gain a perspective on where Raleigh-Durham has been, so that each can contribute to its future.

Todd Bottorff, Publisher

Shoe shiners work their trade on a Durham street, ca. 1940.

A Tale of Two Cities

(1860–1899)

Thanks to media marketing, modern census figures, and a shared international airport, "Raleigh-Durham" exists in the minds of many Americans as a single city in the southeastern United States. However, as native Tar Heels are well aware, Raleigh and Durham are two distinct communities that lie about 25 miles apart within the rolling hills of Piedmont North Carolina. Each has a fascinating history that makes it unique and worthy of individual study.

Created as one of America's earliest planned cities, Raleigh was established in 1792 as the first permanent seat of government for the State of North Carolina. Carved out of an oak forest on 1,000 acres of land purchased from Wake County plantation owner Joel Lane, the new town struggled in its early years, hampered by poor transportation modes, a lack of economic enterprises beyond state government, and—in 1831—the loss of the original 1794 Statehouse in a disastrous fire.

Following the Civil War, the city slowly recovered economically as its main retail avenue—Fayetteville Street—became the commercial capital for Eastern North Carolina. The advent of a streetcar system in the 1880s, and the establishment of no fewer than six institutions of higher learning by 1899, made possible a comfortably affluent middle-class population in the absence of heavy industry and home-grown industrial magnates.

A bit more than half a century younger than Raleigh, Durham grew around a railroad station established in rural Orange County. In 1849, Dr. Bartlett Durham gave less than four acres to the North Carolina Railroad; Durham's station was built and named in his honor. The first post office opened in 1853, but the town was not incorporated until 1869. The new town, wanting a stronger voice, petitioned the state legislature in 1881 to create Durham County from portions of Orange and Wake counties.

The first tobacco factory opened in 1858. Growth was slow until after the Civil War when local industrialists opened their own factories and Durham's main industry began to draw worldwide attention. Textile manufacturing plants were opened to make the cloth bags for tobacco. It was also during this period that Washington Duke and Julian S. Carr donated money and land to Trinity College on the condition that it relocate from Randolph County to Durham. It did so in 1892.

Created as the state's capital city in 1792, Raleigh was laid out according to a plan drawn up by state senator William Christmas. The plan included four main thoroughfares radiating outward from the central statehouse. The southern avenue—Fayetteville Street—became Raleigh's commercial district. This early photograph of Fayetteville Street, thought to be from the 1860s, shows E. Besson's Tailor Shop.

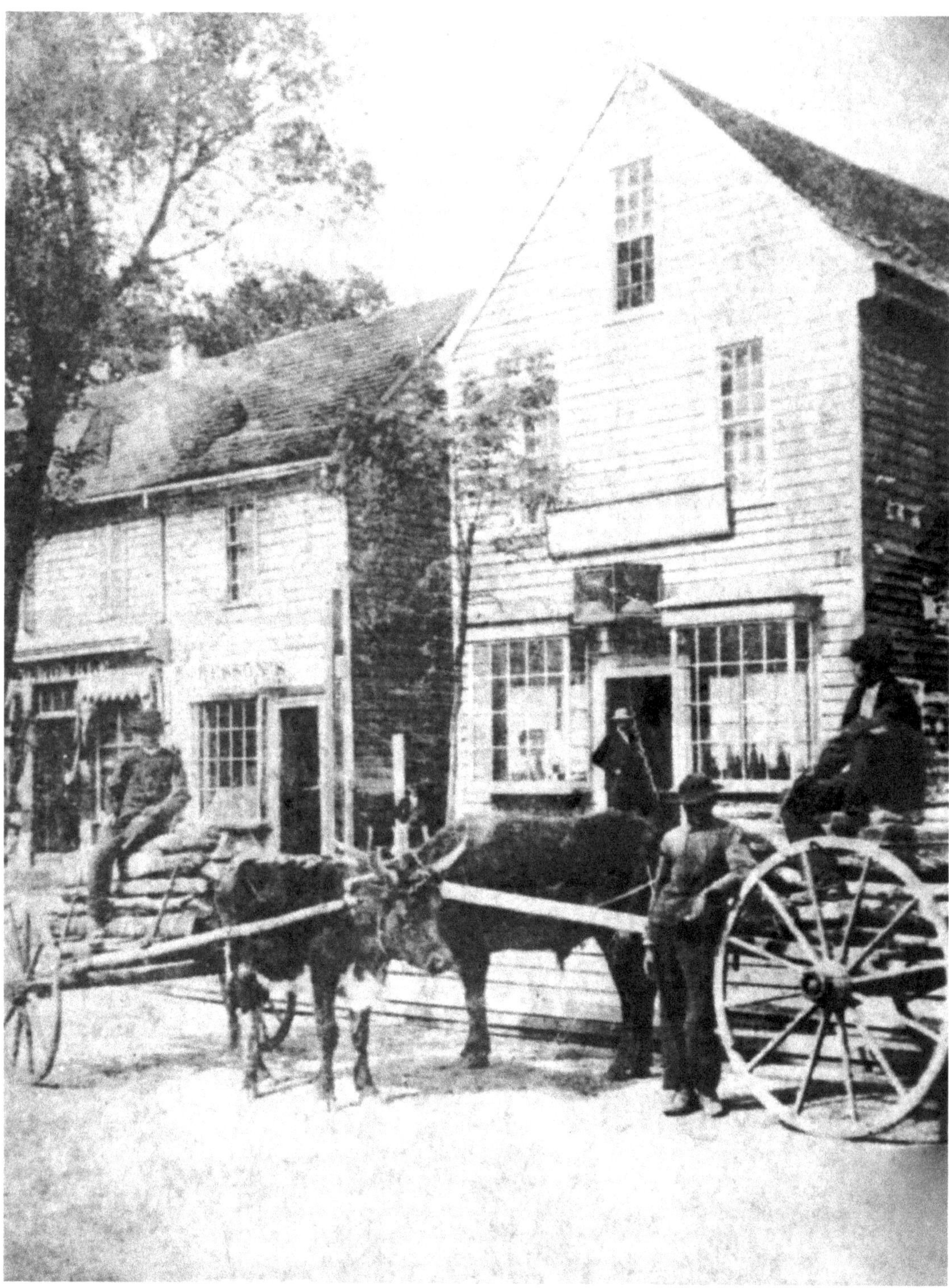

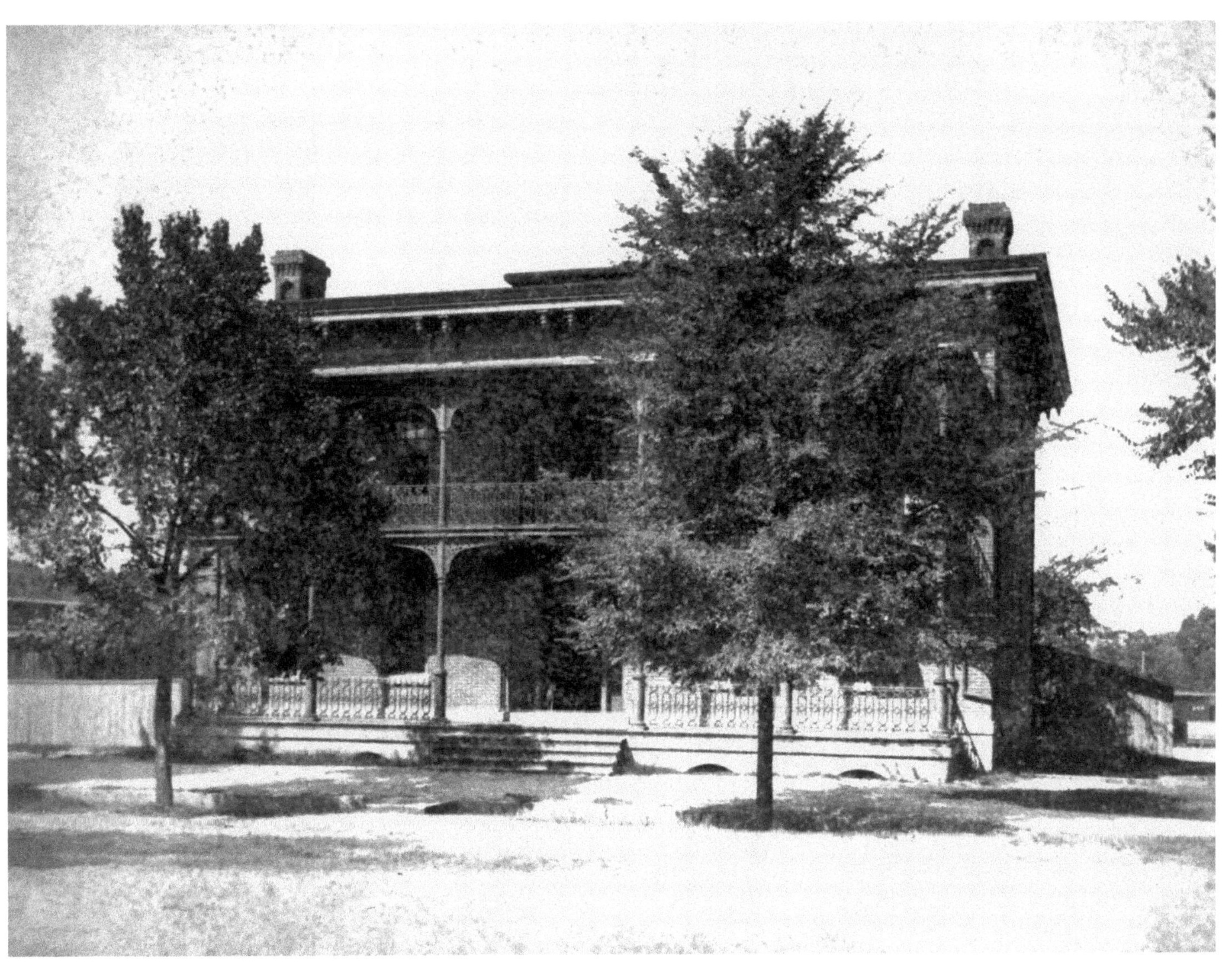

The Raleigh and Gaston Railroad Office Building, ca. 1870s. Constructed in Raleigh during the early 1860s to house offices for the first railroad to serve the capital city, this building was embellished with a wrought-iron front porch in the 1870s. Later known as the Seaboard Coast Line Building, after that railroad absorbed the Raleigh and Gaston line, the structure was moved in 1977 from its original location to its present home at 413 North Salisbury Street.

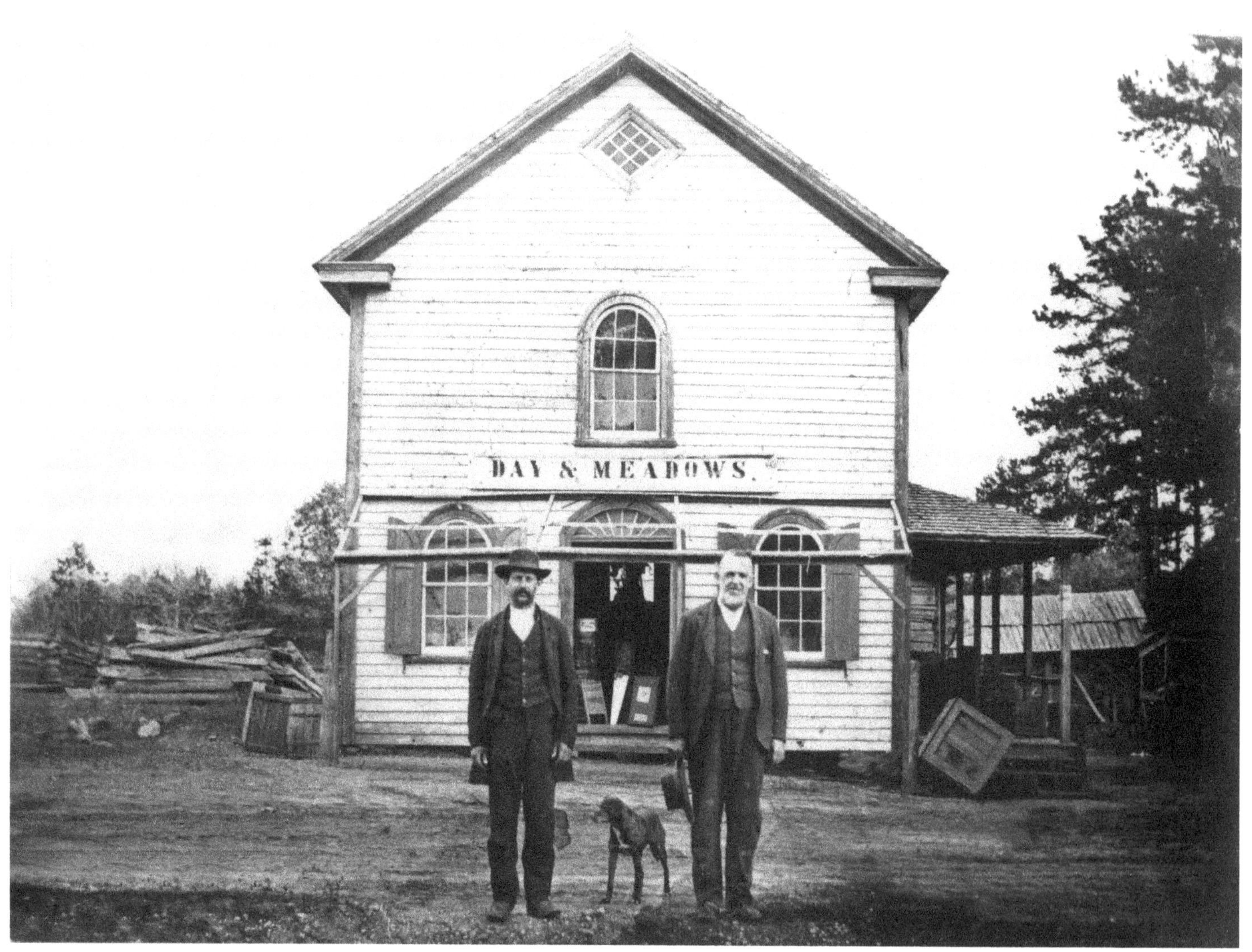

This 1870 image shows merchants Day and Meadows standing in front of their Durham store.

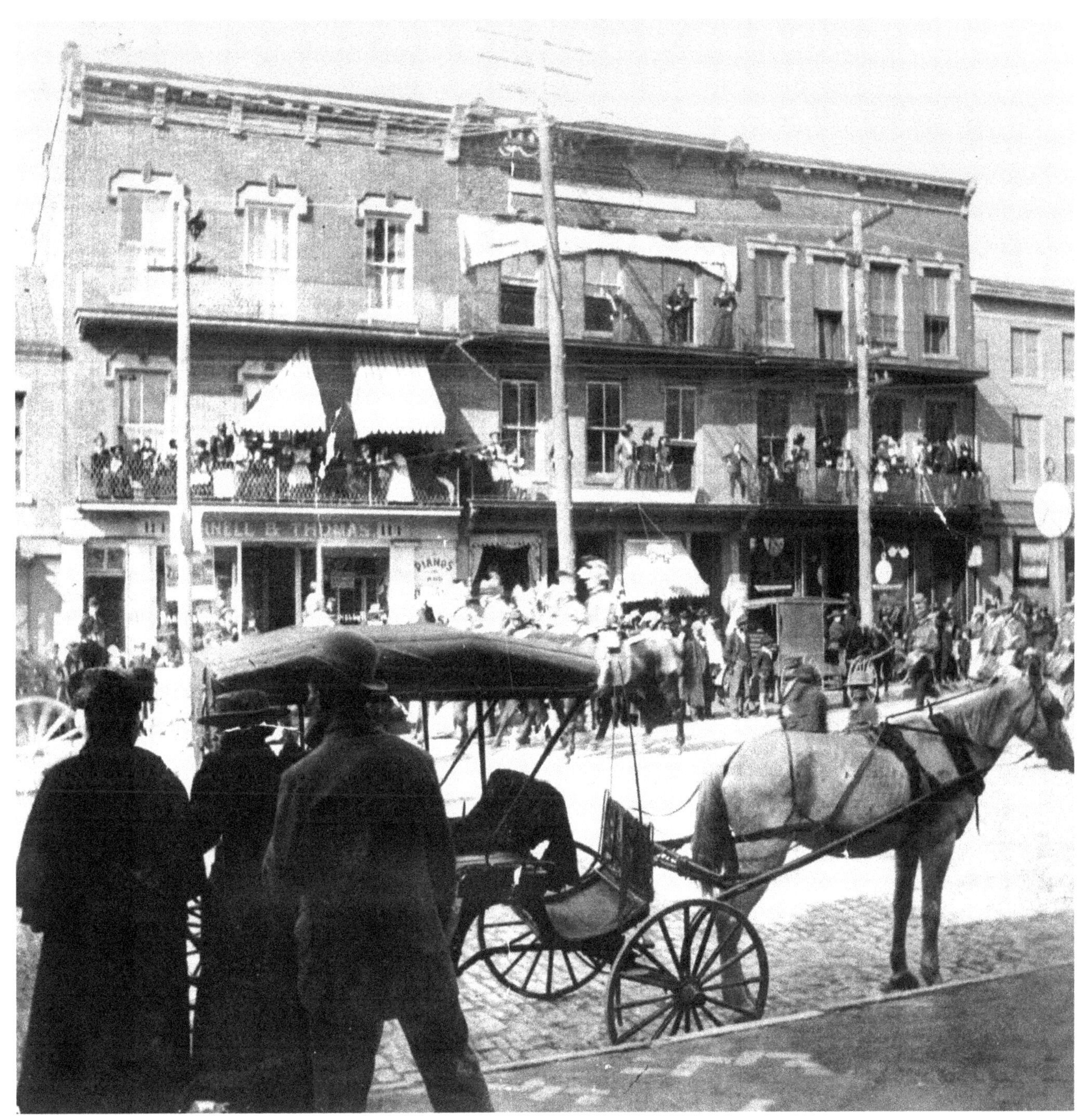

This undated photograph depicts a parade marching along Raleigh's Fayetteville Street.

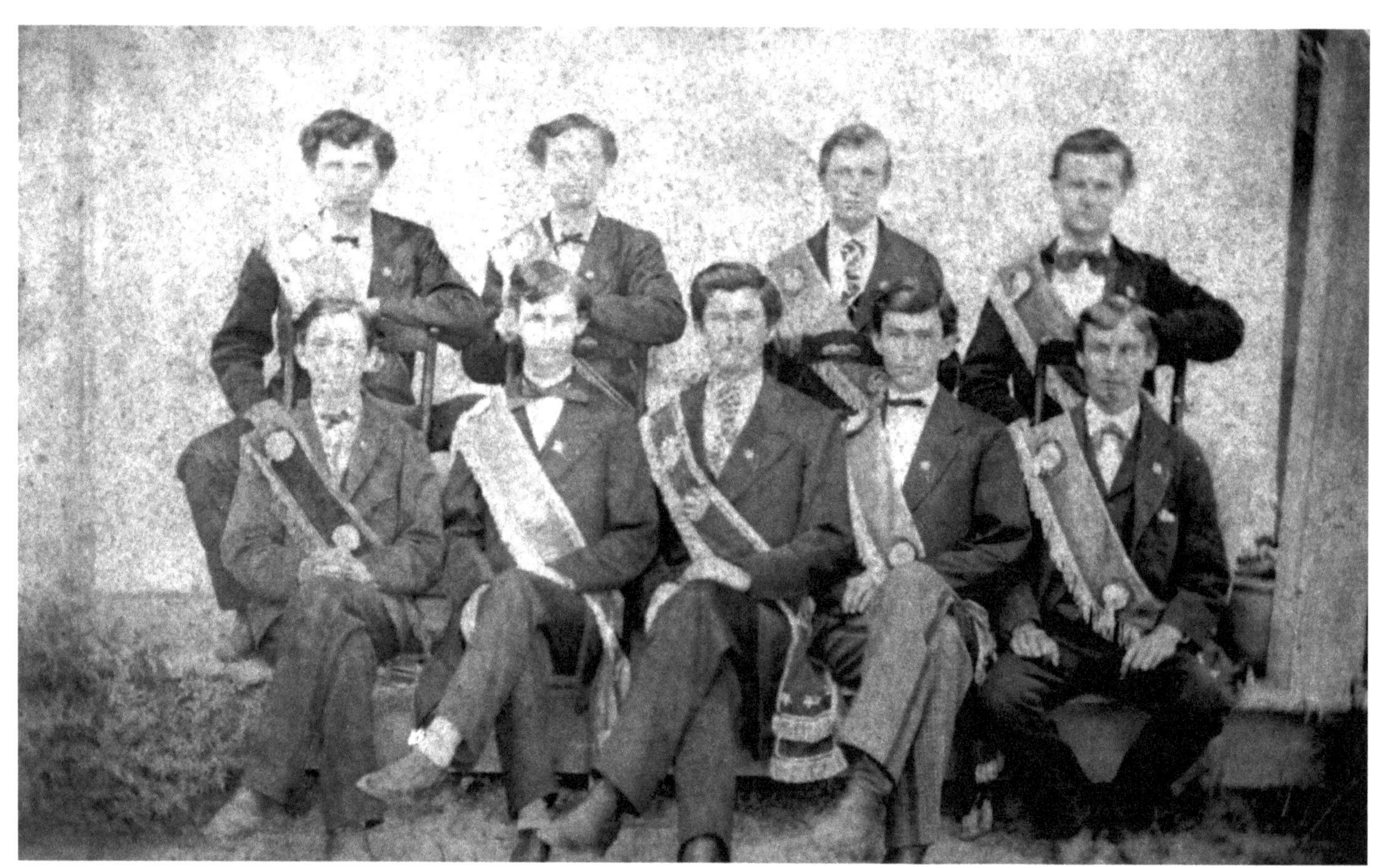

The institution now known as Duke University in Durham can trace its roots back to a Randolph County schoolhouse opened in the late 1830s. Rechartered as Normal College in 1851, the school changed its name to Trinity College in 1859 and continued to operate within Randolph County until the 1890s. These nine Trinity College marshals, wearing sashes and lapel pins, are dressed and ready for a college function, ca. 1871.

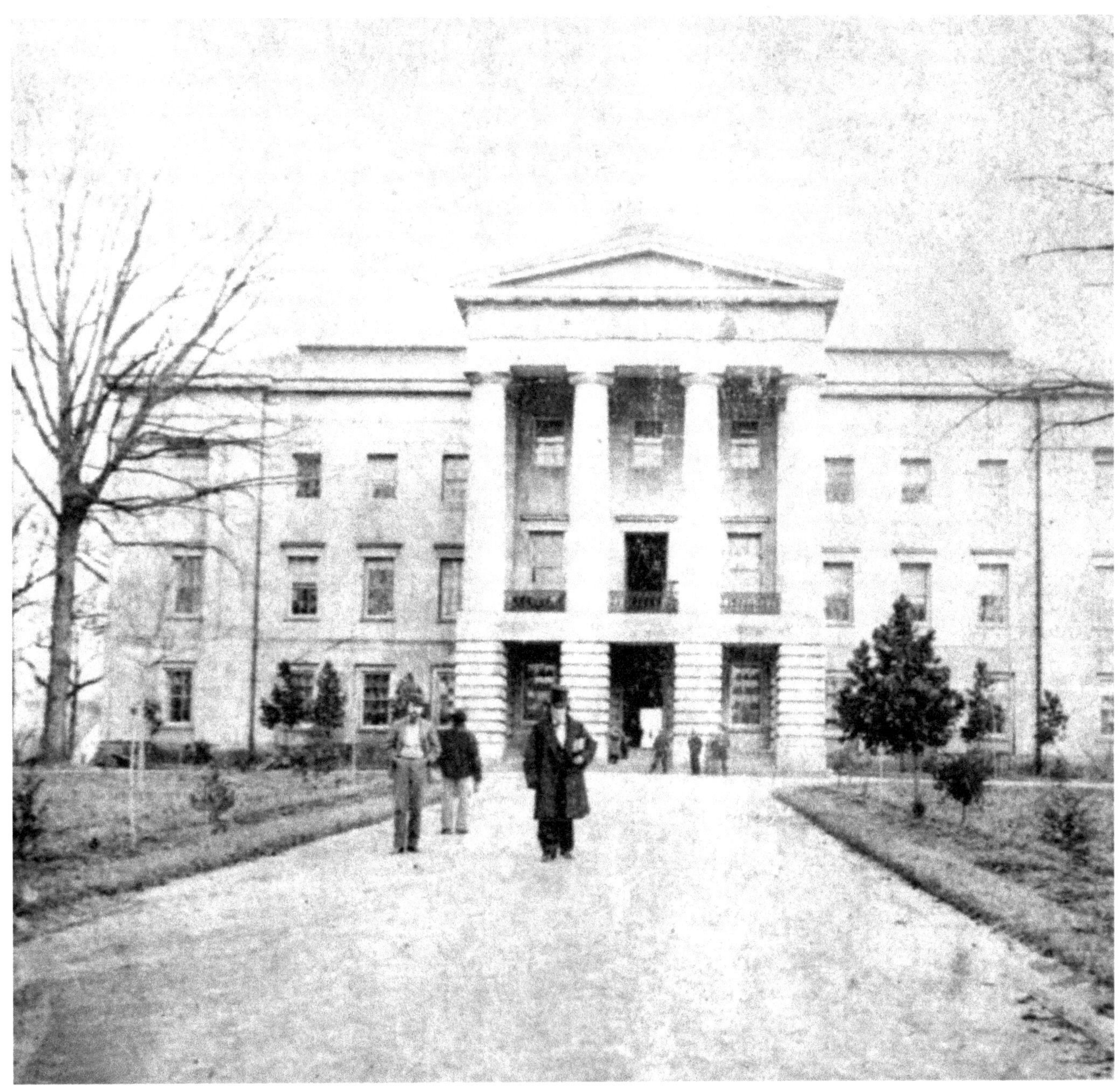

This view of the North Carolina State Capitol was recorded in 1861 and shows Governor David Reid in the foreground. A graceful granite structure that was completed between 1833 and 1840, this statehouse was built to replace an earlier 1794 building that burned to the ground in June 1831.

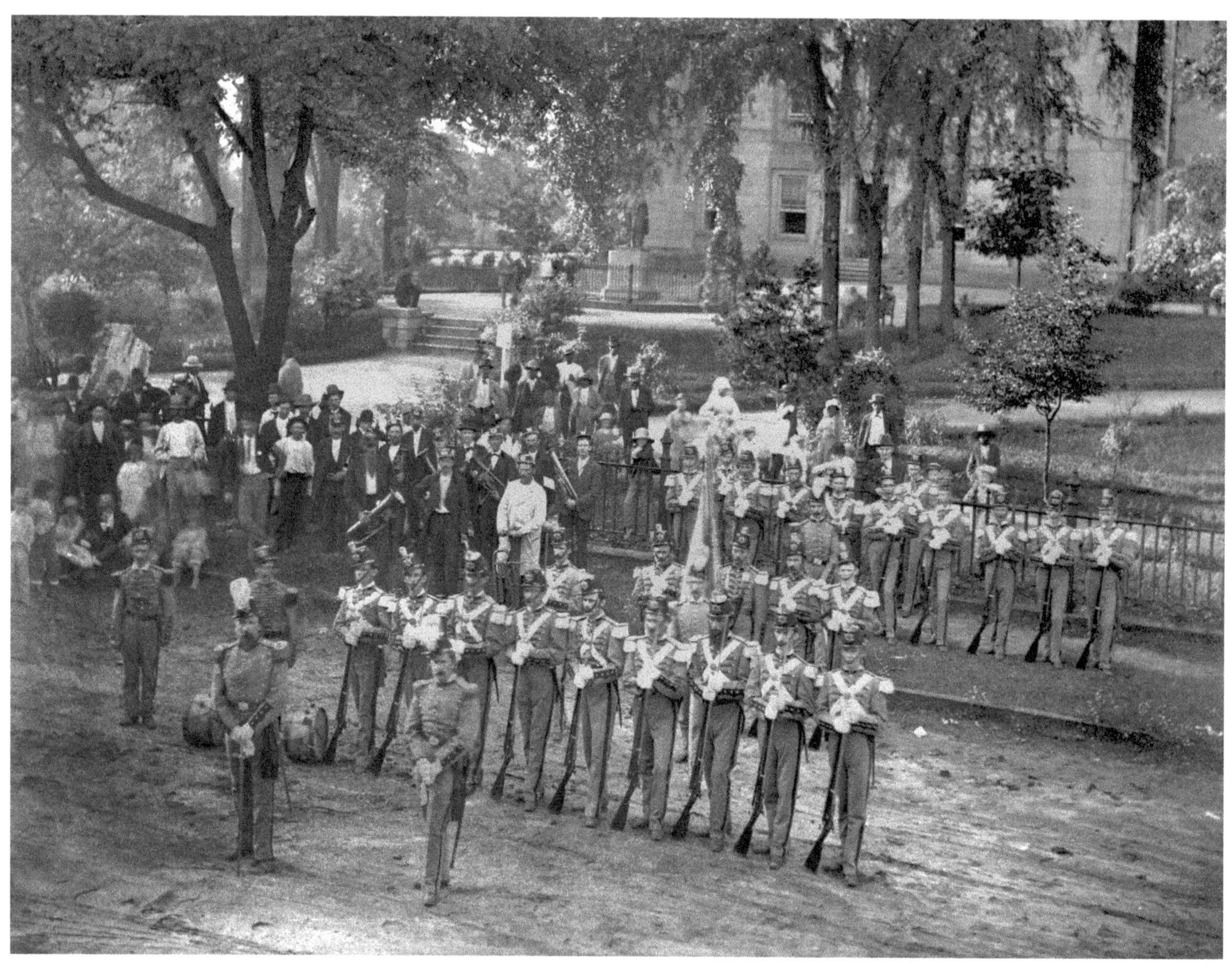

A unit of the Raleigh Light Infantry lines up along Morgan Street just south of the North Carolina State Capitol, ca. 1875.

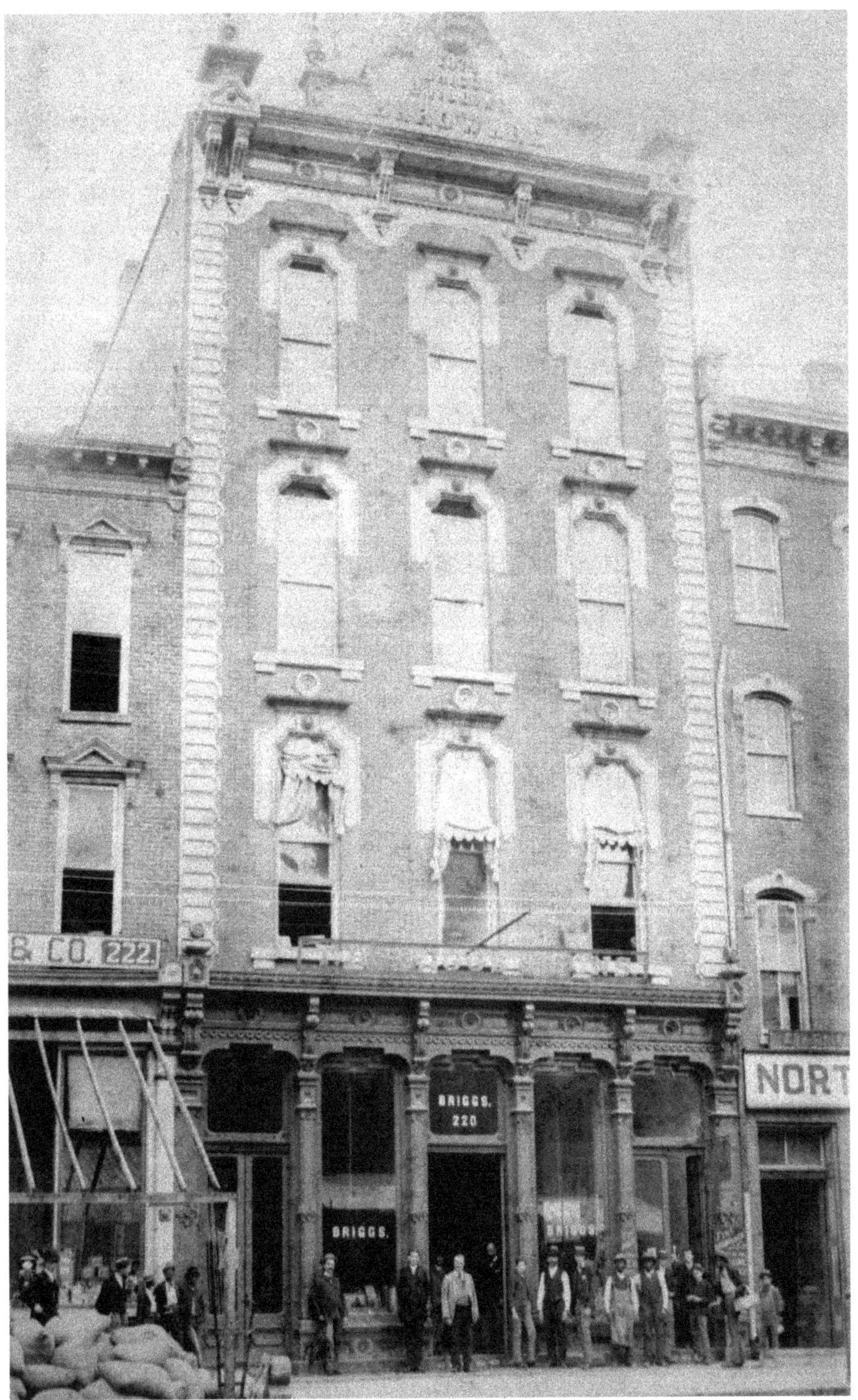

A Raleigh landmark for more than 130 years, the Briggs Building opened in 1874 as a home for Thomas H. Briggs & Sons, a building supply and hardware business. The Briggs family did business on the first floor, renting out the upper floors to other retailers. After the family-owned hardware business moved to a suburban location in 1995, the building was sold and renovated for use by non-profit organizations.

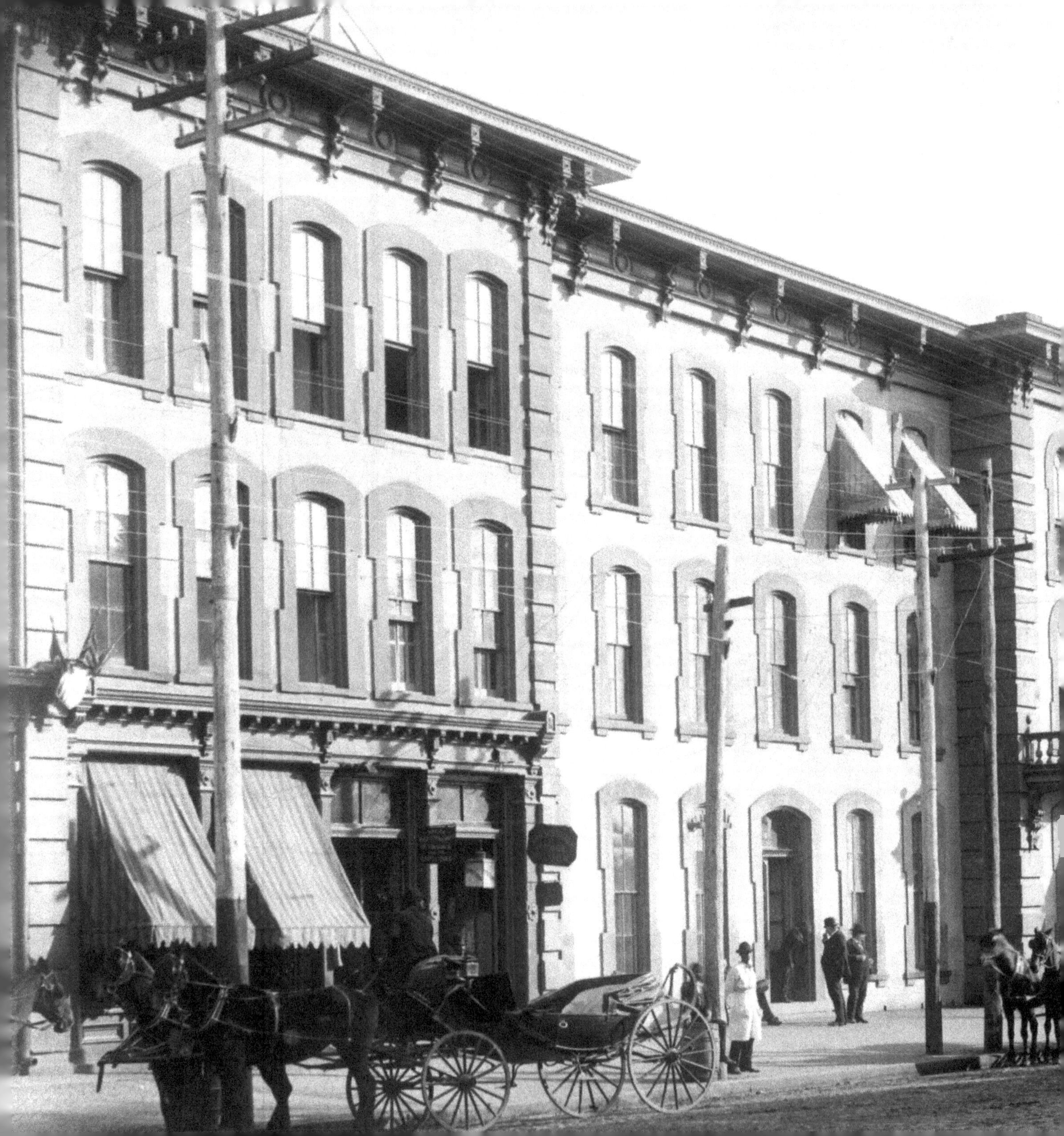

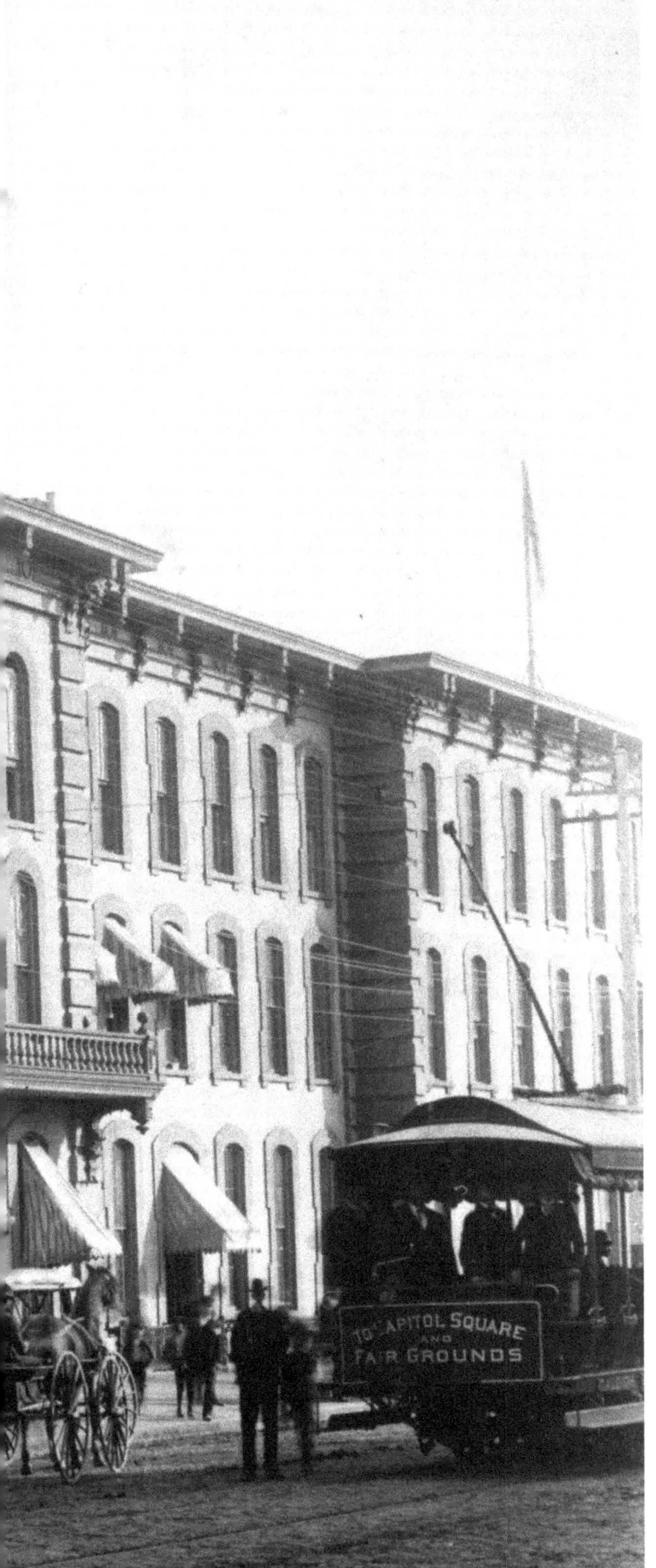

Opened in 1850 on Raleigh's Fayetteville Street, the Yarborough House quickly became known as the city's finest hotel. Over the years it would host the likes of William Jennings Bryan, Andrew Johnson, William Howard Taft, Woodrow Wilson, and—at the height of the Civil War—Mrs. Jefferson Davis, First Lady of the Confederacy. The hotel fell victim to a destructive fire in July 1928 and was not rebuilt.

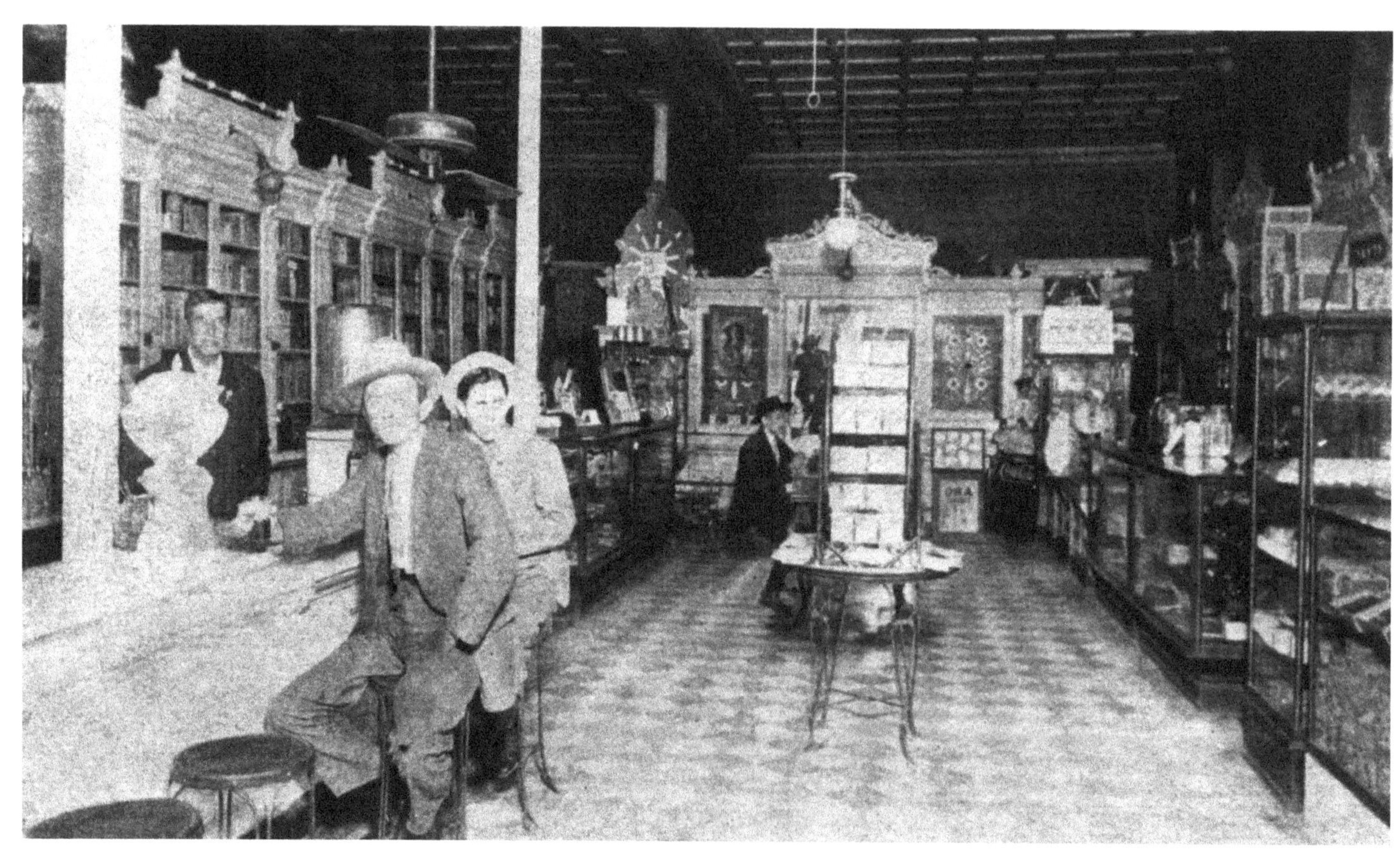

Owner Adrian Healy Michaels stands behind the counter of his Durham pharmacy, ca. 1880.

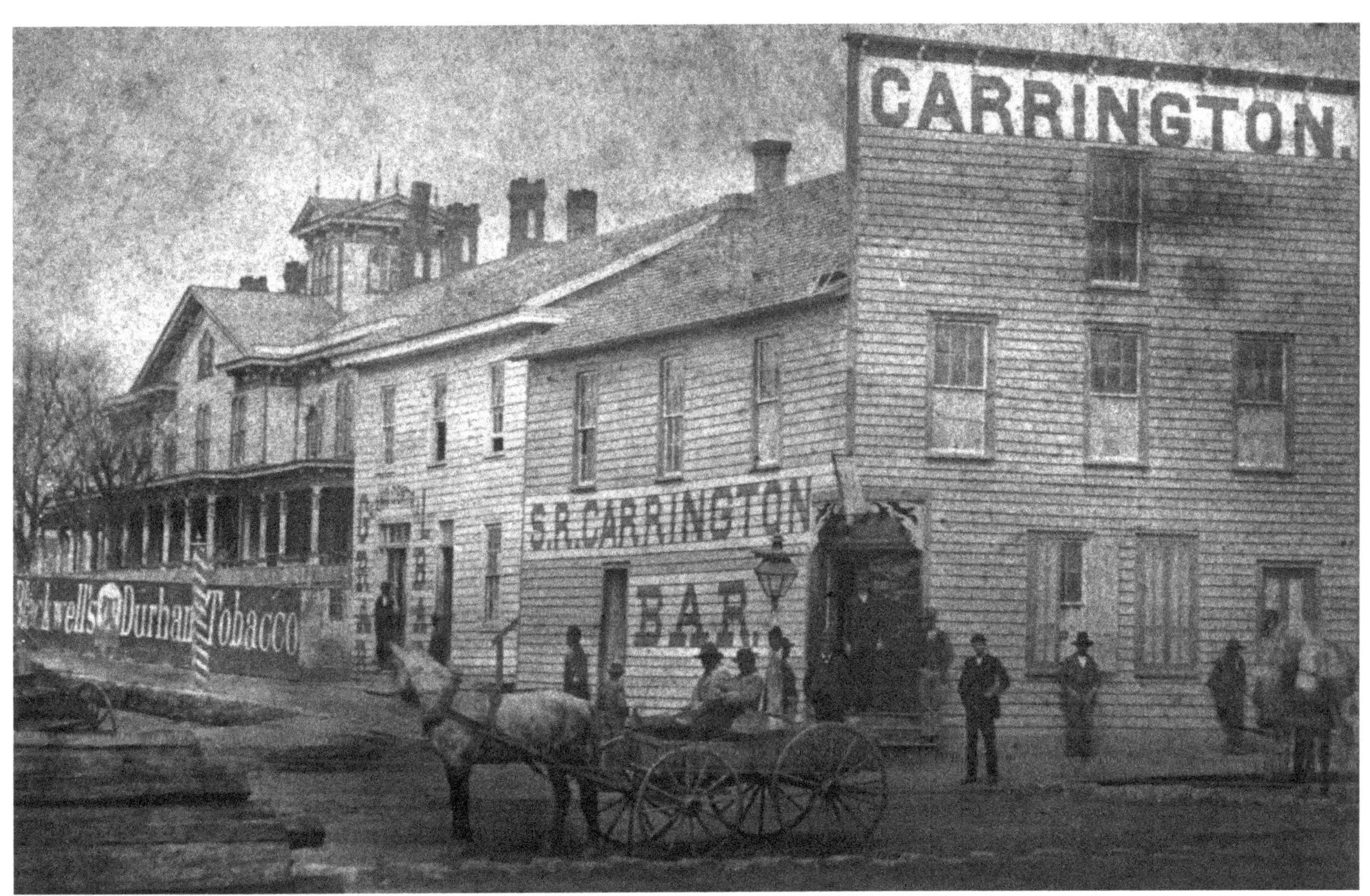

Carrington's Bar and Hotel in Durham, ca. 1880. Against the wishes of Alvis Kinchen Umstead, then chairman of the Durham County commissioners, S. R. Carrington was issued a license to sell beer in early 1882.

The simplest modes of transportation were sometimes relied on in nineteenth-century North Carolina. This image of the North Carolina State Capitol from ca. the 1880s includes an ox-drawn cart.

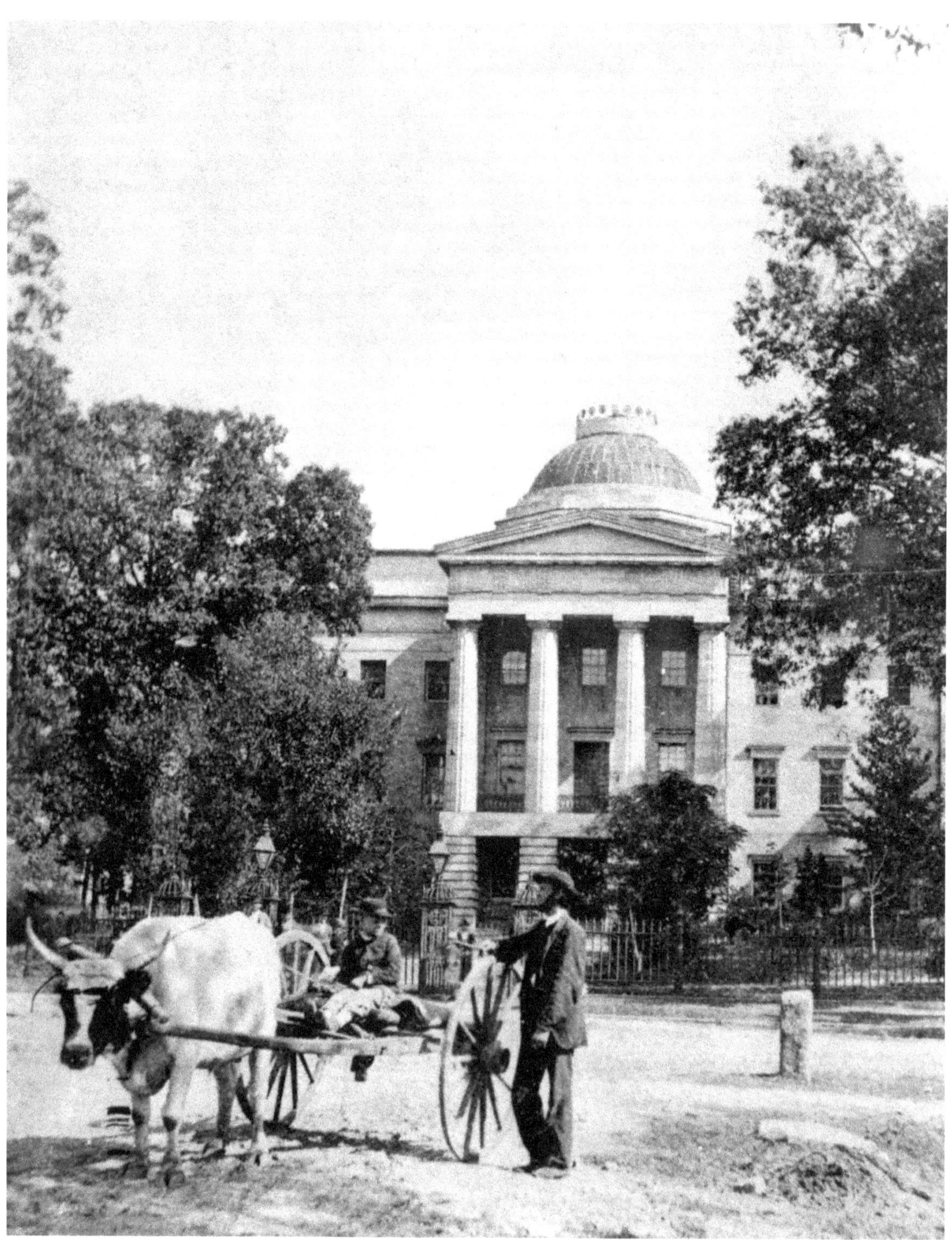

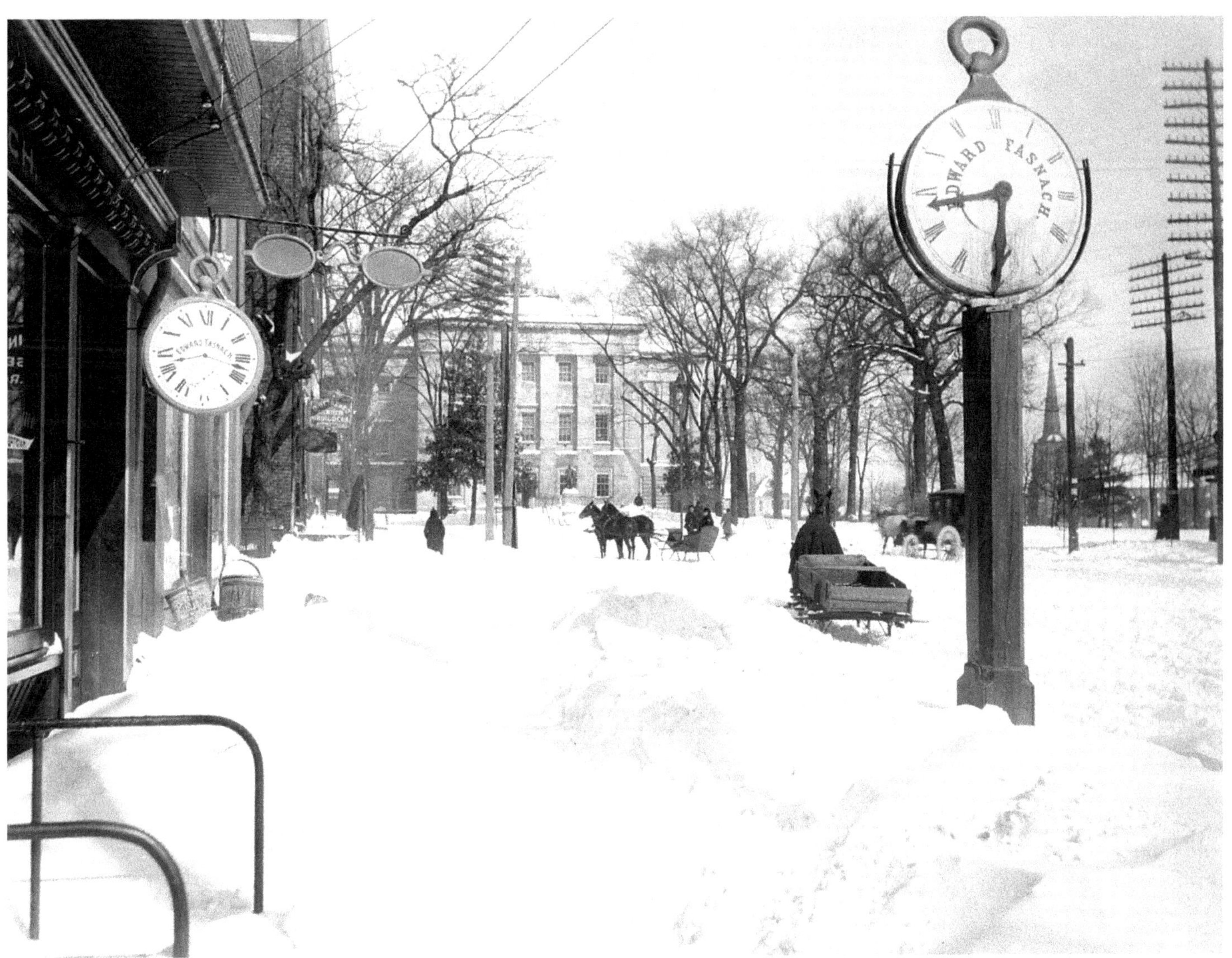

The 100-block of Fayetteville Street in Raleigh following the Great Blizzard of 1899. Striking the Eastern Seaboard in February, the storm brought record snowfall to cities from Georgia to New England. In Raleigh, 17.7 inches of snow fell, a record that stood until 1927.

Merchants along the 200-block of Fayetteville Street in Raleigh dig out from under the snow dumped during the Great Blizzard of 1899.

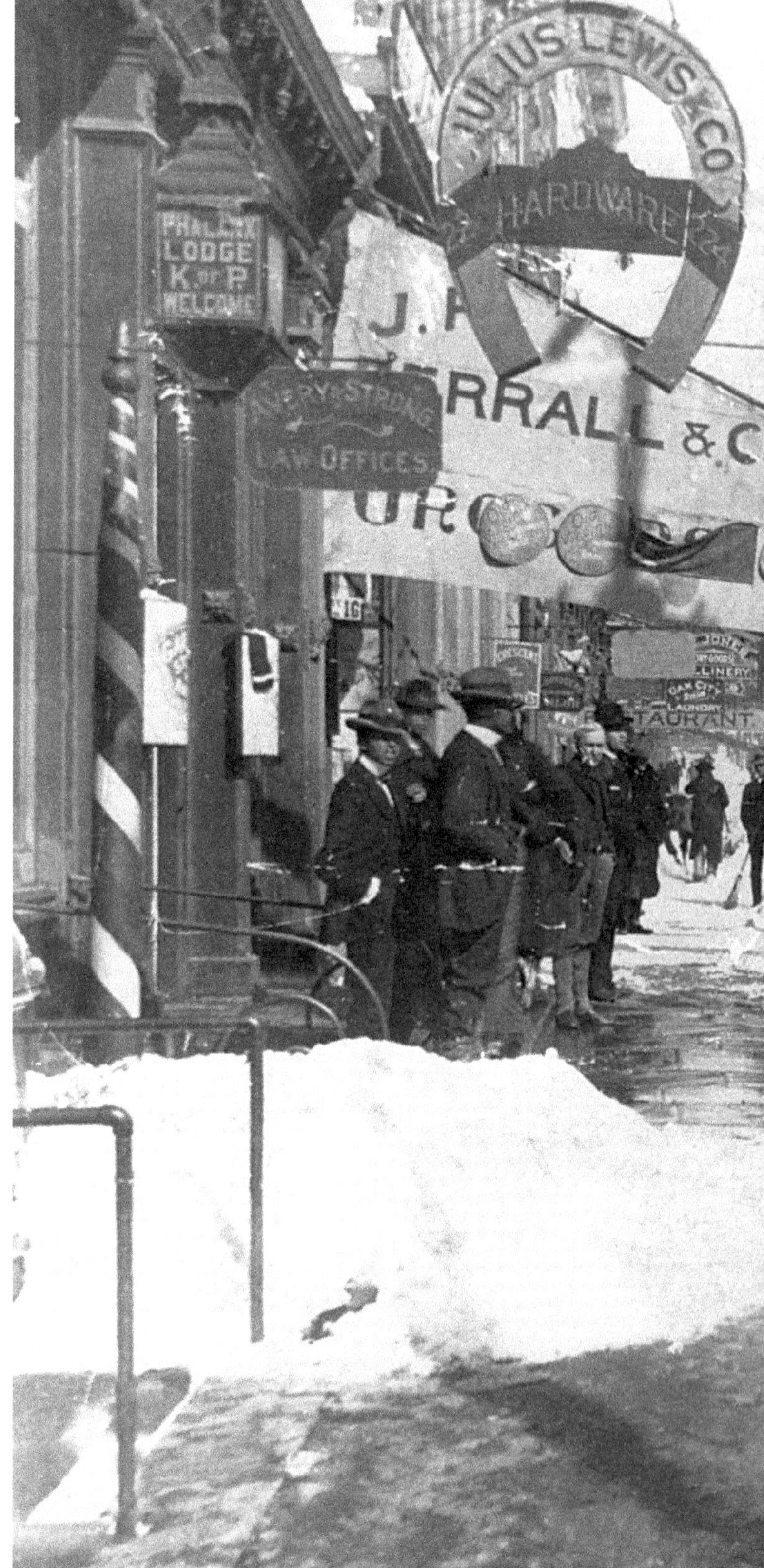

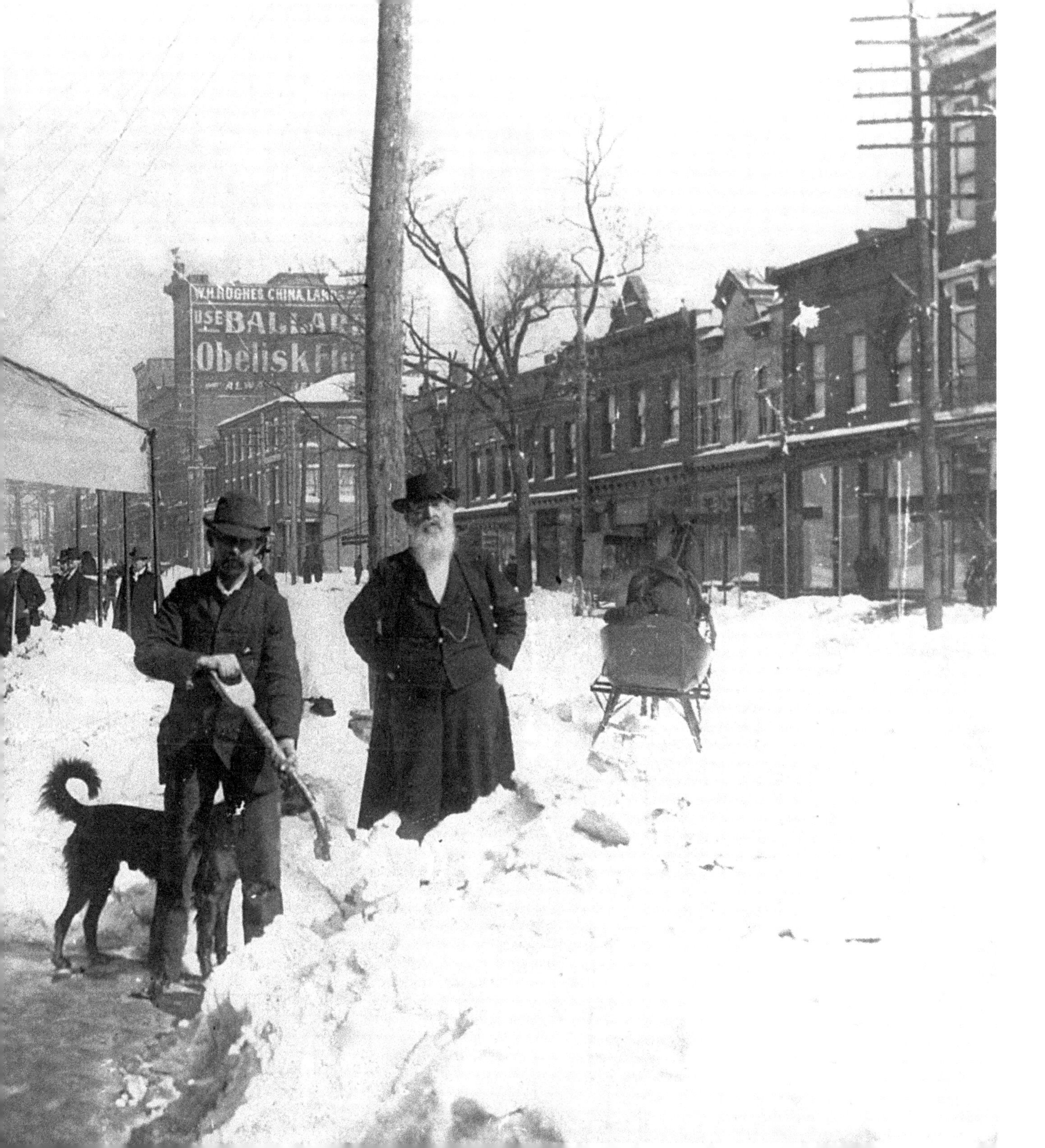
CHINA
USE
Obelisk

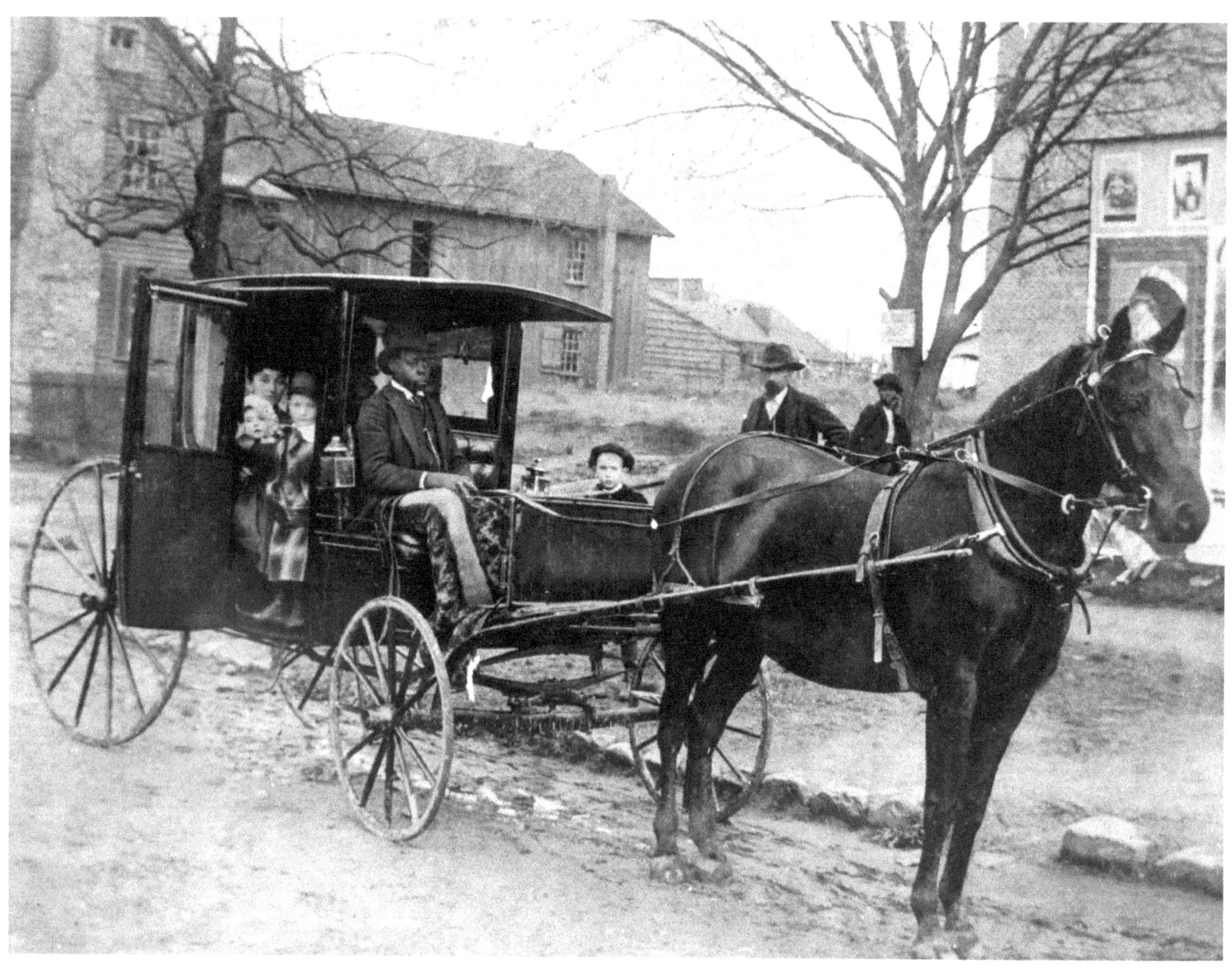

By 1880 W. Duke, Sons & Company had grown into one of America's largest tobacco businesses. Joined by sons Brodie, Benjamin, and James, Washington Duke was one of Durham's leading philanthropists. Seen here are Mrs. Benjamin Duke and her two children as they depart on a winter outing, ca. 1890.

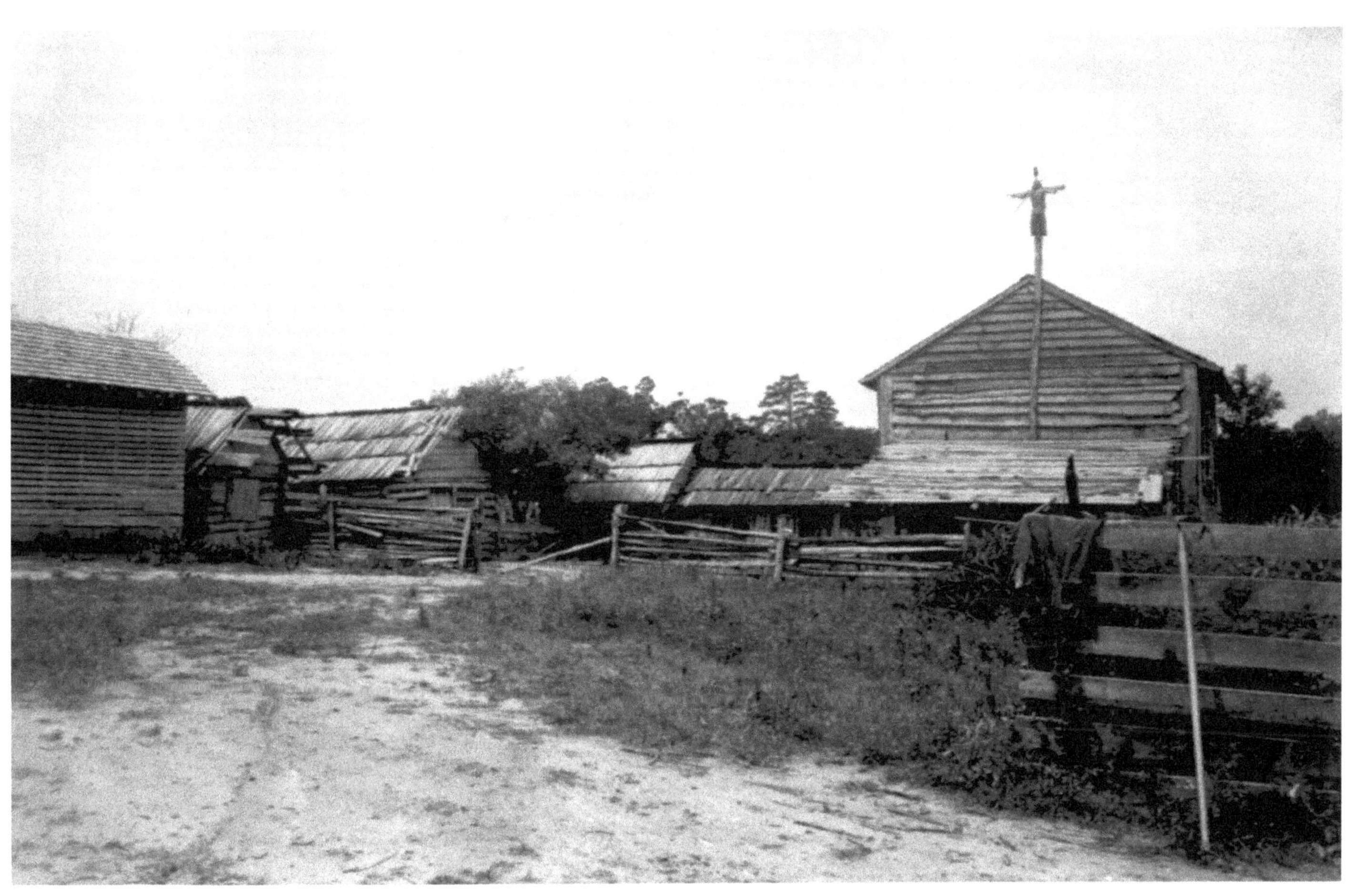

The tobacco factories at the Duke homestead, ca. 1890.

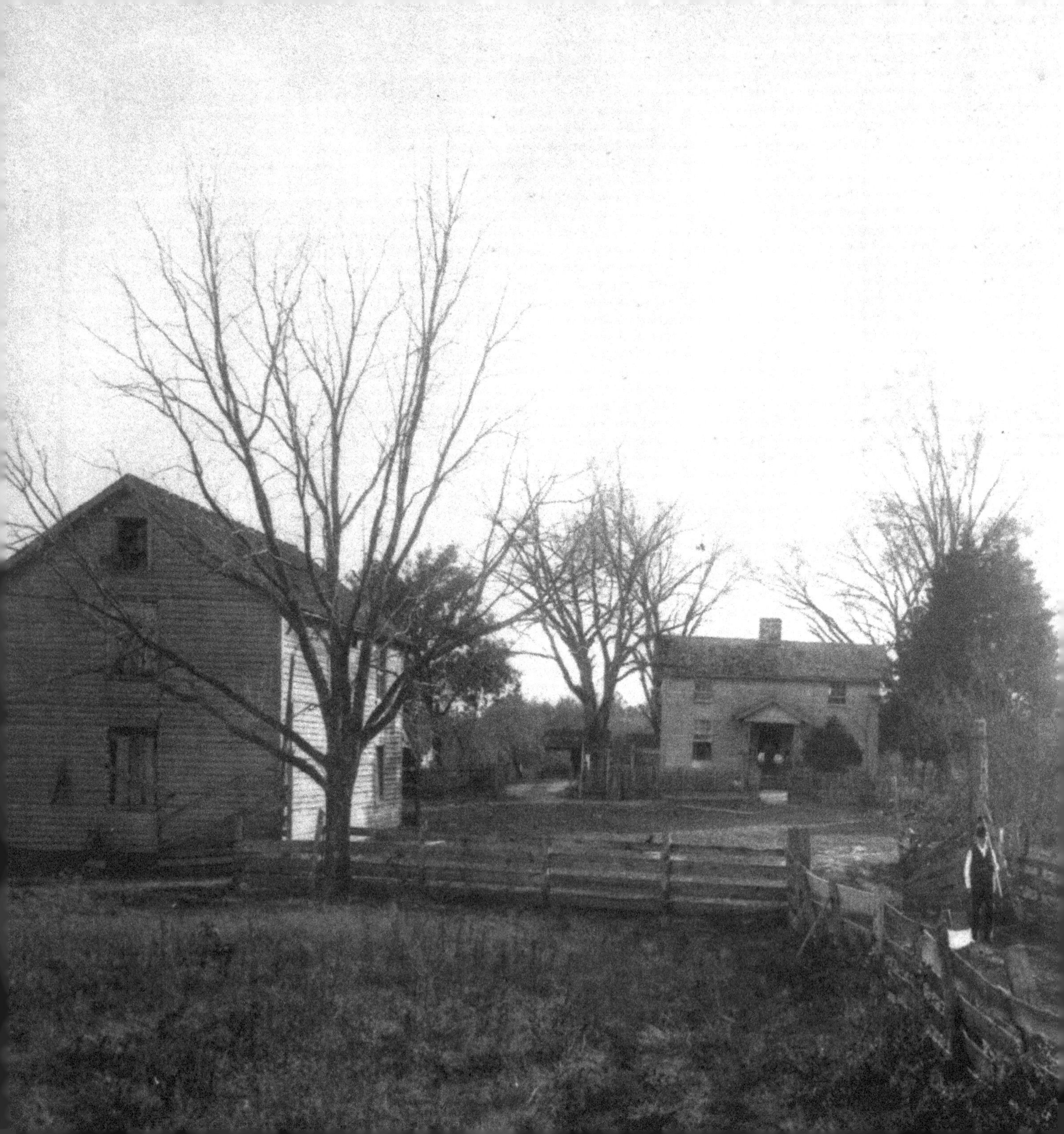

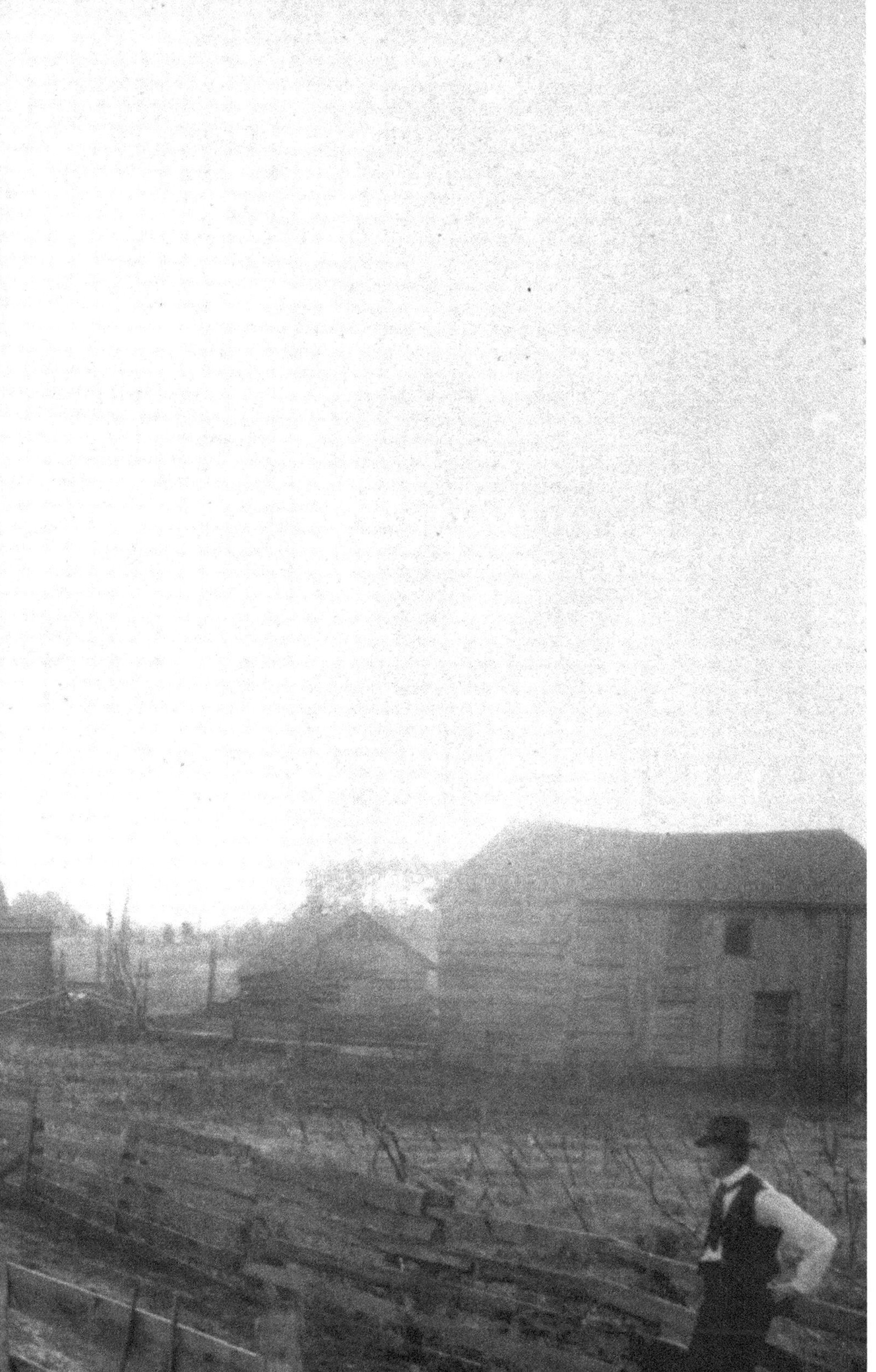

Washington Duke (at center, with hoe) walks in front of his house and early tobacco factories, ca. the late nineteenth century. The frame house, built in 1852, originally consisted of two rooms on each floor on either side of a central chimney. Duke began growing tobacco at this farm during and shortly after the Civil War. He eventually turned his crop into one of the largest tobacco works in America.

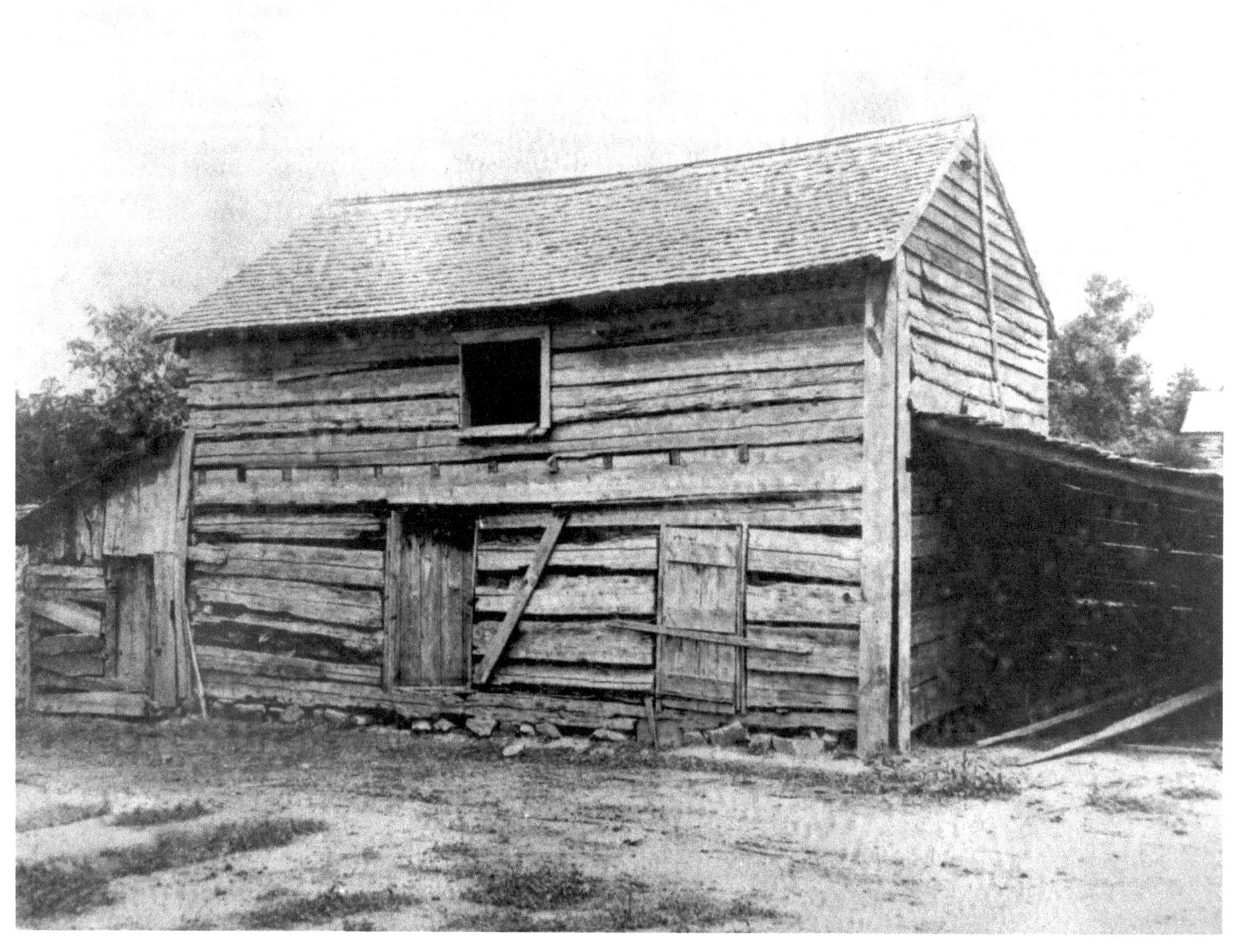

Washington Duke's second tobacco factory. With an increase in production in 1866, Duke was forced to convert an old stable into his second factory.

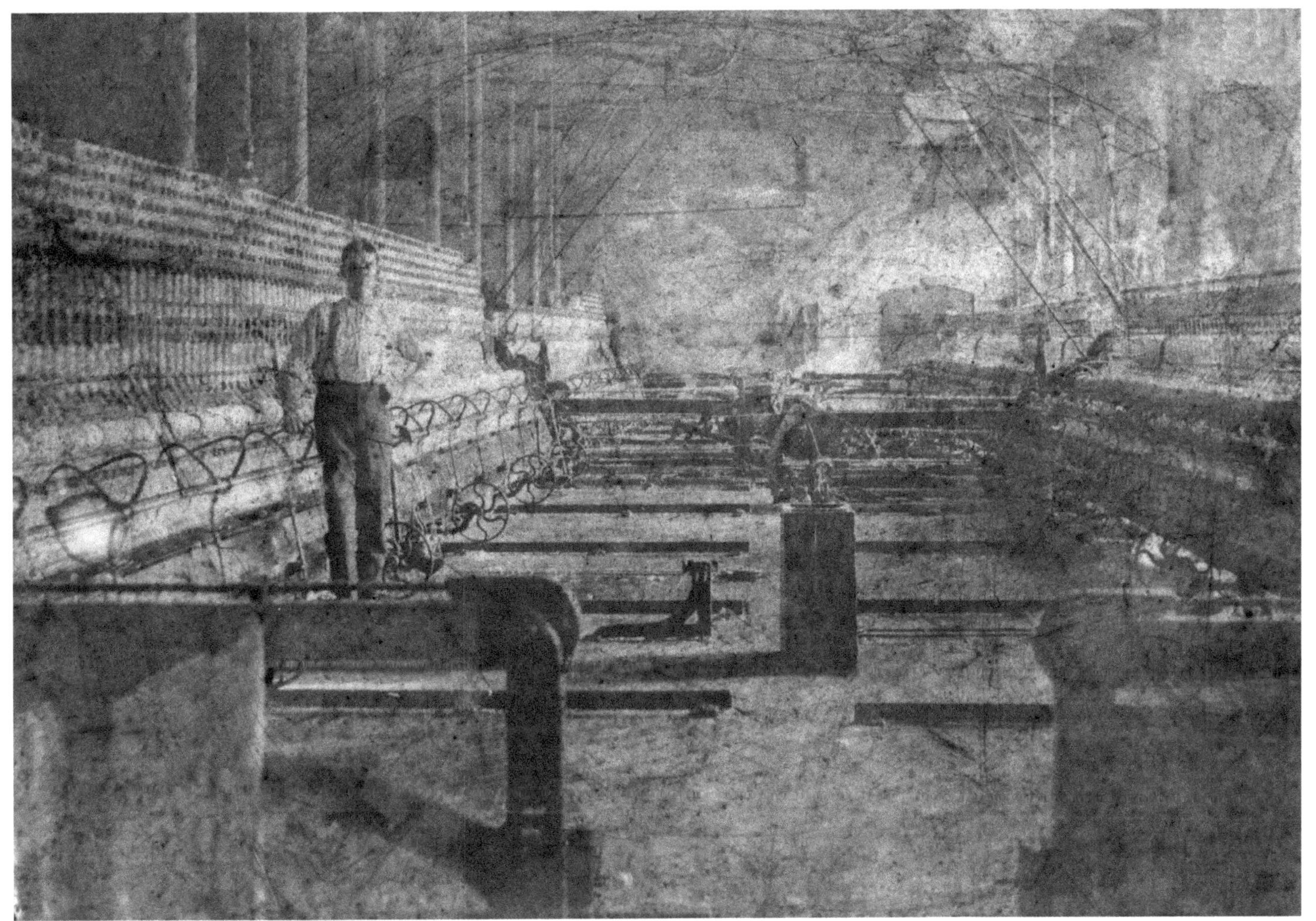

The interior of a Durham County textile mill, ca. 1890. In the years before child labor laws, it was not unusual to see young children and adolescents working alongside adults at textile mills like this one.

The Durham Fire Department began service on December 8, 1872. This undated photograph shows the department's hose wagon #2.

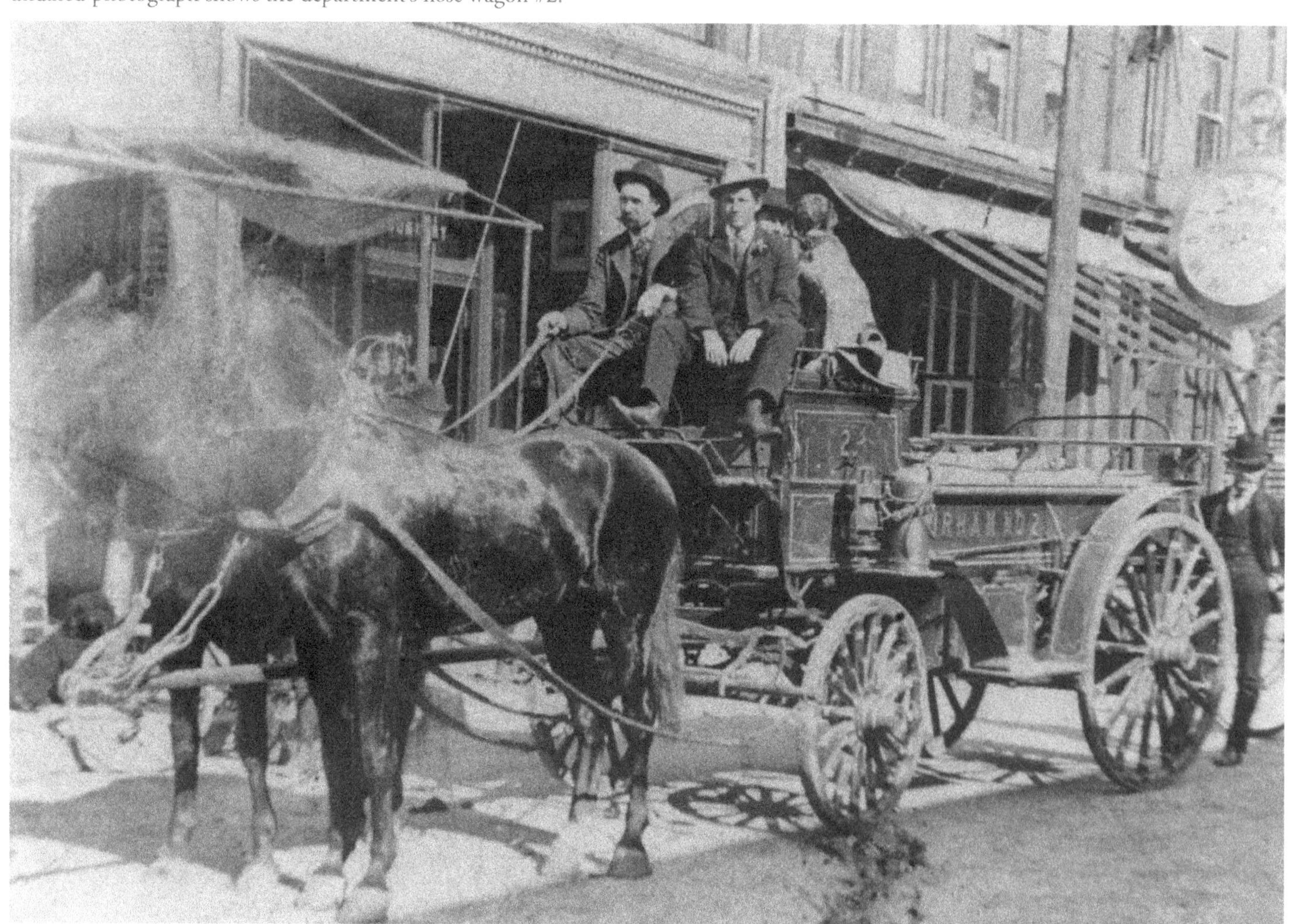

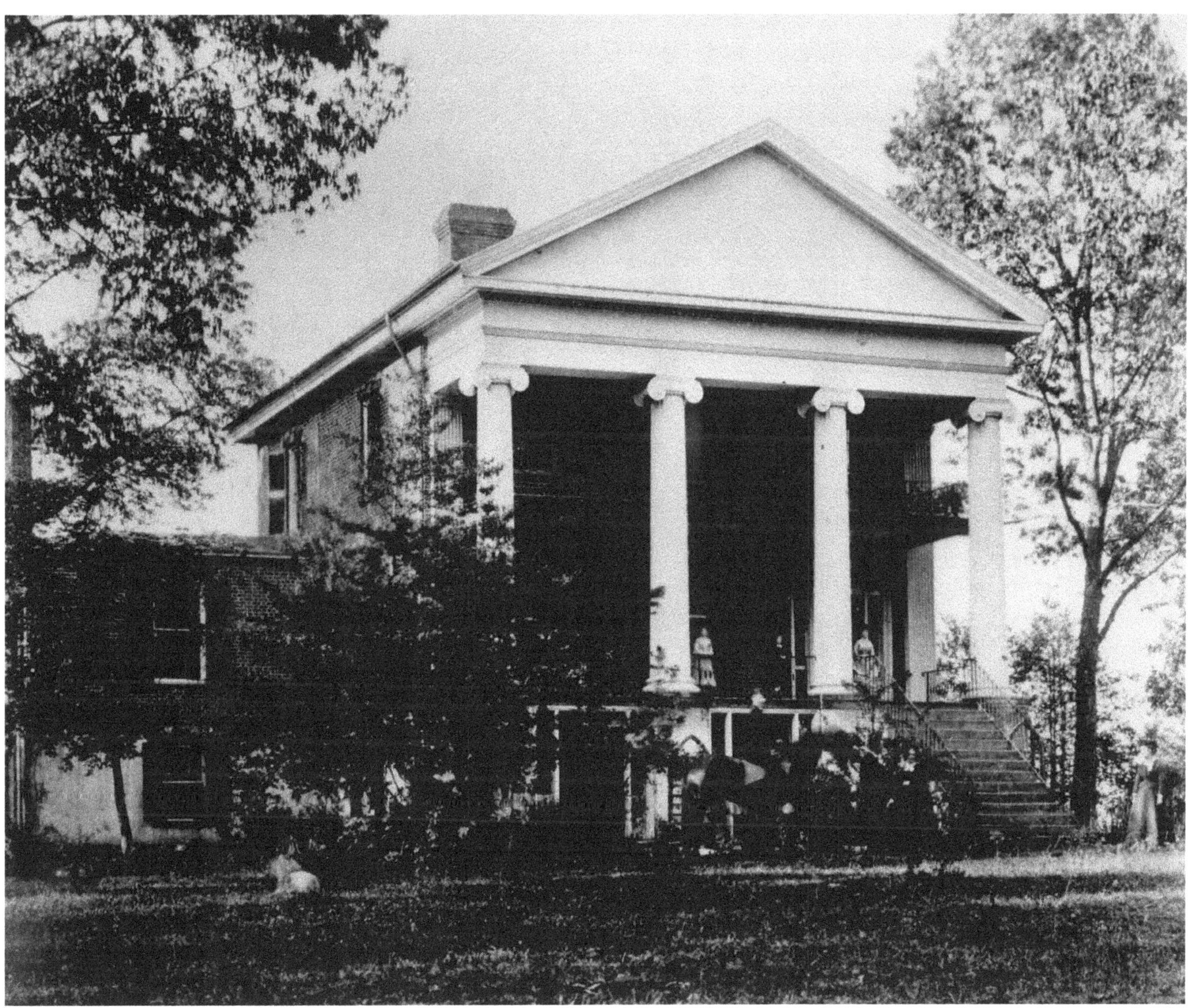

This Greek Revival–style mansion once graced Raleigh's Peace Street and served throughout much of the nineteenth century as one of the city's most prominent homes. Built in the 1840s by Nancy Lane Mordecai, the residence earned the name "Devereux House" when Mordecai's daughter Margaret married John Devereux and then lived here. The house was razed ca. 1900 after the estate was subdivided into smaller lots.

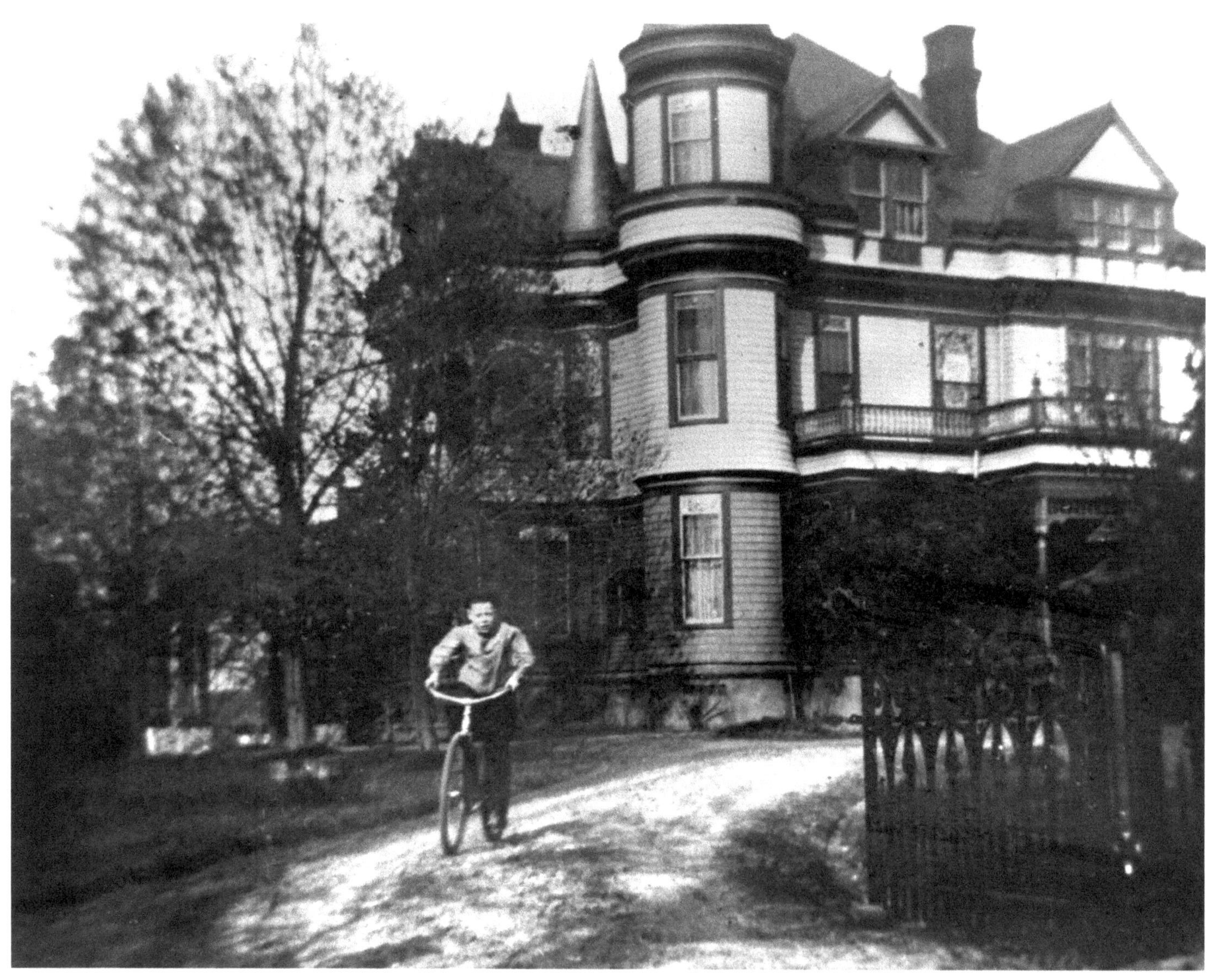

Following his retirement from W. Duke, Sons & Company in 1880, founder Washington Duke erected a huge Victorian-style mansion on Main Street in Durham within walking distance of the Duke tobacco factories. Named "Fairview," the many-gabled home included elaborate gardens.

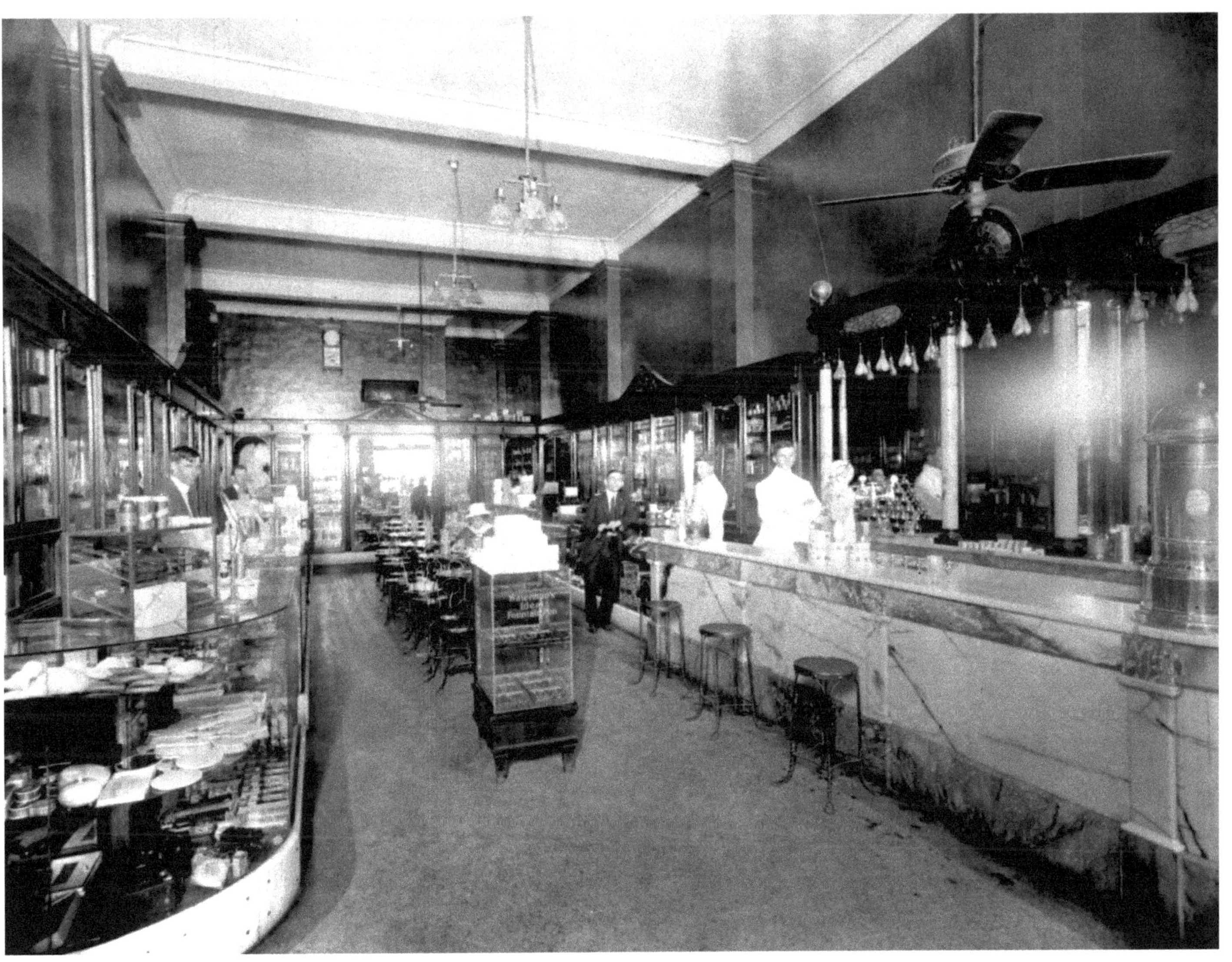

In the late 1800s and early 1900s, several privately owned drugstores operated along a four-block stretch of Fayetteville Street in downtown Raleigh. One of the most popular of these establishments was Brantley's Drug Store. Located at the corner of Fayetteville and Hargett streets, it was popular both for its soda fountain and its medicinal potions.

This image shows the proximity of Washington Duke's mansion, "Fairview," to the Duke Tobacco Company works on Main Street in Durham, ca. 1880s–1890s.

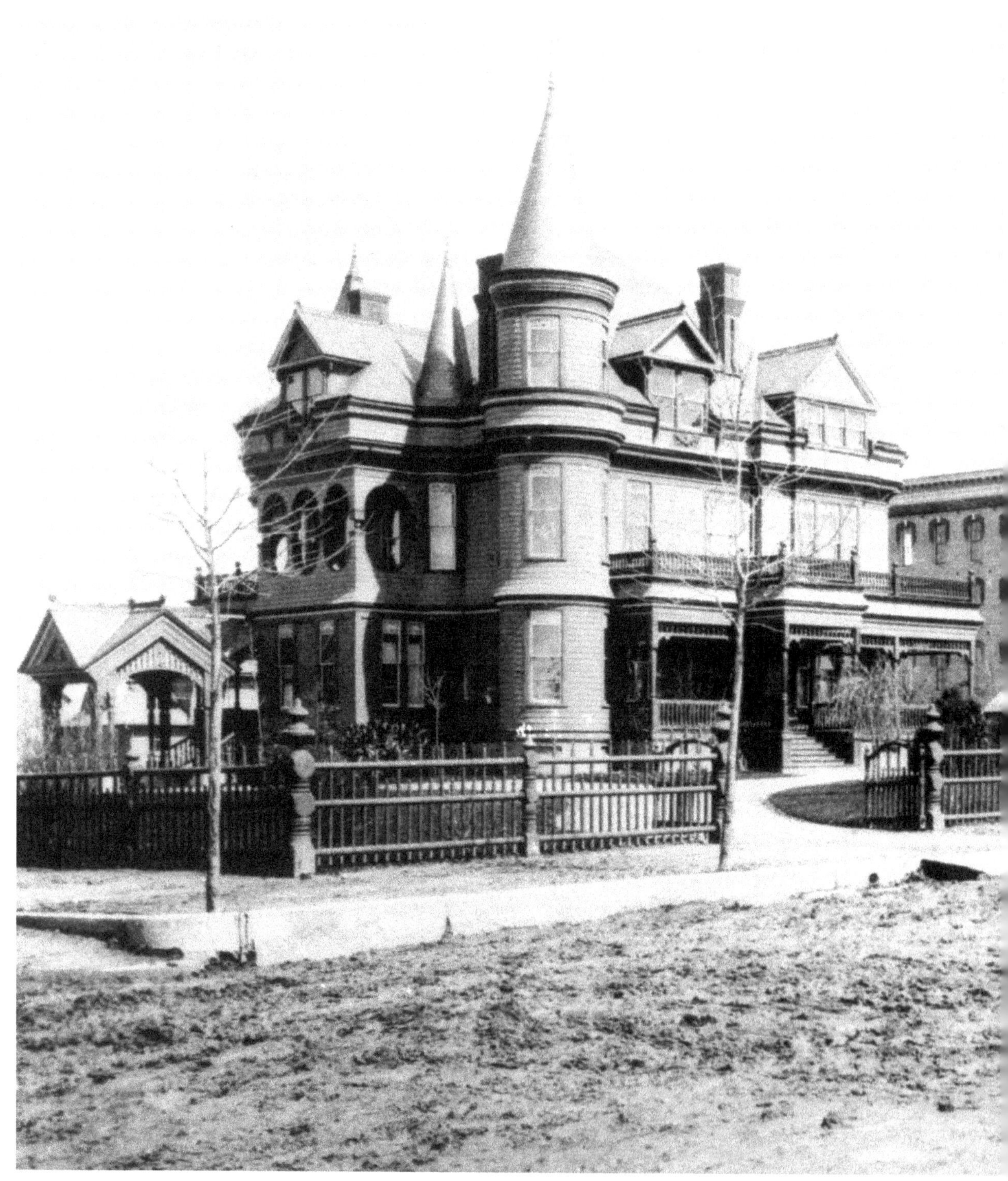

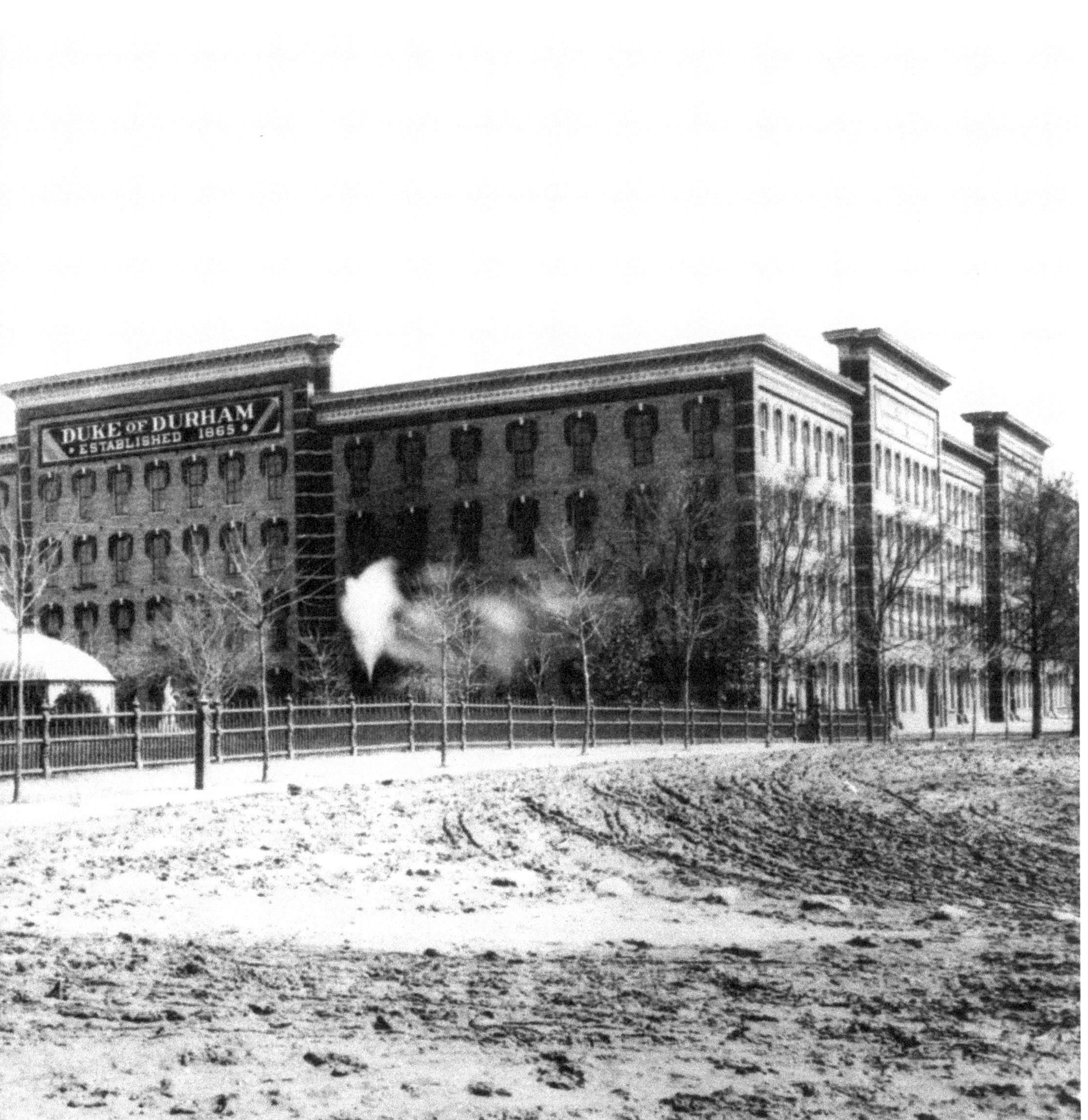
DUKE OF DURHAM
ESTABLISHED 1865

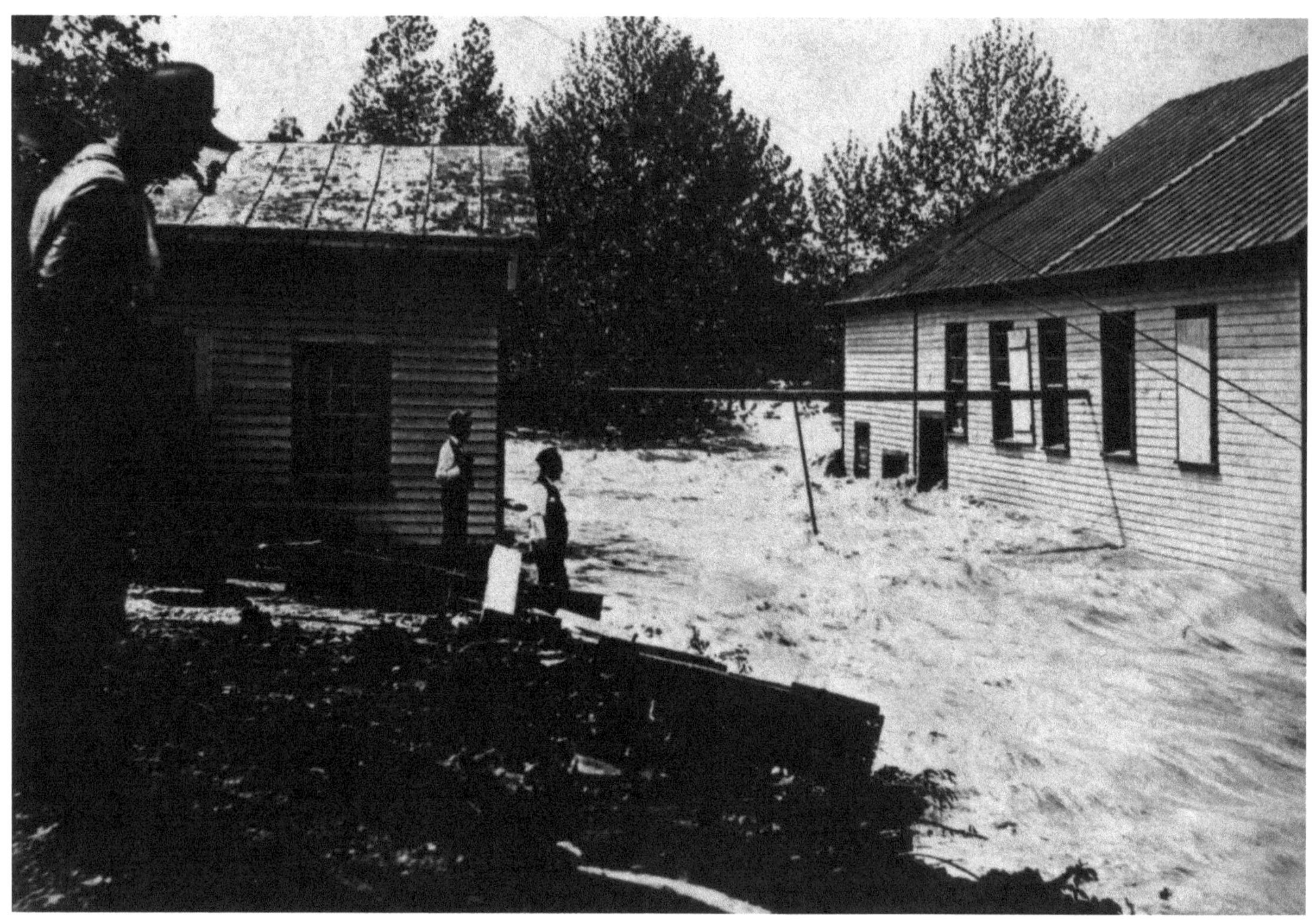

Flooding of the Eno River in 1899 envelops Eno Station Mill.

James B. Duke, son of Washington Duke and father of heiress Doris Duke, expanded the family's fortunes into textile mills and power companies. The younger Duke used some of his wealth to create an elaborate estate in Somerville, New Jersey, in 1893. Known as Duke Farms, it included a celebrated assortment of greenhouses and gardens that remain today and operate as a tourist attraction.

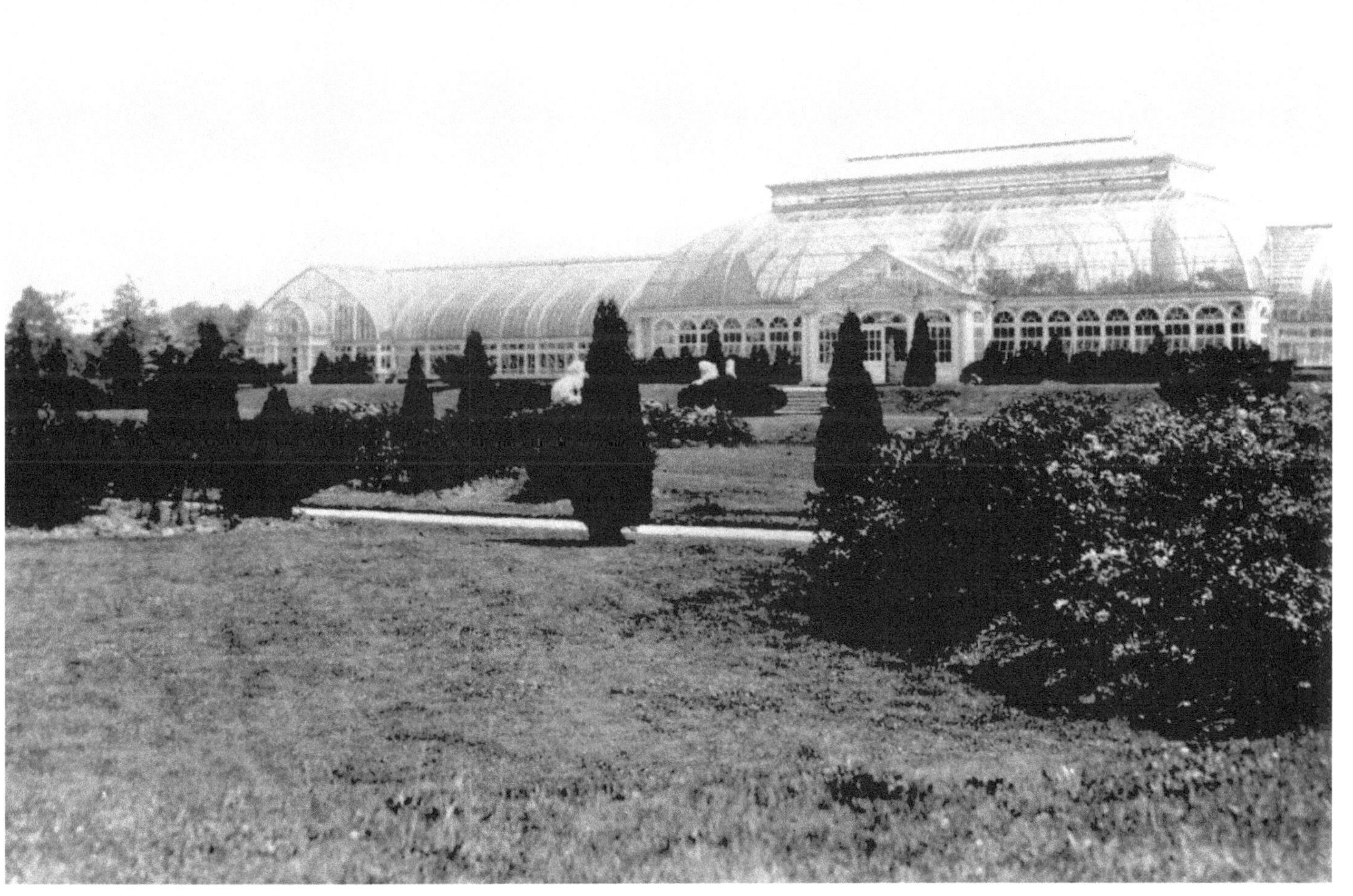

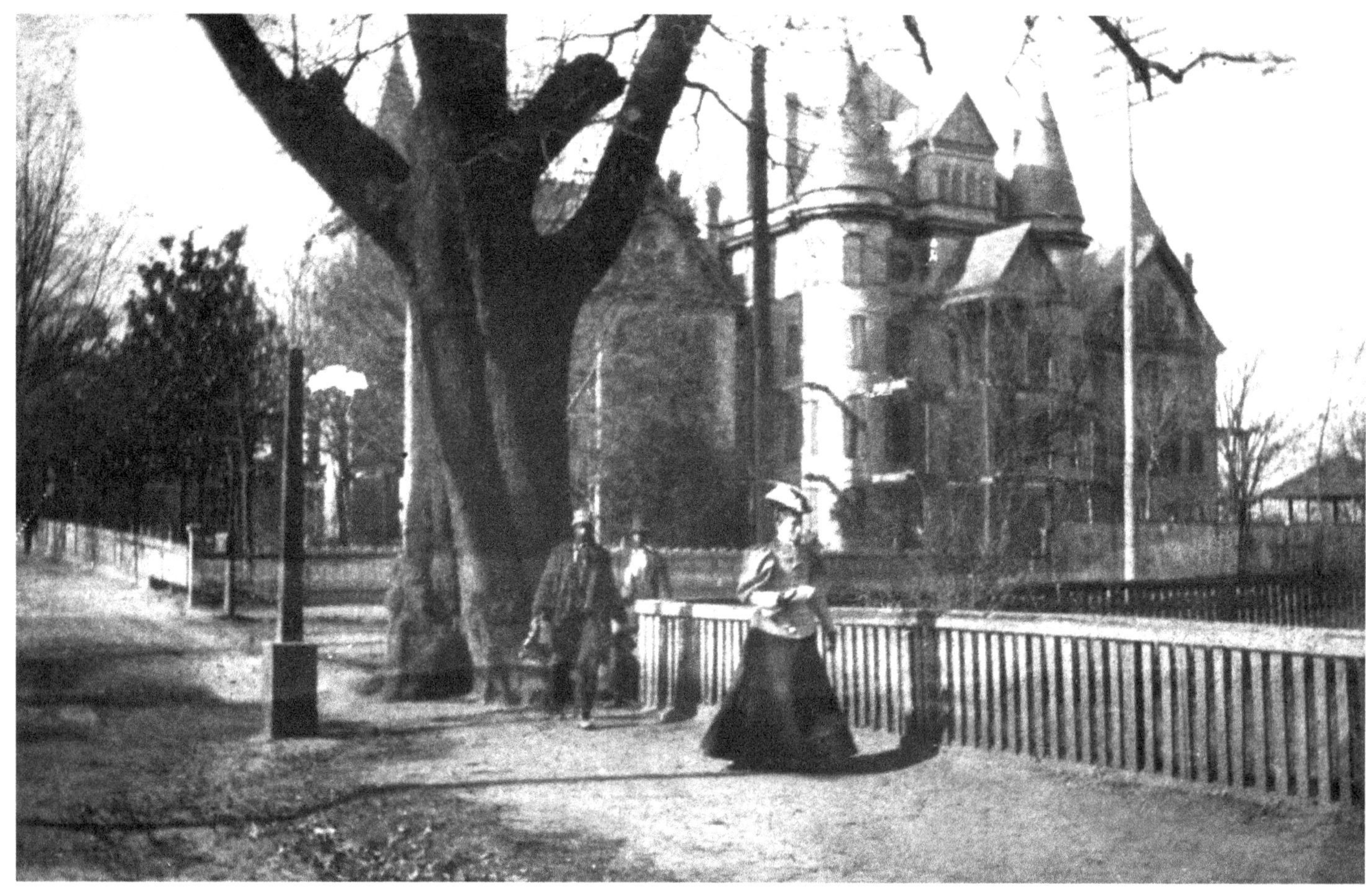

Chartered in 1891, the Baptist Female University opened its first campus in a large Queen Anne–style structure at Edenton and Blount streets in Raleigh. The school quickly expanded, changing its name to Meredith College in 1909.

Tobacco Trusts and Trolley Cars

(1900–1919)

At the dawn of the twentieth century, American enterprise thrived as the Industrial Revolution brought unprecedented change to the working lives of average men and women across the country. The era also created unprecedented wealth for a handful of canny (and lucky) entrepreneurs who were able to grab a foothold of opportunity in the new economy and its thirst for novel inventions and innovative products.

Manufacturing continued to grow as more tobacco factories, textile mills, and machinery plants opened in Durham.

Parrish Street became a center of African American business activity in Durham. It was here that John Merrick built the headquarters for North Carolina Mutual and Provident Association, which would eventually become the largest black-owned business in the world. Mutual was joined in the neighborhood by several other businesses including a bank, barbershop, clothing stores, drugstore, and a hosiery mill. As a result, Parrish Street became known as Durham's "Black Wall Street."

By the 1900s Raleigh enjoyed a solid, stable economy built upon state government and education. The growth of the city's streetcar system created new neighborhoods that were just a ten-cent ride away from downtown. Its prosperous, middle-class citizenry helped fuel a flourishing retail district along Fayetteville Street, a main thoroughfare running due south of the North Carolina State Capitol. The avenue's first four blocks soon housed hundreds of family-owned enterprises that served as a shopping mecca for families throughout Eastern North Carolina.

Raleigh's African American community had its own, separate retail world. Initially, Wilmington Street served this purpose. By the 1920s, however, many successful businesses owned or operated by blacks would move to East Hargett Street, anchored by the Lightner Arcade, an office building and hotel opened by Calvin Lightner.

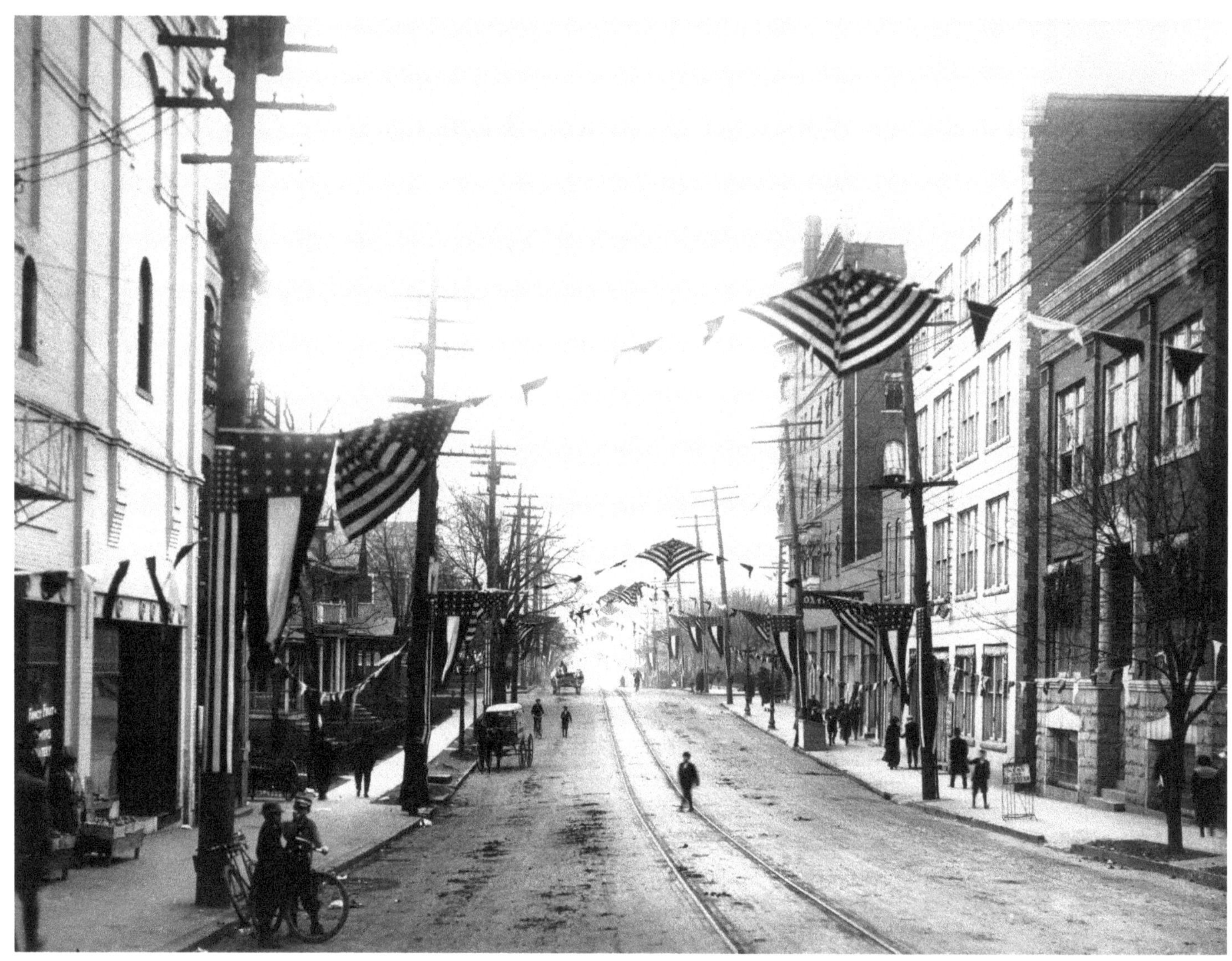

During the early 1900s Raleigh's main electric company, Carolina Power & Light, took a vast number of downtown images to archive their power line system. This CP&L photograph depicts Martin Street, looking west from Salisbury Street. In the distance, just to the right of center, can be seen the Raleigh Hotel and Nash Square.

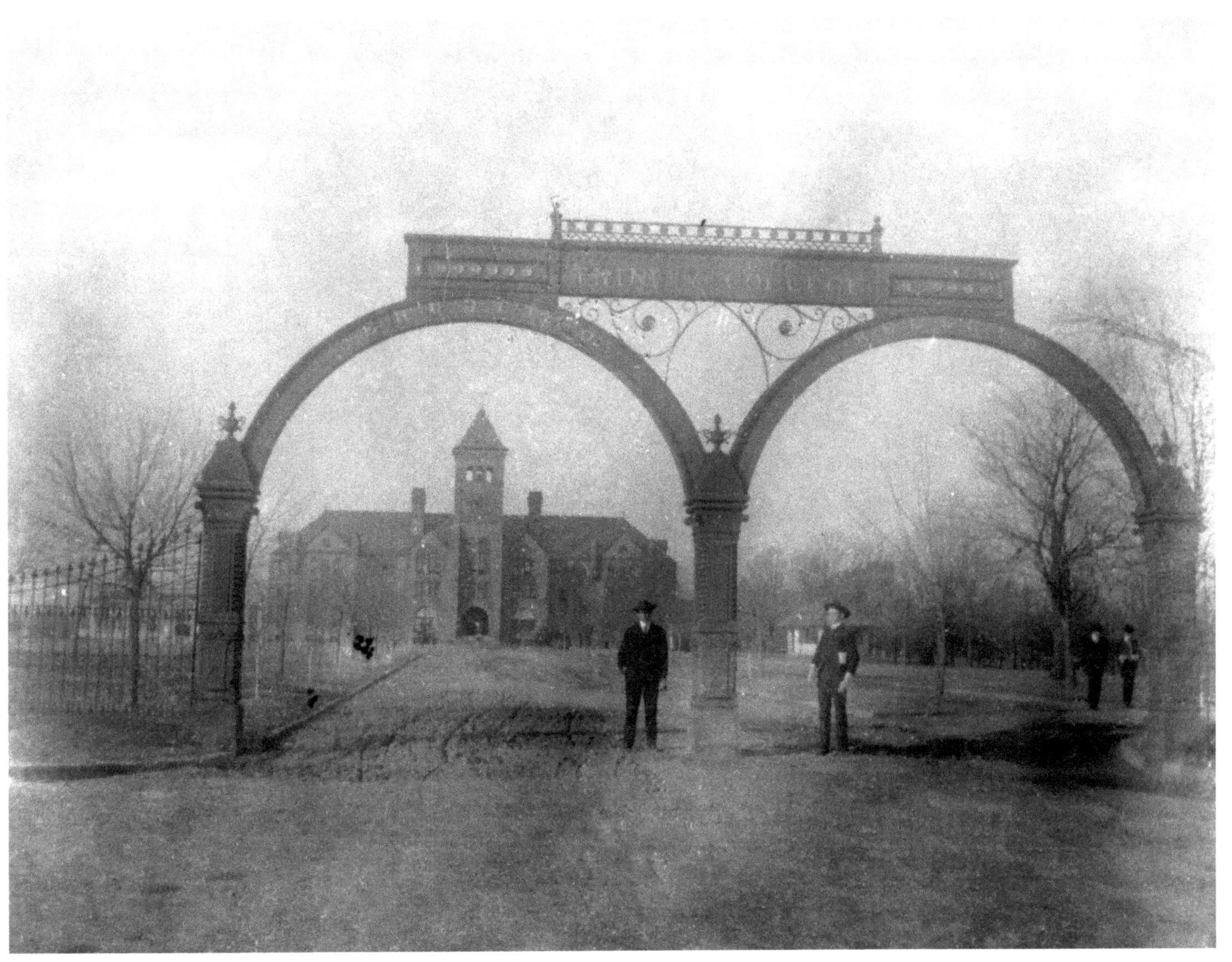

In 1892 Trinity College relocated from rural Randolph County to the more urban setting of Durham. The Duke family, rich from their tobacco businesses, became great benefactors of the new campus and financed many of its first structures. This image shows the Main Gate at Trinity College in 1904. The Washington Duke Building, completed in 1892, is in the background and Stagg Pavilion is to the right.

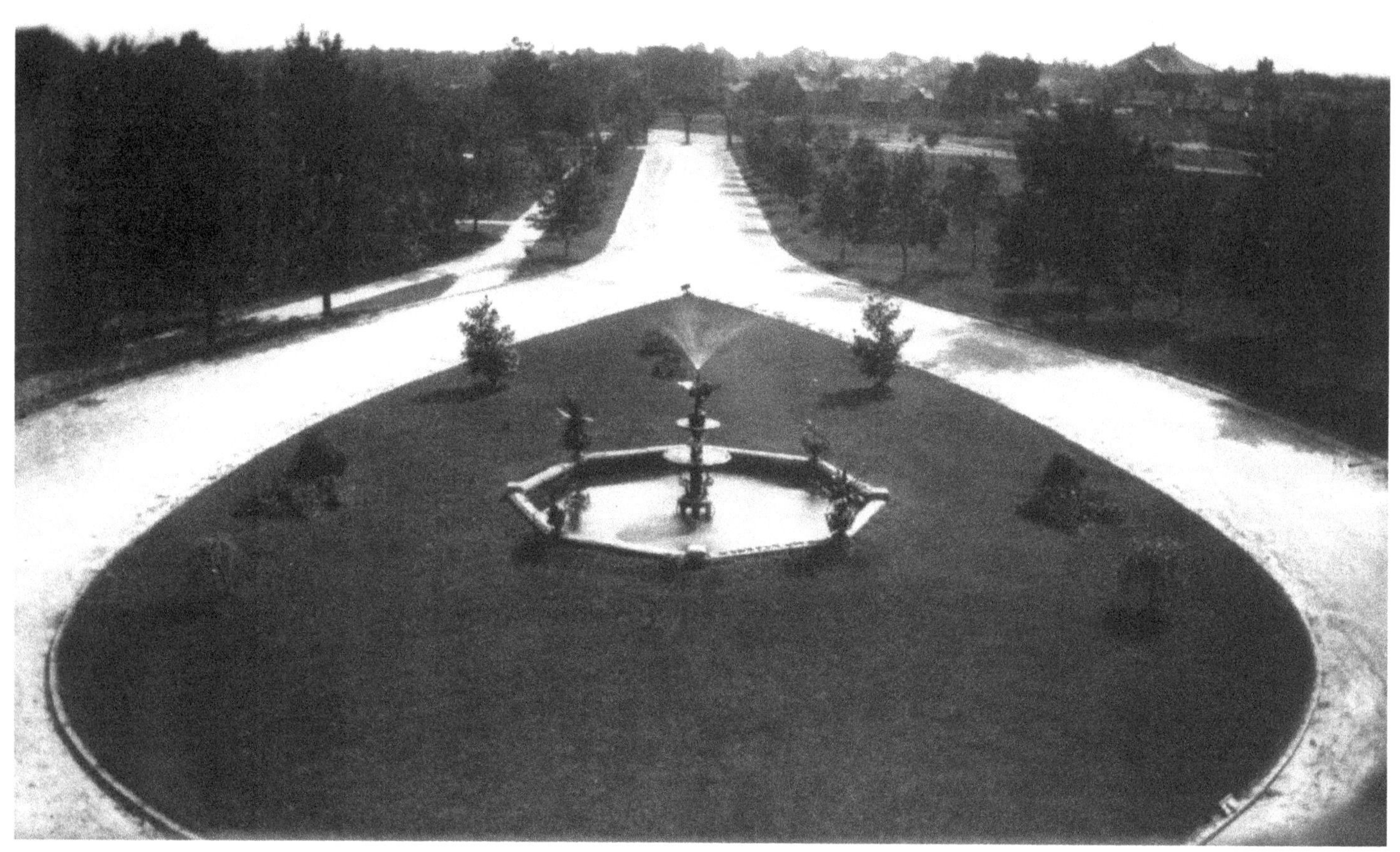

Entrance to Trinity College as seen from the Washington Duke Building, ca. 1900. One of the campus's original structures, the Duke Building was destroyed by fire in 1911. The statue of Washington Duke now occupies the circle.

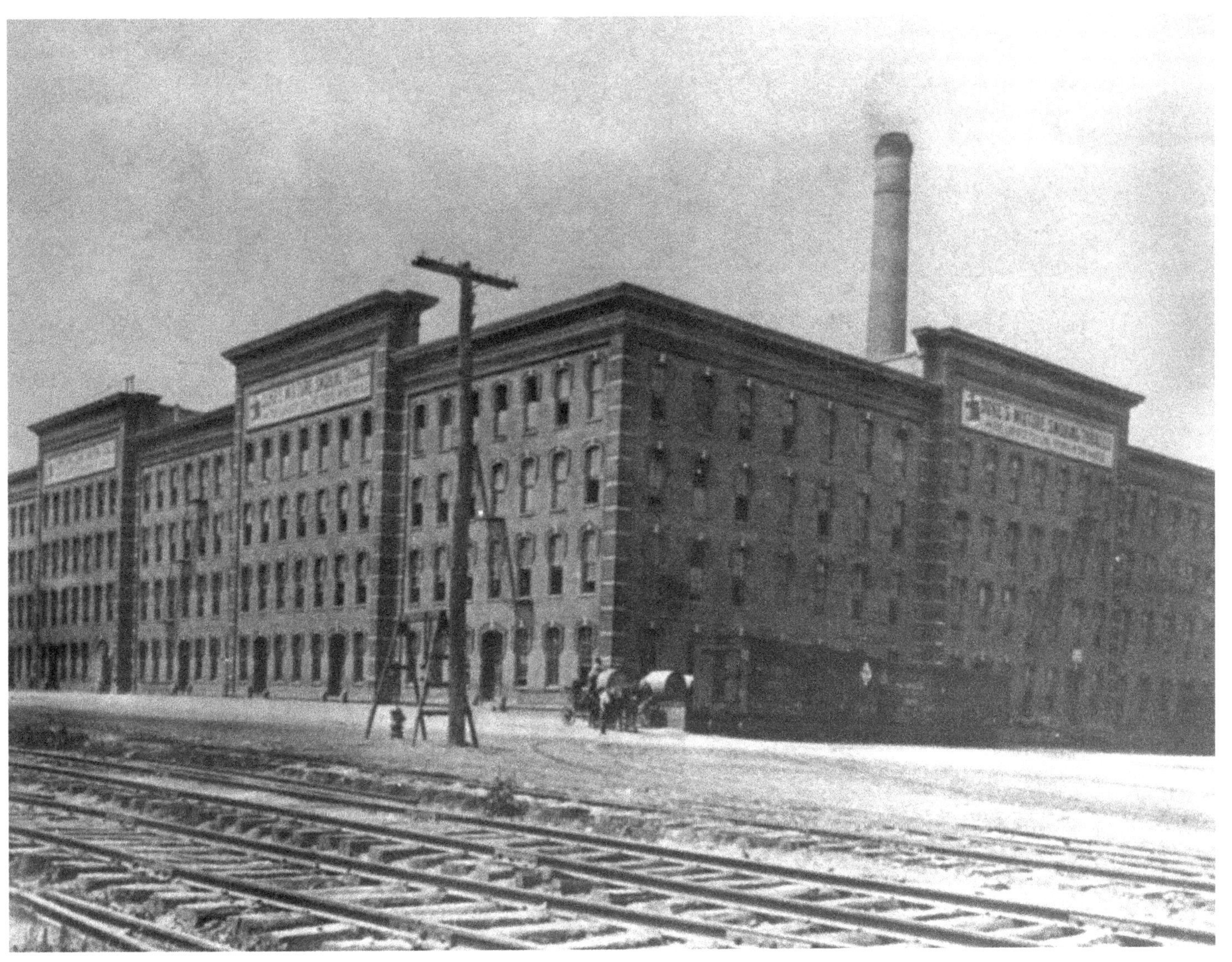

By 1890 James B. Duke had persuaded his four largest competitors to join forces with him to form the American Tobacco Company. For nearly two decades it would monopolize tobacco sales in the U.S. This 1900 photograph shows the Durham factory.

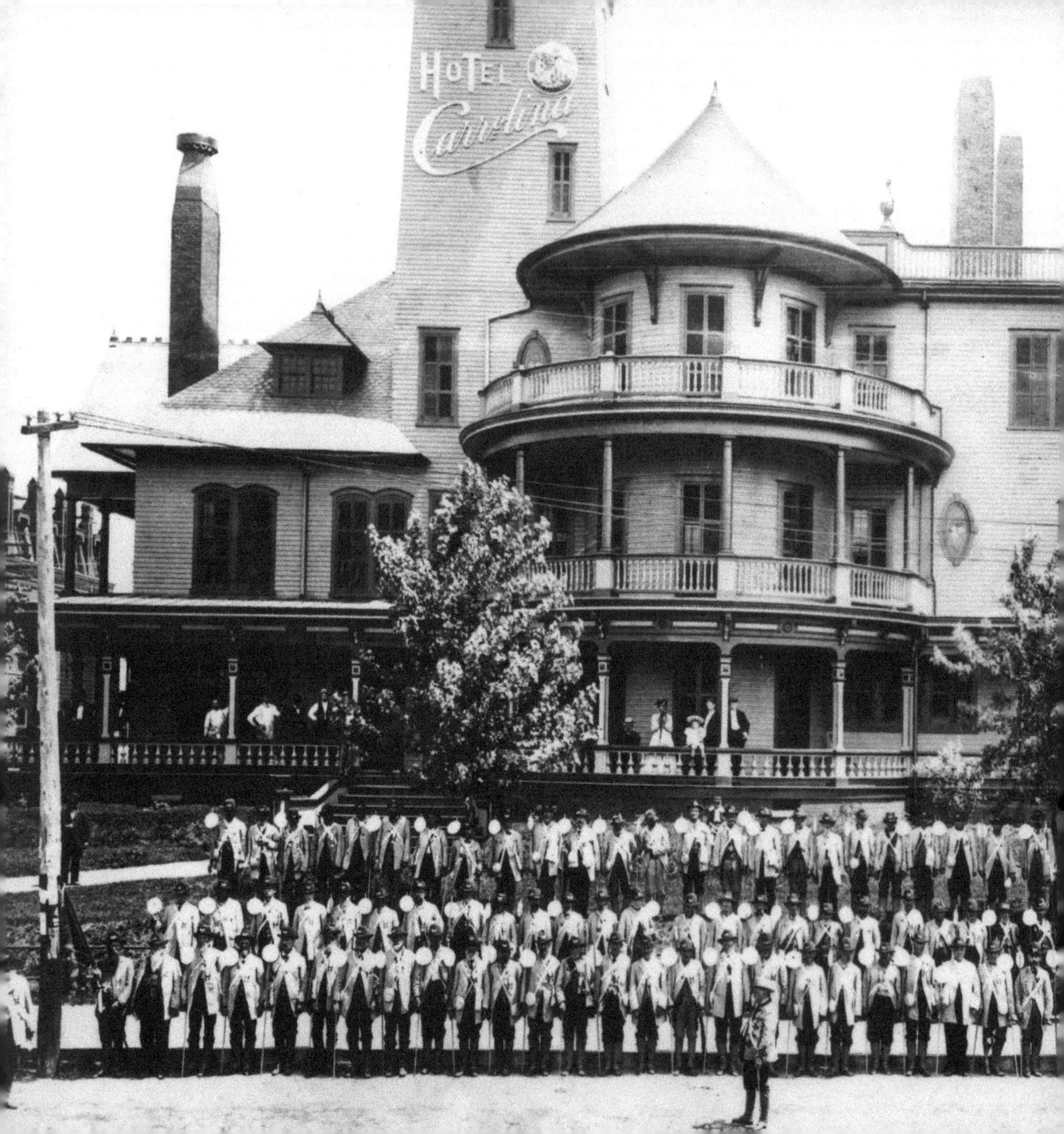
HOTEL
Carolina

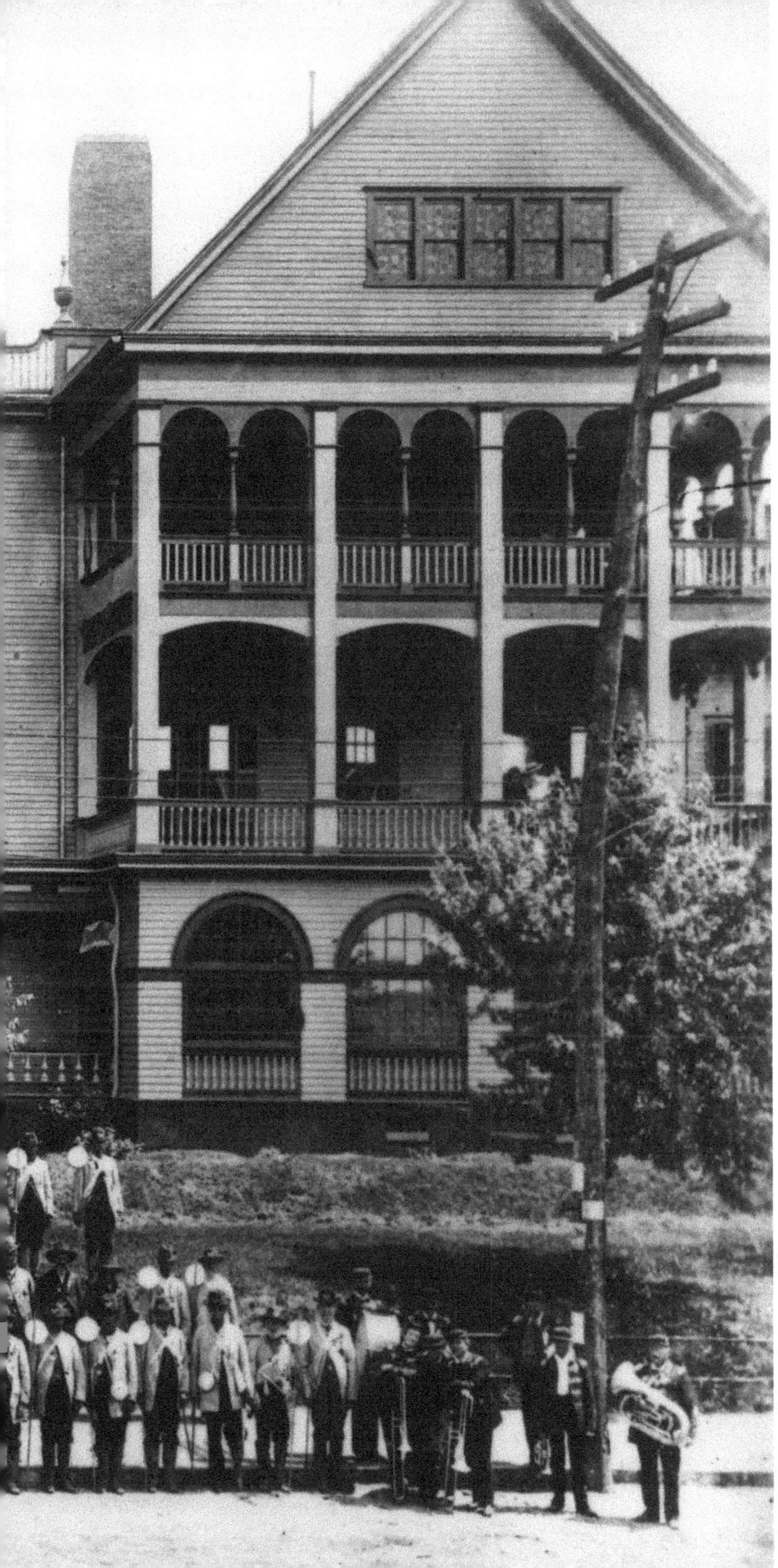

Opened in 1891 by Julian S. Carr, another Durham-based tobacco magnate, the Hotel Carrolina (correct spelling) was a fanciful Queen Anne–style complex that stood proudly at the end of South Corcoran Street in Durham. Lost to fire in 1907, it reigned for nearly two decades as one of the South's finest inns. Here, a group of veterans from the Spanish American War pose in front of the hotel, ca. 1900.

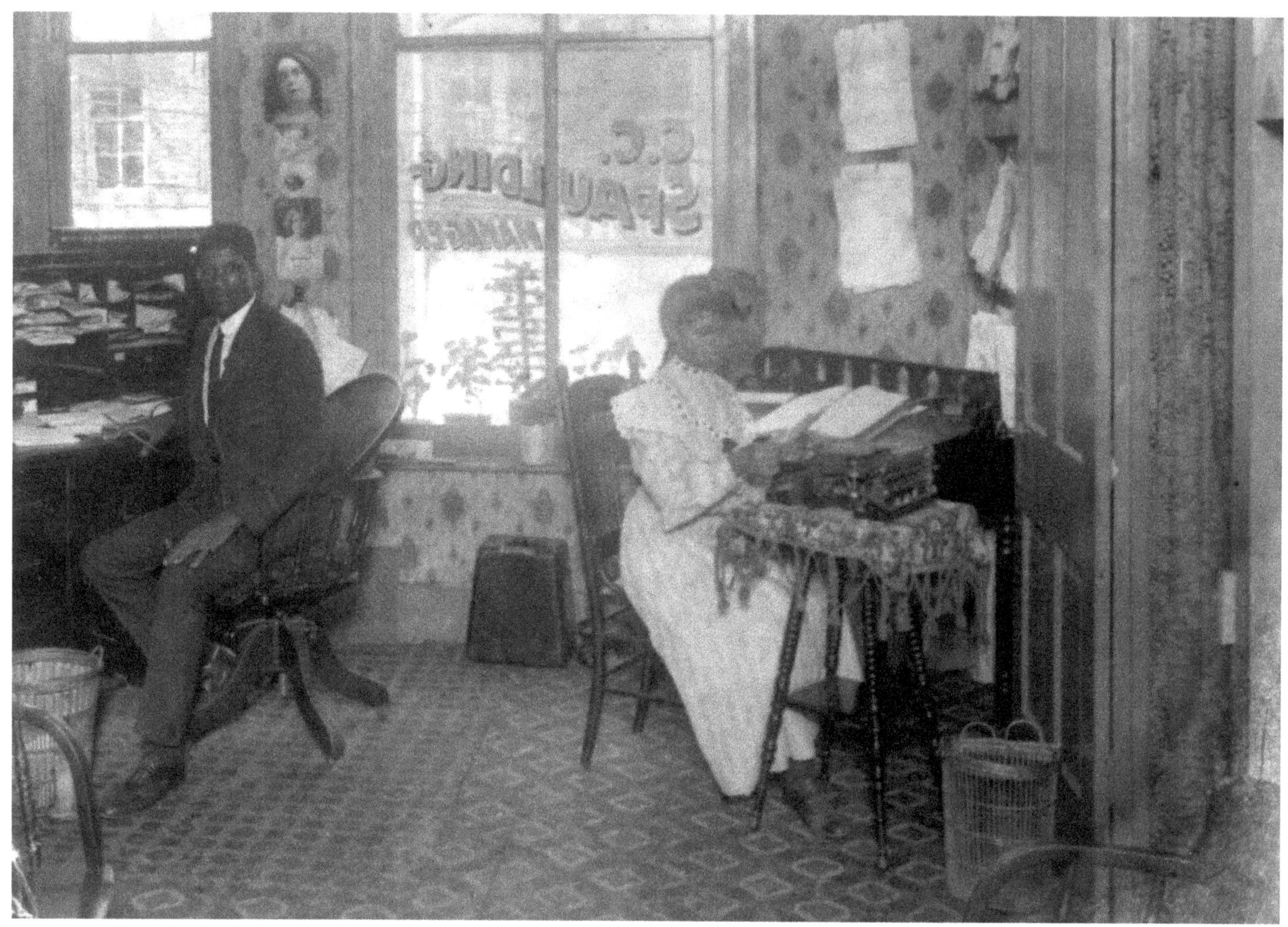

First office of the North Carolina Mutual and Provident Association. The largest black-owned insurance company in the world was started in Durham in 1898 by John Merrick and A. M. Moore. C. C. Spaulding, Merrick's nephew, joined the firm shortly after finishing high school. He rose from part-time clerk to general manager in less than a year. In this 1902 photograph, Spaulding is seated to the left, with his clerk, Miss Dore Whitted, to the right.

Alspaugh Hall on the campus of Trinity College, ca. 1904.

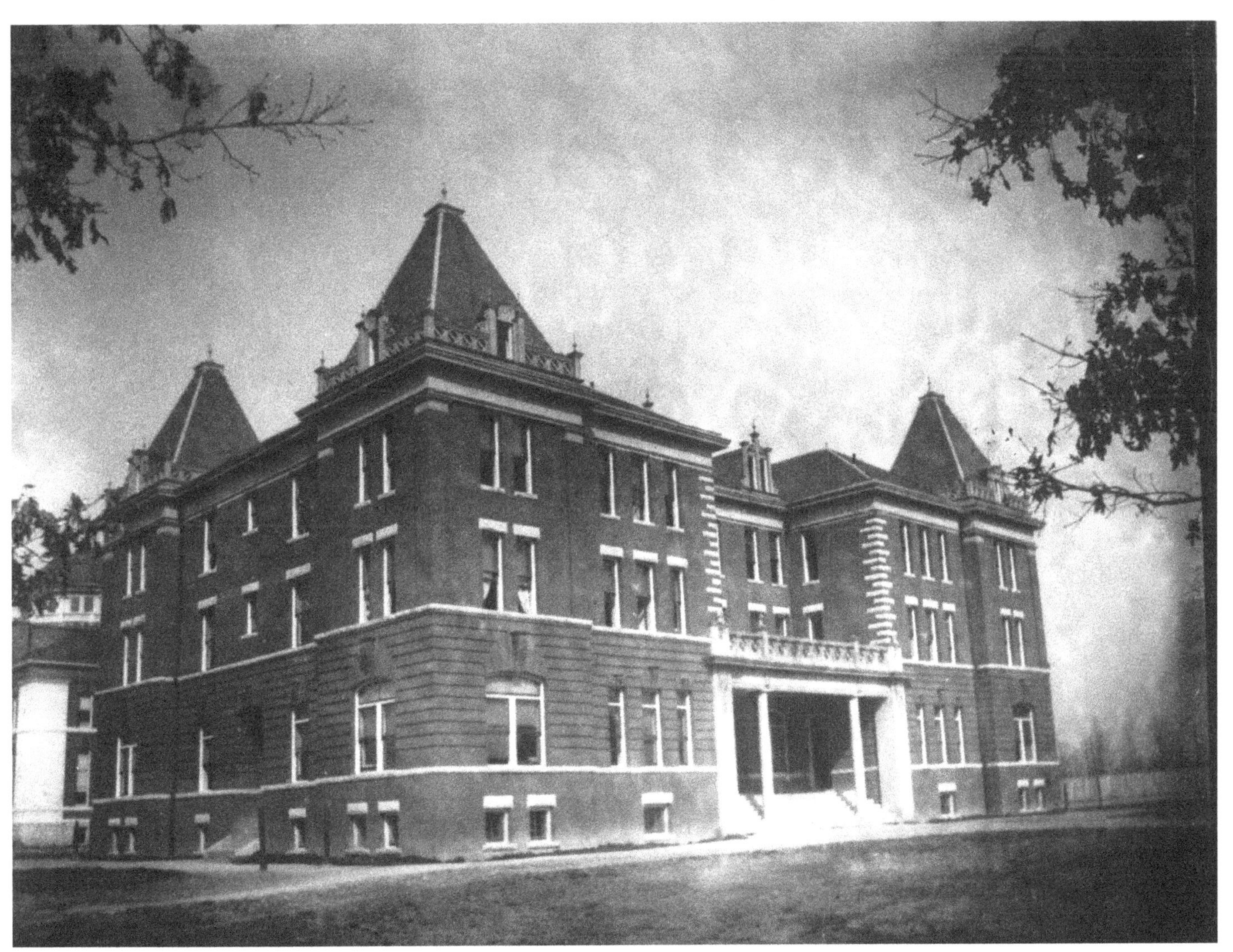

The house and barn of James and Nancy Bennitt where, on April 26, 1865, General Joseph E. Johnston surrendered to Union general William T. Sherman, ending the Civil War within the Carolinas, Georgia, and Florida. Located outside Durham, the original farmhouse and kitchen were destroyed by fire in 1921.

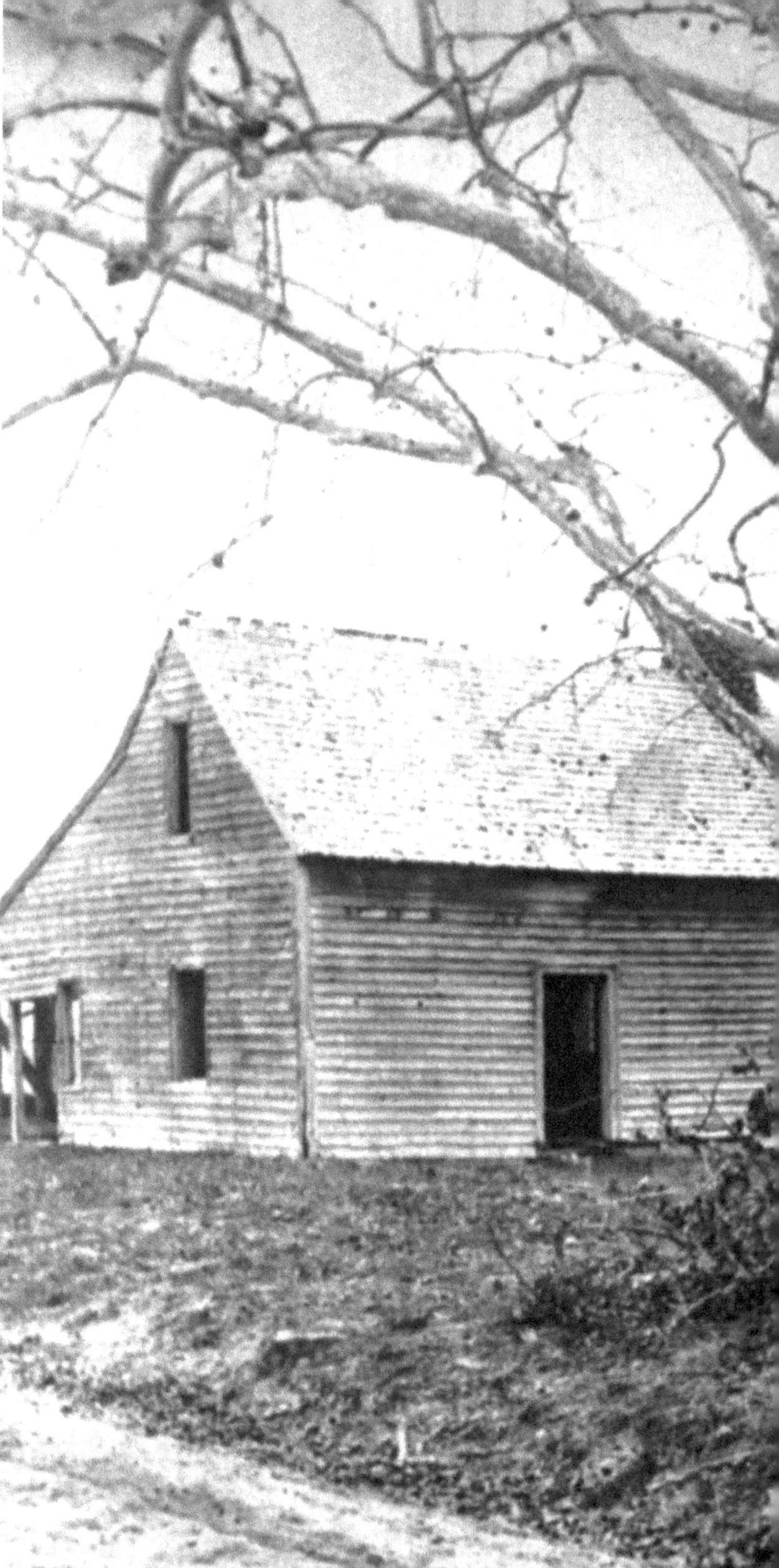

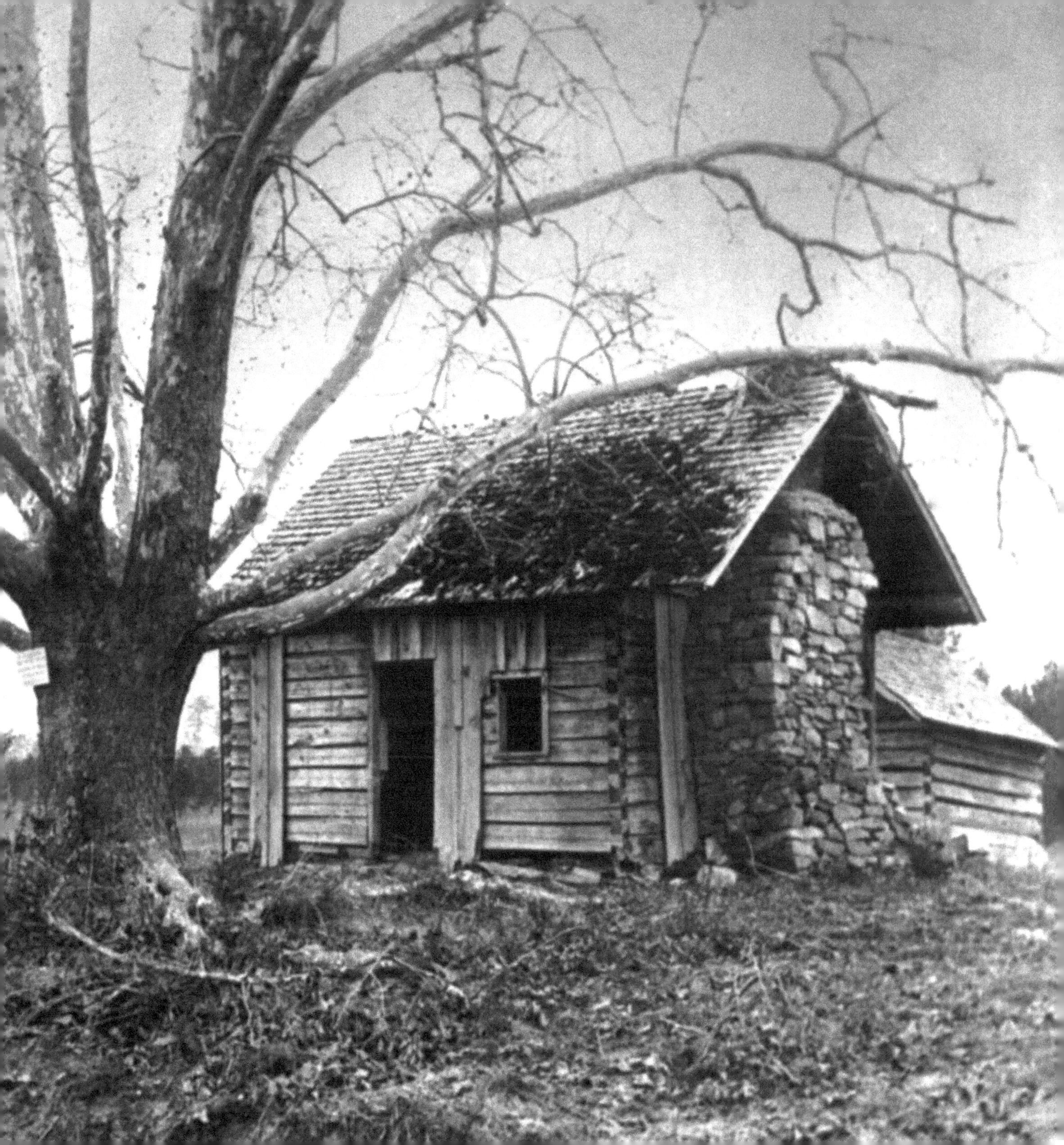

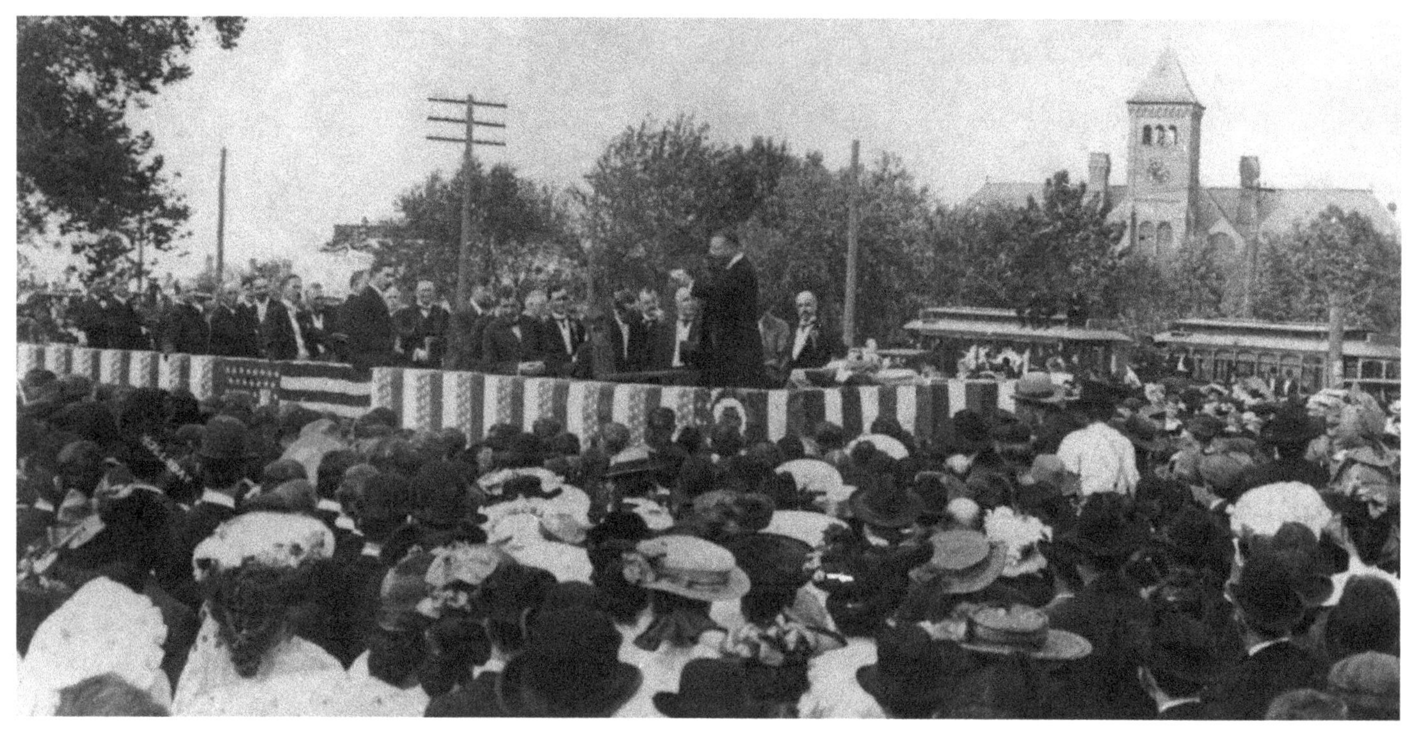

With the Duke Building as a backdrop, President Theodore Roosevelt delivers "The Importance of Academic Freedom" at Trinity College on October 19, 1905. Roosevelt also spoke at the North Carolina State Fair in Raleigh during the same visit.

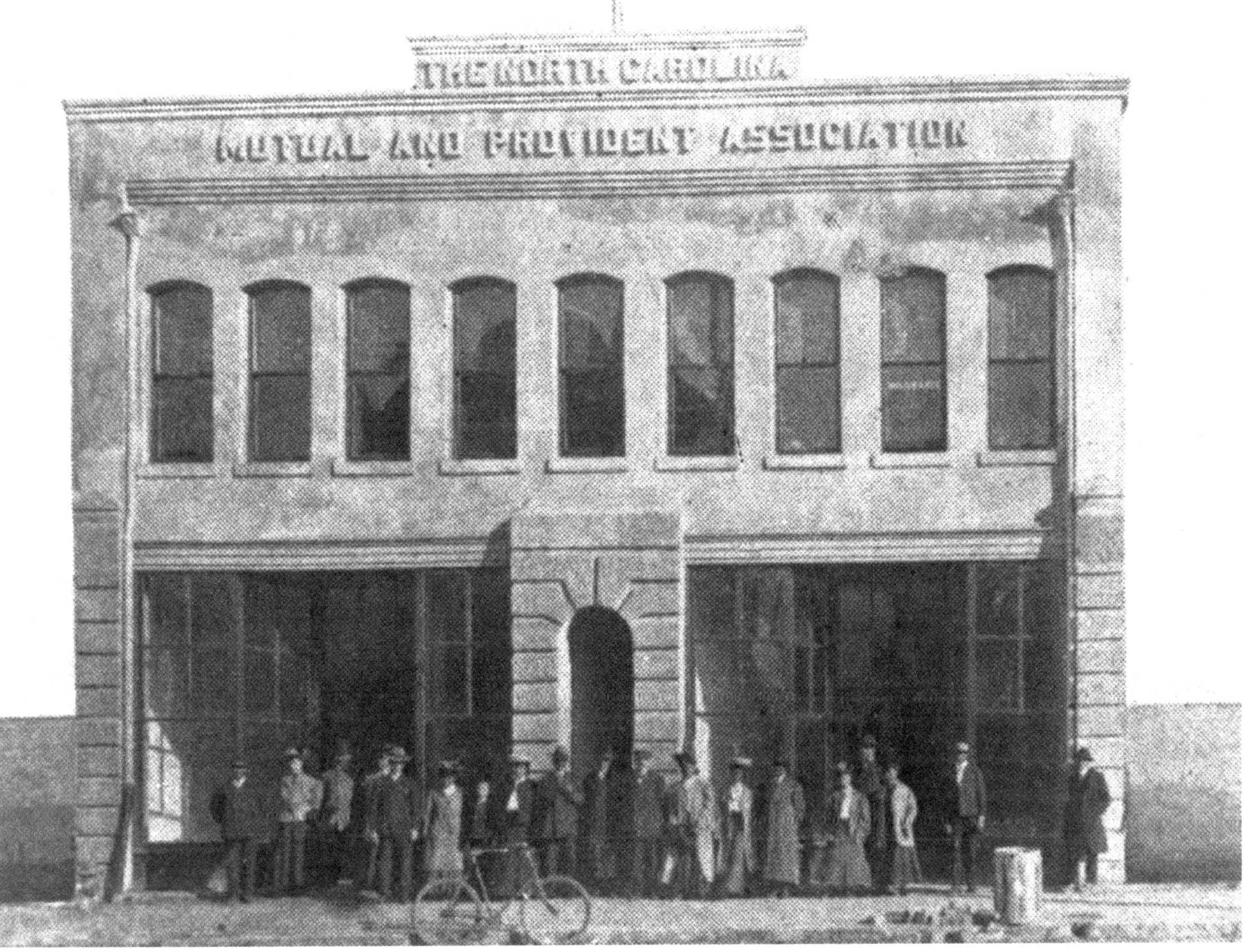

Seven years after its beginning, the North Carolina Mutual and Provident Association built its first office building on Durham's Parrish Street. The company, later known as North Carolina Mutual Insurance Company, occupied this building until 1920, when the building was replaced with a larger structure.

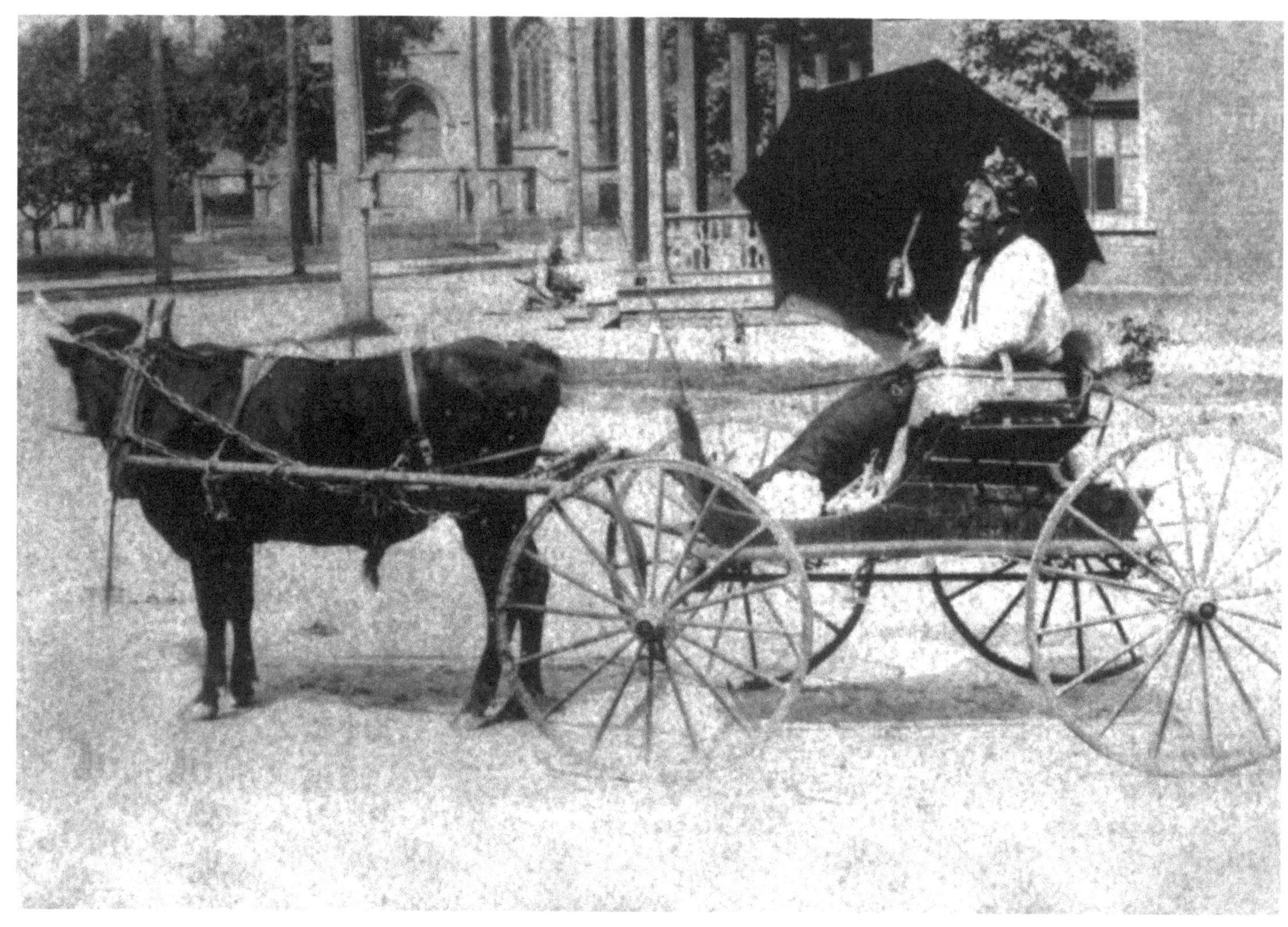

"Aunt Betsy" was a popular postcard image from Raleigh in the early 1900s.

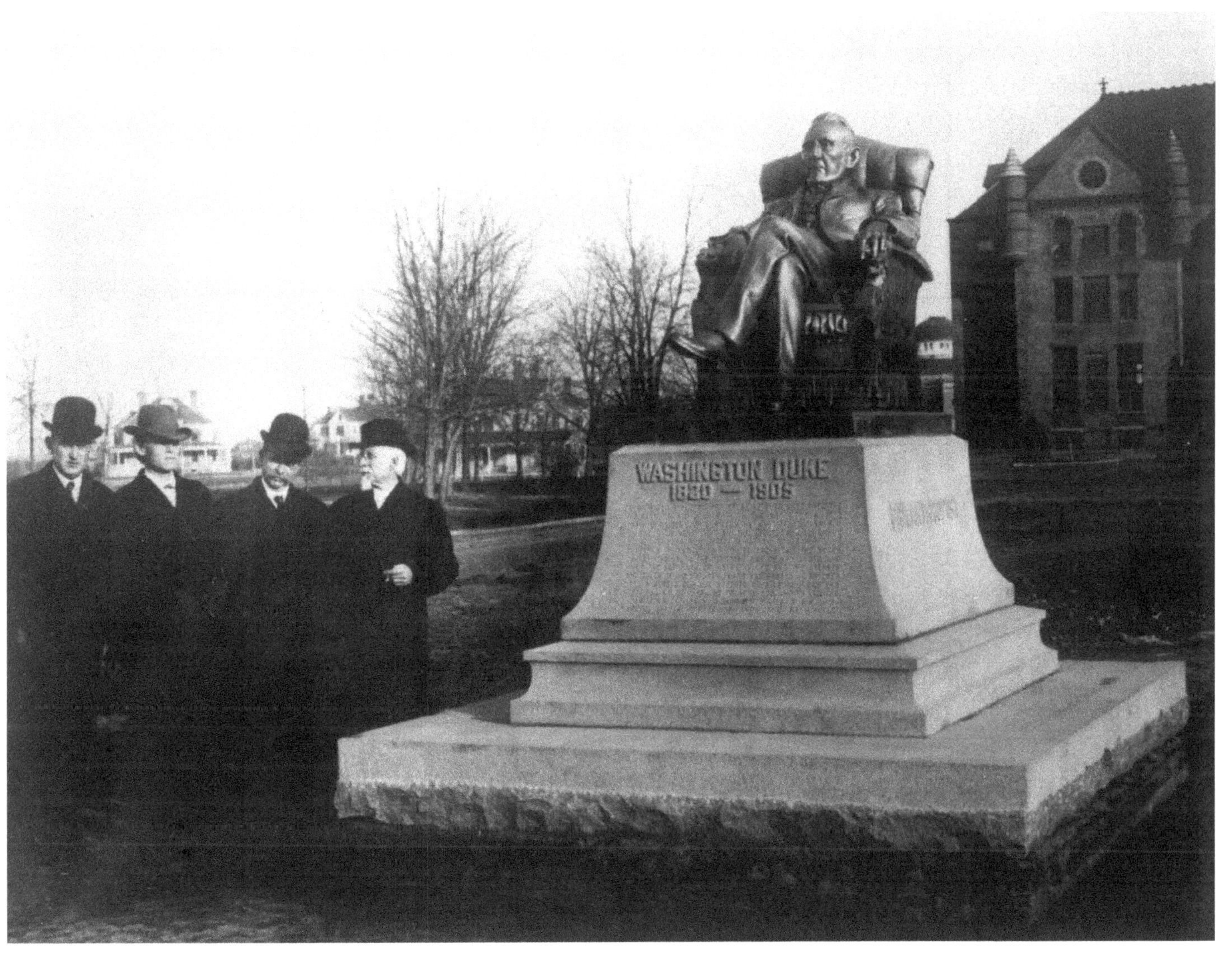

Shortly after his death in 1905, friends of Washington Duke began making plans to erect a monument in his honor. Created by Virginia sculptor Edward Virginius Valentine, the monument is shown here during its dedication and before its permanent placement in 1908 near the entrance of Trinity College.

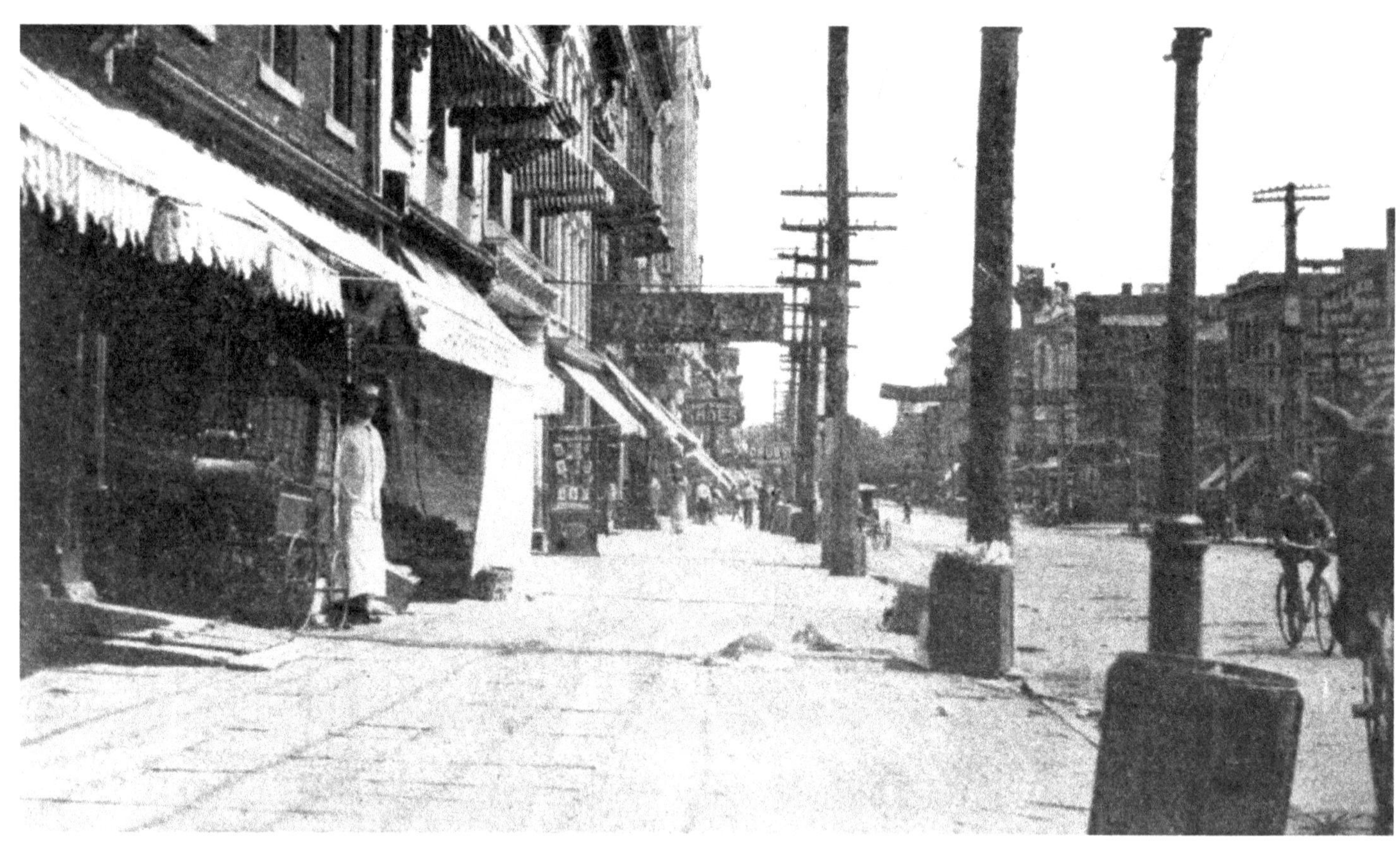

A Raleigh merchant poses on the east side of the 100-block of Fayetteville Street, ca. 1910. In the background is the marquee for the Grand Theater, one of the city's earliest motion picture houses.

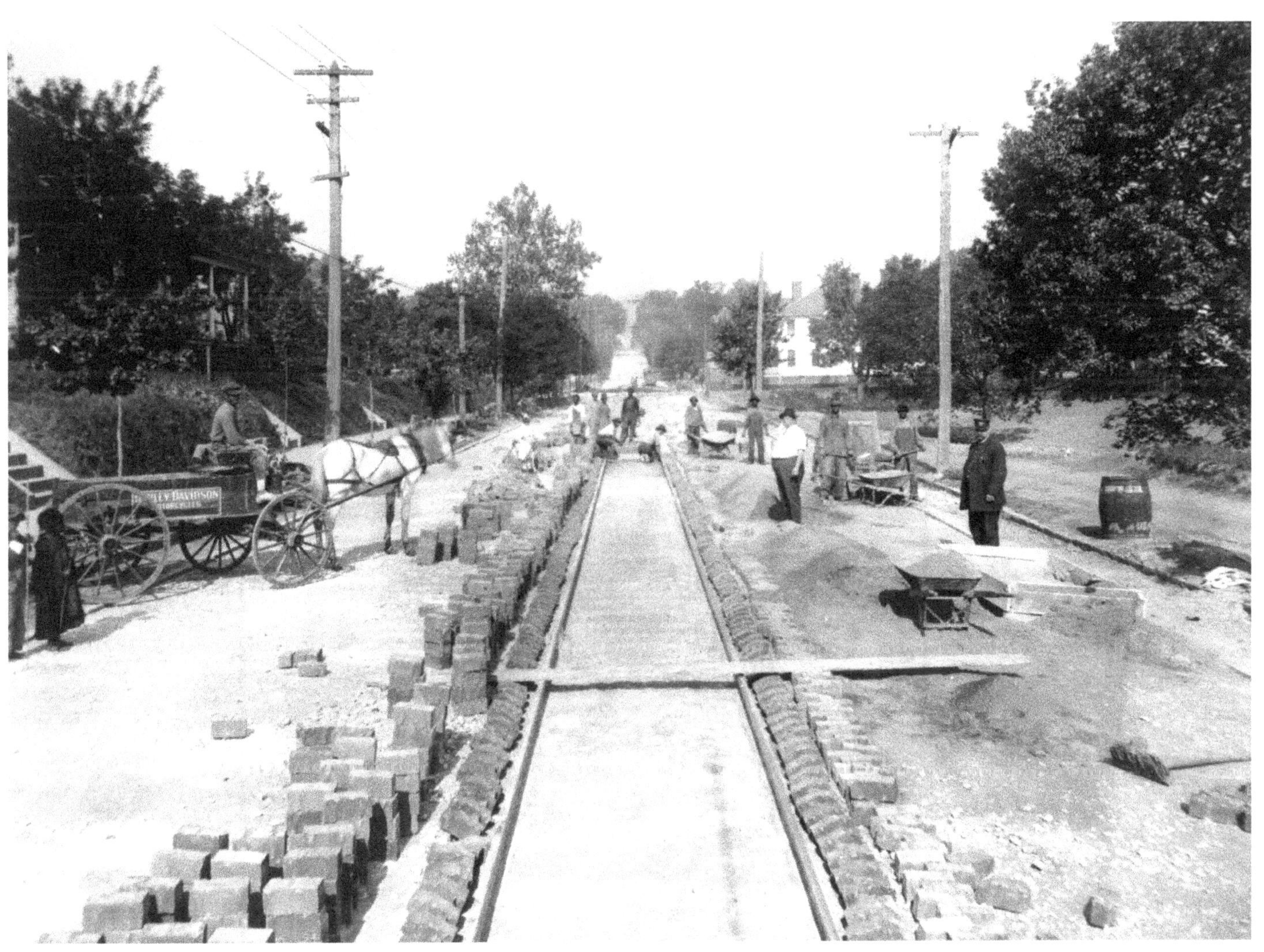

Workers pave East Lane Street in Raleigh during the summer of 1906. The wagon at far-left advertises Harley-Davidson motorcycles.

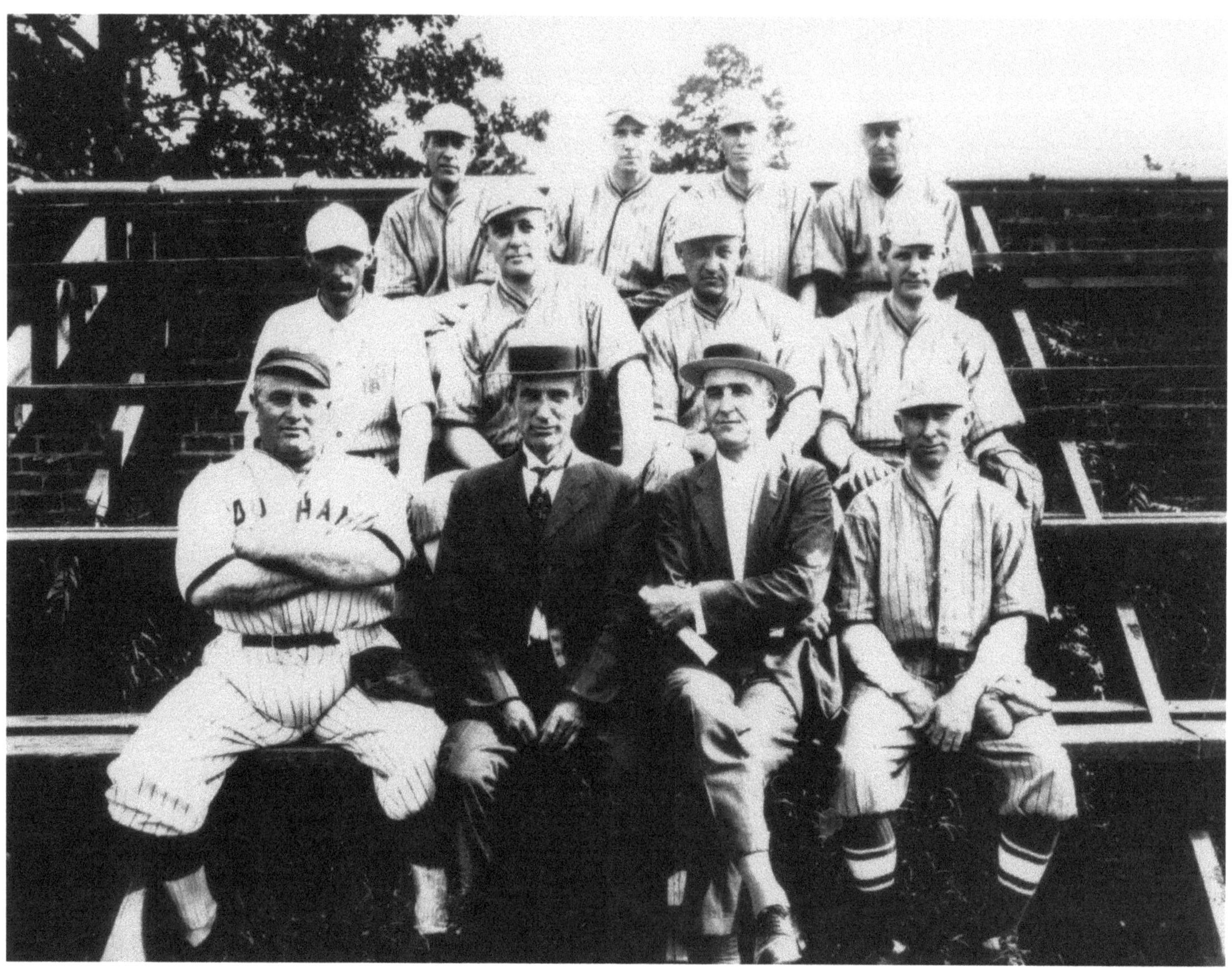

Trinity Baseball Club, ca. 1908.

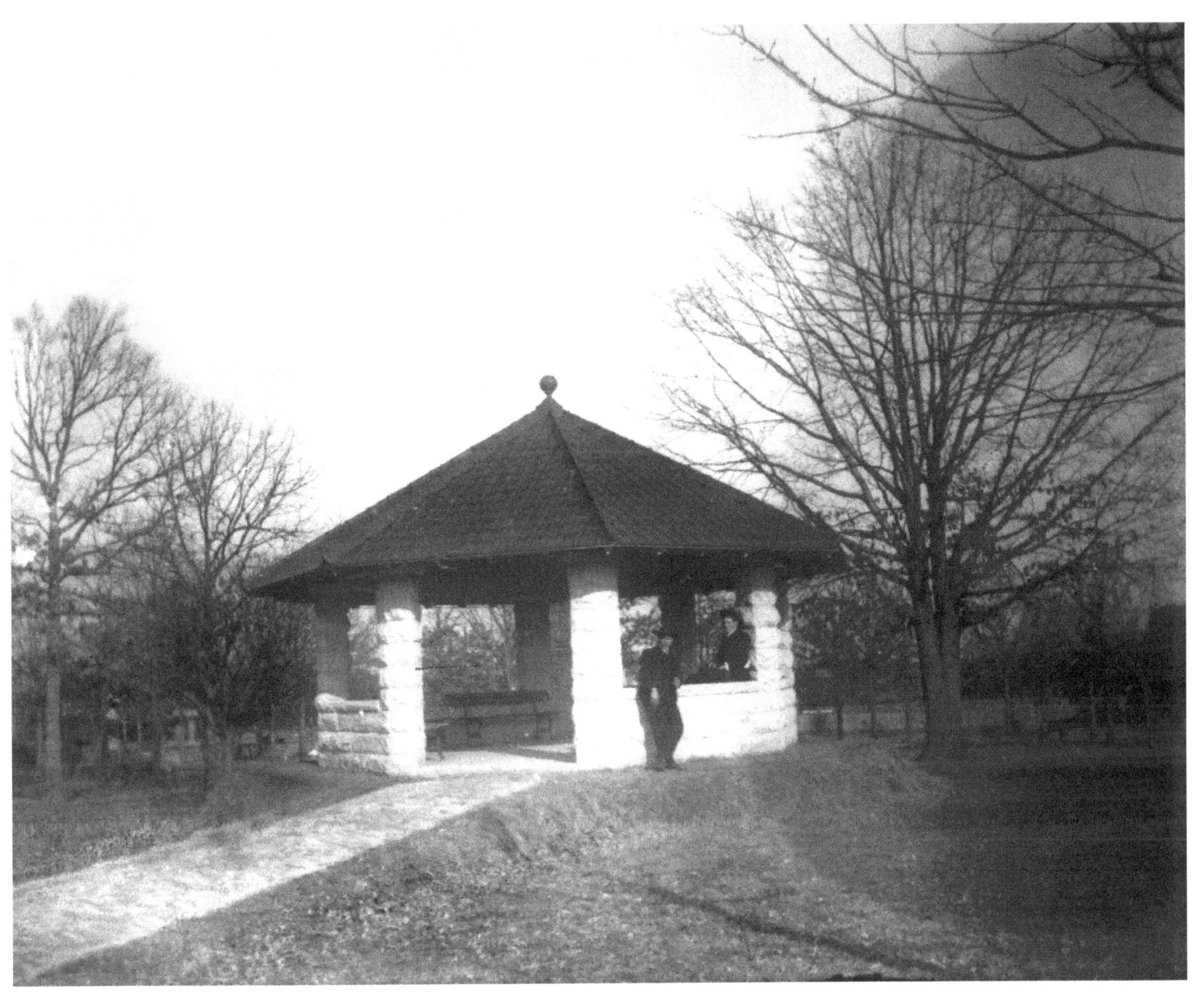

Stagg Pavilion was given to Trinity College by Mary Lyon Stagg, daughter of Mary Elizabeth Duke, sister of James and Benjamin Duke. The gazebo is named in honor of her husband, James Edward Stagg, a college trustee.

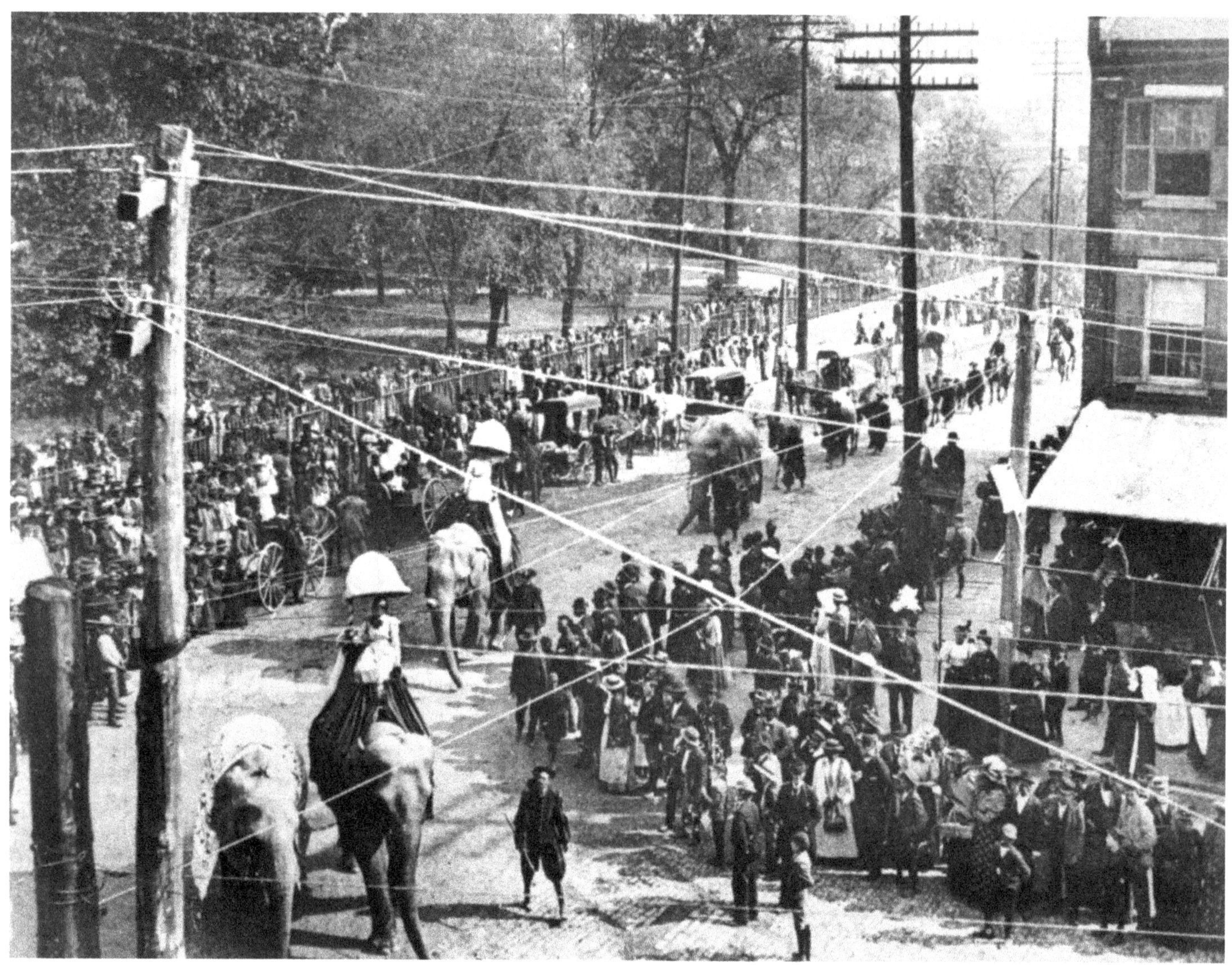

A circus parade—complete with elephants—turns the corner of Fayetteville and Morgan streets in Raleigh, ca. 1900. Fayetteville Street served as the city's central parade route and celebration site until its conversion into a pedestrian mall in the late 1970s.

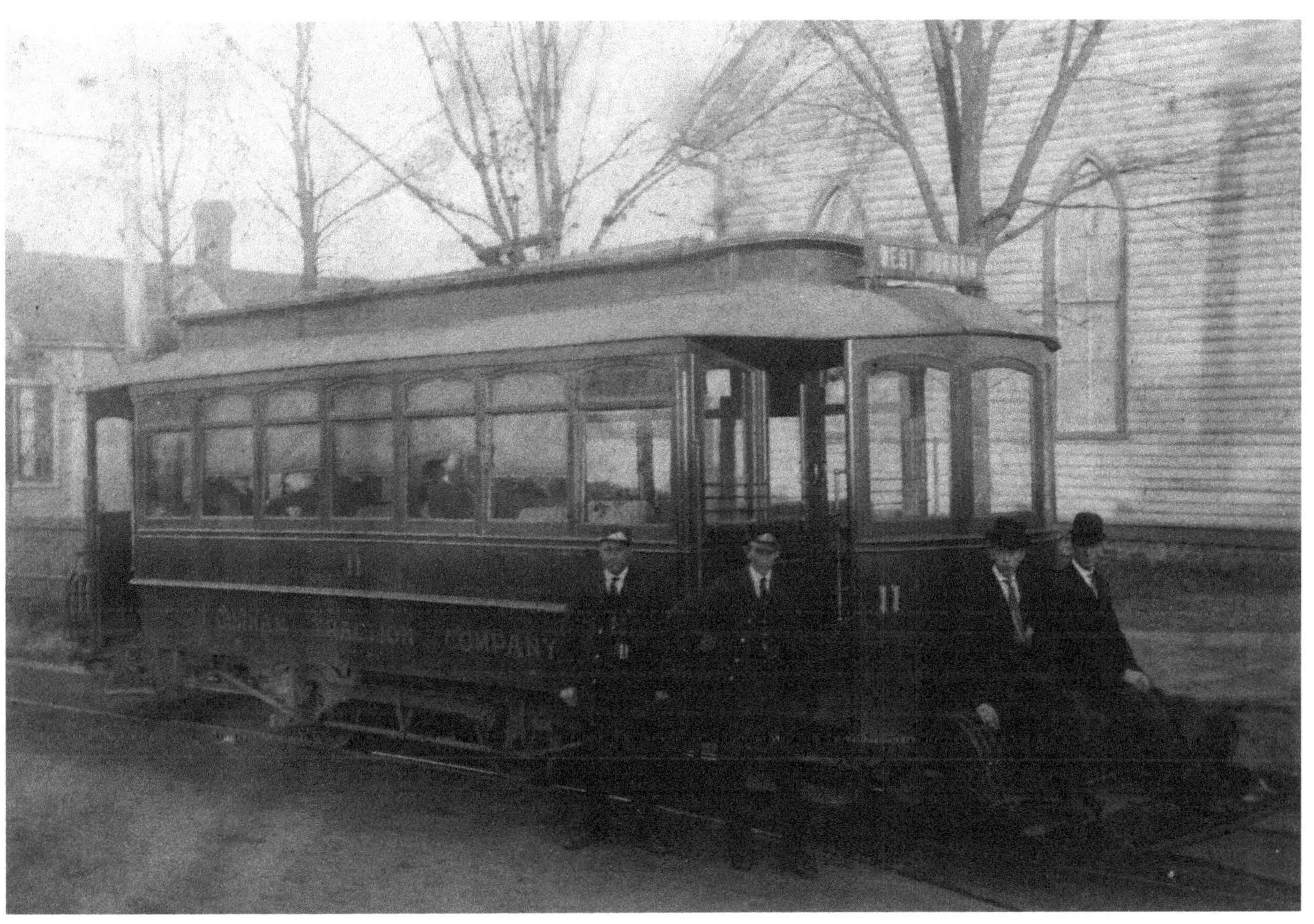

Durham's first streetcar system, the Durham Street Railway Company, began service in 1888 but soon folded owing to safety issues. In 1902 the city's first electric streetcar system, the Durham Traction Company, debuted. It would operate an electric trolley system for the city until the 1930s, when motorized buses became more economical. One of the Durham Traction Company's trolley cars is shown here, ca. 1908.

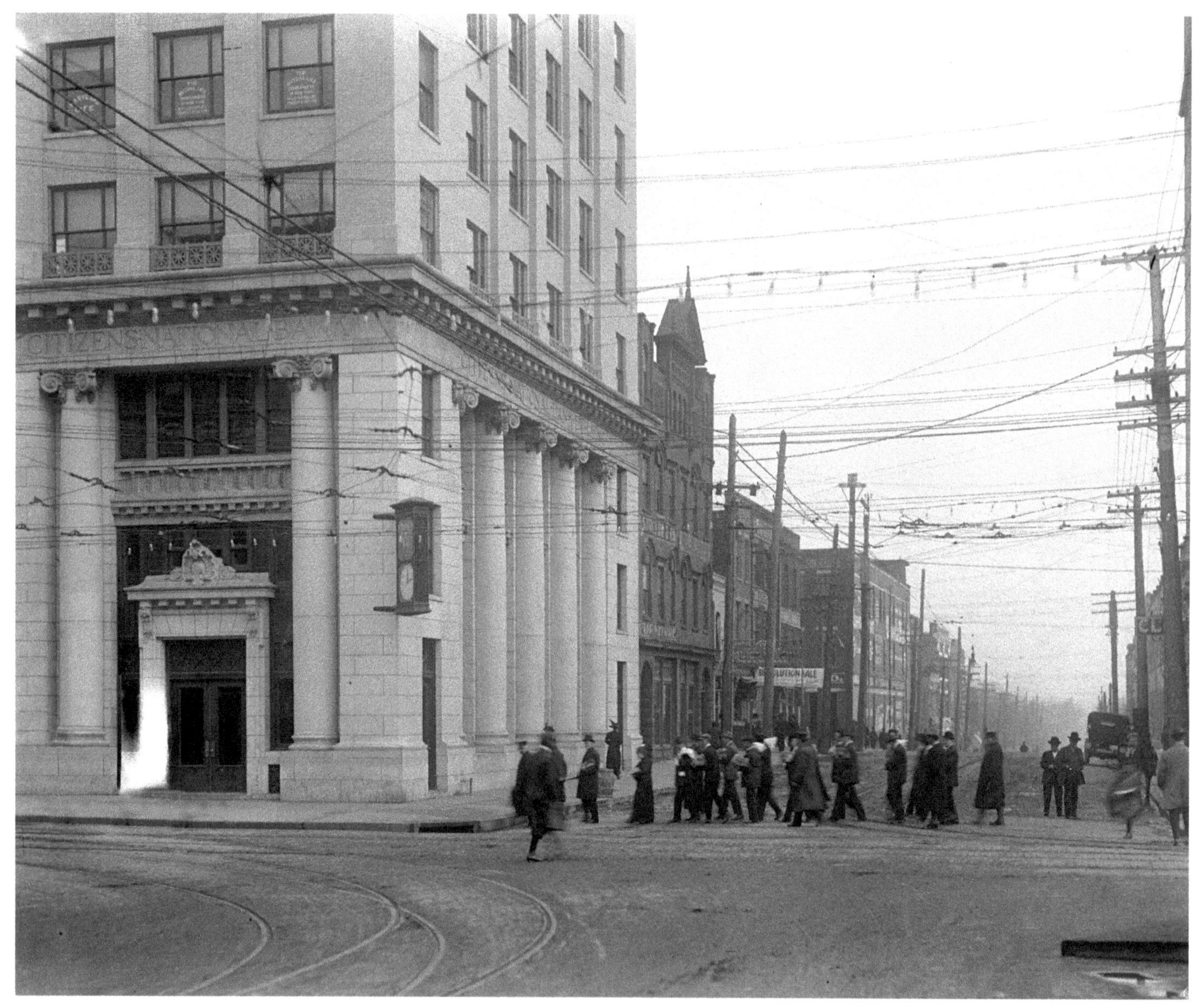

The northeast corner of Fayetteville and Martin streets in Raleigh housed the Citizens National Bank by 1914, when this photograph is believed to have been taken. Constructed a year earlier, the ten-story edifice was the city's tallest structure at the time.

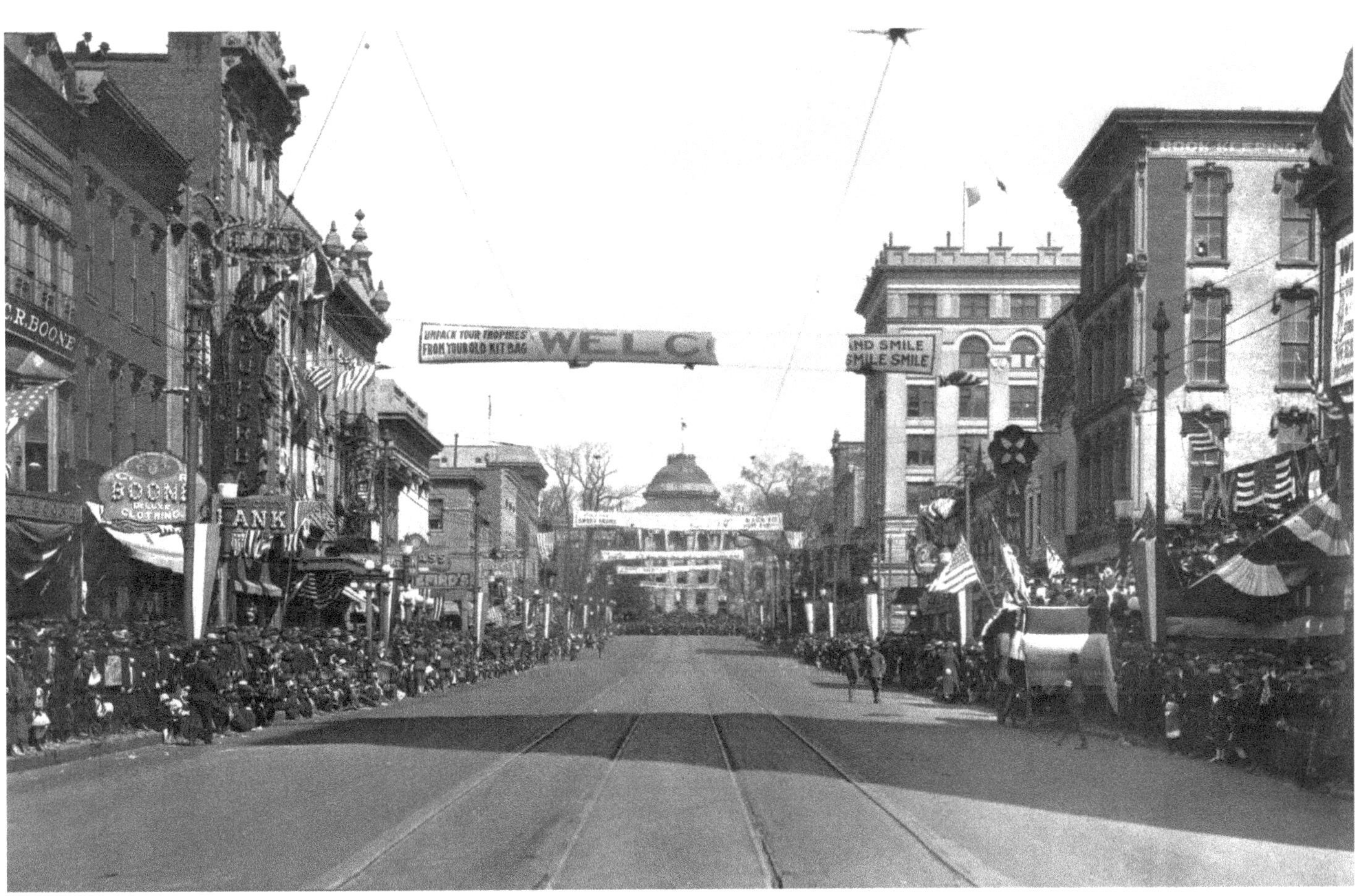

In March 1919, the 200-block of Fayetteville Street in Raleigh is festooned with banners as a crowd awaits the beginning of a parade to honor the state's returning World War I veterans. The North Carolina State Capitol is visible in the center background.

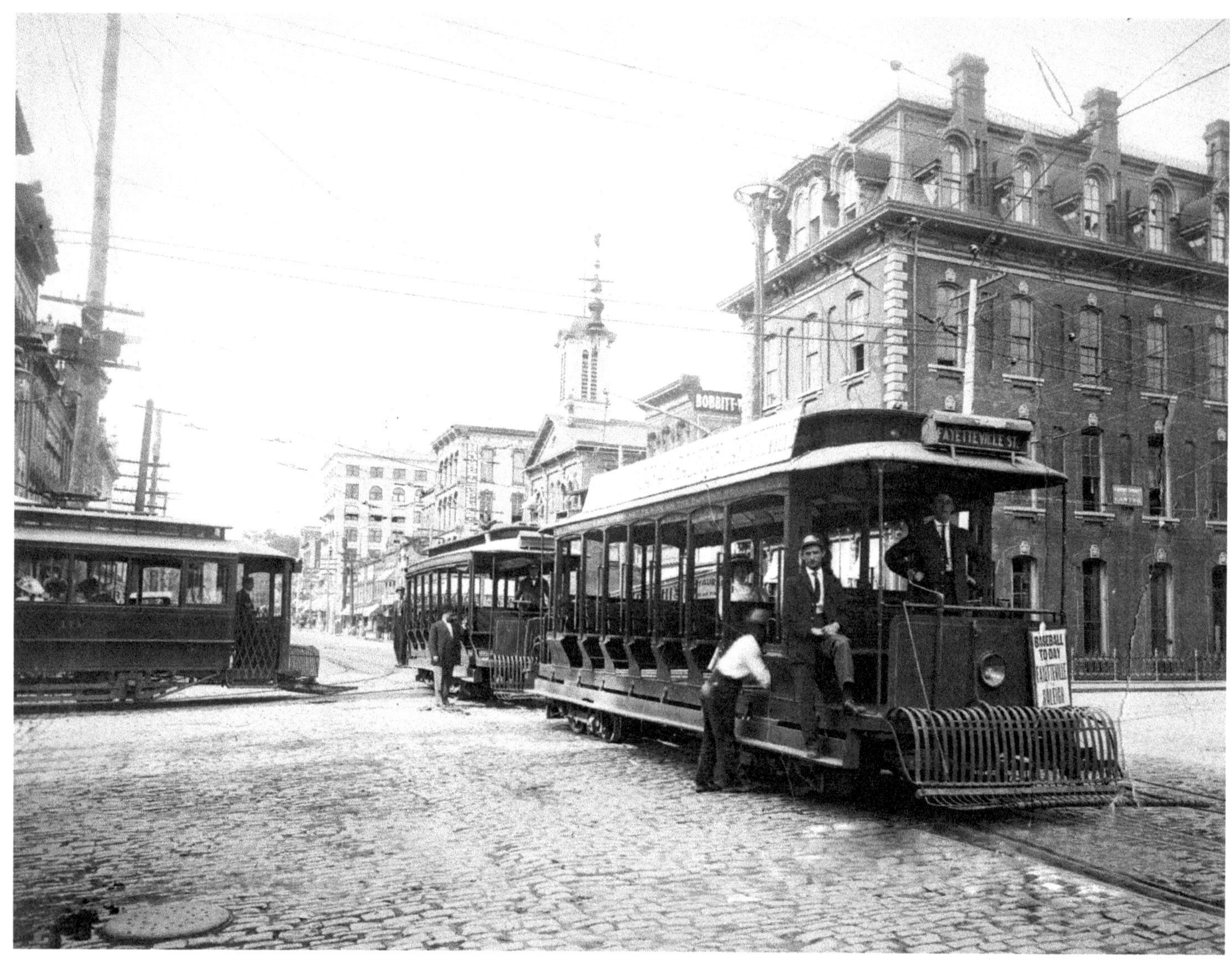

Raleigh premiered the state's first streetcar system on Christmas Day 1886. Originally powered by mules, the system was electrified in 1891. Called the Raleigh Street Railway, the operation would later fall under the ownership of the Carolina Power & Light Company. In this 1910 photograph, a Raleigh trolley car crosses Martin Street as it moves down tracks along Fayetteville Street.

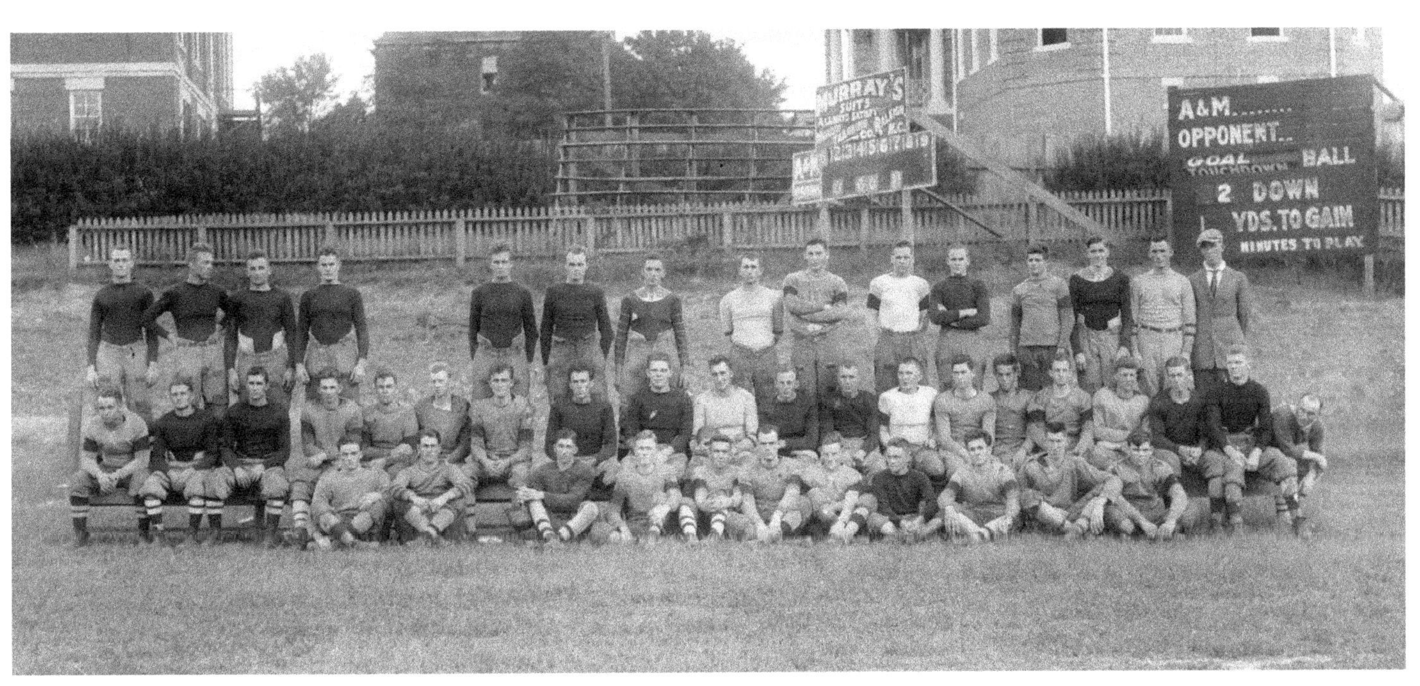

By the 1900s football began to compete with baseball as the most popular spectator sport on America's college campuses. Despite being frowned upon by faculty (and parents) who found it too violent, college football grew in popularity during the 1920s and 1930s. This image depicts the North Carolina A&M College (now North Carolina State University) football squad from ca. 1905 to 1910.

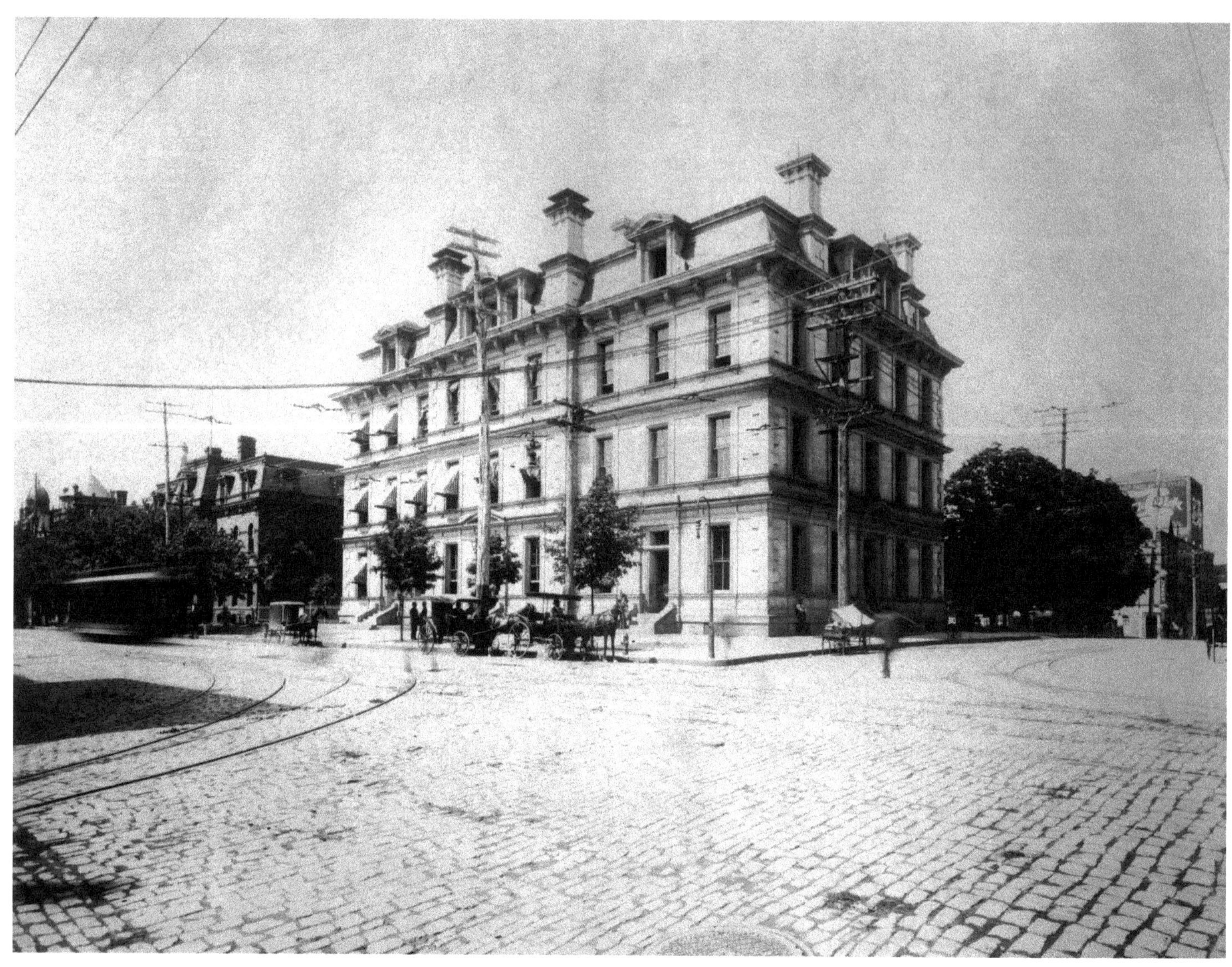

Constructed between 1874 and 1879 on the southwest corner of Fayetteville and Martin streets in Raleigh, the Century Post Office Building was the first federal structure erected in the South after the Civil War. The building continues to serve as a downtown post office today.

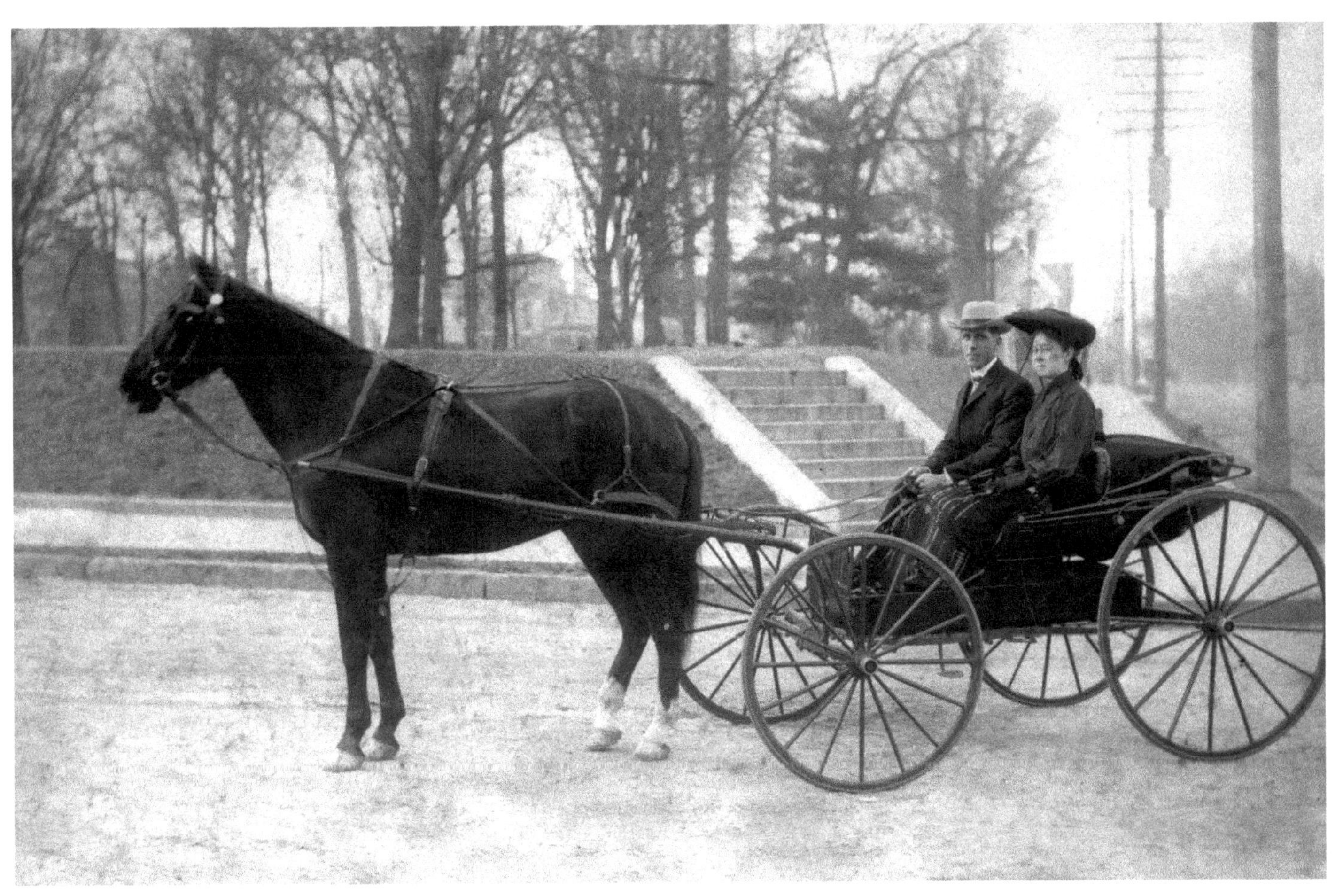

A horse-drawn buggy carrying William Henry Smith and Margaret Alice Baugh passes Union Square and the North Carolina Statehouse in Raleigh, ca. 1908.

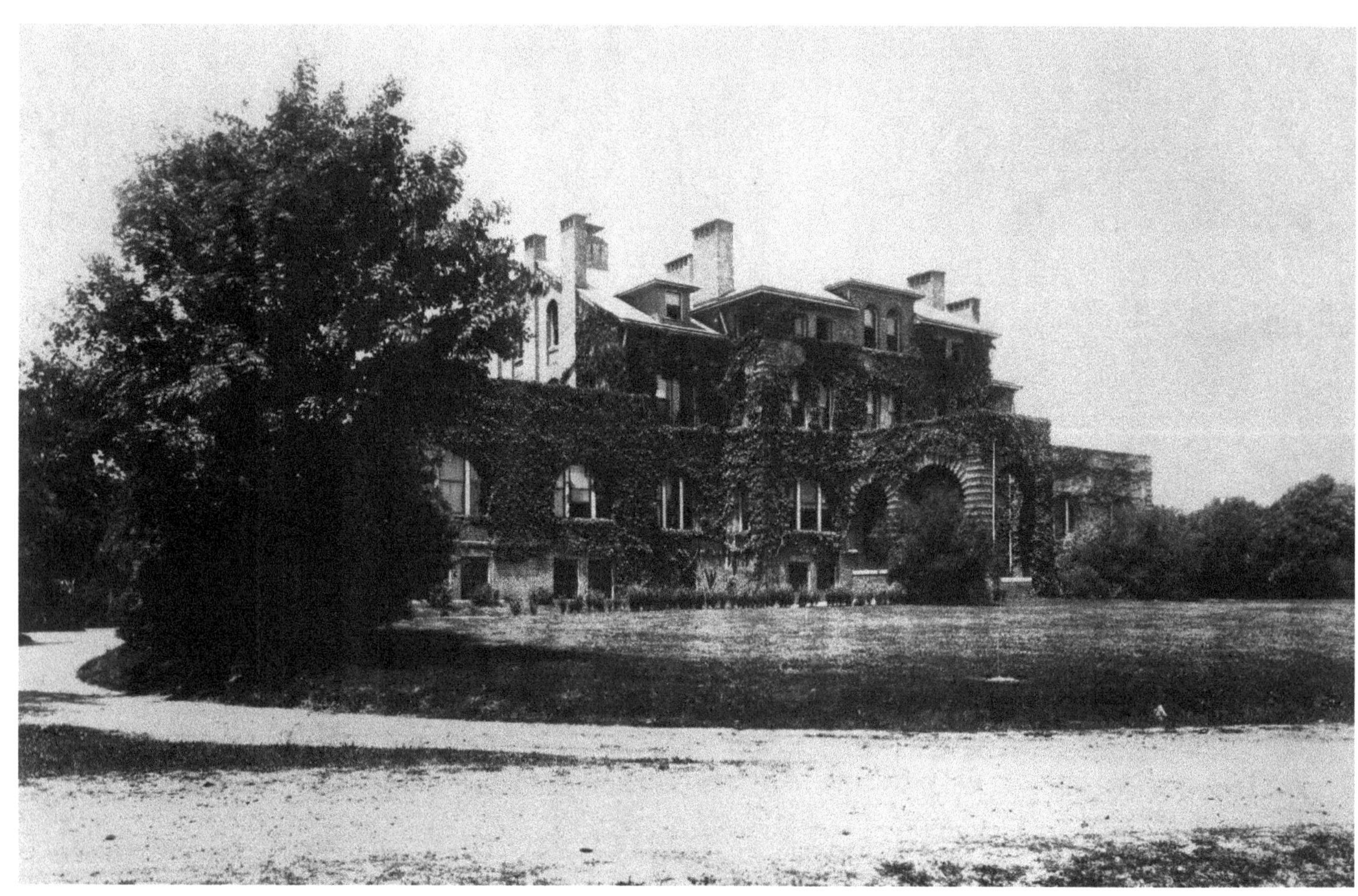

Chartered by the General Assembly in 1887, North Carolina A&M College (now known as North Carolina State University) first opened its doors to students in Raleigh on October 3, 1889. The first building constructed on the new campus was Holliday Hall, pictured here in 1909.

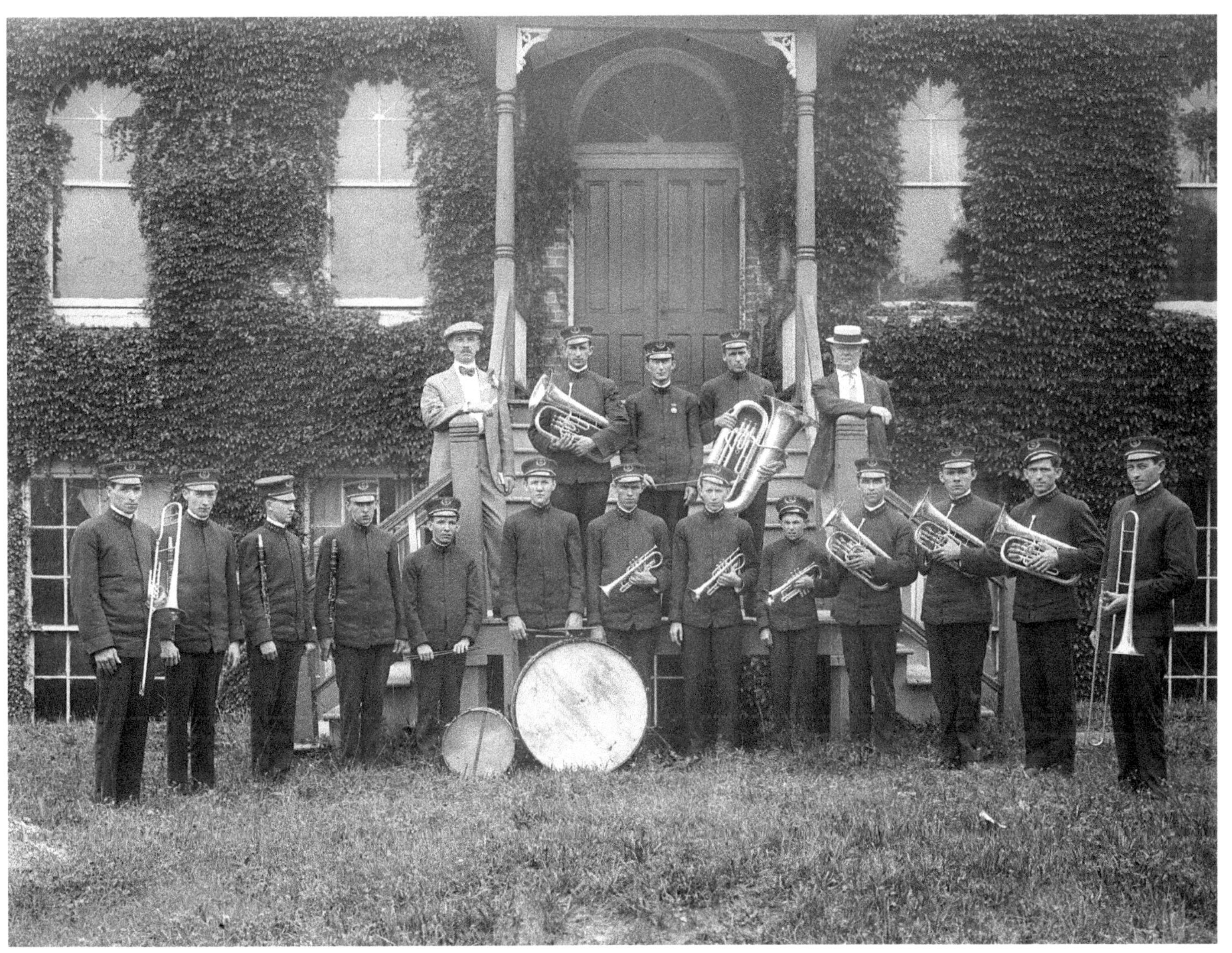

Built between 1892 and 1910, Pilot Mill was one of only a handful of textile mills located in Raleigh. Most North Carolina textile mills sponsored musical and athletic clubs for their employees to participate in. The Pilot Mill Cotton Band poses here for a portrait in this undated photograph.

First hosting students in 1899, the Main Building of Raleigh's Baptist Female University (later Meredith College) was designed by A. G. Bauer. Its lower floors held classrooms and meeting spaces while the upper floors served as dormitories for both students and instructors. When Meredith moved to a new campus in West Raleigh in 1926, the building became the Mansion Park Hotel. It was demolished in 1967.

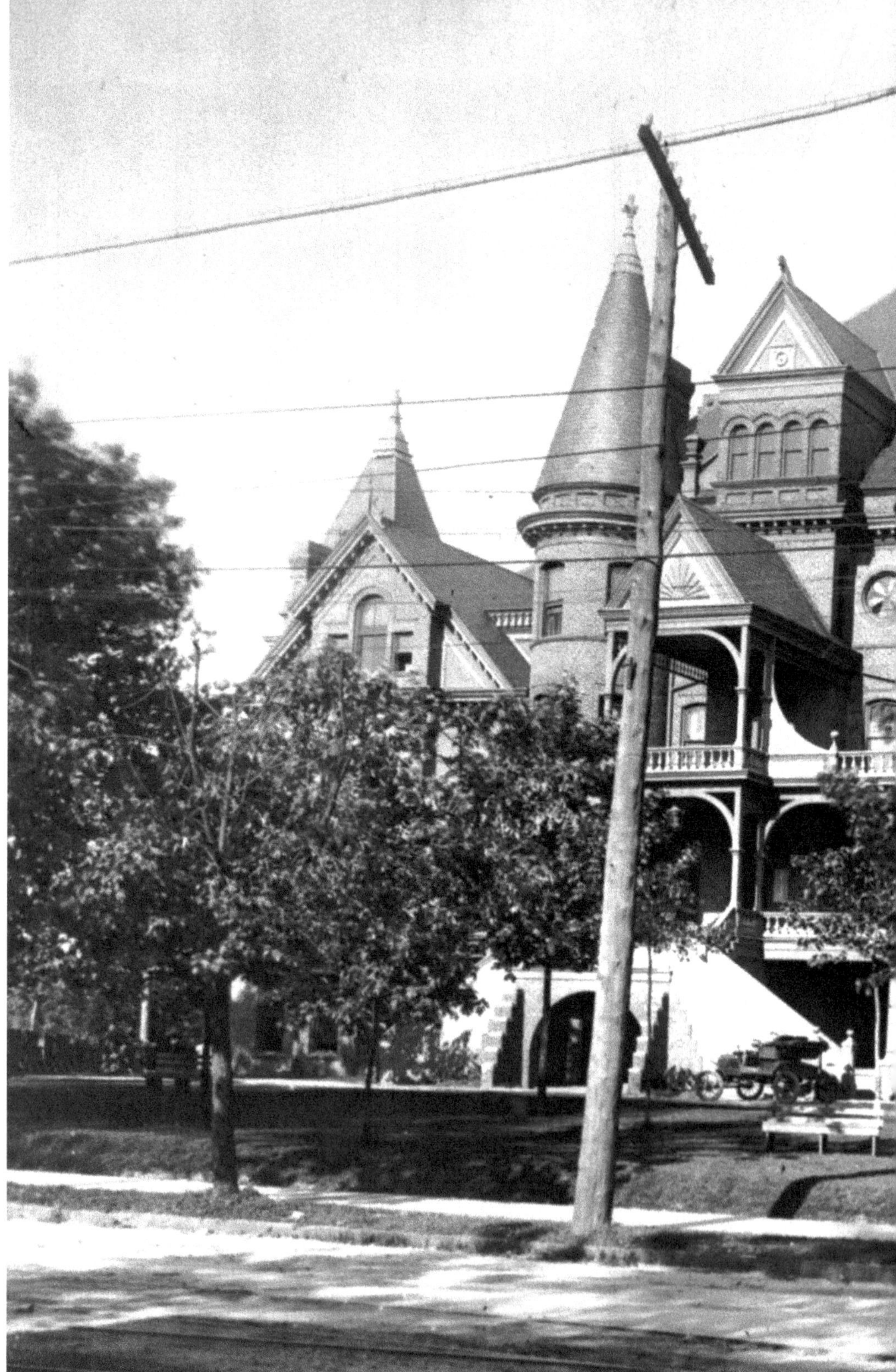

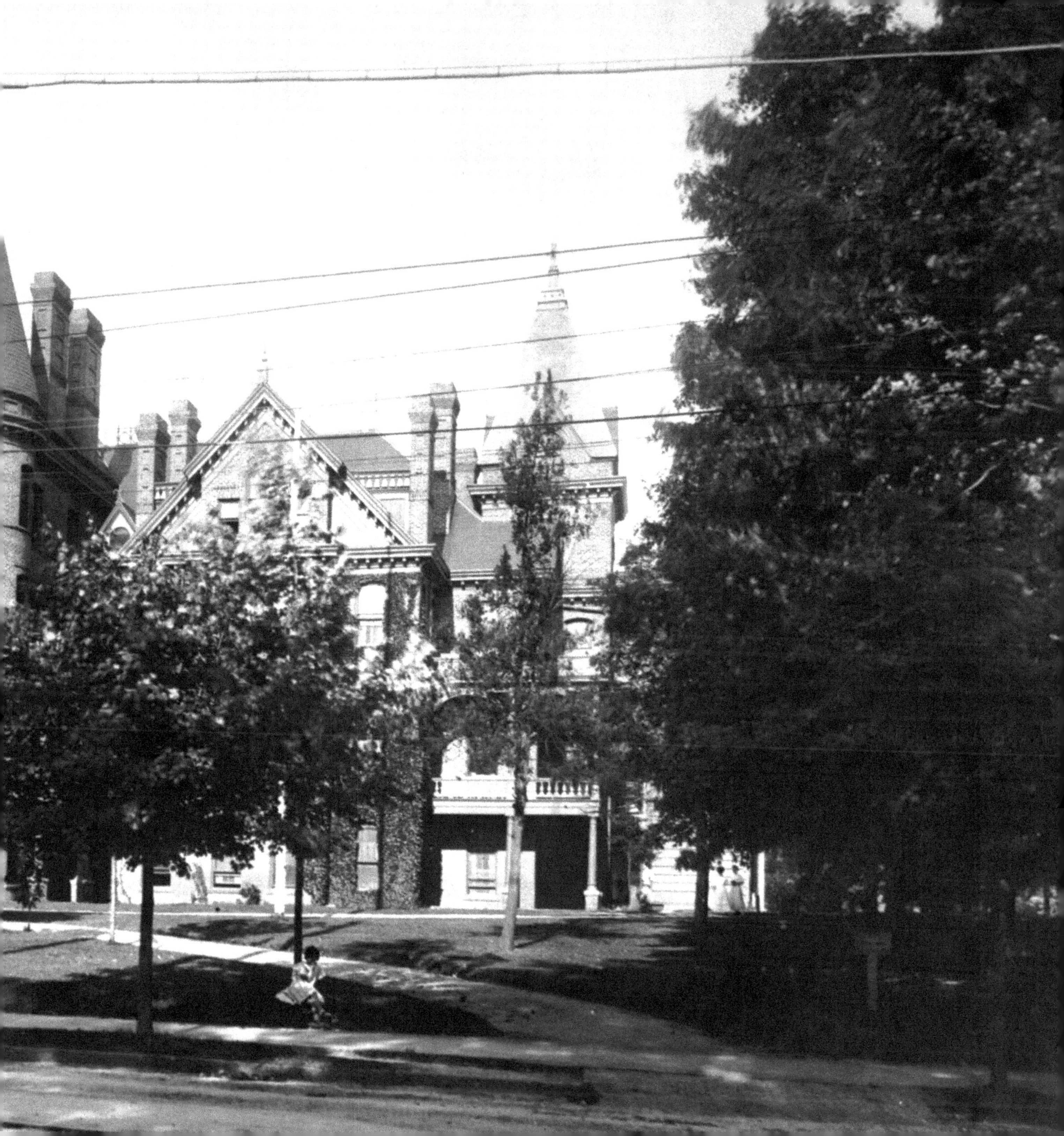

Raleigh has been the site for the North Carolina State Penitentiary since 1870, when construction began on this imposing Gothic structure. Known as "Central Prison," the building was designed by Ohio architect Levi Scofield. Taking 14 years to complete at a cost of $1.25 million, the structure housed the state's prison population until the 1980s, when a modern facility was built to replace the aging edifice.

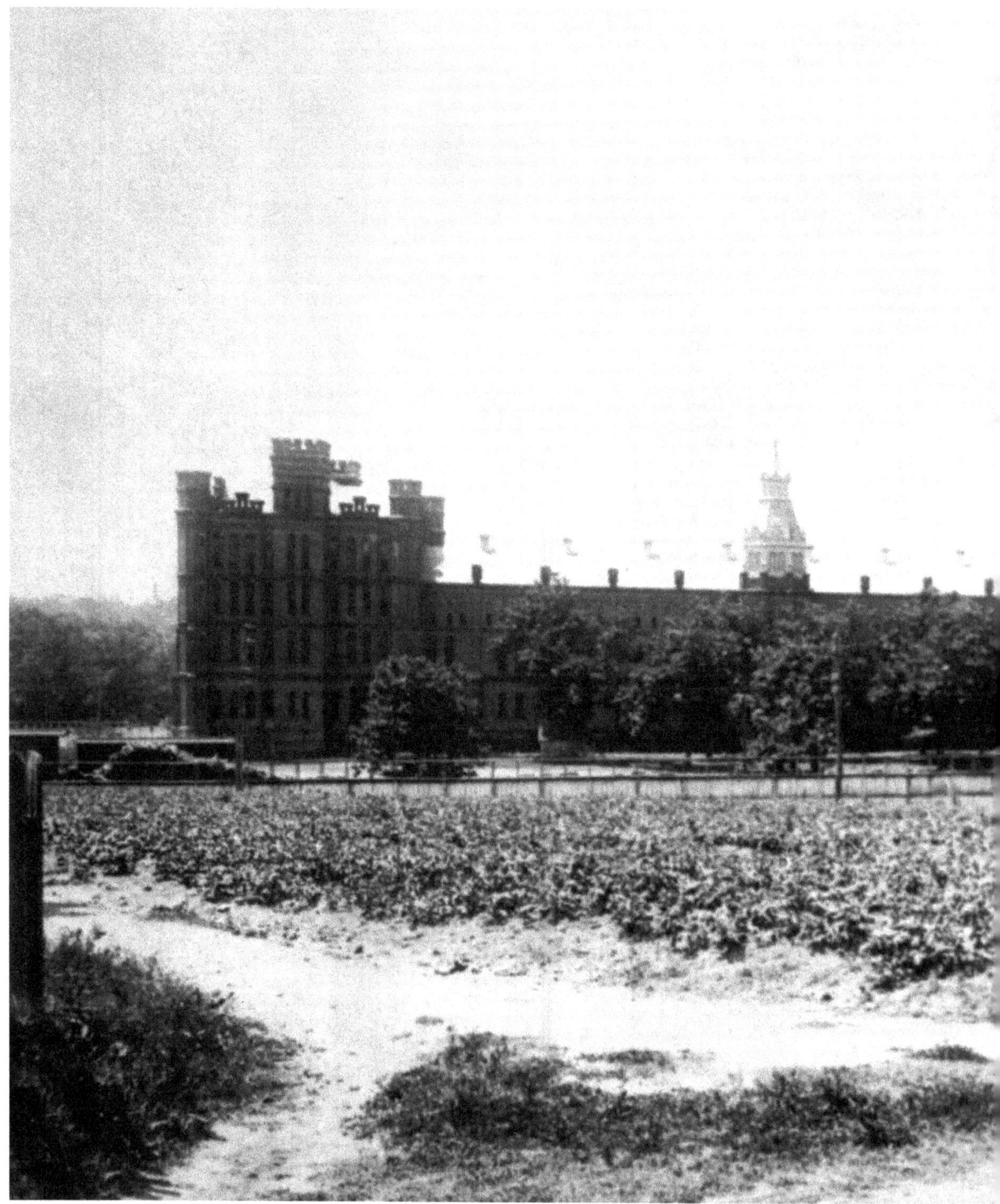

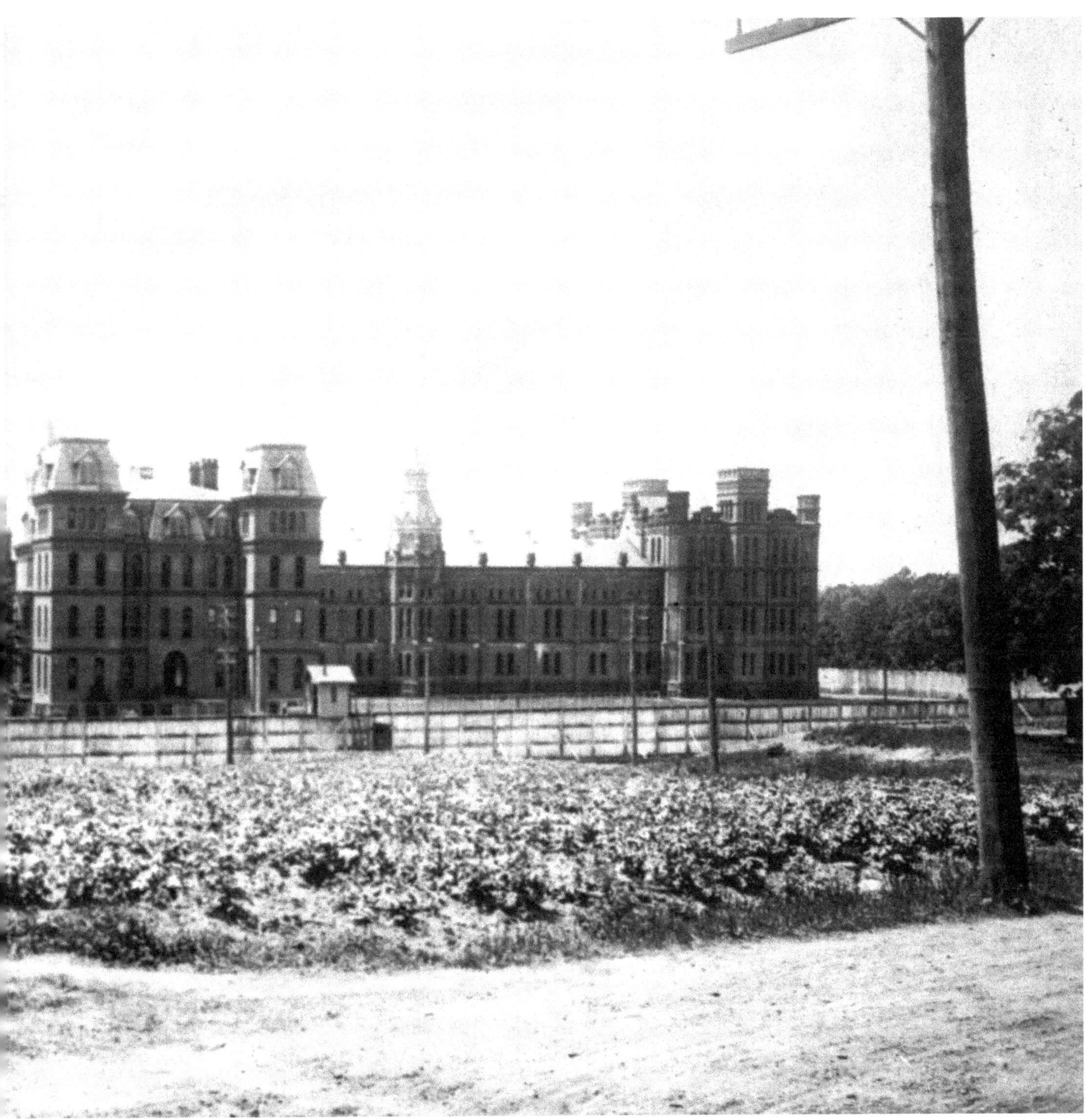

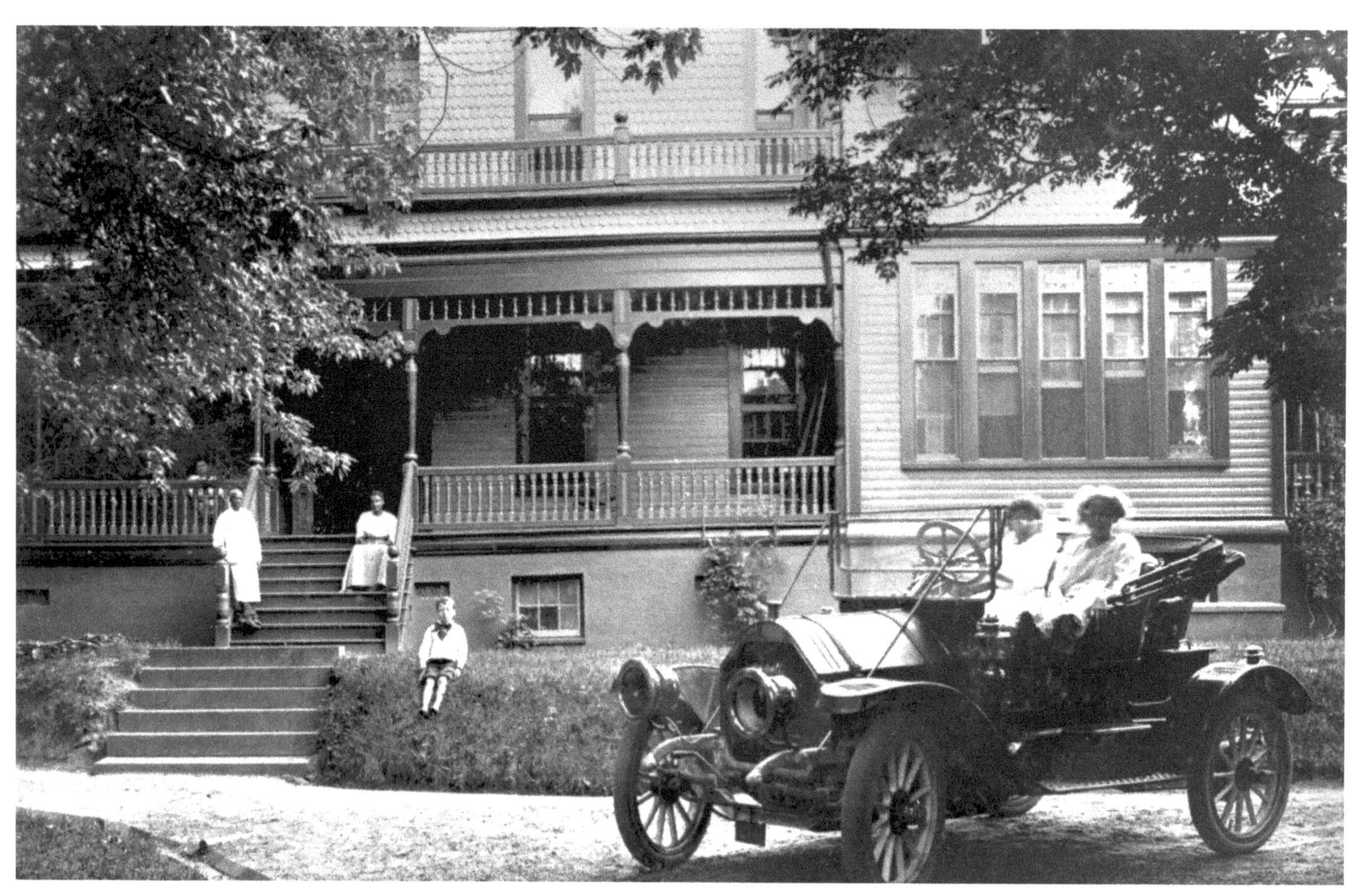

Unidentified people pose with an early automobile outside "Fairview," Washington Duke's home in Durham.

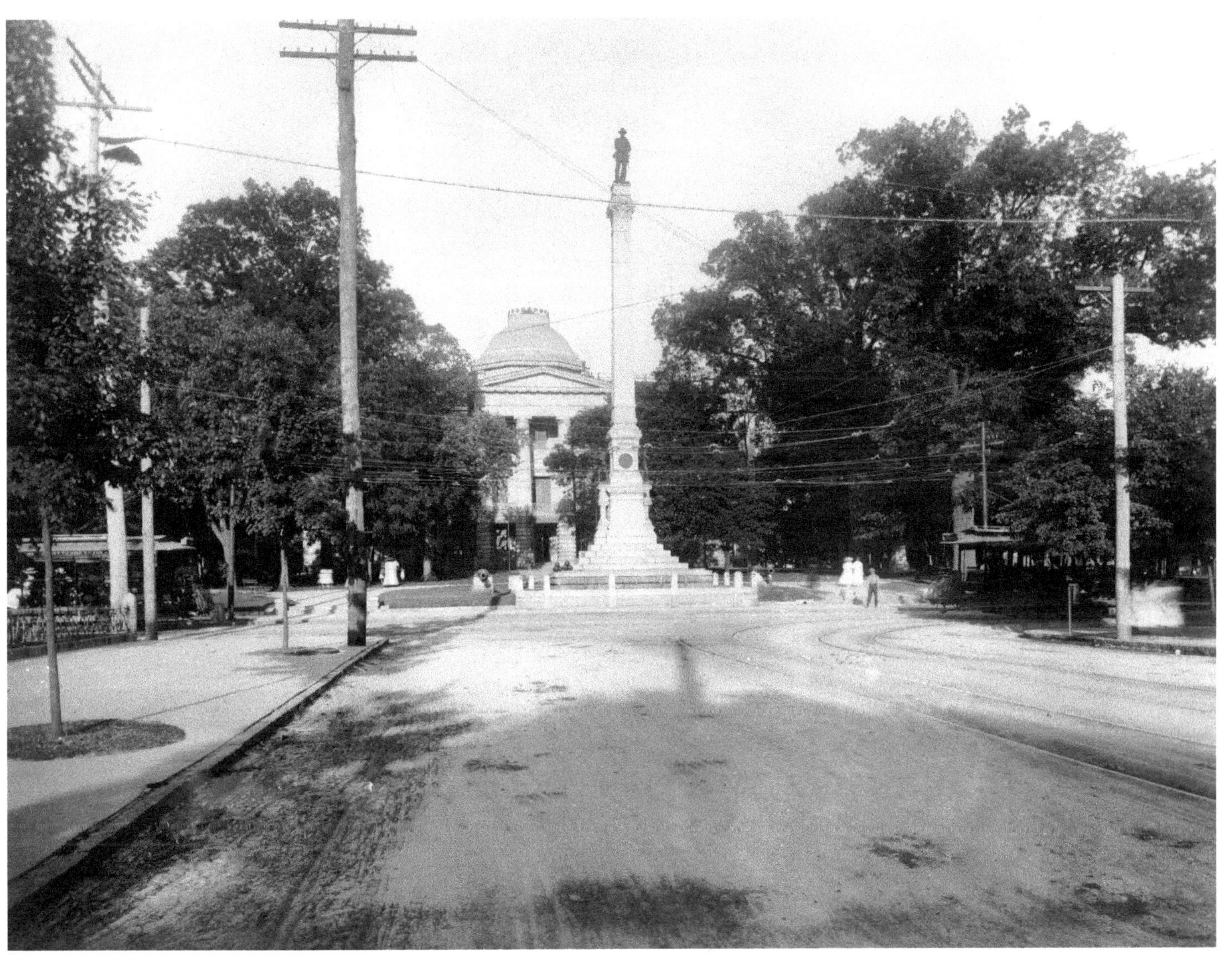

Looking east on Hillsborough Street in Raleigh toward the west front of the North Carolina State Capitol, 1909. Prominent in the photograph is the Confederate Memorial, a monument honoring North Carolinians killed during the Civil War.

This rooftop image, probably taken from atop the former Commercial National Bank building in Raleigh, faces west down Martin Street from its intersection with Fayetteville Street, ca. 1915. Standing prominently in the center of the image is the Tucker Building.

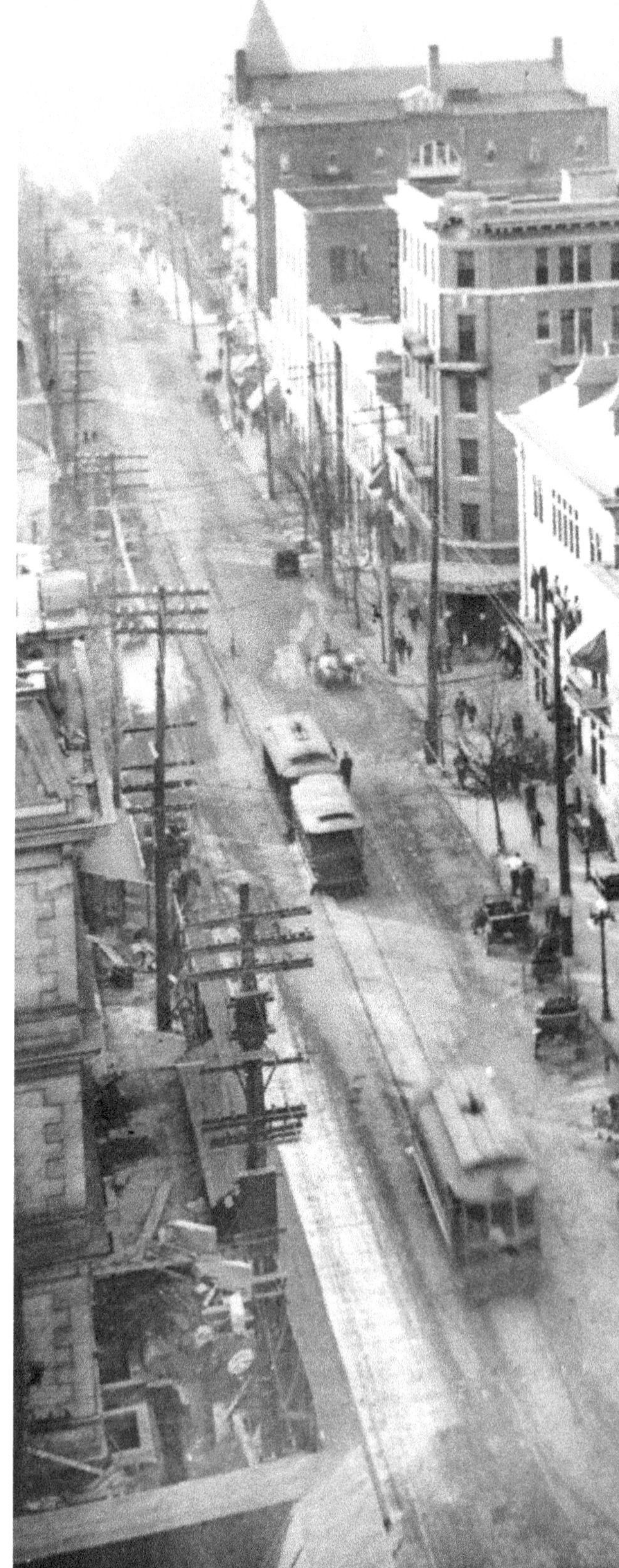

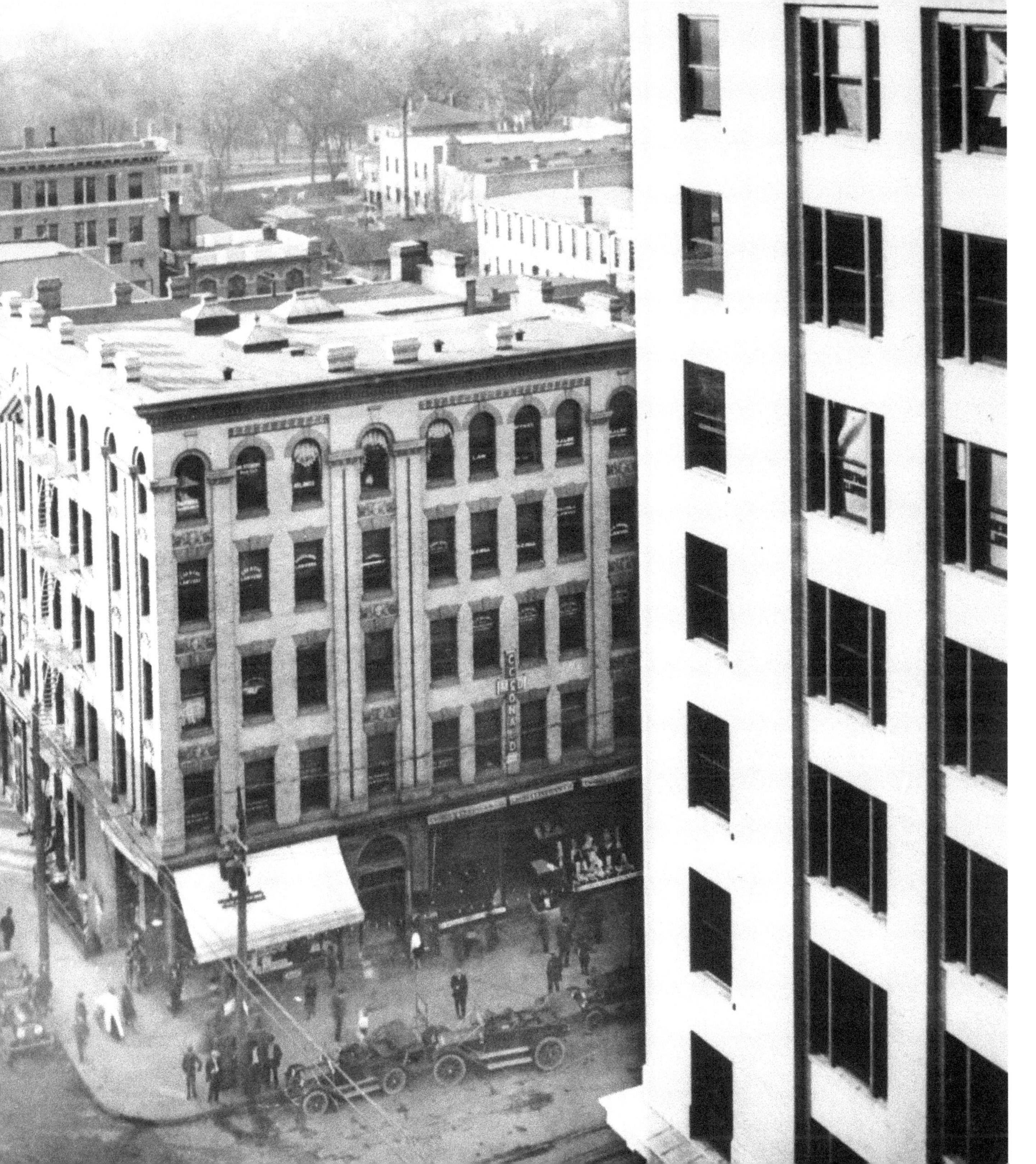

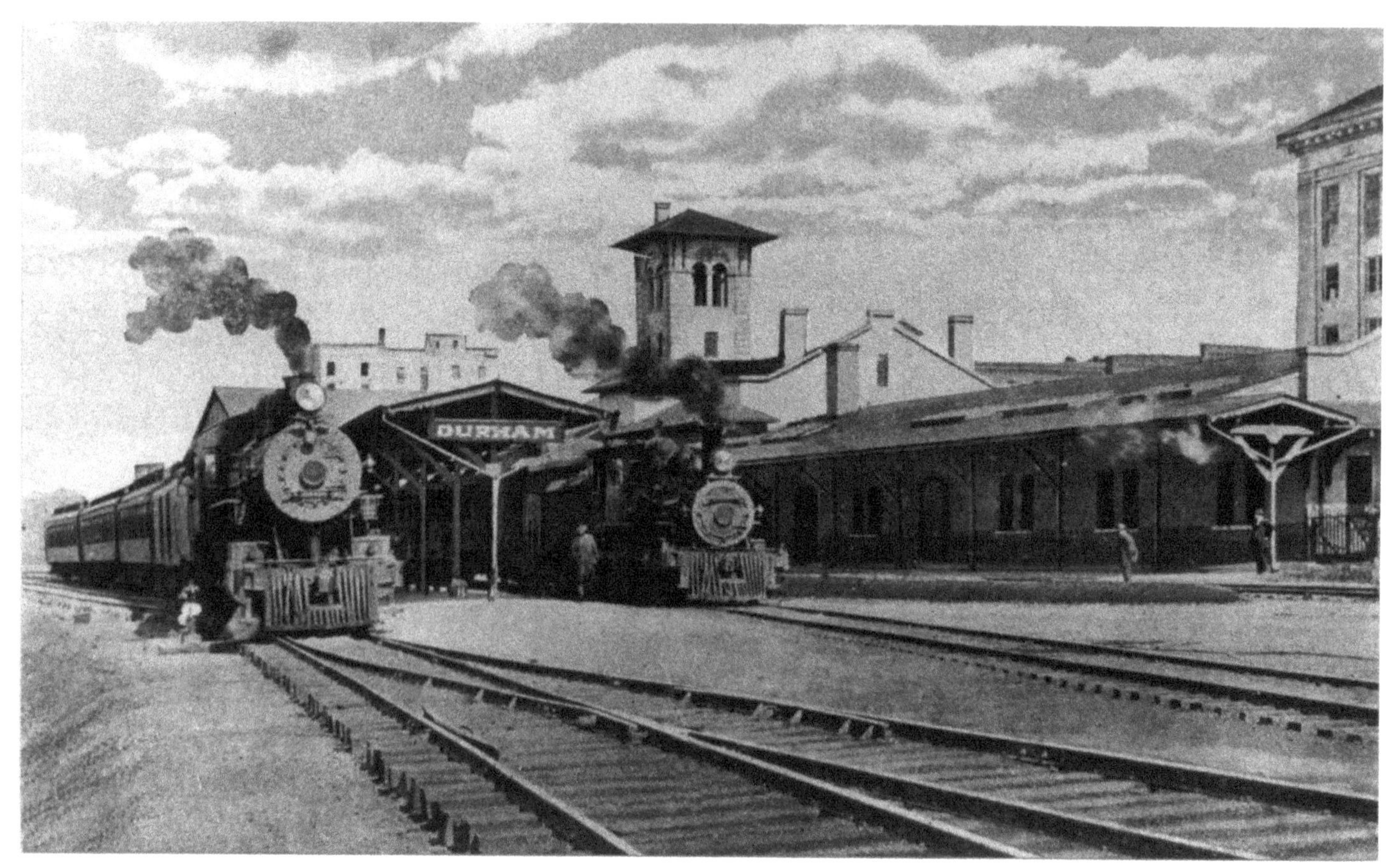

This image, from a postcard, shows two steam engines idling at Durham's Union Station, ca. 1910.

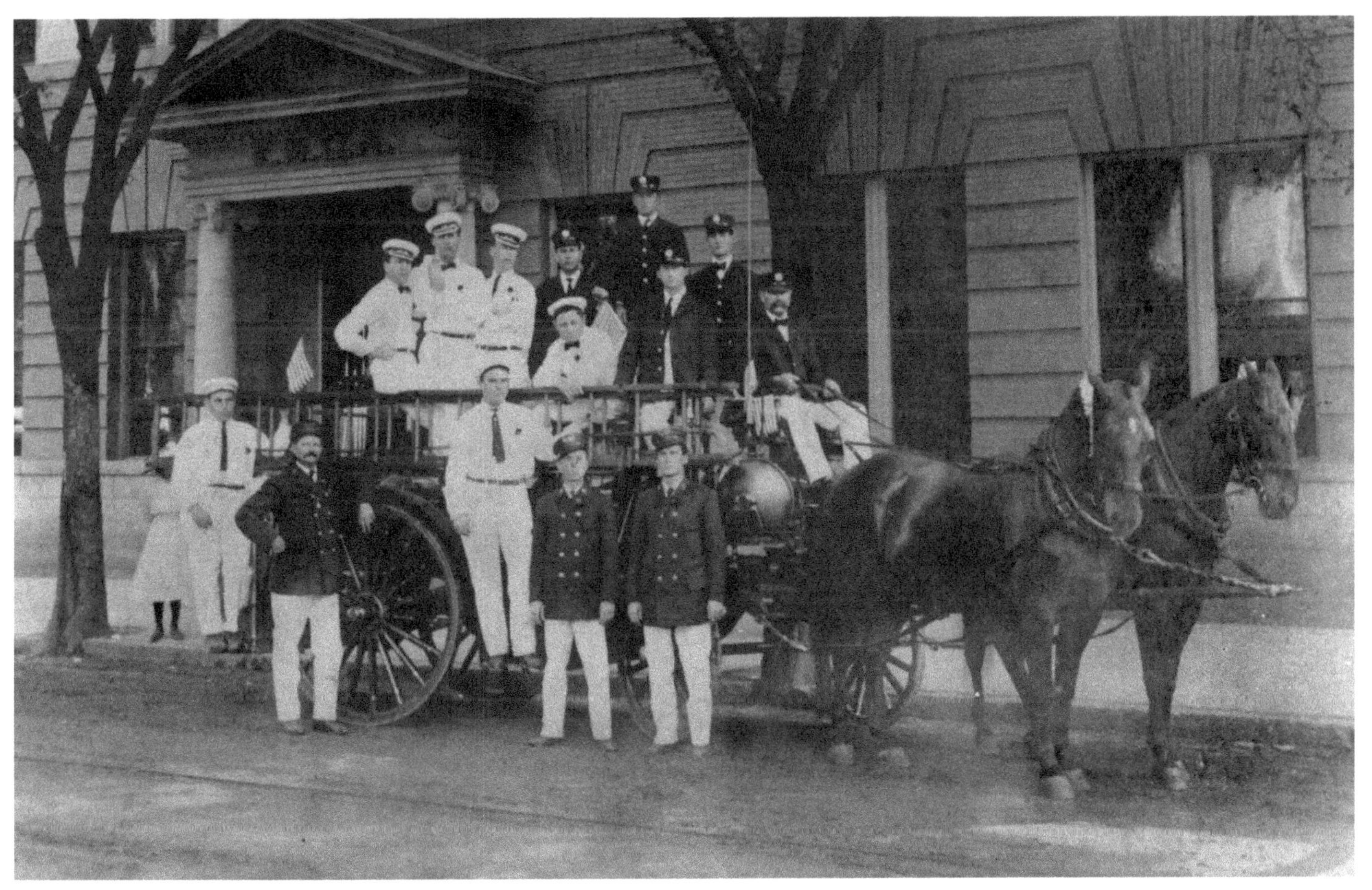

A Durham Fire Department horse-drawn hose wagon and crew stand in front of the YMCA, ca. 1910.

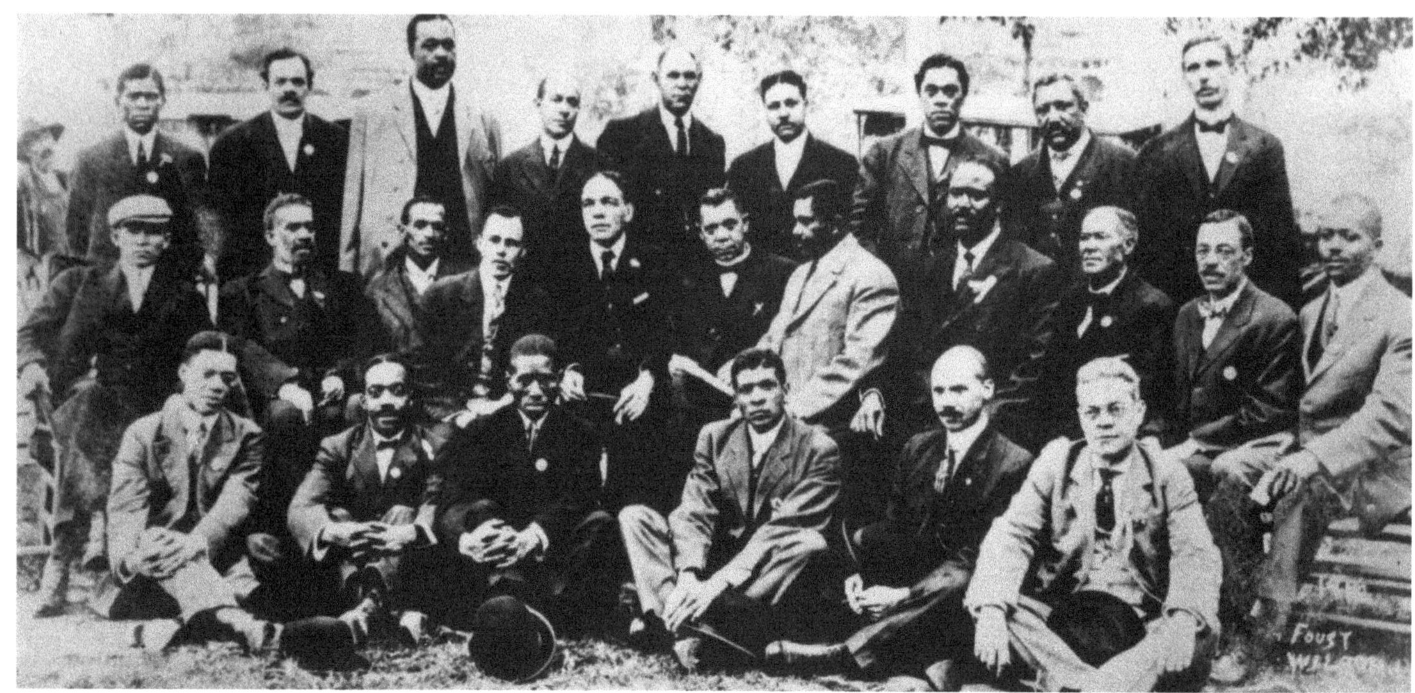

After visiting Durham in 1910, Booker T. Washington (shown here in a group photograph, second row, sixth from right) called Durham "the city of Negro Enterprises."

S. E. Rochelle, far left, a Durham bicycle and motorcycle dealer, shows off his motorcycles in front of the "Whirl of Death," a motorcycle arena created by the American Motordrome Company for traveling carnivals, ca. 1910.

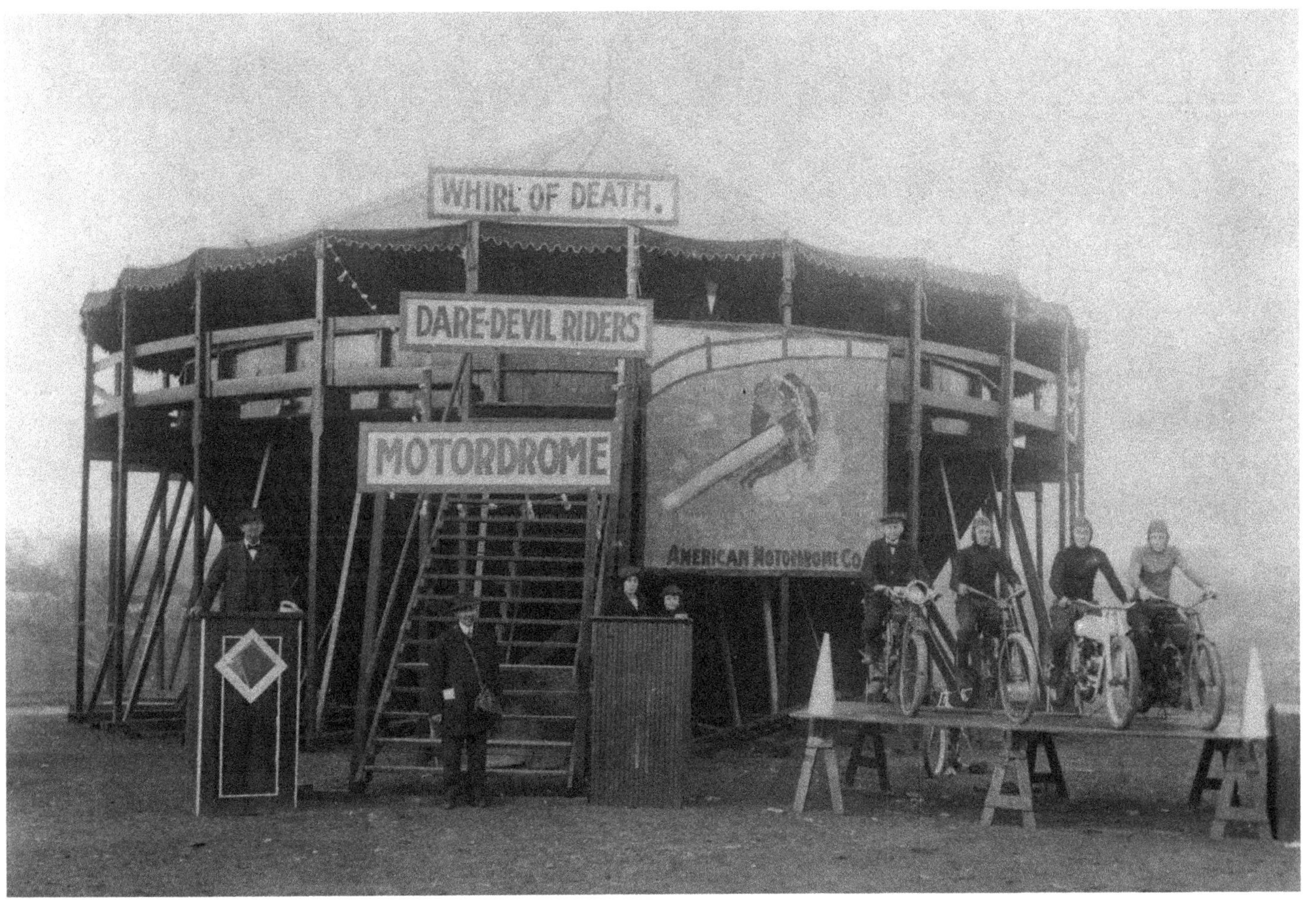

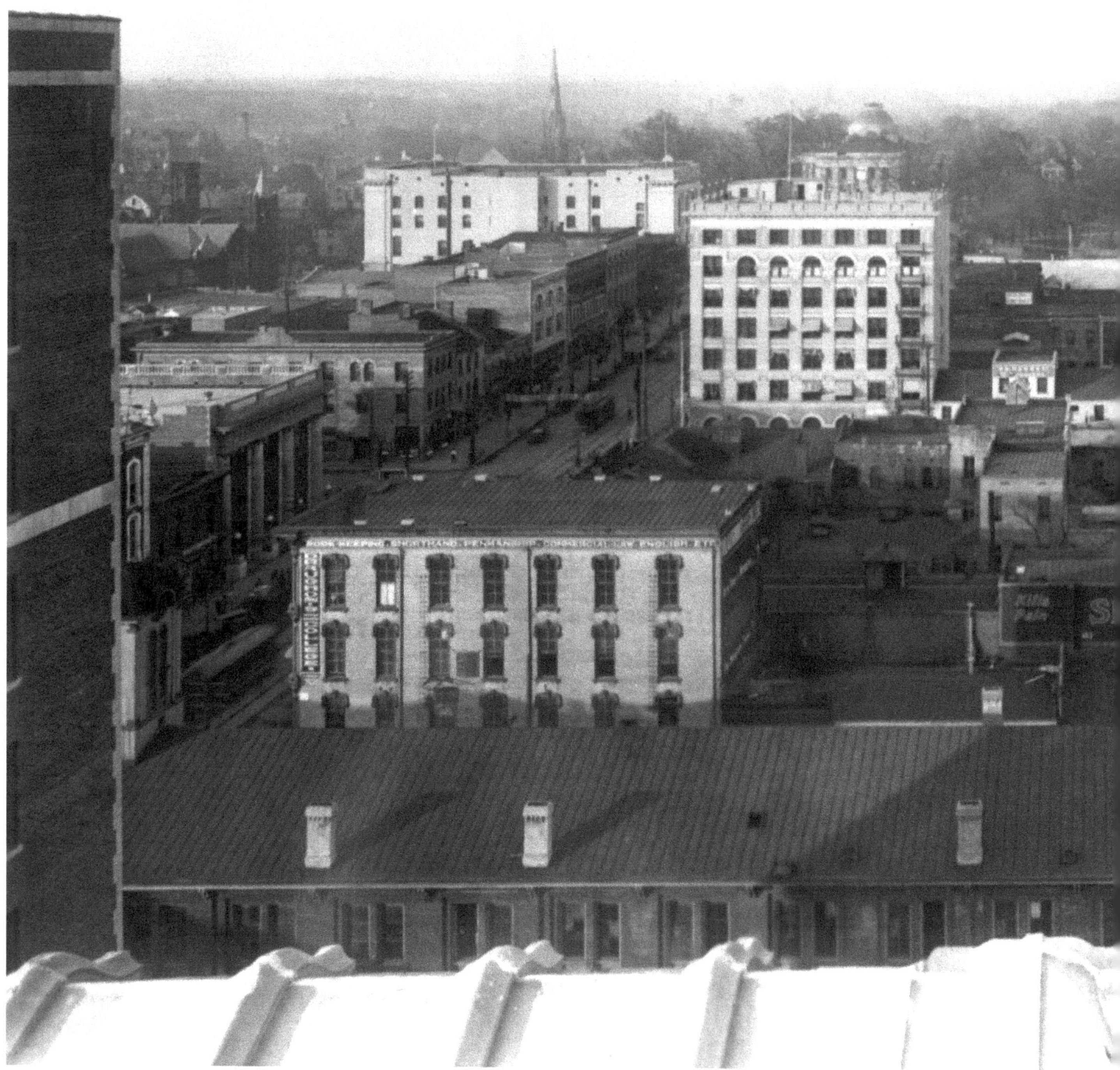

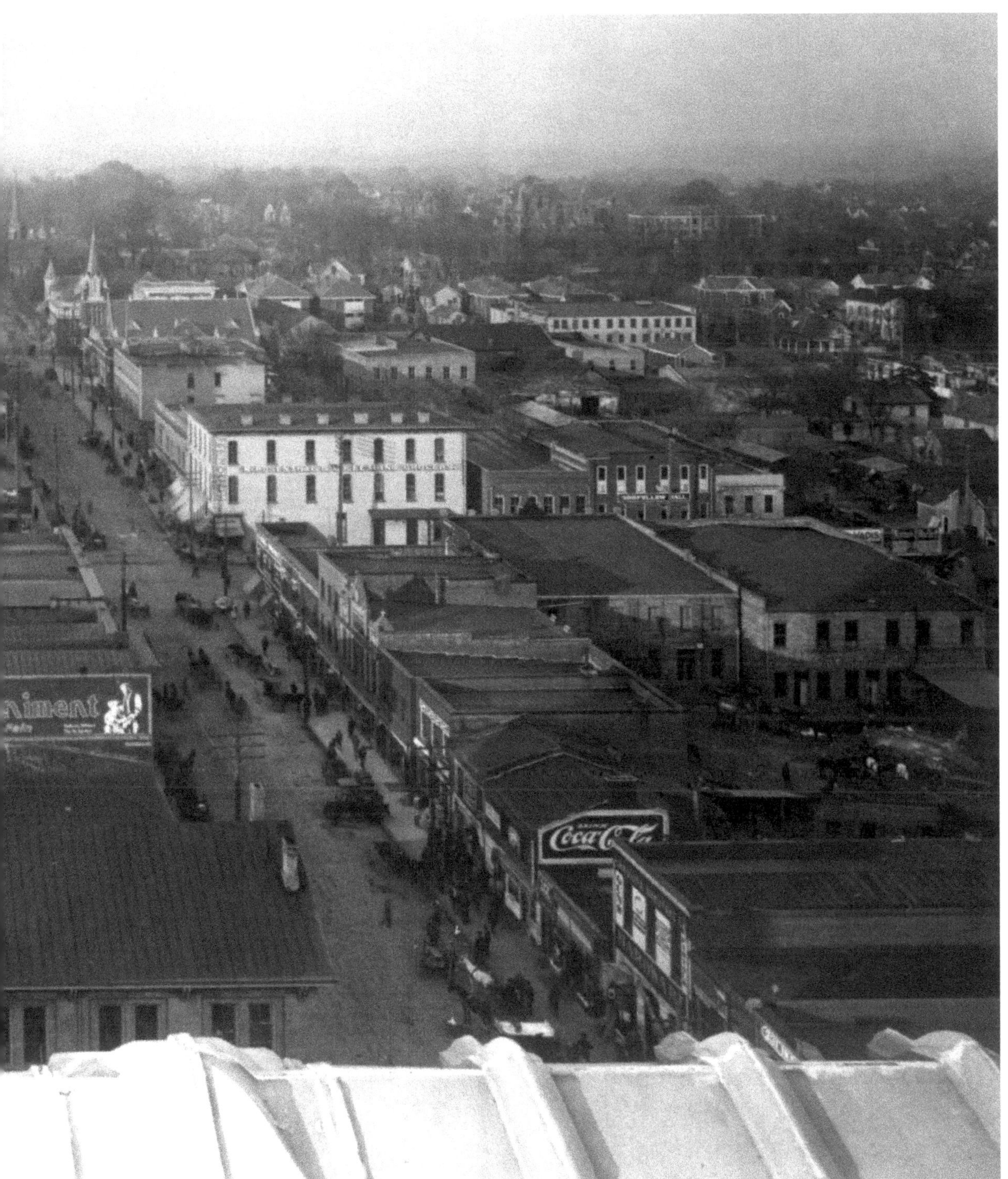

A panorama of downtown Raleigh, ca. 1915, faces north toward the distant State Capitol, with Fayetteville Street to the left and Wilmington Street running up the right.

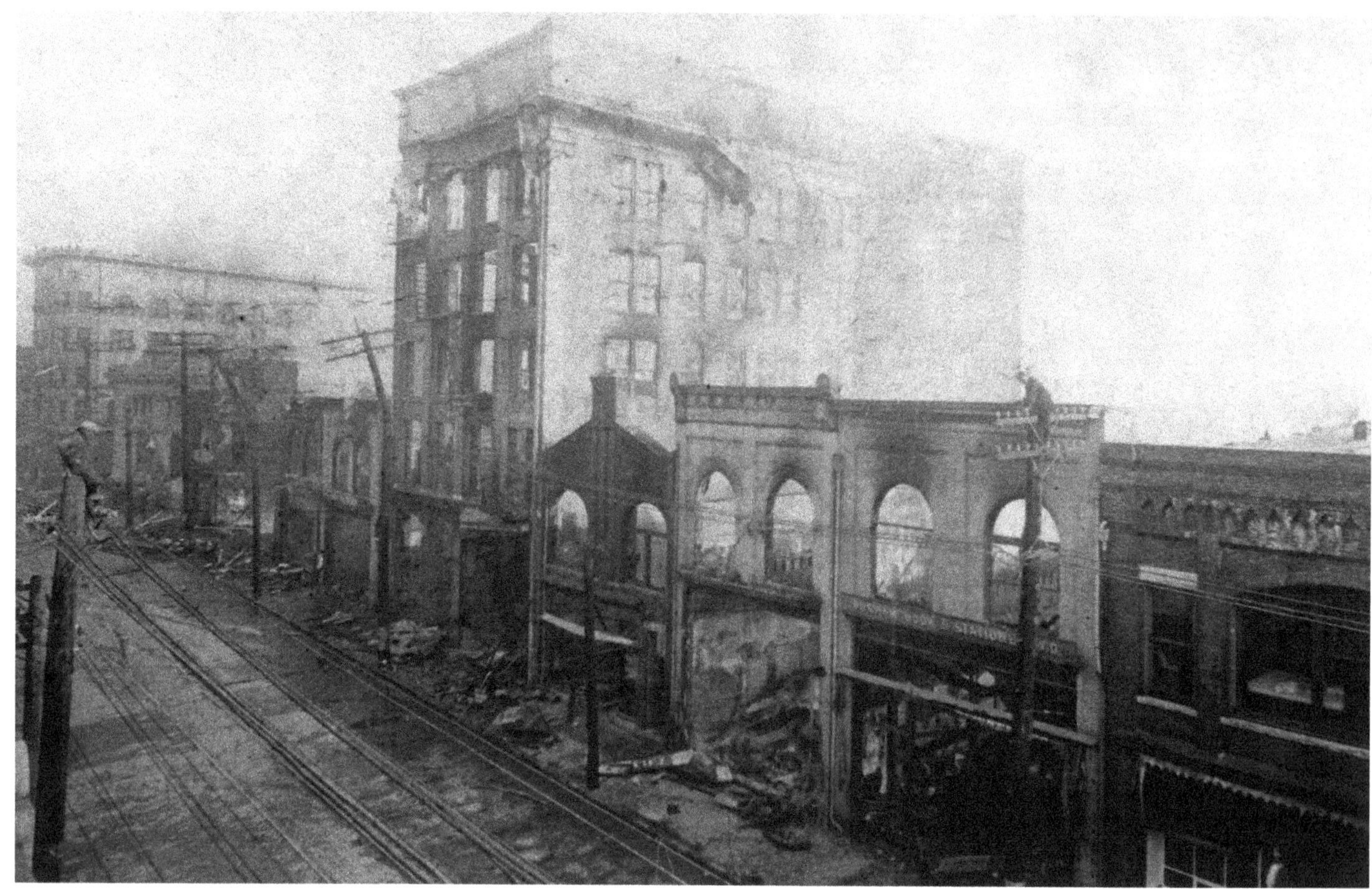

A postcard image of burned-out Main Street in Durham, 1914. A broken water main on Mangum Street left fire fighters with insufficient water pressure to fight this fire, which burned out the entire block between Mangum and Corcoran streets. The men on the poles appear to be attempting to disconnect the power.

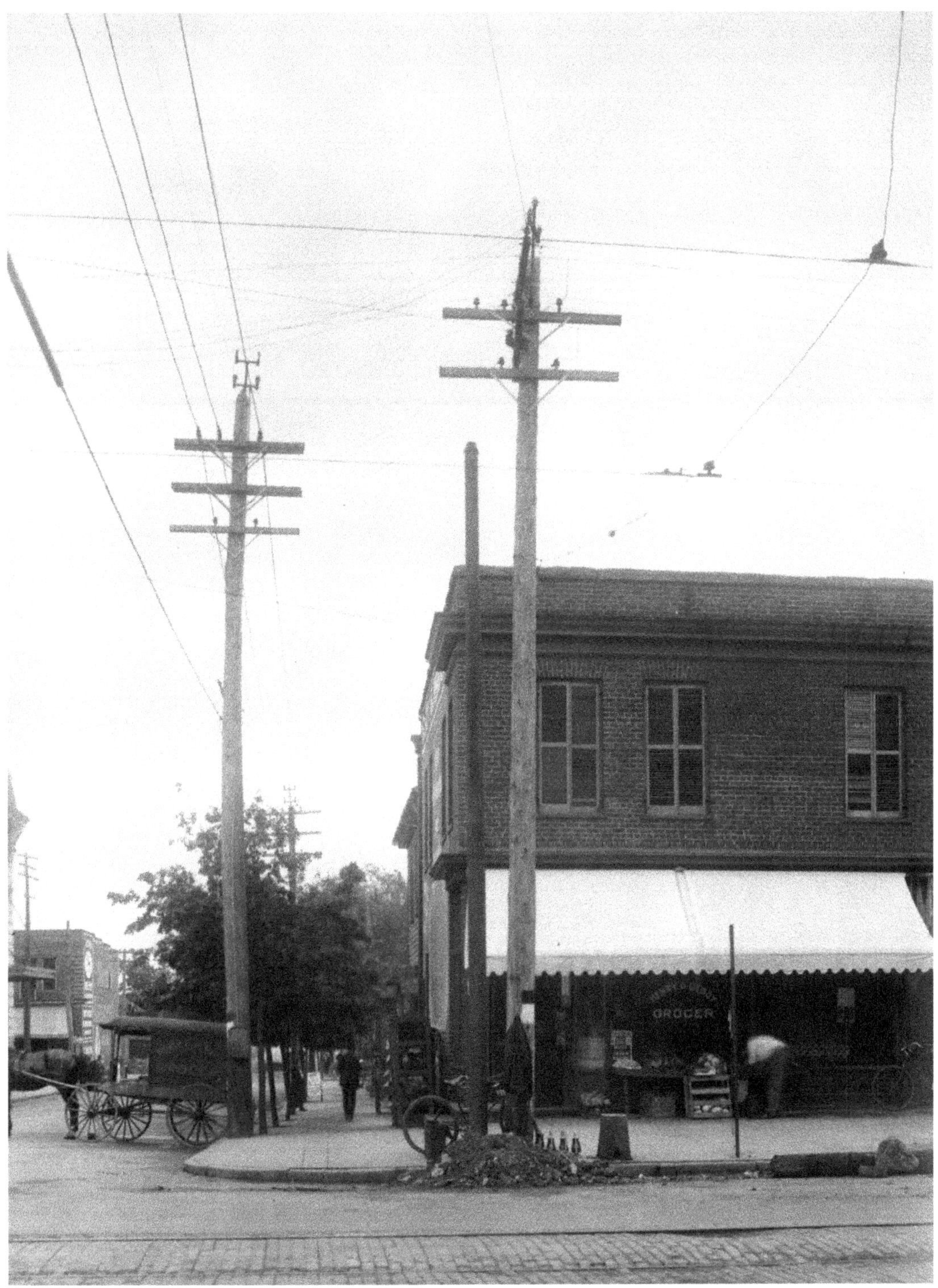

Horse-drawn delivery carts, such as this one (far left) for Henry G. DeBoy's Grocery Store at Fayetteville and Davie streets in Raleigh, were common at the turn of the century.

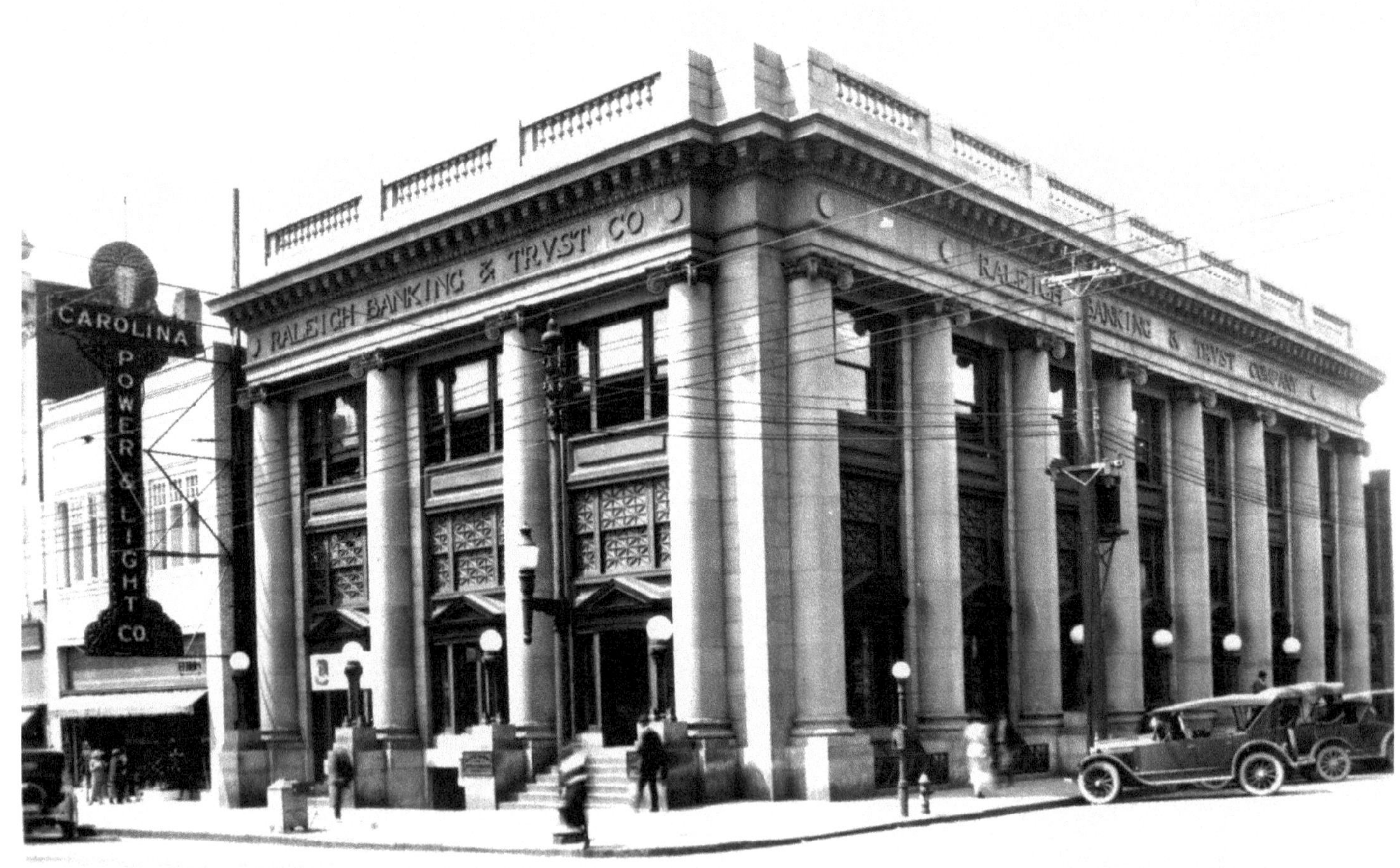

The Raleigh Banking & Trust Company was erected on the southwest corner of Fayetteville and Hargett streets in Raleigh in 1913. It replaced an 1868 structure that was affectionately known as the "Round Steps Bank" owing to its curved stairway. In 1928–1930, the bank added an additional eight stories above the original three-story facility, creating an eleven-story skyscraper.

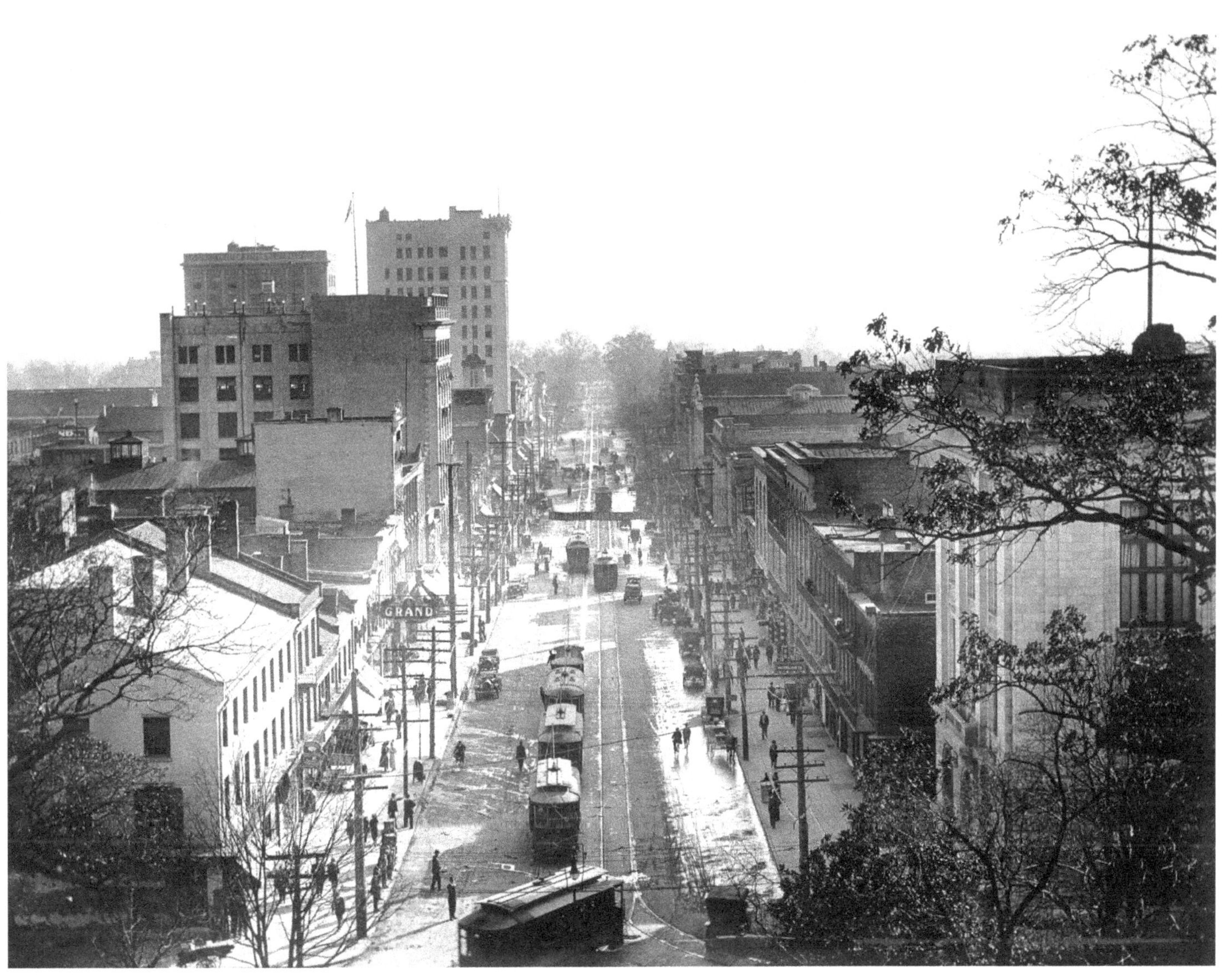

From the dome of the North Carolina State Capitol, a photographer captures Raleigh's Fayetteville Street in the mid 1910s. Visible here are the busy streetcar track running down the avenue, the Grand Theater marquee (left), and the Citizens National Bank building (left-center), then Raleigh's tallest structure.

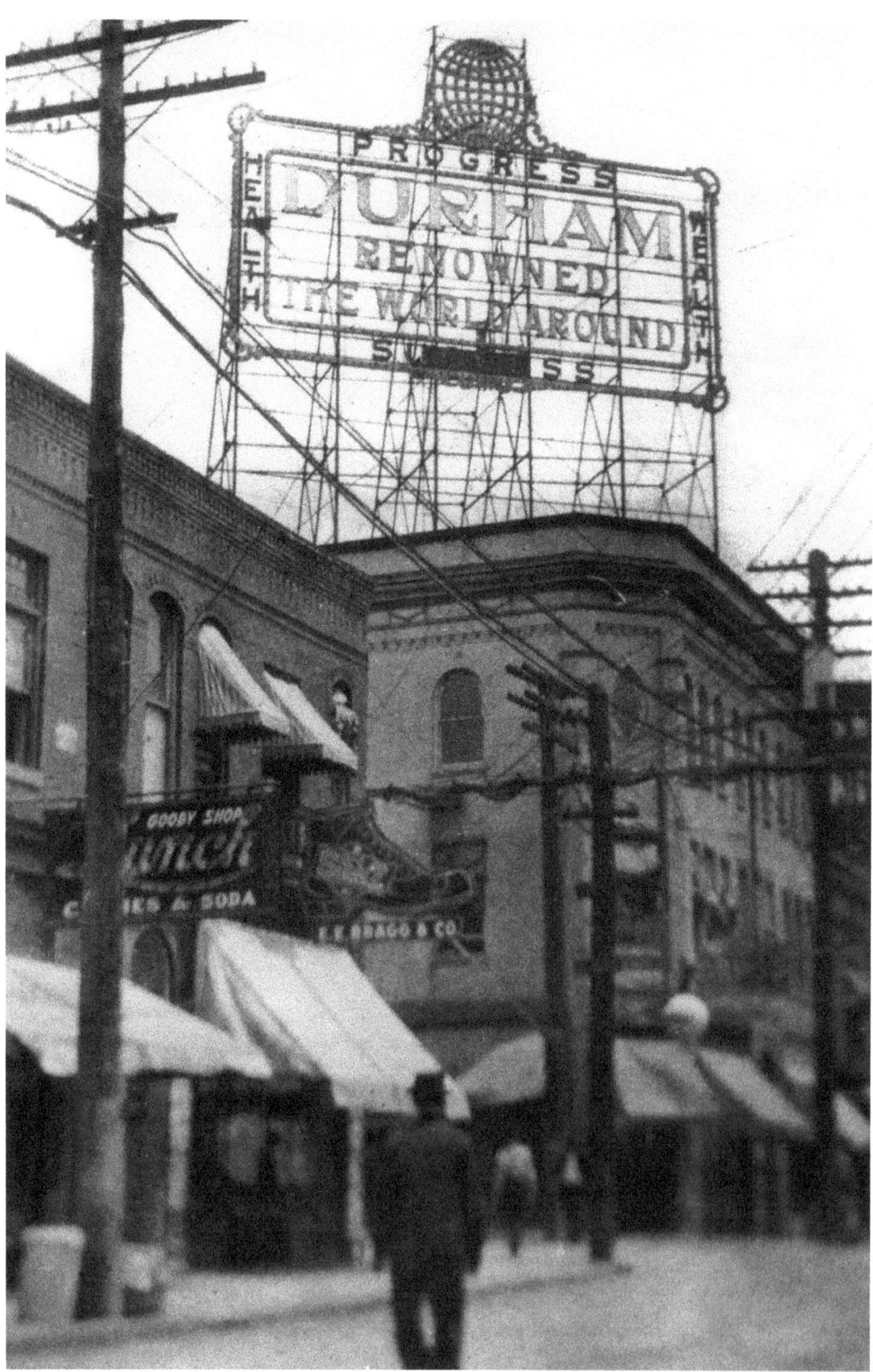

Illuminated for the first time on December 15, 1913, this sign was a gift to the city from the Durham Traction Company. It stood mounted on the roof of a three-story building on the corner of Main and Church streets until it was destroyed by wind in 1919.

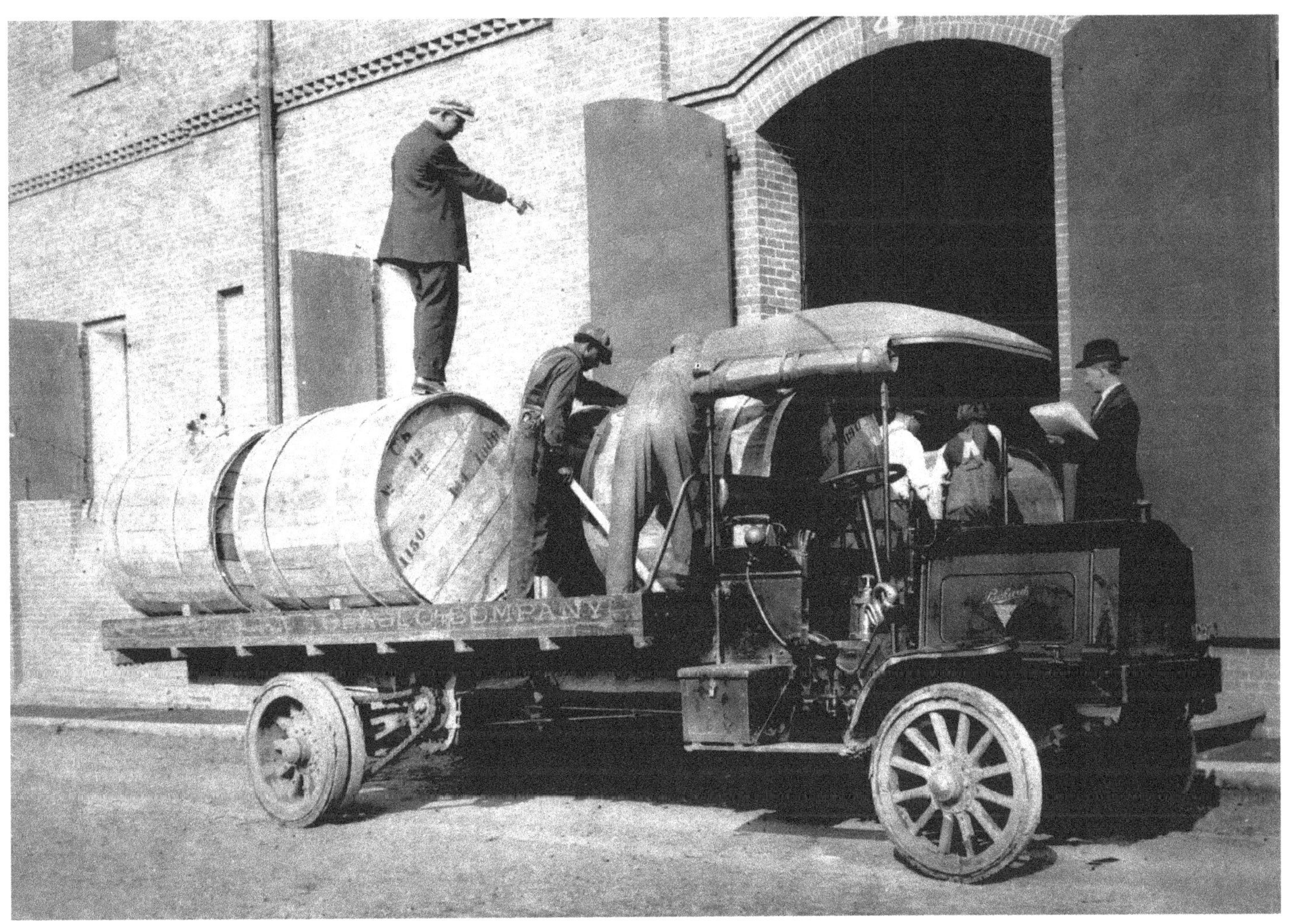

Workers unload tobacco barrels, or hogsheads, from a truck at the American Tobacco Company Warehouse.

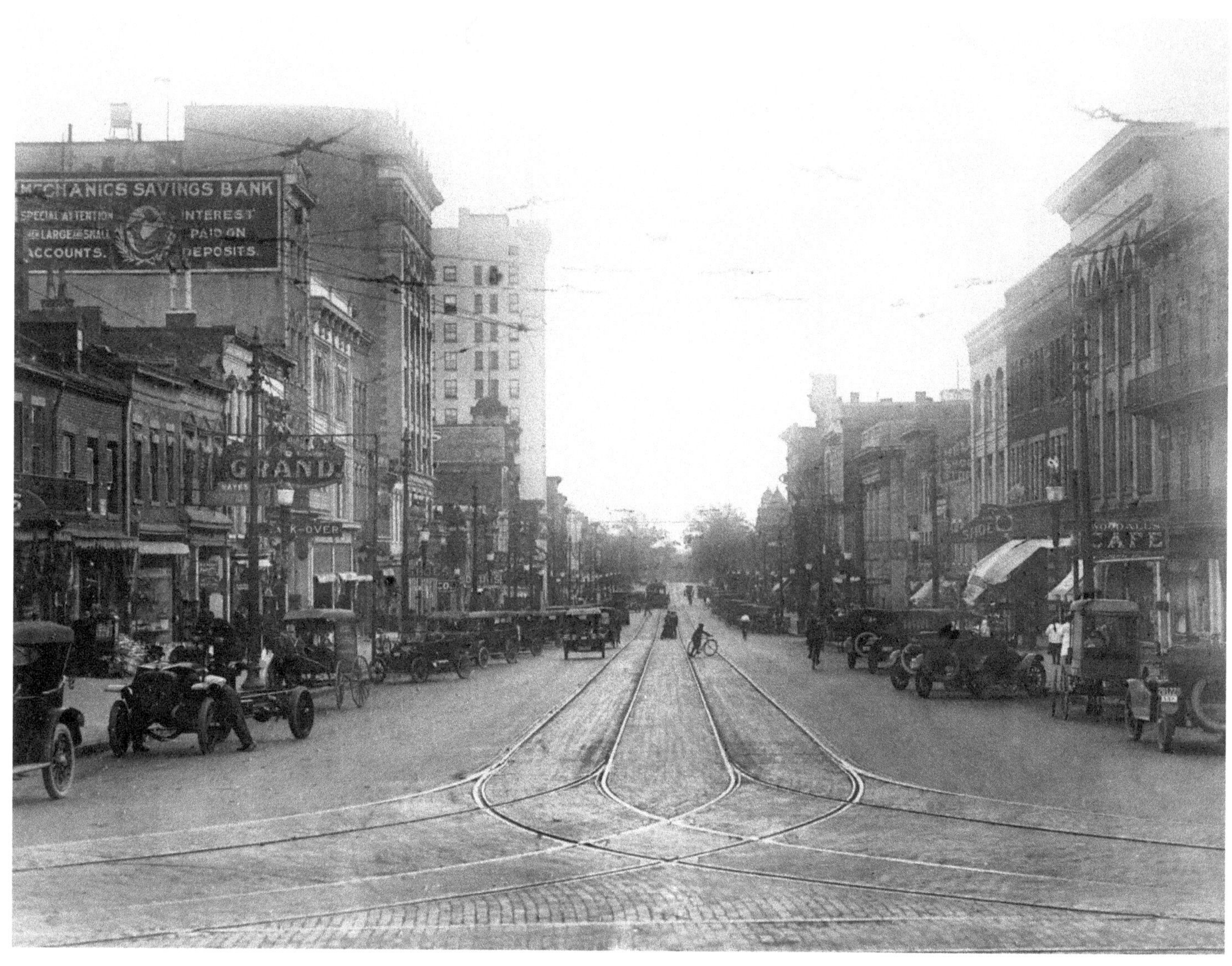

Fayetteville Street in downtown Raleigh, 1917.

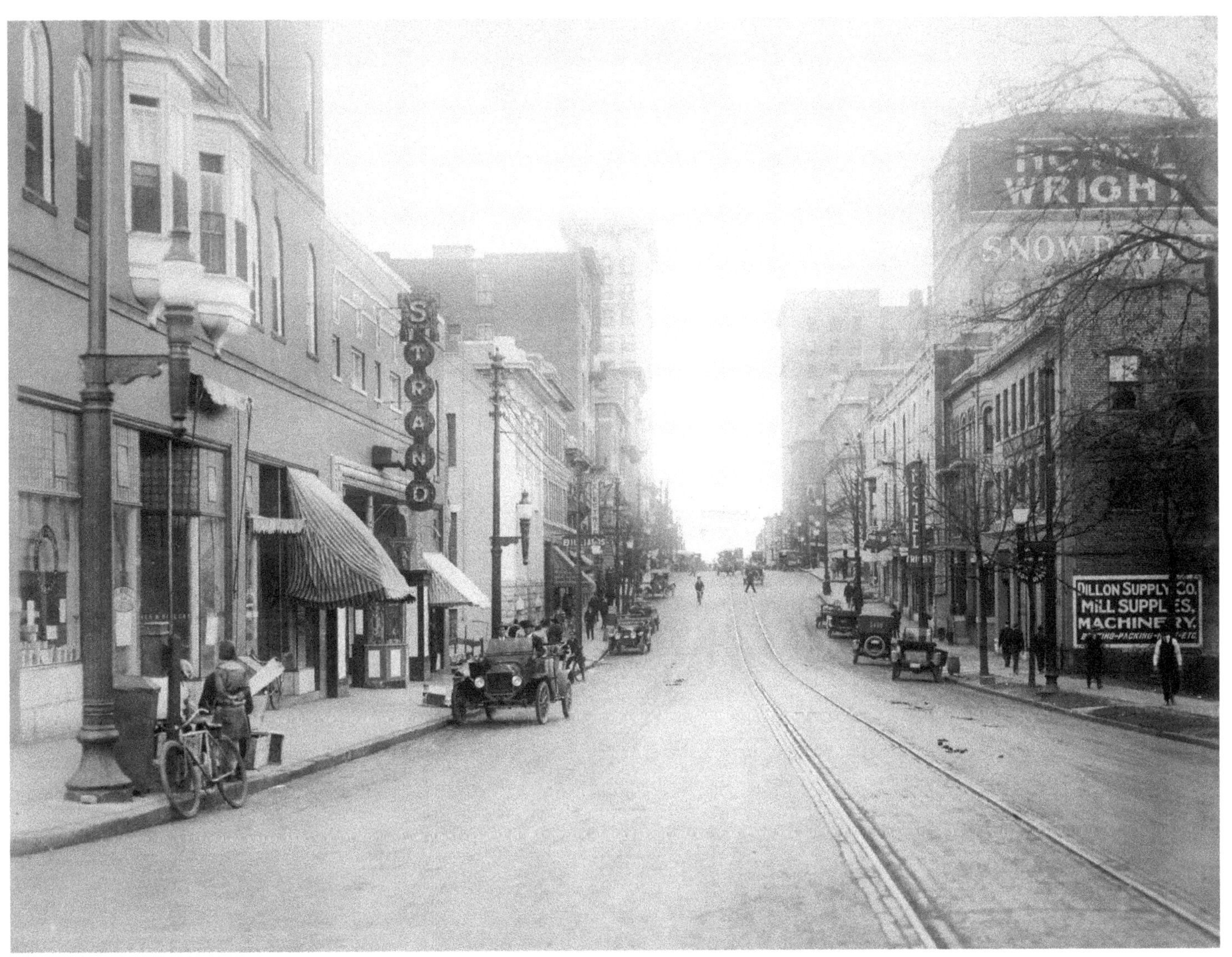

Raleigh's Martin Street as it appeared in 1917, facing east from the intersection at McDowell Street. A portion of the Raleigh Hotel is visible at far-left, followed by the Strand Theater.

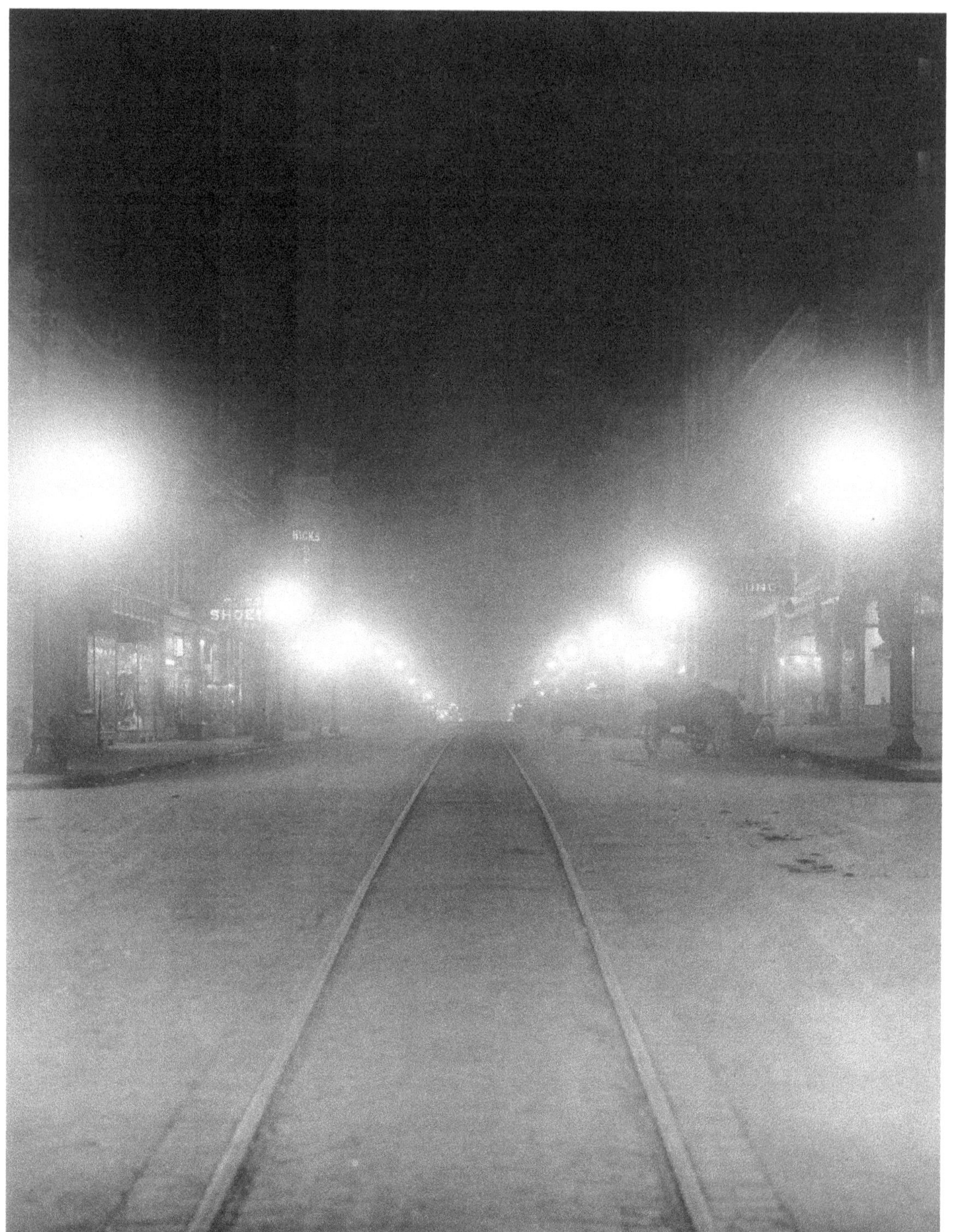

Another 1917 view of Martin Street, looking west from Wilmington Street toward Fayetteville Street, captures the Raleigh business district at night.

Happy Days Are Here . . . and Gone (1920–1939)

Following the ravages of World War I, Americans entered a ten-year joy ride known as the Jazz Age. The 1920s would challenge the country's existing social mores while simultaneously setting the stage for an economic downturn that struck on October 24, 1929. Called "Black Thursday," by day's end the stock market crash that rolled through the world's currency markets had launched a stark, new era—the Great Depression.

The 1920s brought unparalleled progress in local transportation. Spurred by a statewide movement to improve road conditions, new paved highways were constructed connecting Raleigh to Durham and other neighboring communities. Air travel gained a foothold as small, private airstrips rose out of farm fields. In the early 1930s Raleigh Municipal Airport was dedicated south of town on Garner Road. For a decade it provided air service to and from Raleigh via Eastern Airlines until its runways became too short to accommodate the modern DC-3 aircraft.

Raleigh withstood the Great Depression better than other cities thanks to its bedrock "industry," state government. Nevertheless, hard times were felt by many as businesses closed and all but one of the city's banks—the Mechanics & Farmers Bank on East Hargett Street—suffered either closure or a bank run. One bright spot during this period was the city's new baseball park, Devereux Meadow. Constructed in 1938 as a Works Progress Administration project, the park would host the Raleigh Capitals ball club for many seasons.

The construction of Duke University and the expanding tobacco industry also softened Durham's experience of the Great Depression. The era was nonetheless a time of stress and great difficulty for most, especially for those with little to begin with. As the city began to recover, federal programs helped engender the construction of roads and bridges, land improvements, a new sewer plant, new structures at North Carolina College for Negros, and several new public schools.

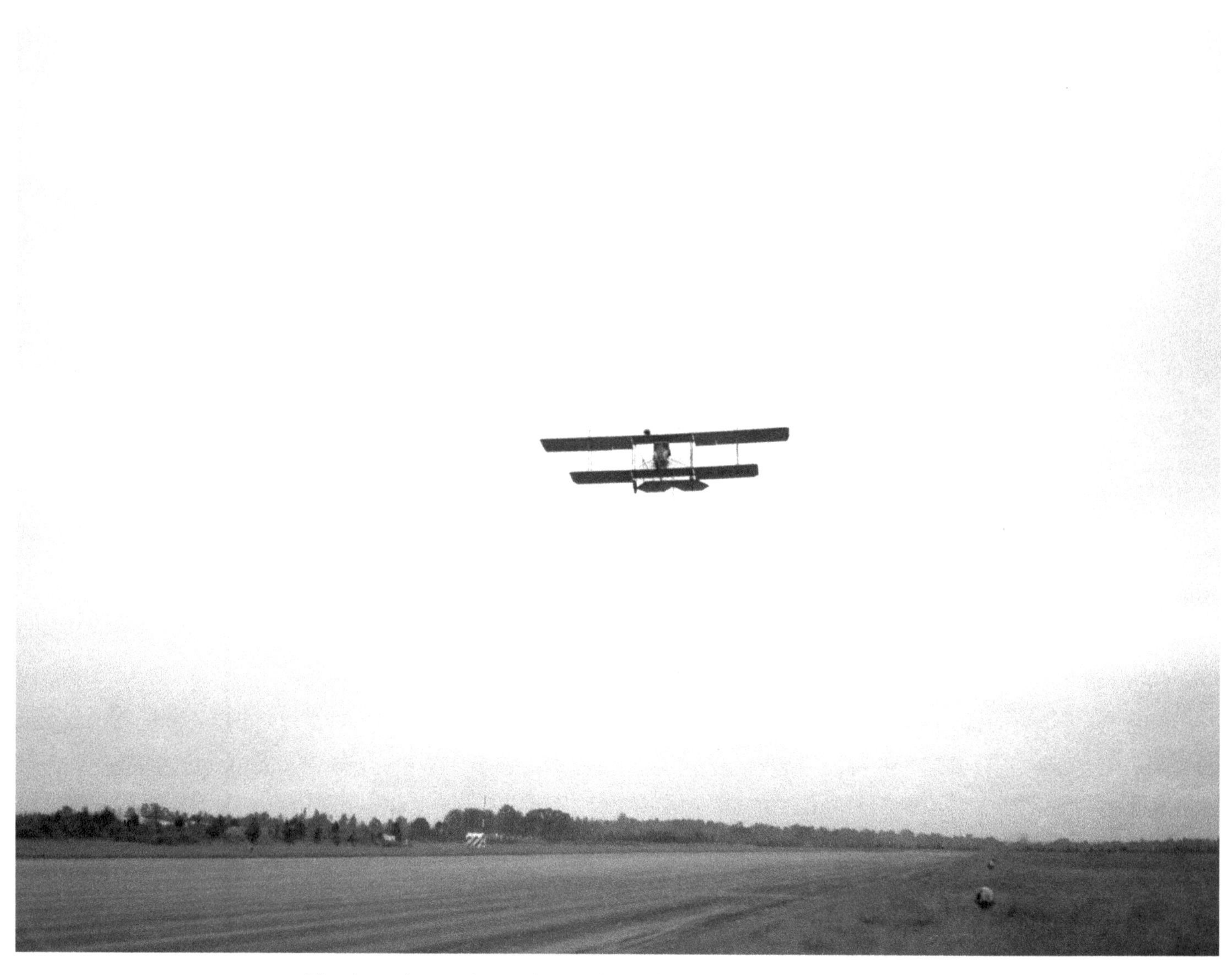

Thanks to the Wright Brothers and their historic flight at Kitty Hawk in December 1903, North Carolina considers itself "First in Flight." The cities of Raleigh and Durham maintained small municipal airports until the early 1940s, when Raleigh-Durham Airport debuted on land located between the two cities. Here, a biplane departs Raleigh-Durham Airport early in its career.

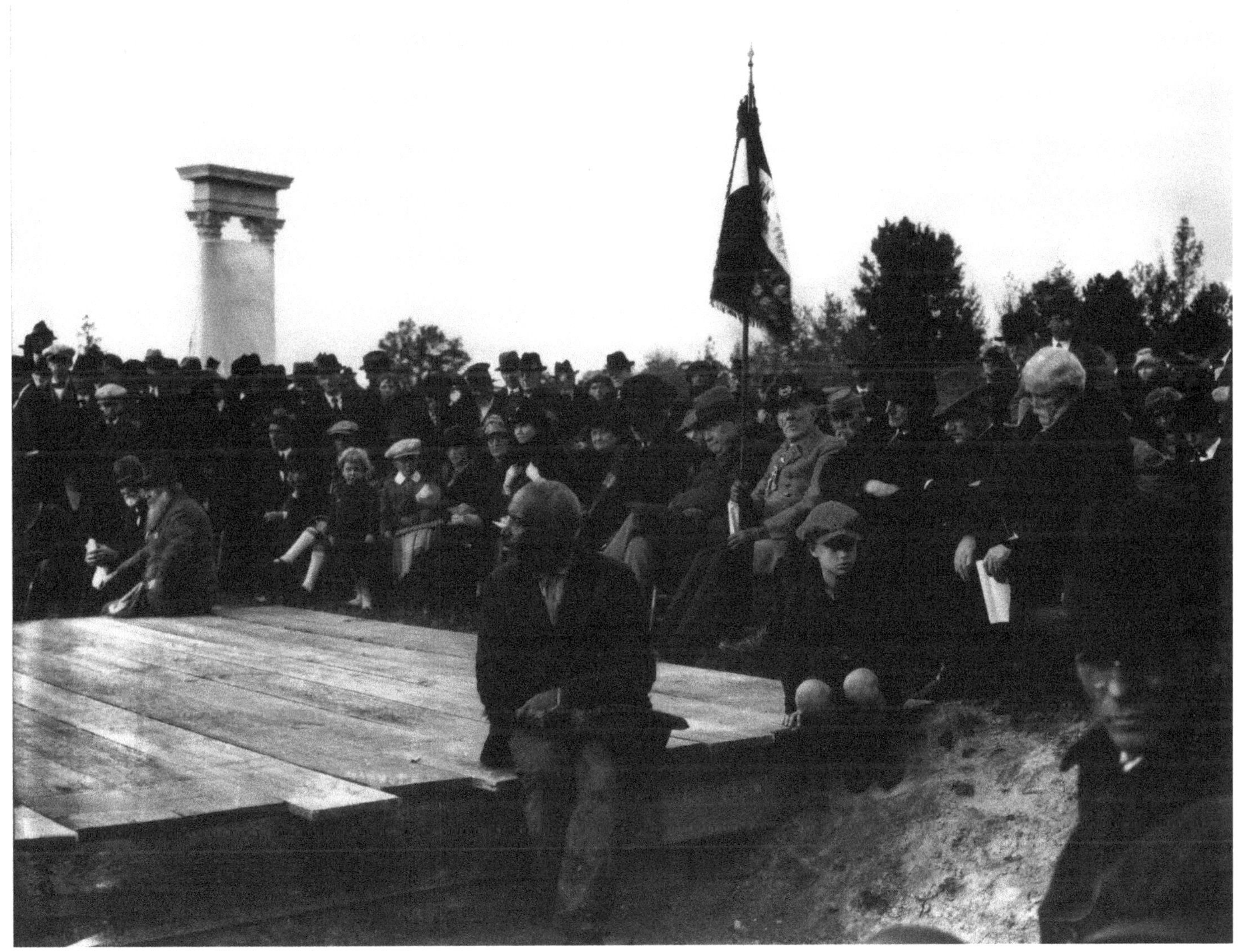

Surviving Civil War veterans and their families gather at Bennett Place near Durham for the dedication of the farm as a historic site, ca. 1920. The nineteenth-century farm hosted the surrender of Confederate general Joseph Johnston to Union general William T. Sherman in April 1865.

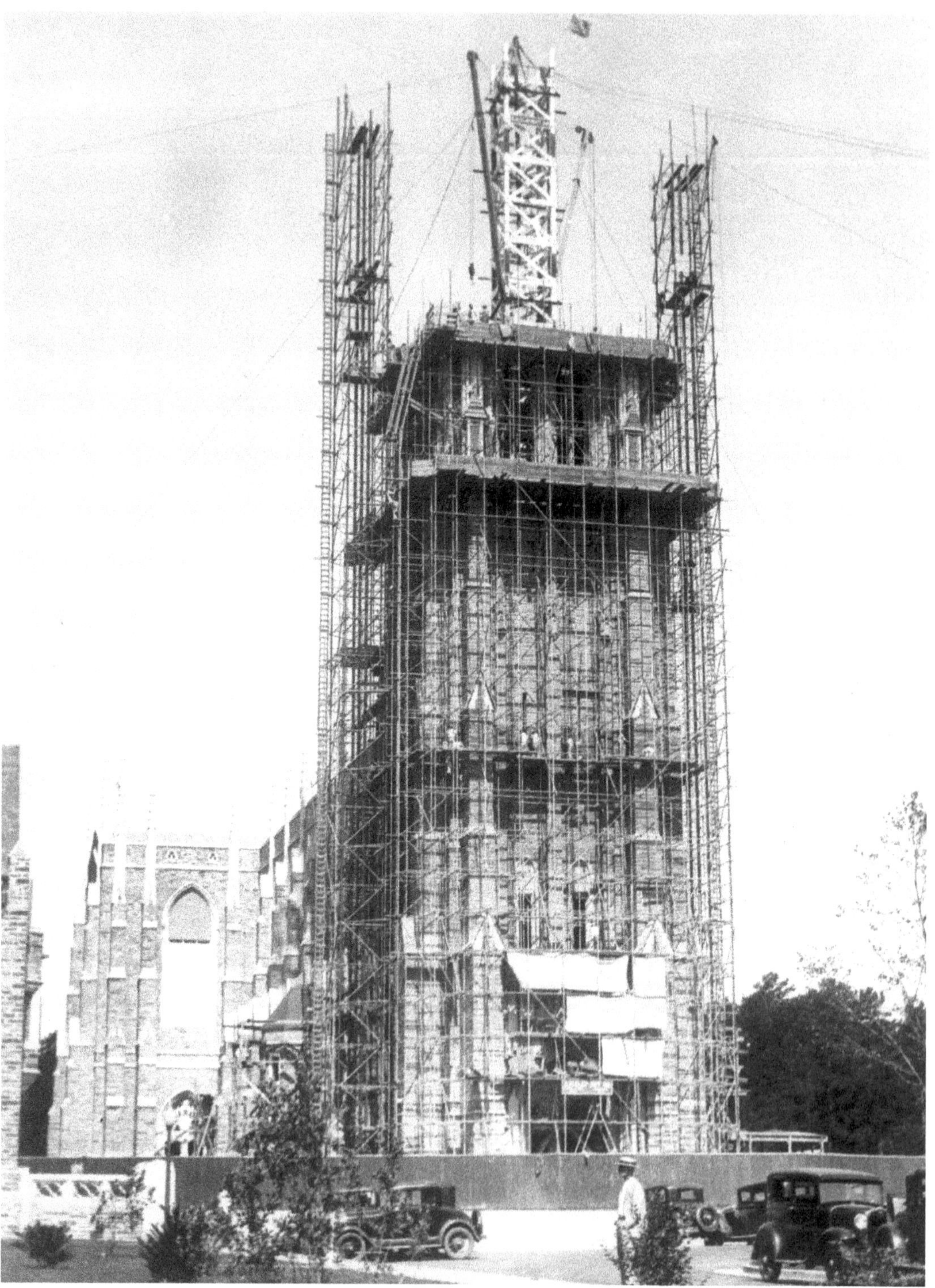

Designed by Julian Abele, the first African American architect to garner recognition, Duke Chapel was constructed on the West Campus of Duke University between 1930 and 1935.

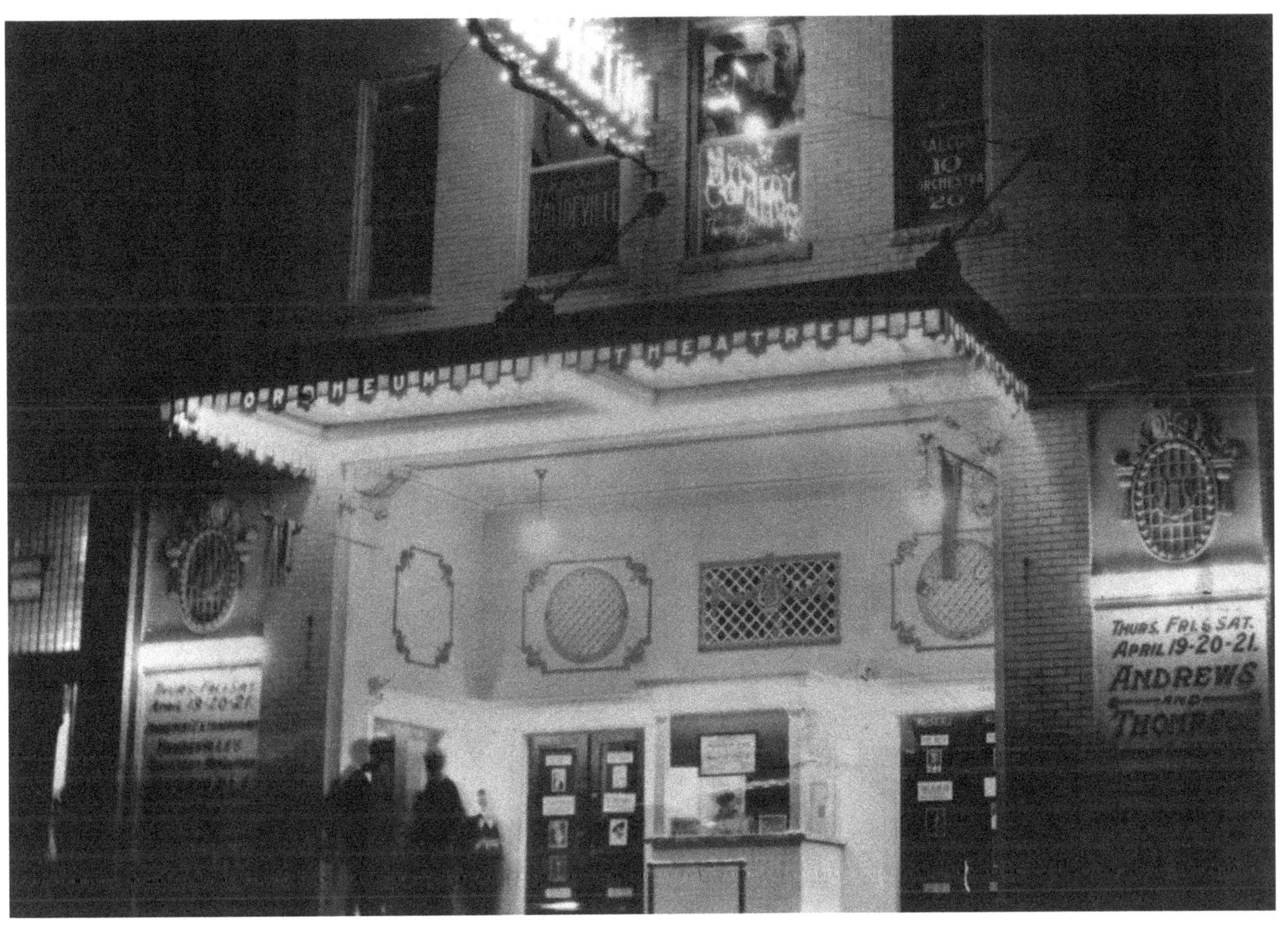

Located on Main Street between the Durham Cafe and the Hotel Malborne, the Orpheum Theatre (shown here ca. 1920) hosted many vaudeville acts.

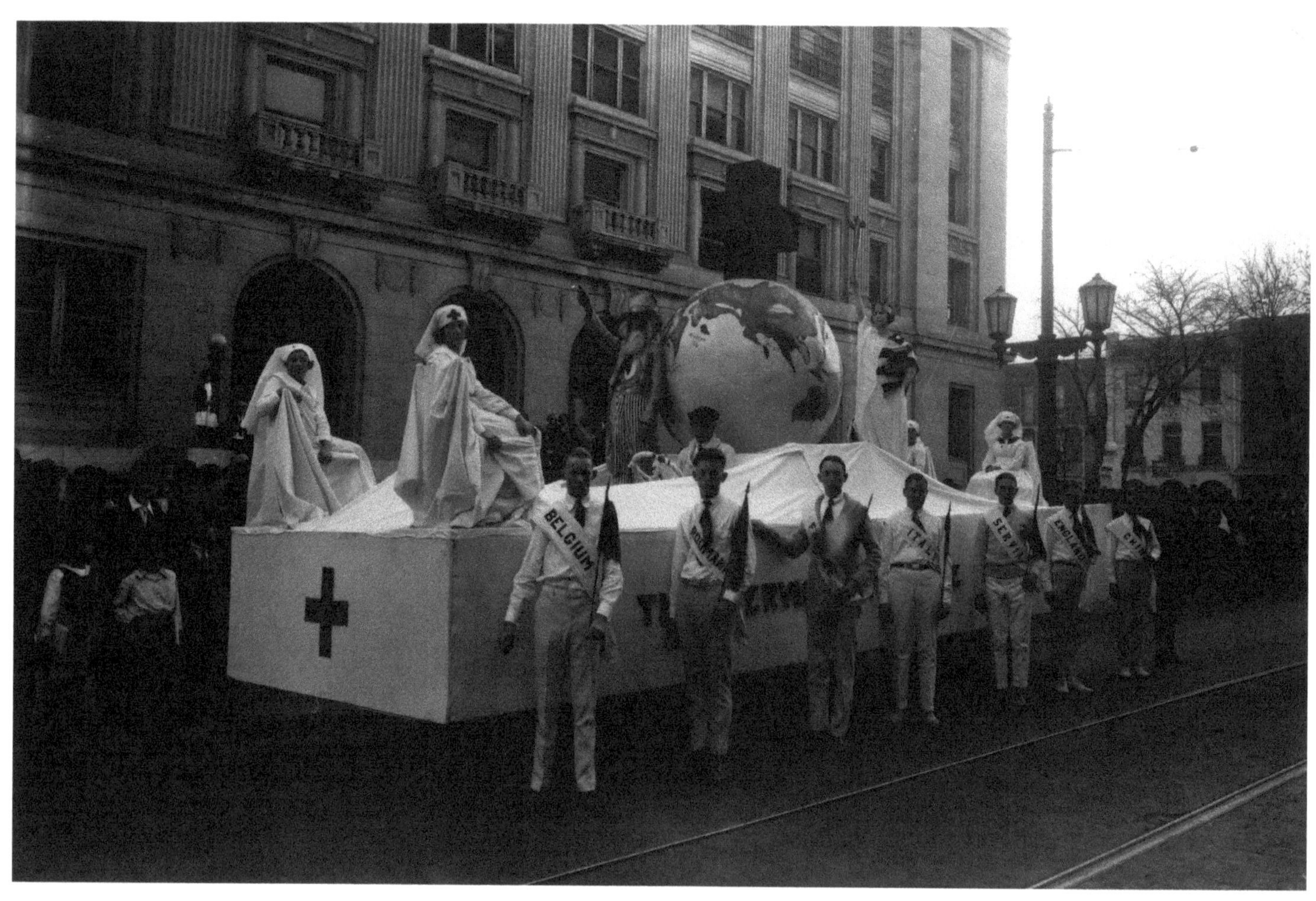

A Red Cross float, recognizing the global presence of the organization, passes in front of the Durham County Courthouse, ca. 1920.

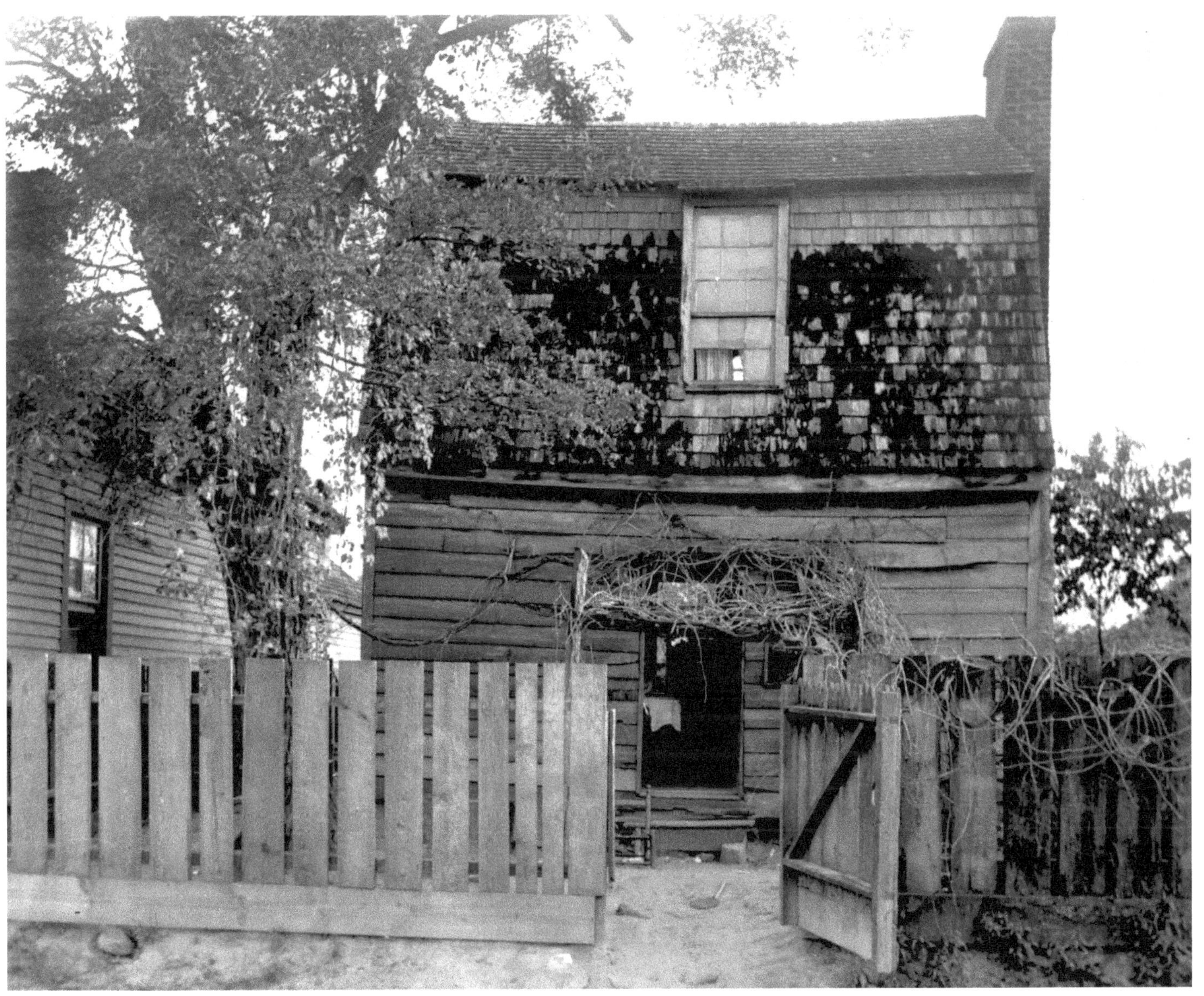

Andrew Johnson, 17th president of the United States, was born in Raleigh on December 29, 1808, inside this detached kitchen outbuilding on Fayetteville Street. The structure has been preserved and stands today in Raleigh's Mordecai Historic Park.

A night view of Raleigh's Fayetteville Street, from the top of the North Carolina State Capitol, in 1924.

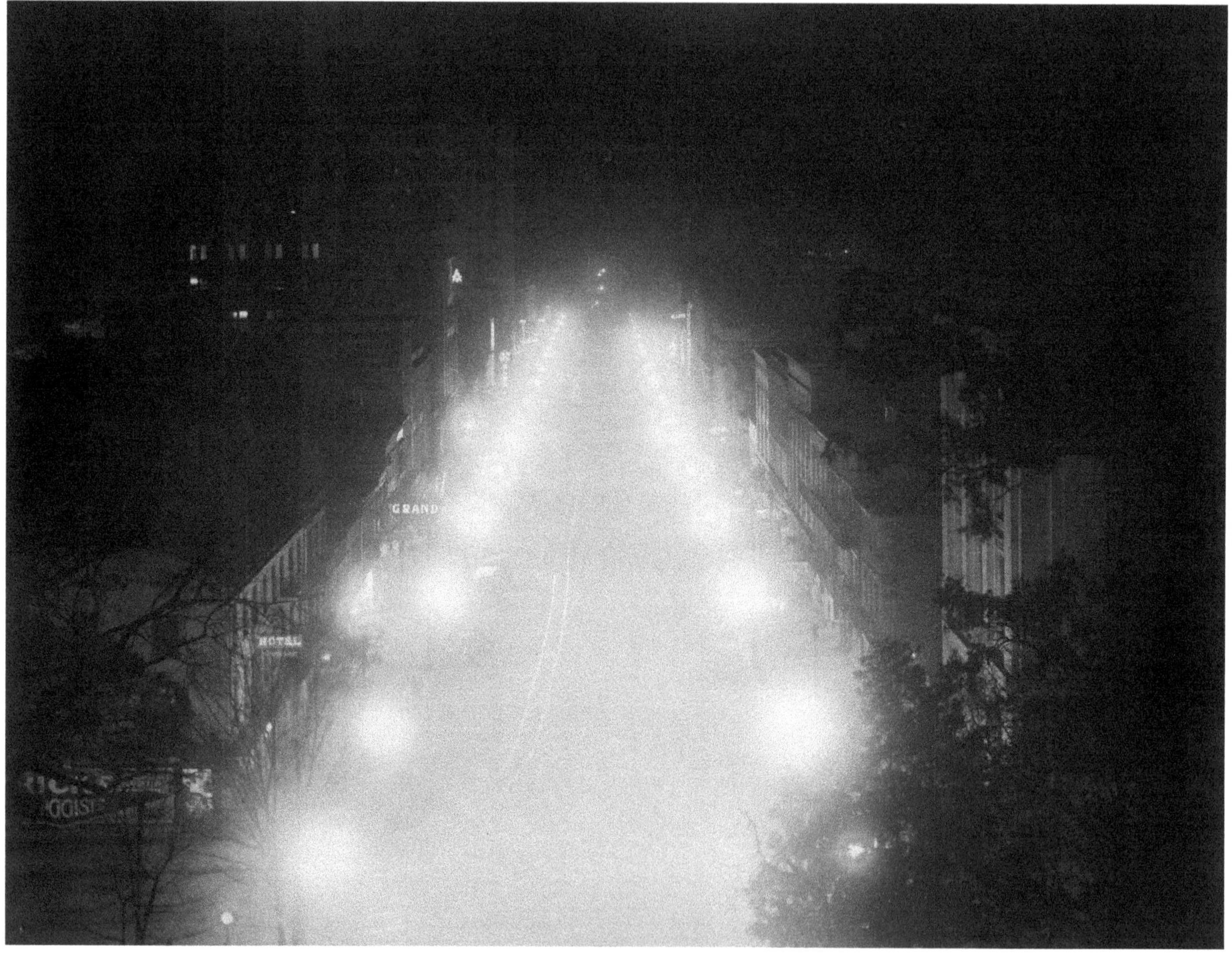

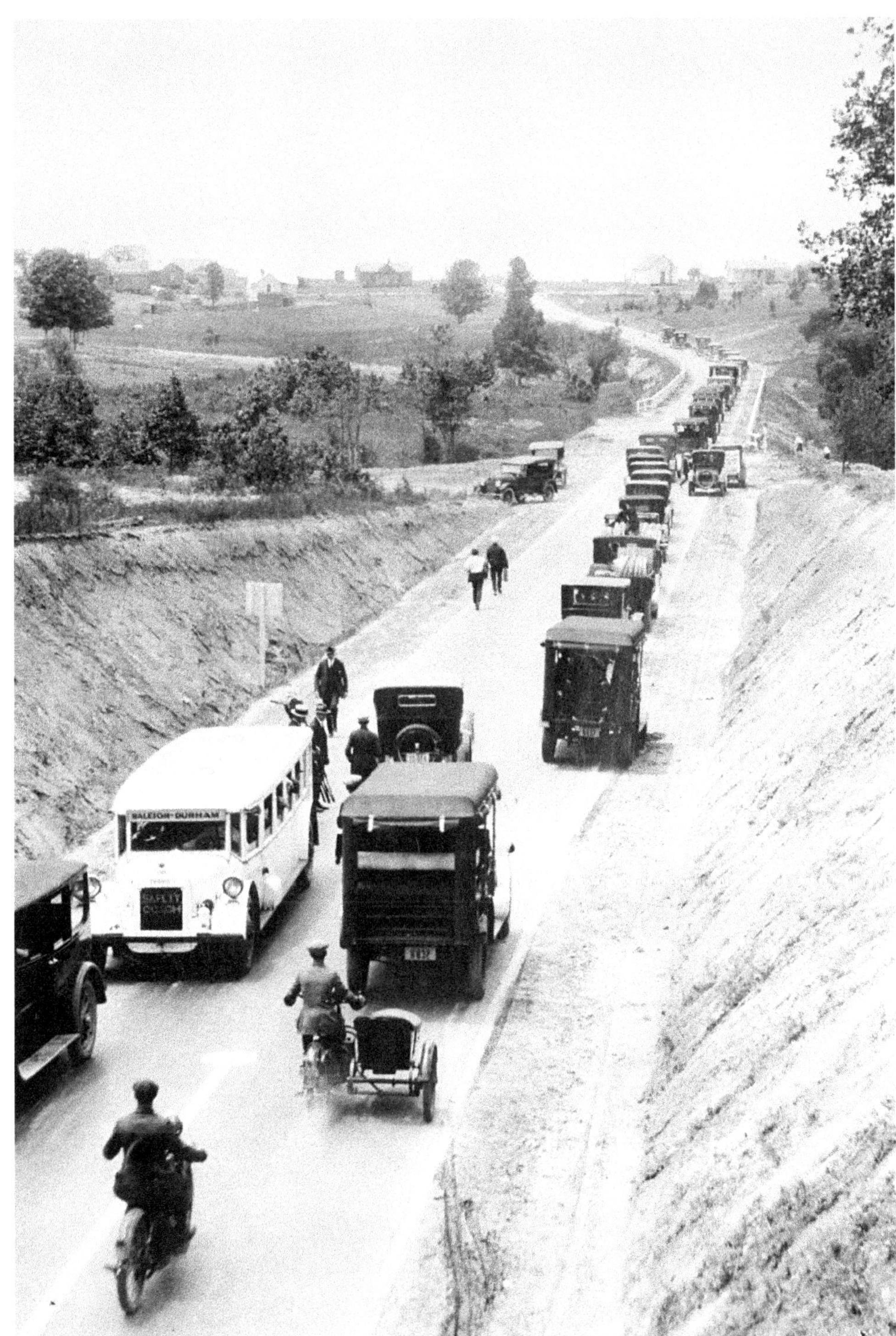

Known by the dubious moniker "the Rip Van Winkle State" in the nineteenth century for its poor roads and limited means of transportation, by the 1920s North Carolina had become known as "the Good Roads State" for its construction of paved roads and miles of state-owned highways. Construction along the Raleigh-Durham Highway is shown here in 1924.

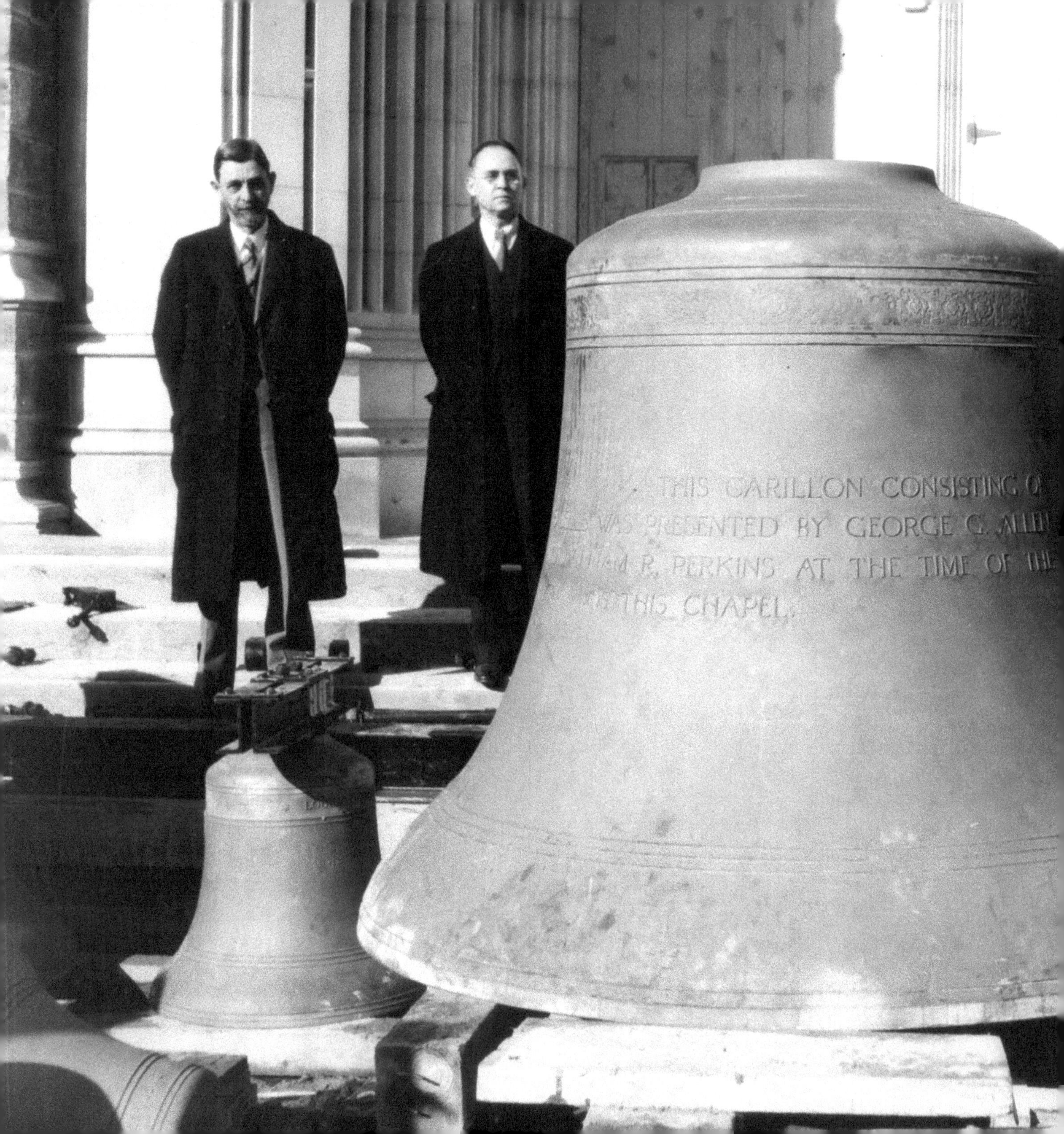
THIS CARILLON CONSISTING
PRESENTED BY GEORGE G.
R. PERKINS AT THE TIME OF
THIS CHAPEL

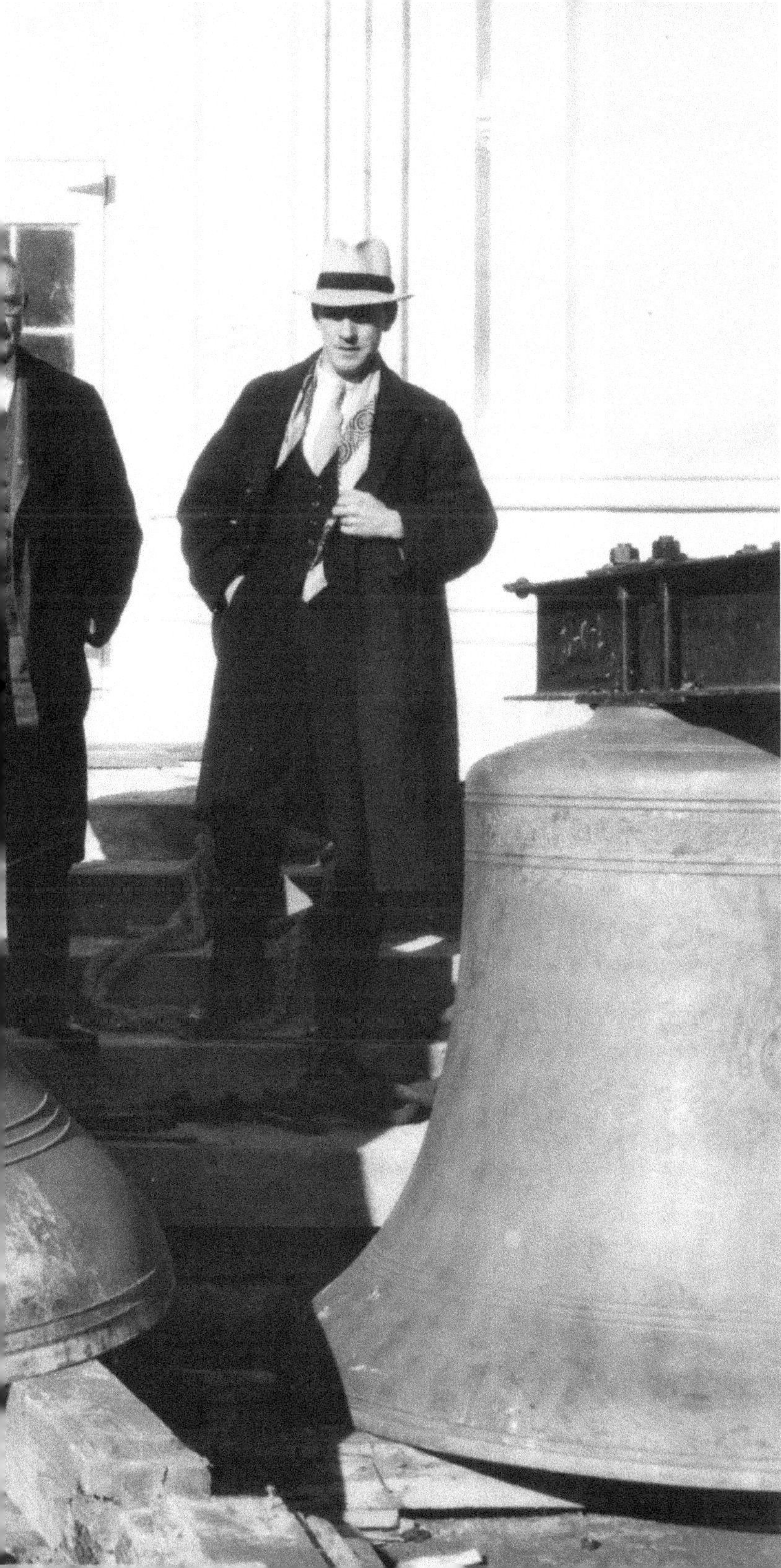

The 50-bell carillon in Duke Chapel at Duke University was dedicated in 1932. Forged in England, the bells were a gift from George G. Allen and William R. Perkins.

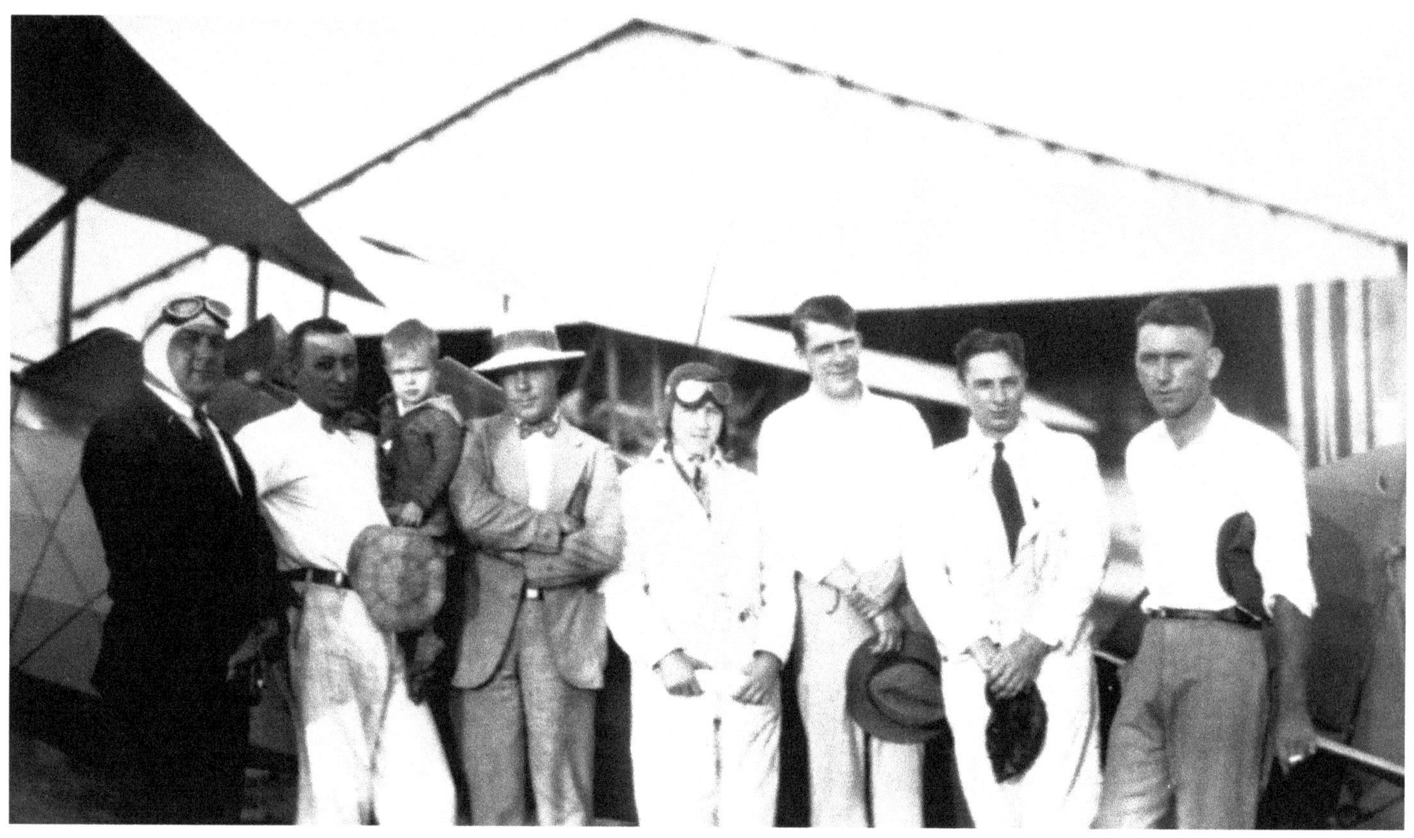

Several small, private airfields operated around Raleigh in the 1920s before a municipal site was dedicated. One of them, Marshburn-Robbins Airfield, was located along Old Garner Road south of the city. Pictured in 1927 are the Mills family and aviator Alton Stewart (fourth from the right), a Harnett County native.

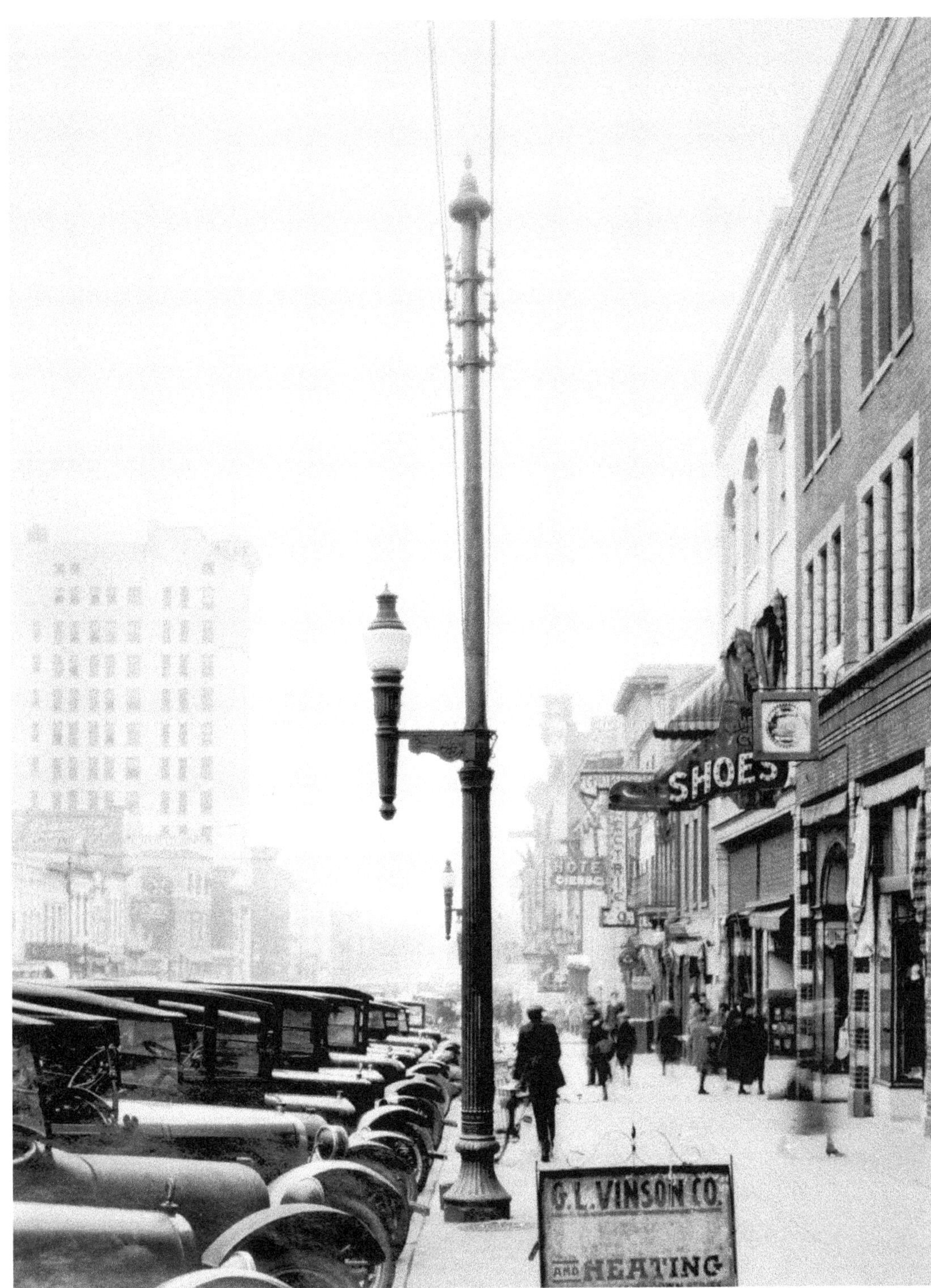

The sidewalk on the 100-block of Fayetteville Street in Raleigh, ca. 1920s.

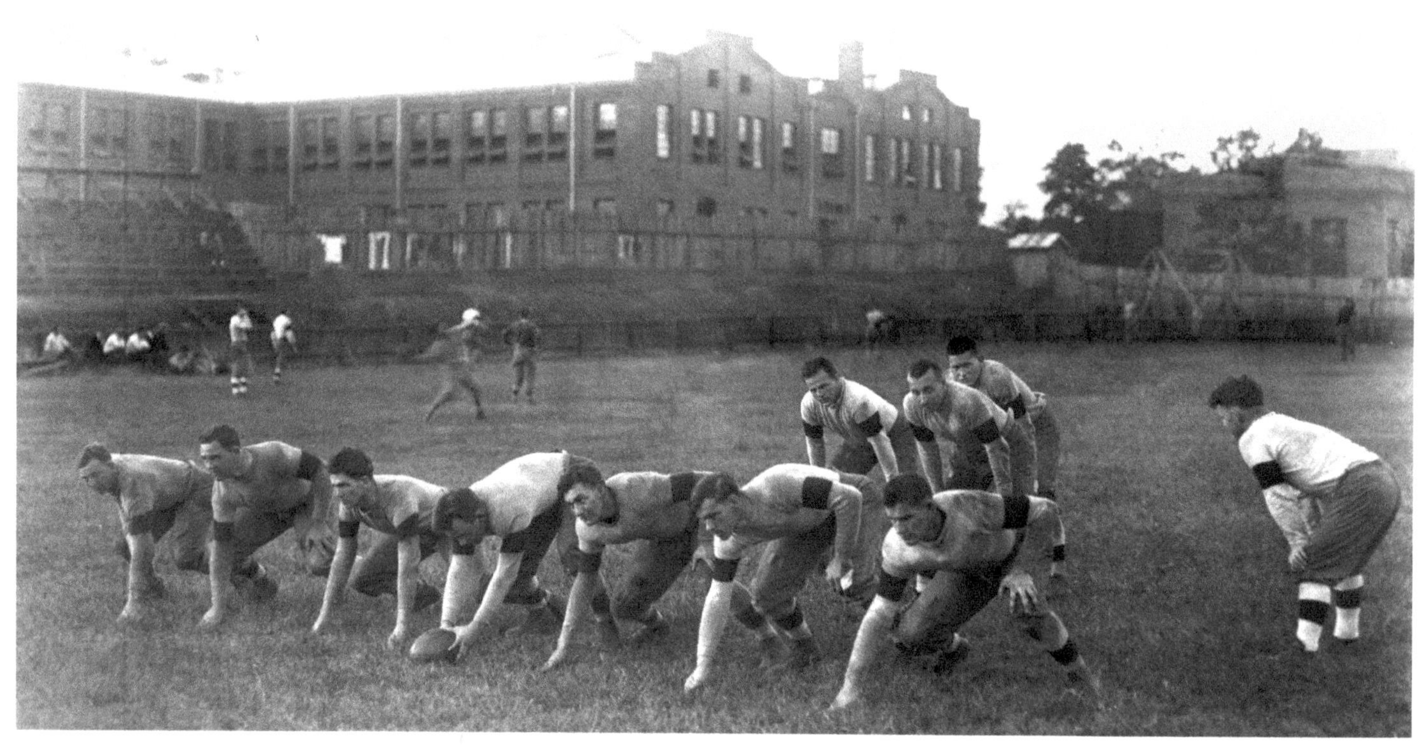

The football team at North Carolina A&M College (now North Carolina State University) practices on Riddick Field, in the early twentieth century.

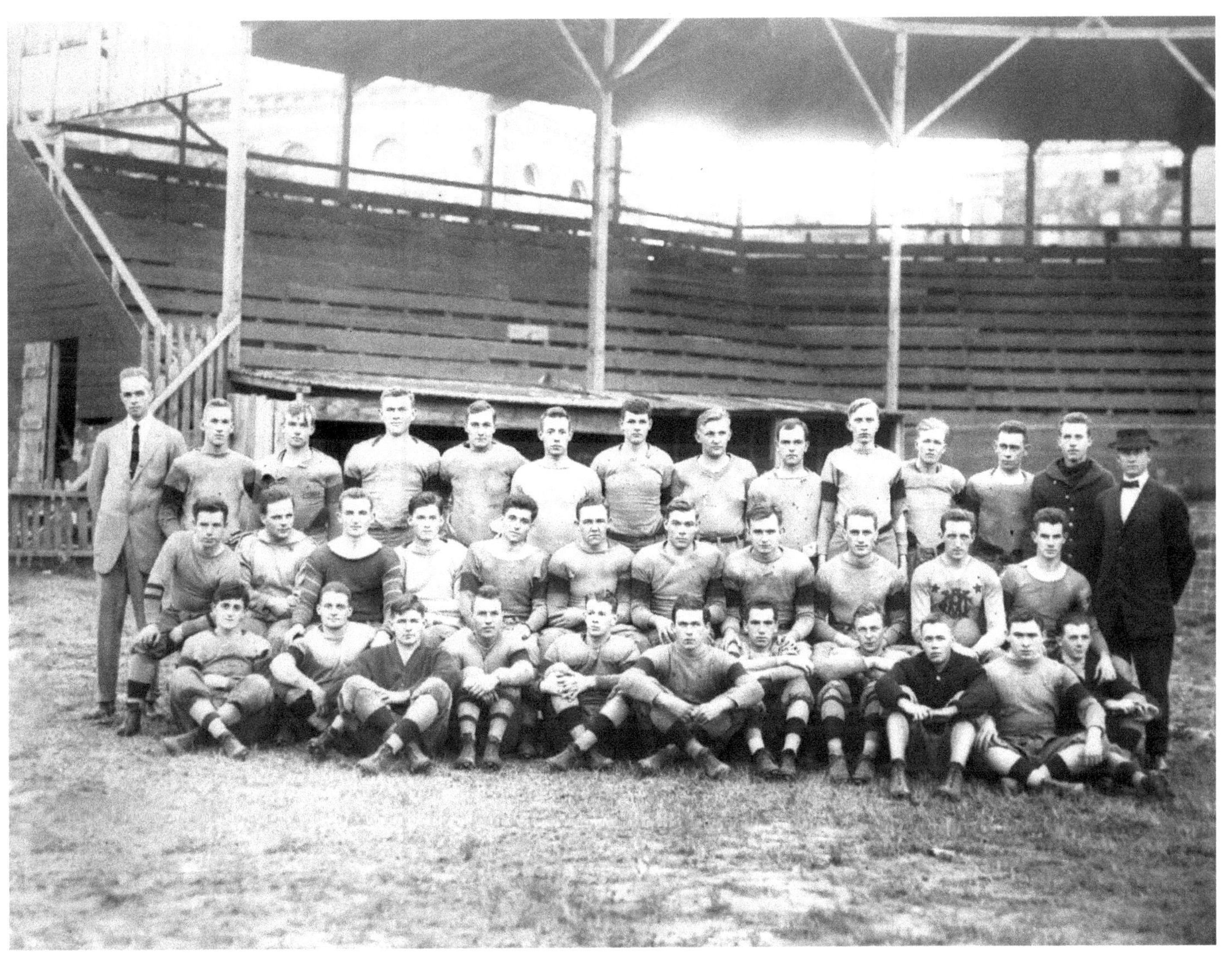

The North Carolina A&M College football squad poses in front of the grandstand at Riddick Field, in the early twentieth century.

A narrow-gauge railroad was used to transport materials during the construction of the National Highway through Durham County in 1919.

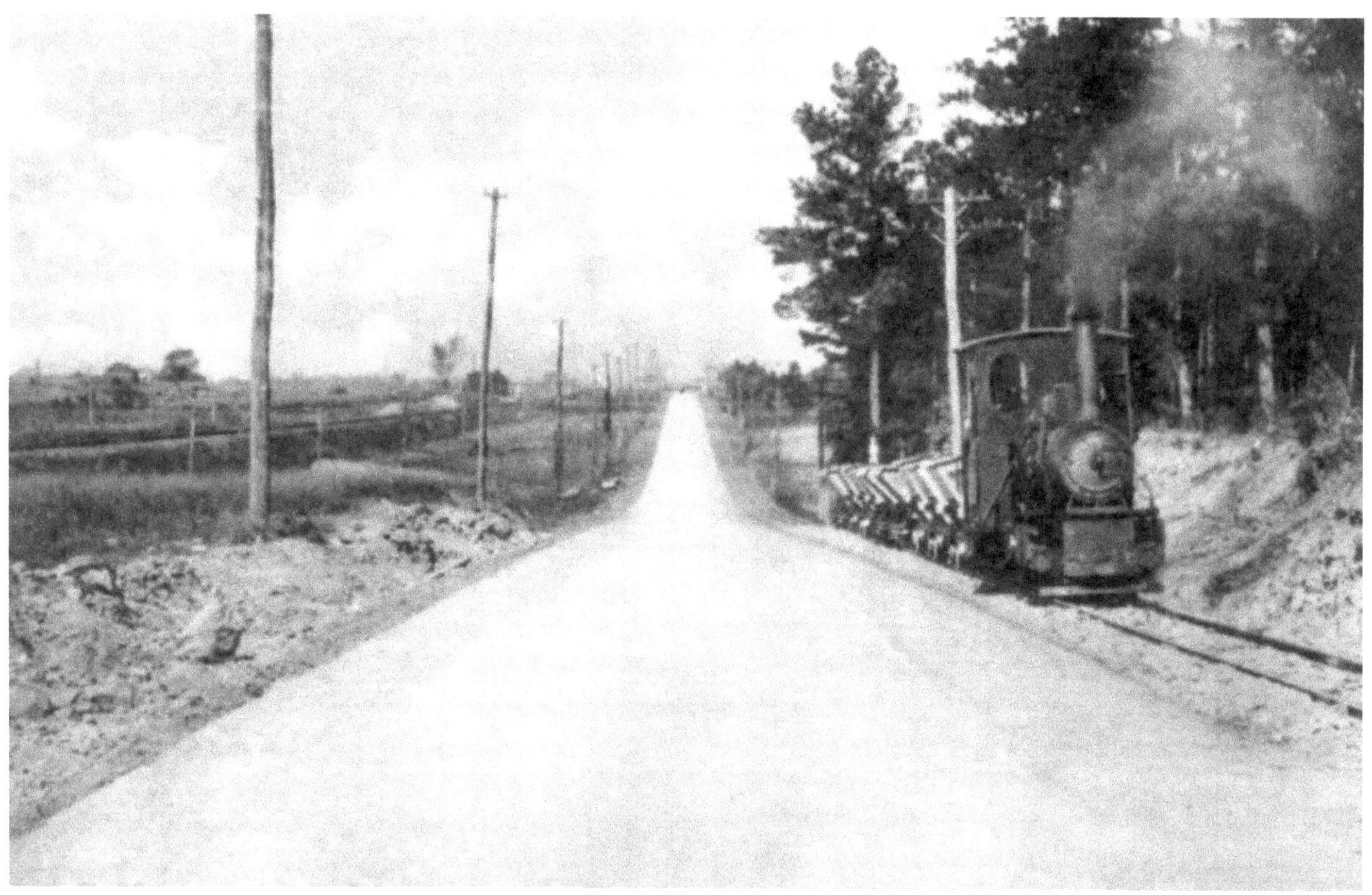

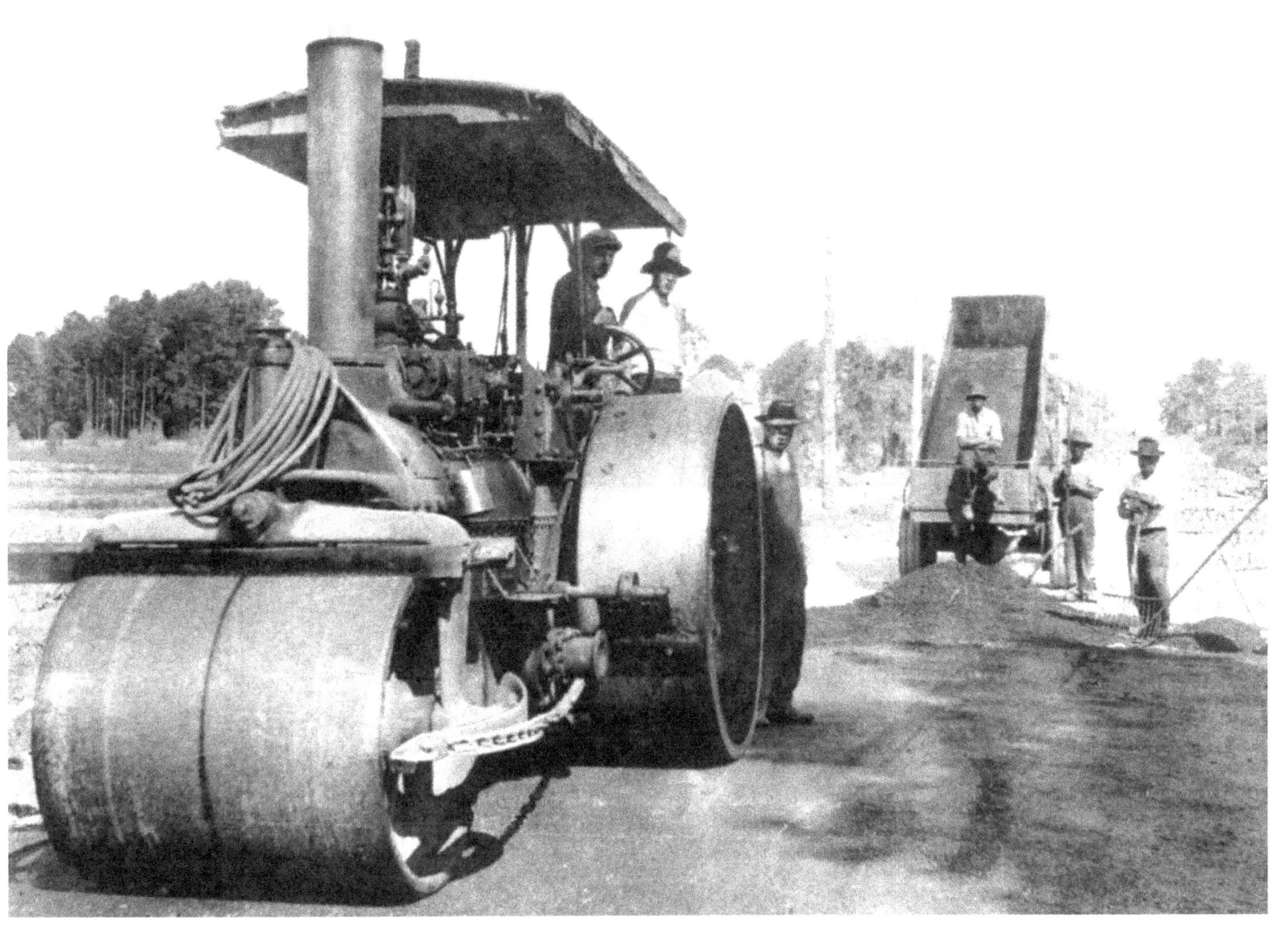

Workers lay the road surface during the construction of the Roxboro Road section of the National Highway in Durham County, ca. 1919.

Debuting October 5, 1929, the Duke University football stadium was the first facility used at the new West Campus location.

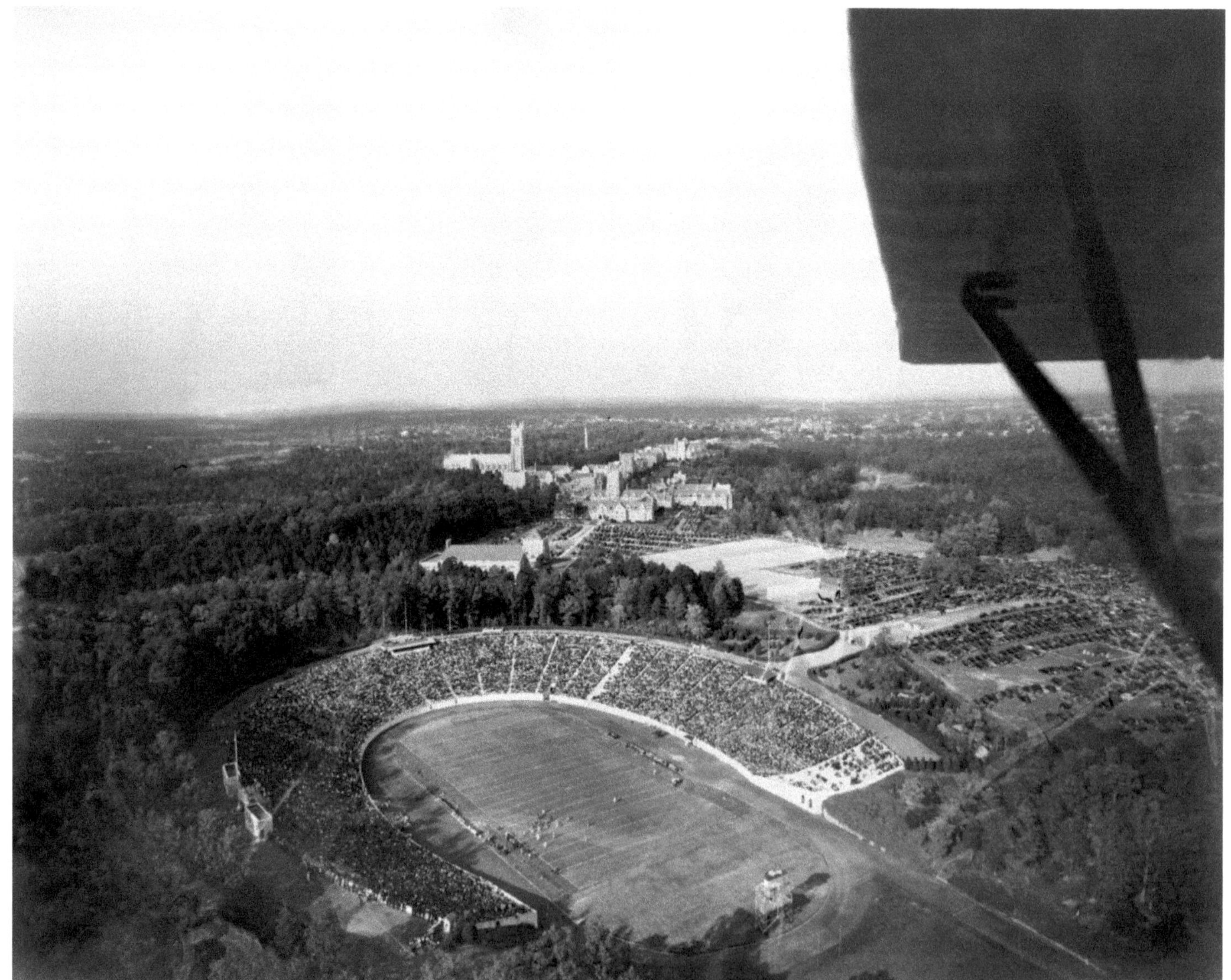

Built in 1892 on Dawson Street west of Nash Square, Raleigh's Union Depot served railroad passengers until 1950. Parts of the structure are still in use today as offices.

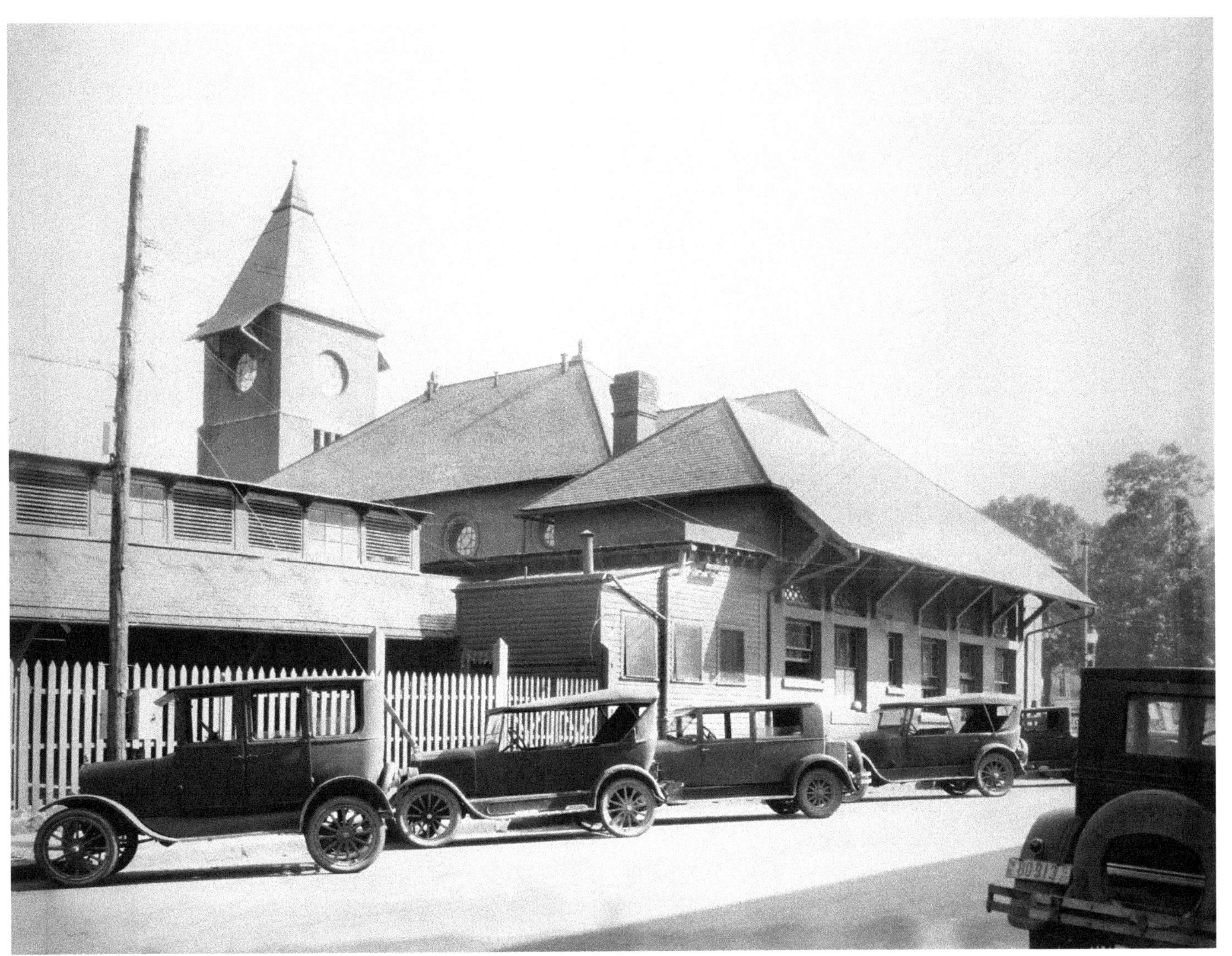

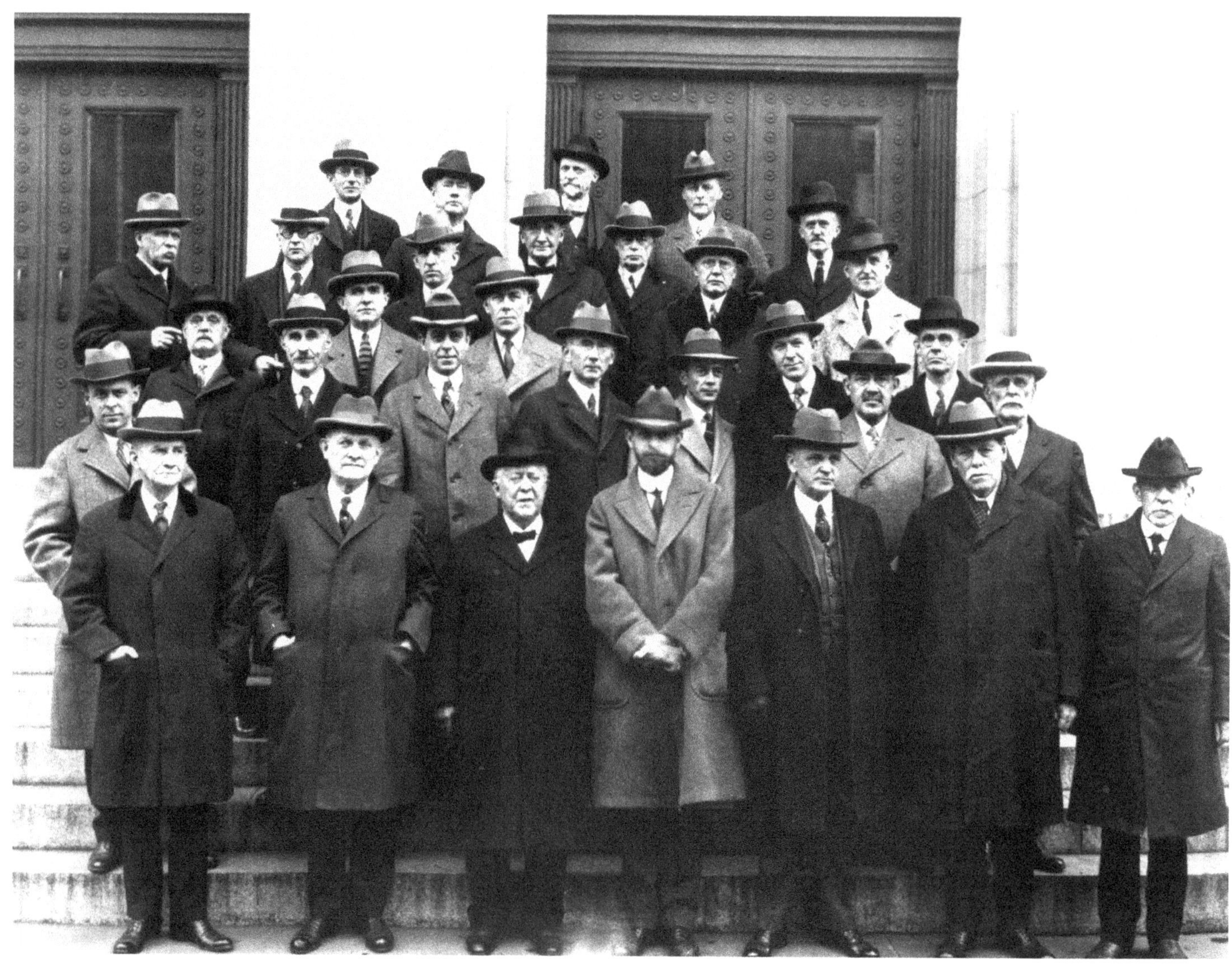

James B. Duke established the Duke Endowment in 1924, a philanthropic trust fund to benefit a variety of organizations in North Carolina. One of the beneficiaries was Trinity College, whose board (pictured here) recommended a name change in honor of the gift and the generosity of the Duke family. The change—to Duke University—became official on December 29, 1924.

This view from an upper window of the Masonic Temple Building at 133 Fayetteville Street in Raleigh shows the Raleigh Banking & Trust Building on the corner of Fayetteville and Hargett streets after its expansion from three to eleven stories in 1930.

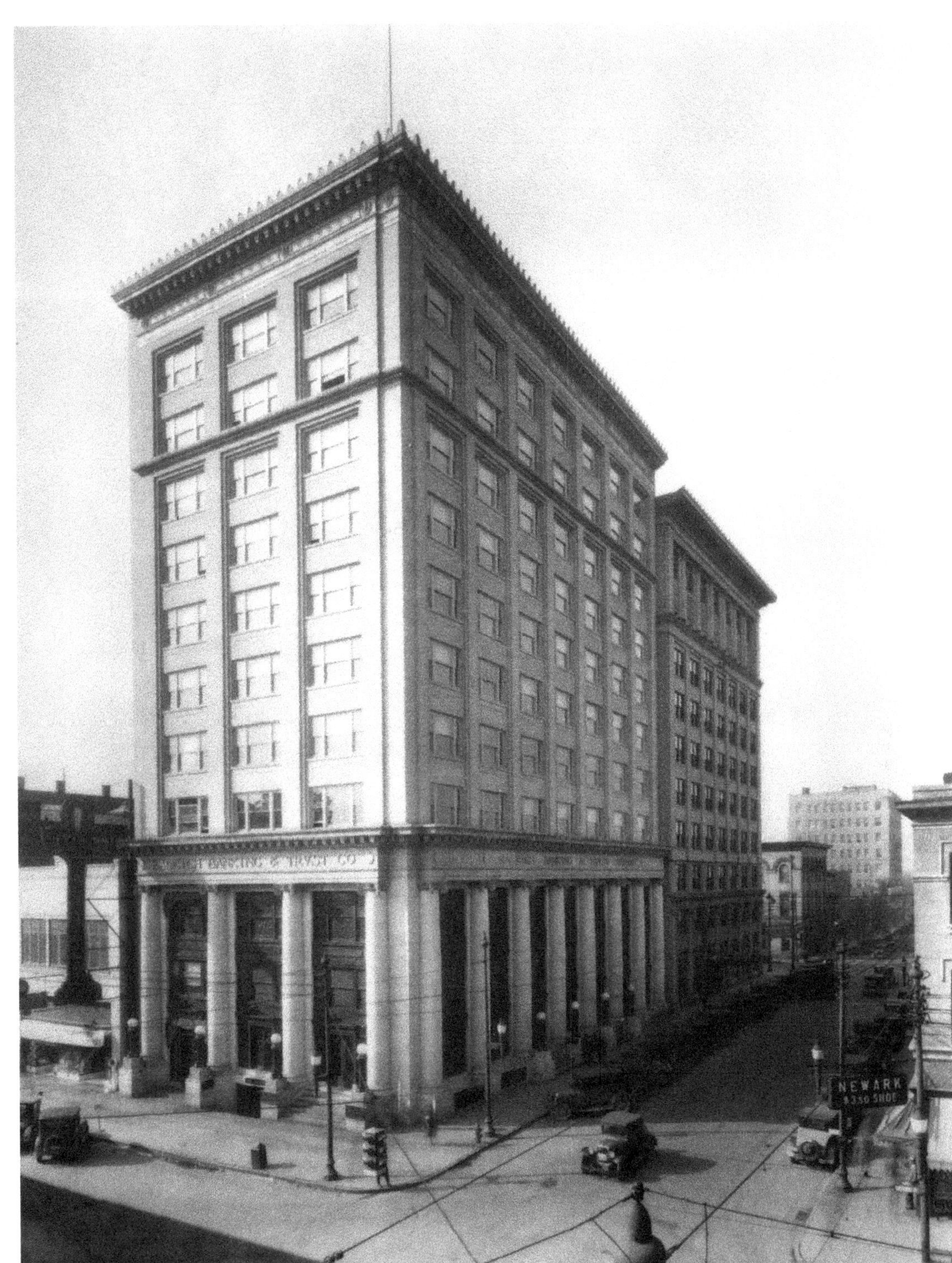

This aerial view of Duke's East Campus shows the West and East Duke buildings with the statue of Washington Duke in between. The domed building in the rear is the Women's College Auditorium.

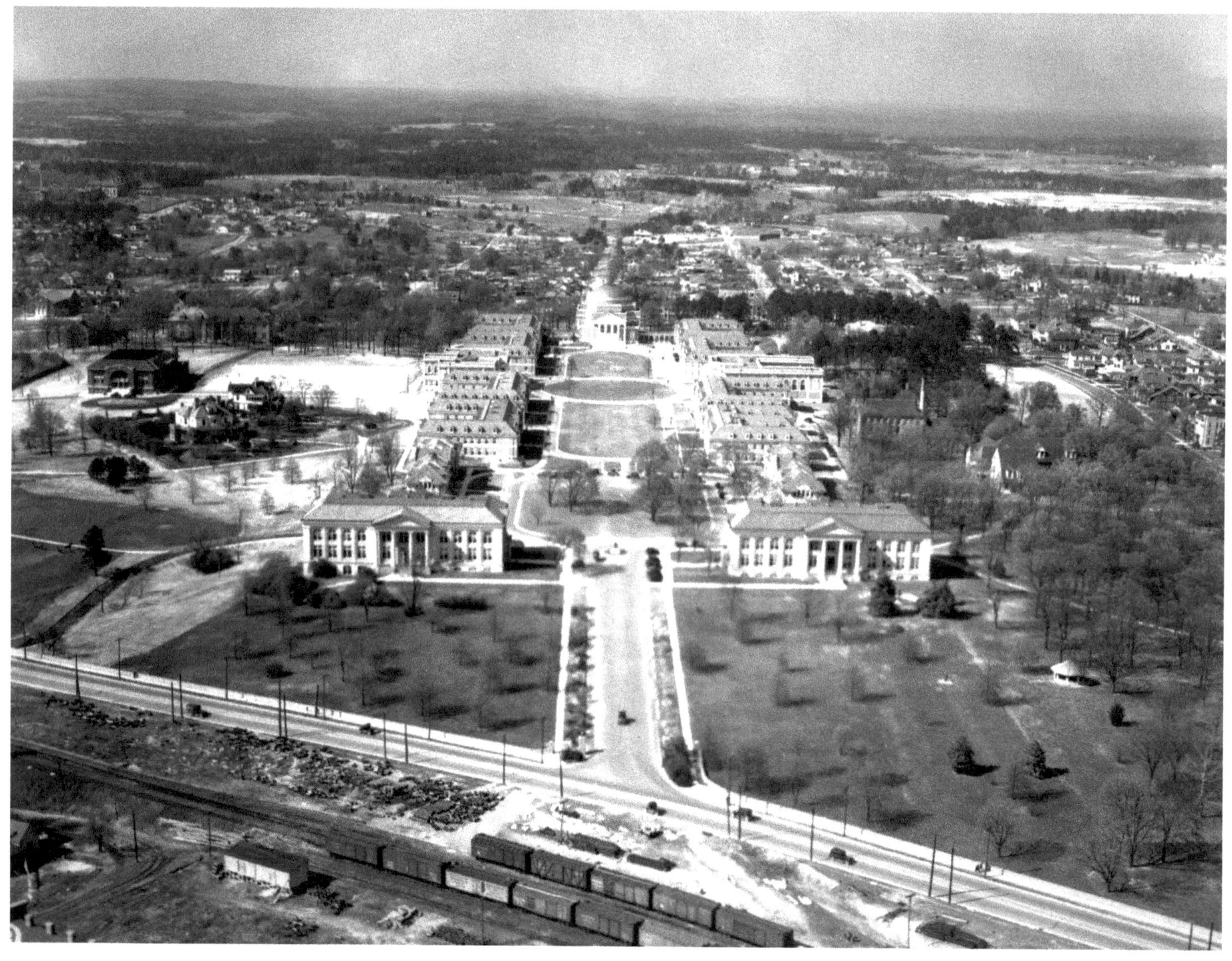

Carolina Air Lines operated briefly during the 1920s out of Marshburn-Robbins Field south of Raleigh. This photograph depicts a young man in the cockpit of one of the company's Waco II airplanes.

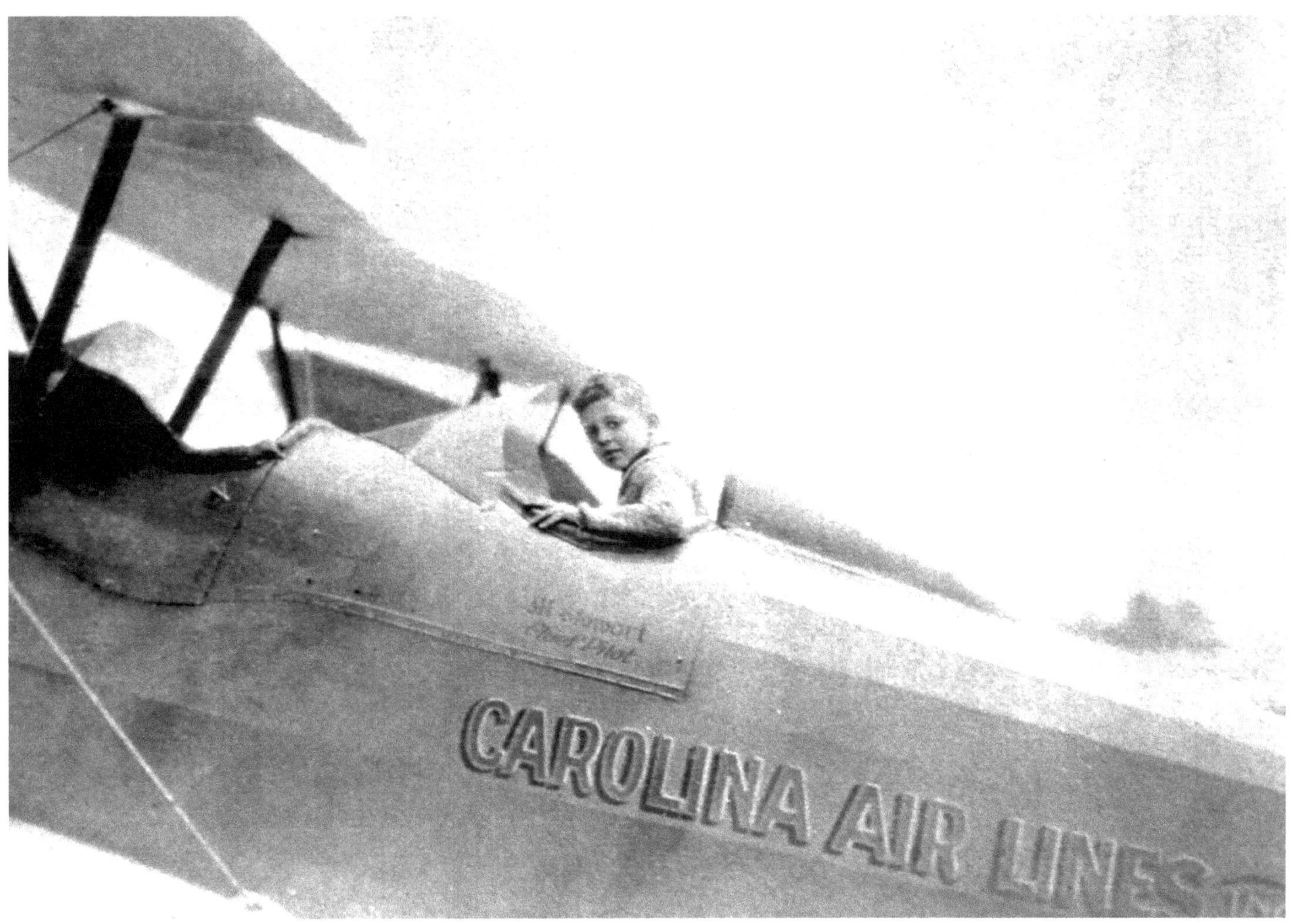

Following Spread: These two Waco airplanes were delivered to the Curtis Travel Air Service in Raleigh in the late 1920s.

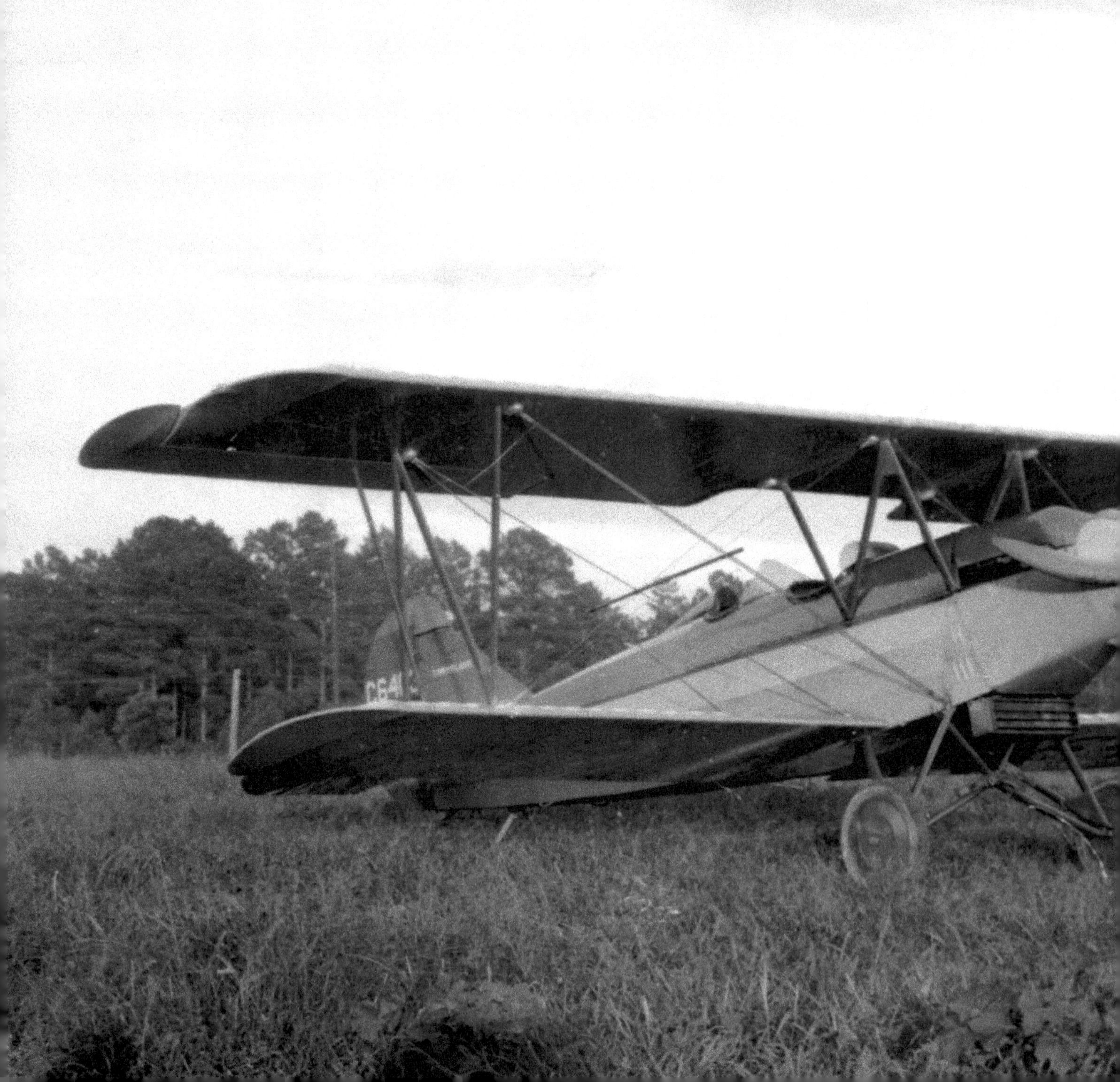

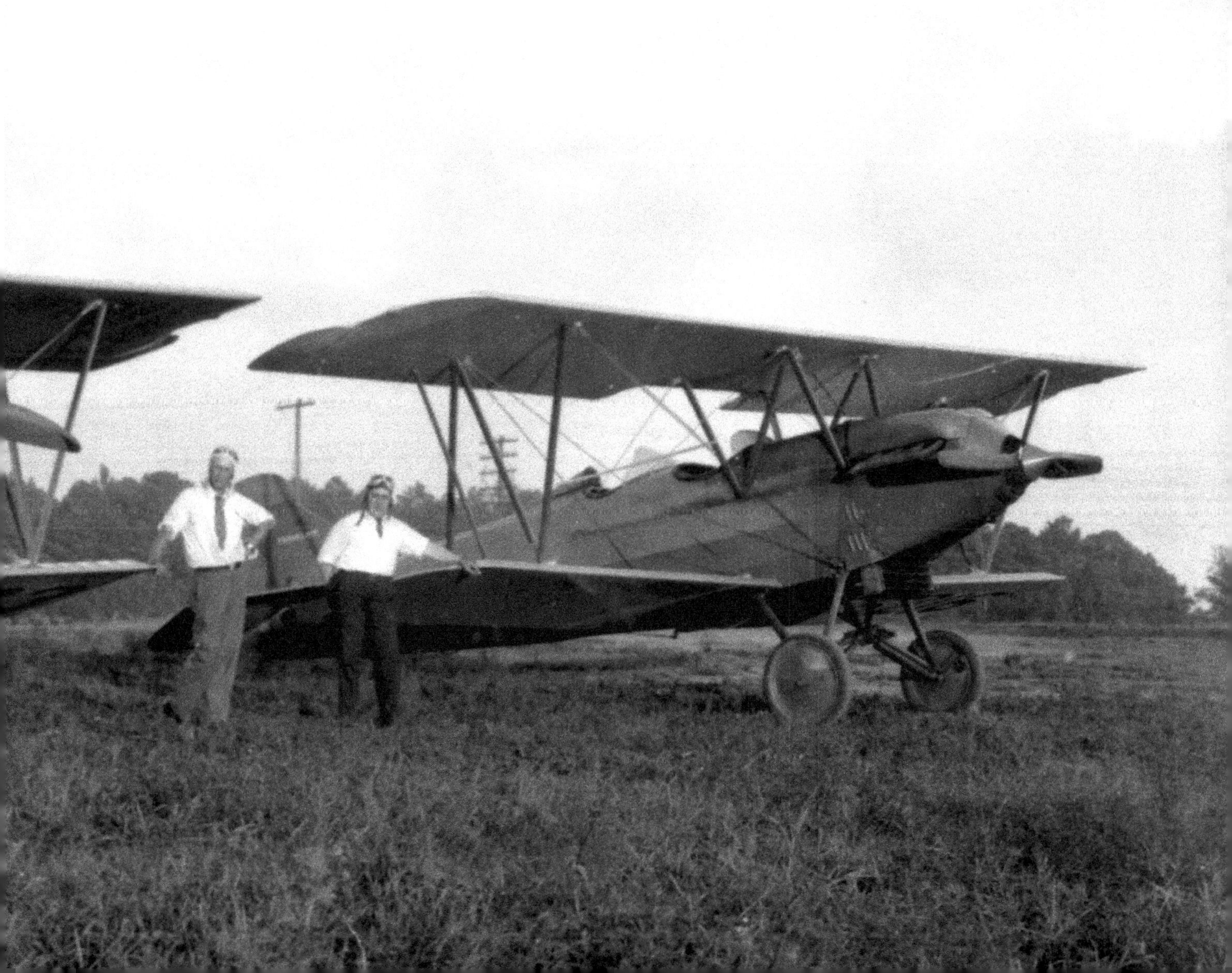

The Academy of Music Building (center, with "North Carolina Cotton Growers Co-operative" signage) was erected on the southwest corner of Salisbury and Martin streets in Raleigh in 1893. The structure served as a home for the finest theatrical productions in the city for two decades. Will Rogers, W. C. Fields, Ethel and John Barrymore, and other celebrated performers strode across its stage.

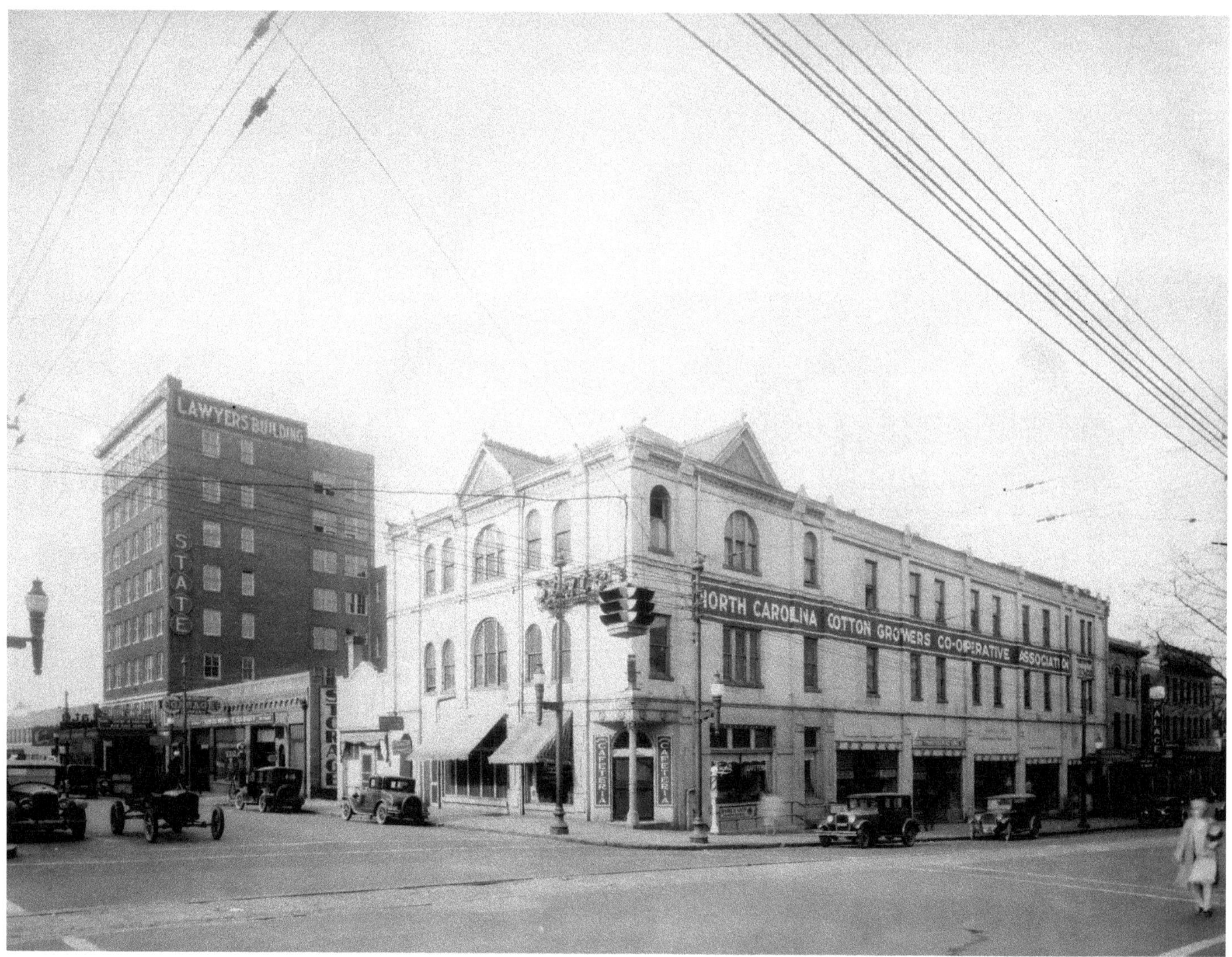

Opening on July 4, 1912, Bloomsbury Park was an early Raleigh amusement park at the end of the new Glenwood Avenue trolley line. Here, the Bloomsbury Park trolley travels alongside the dirt-paved route to the park in 1913.

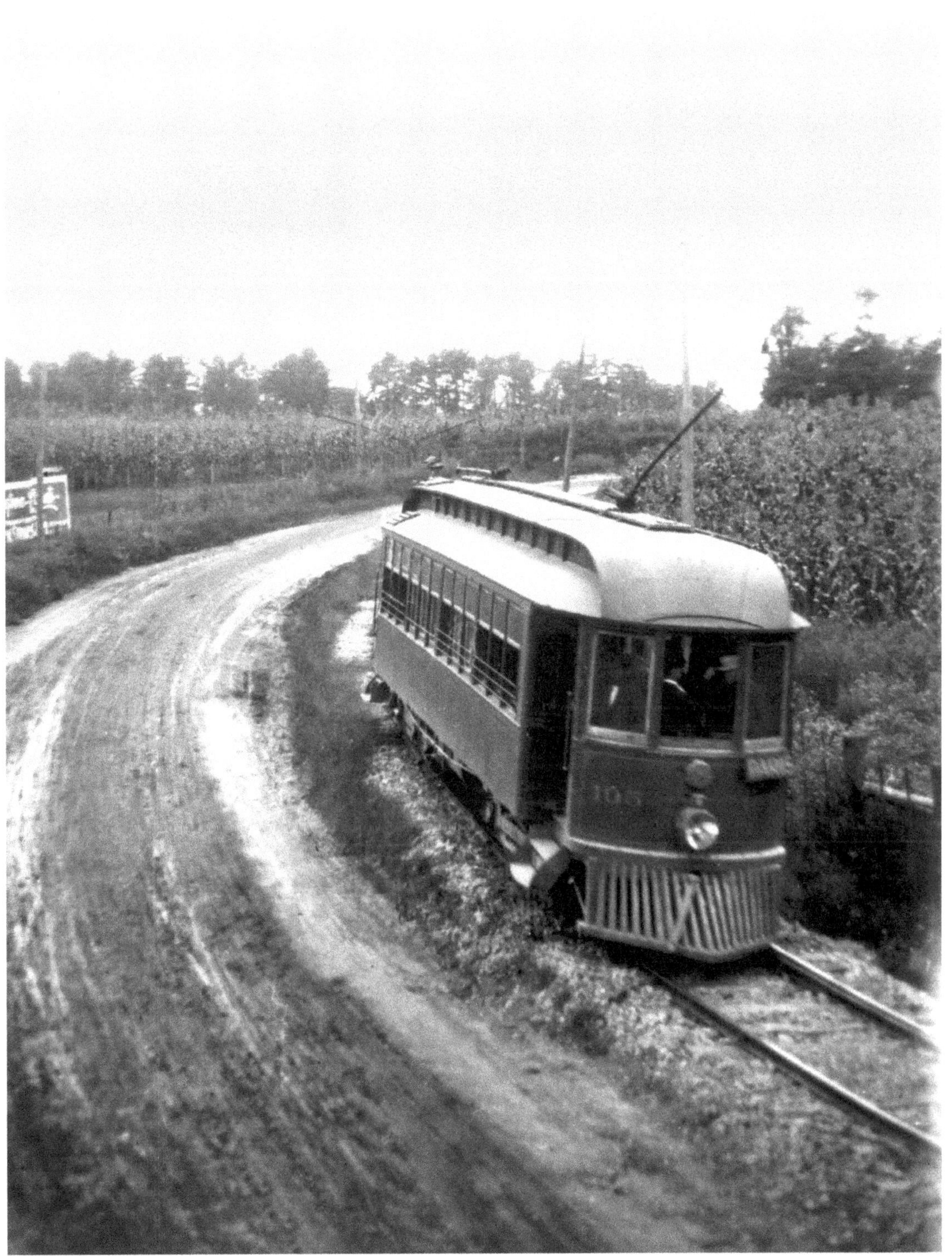

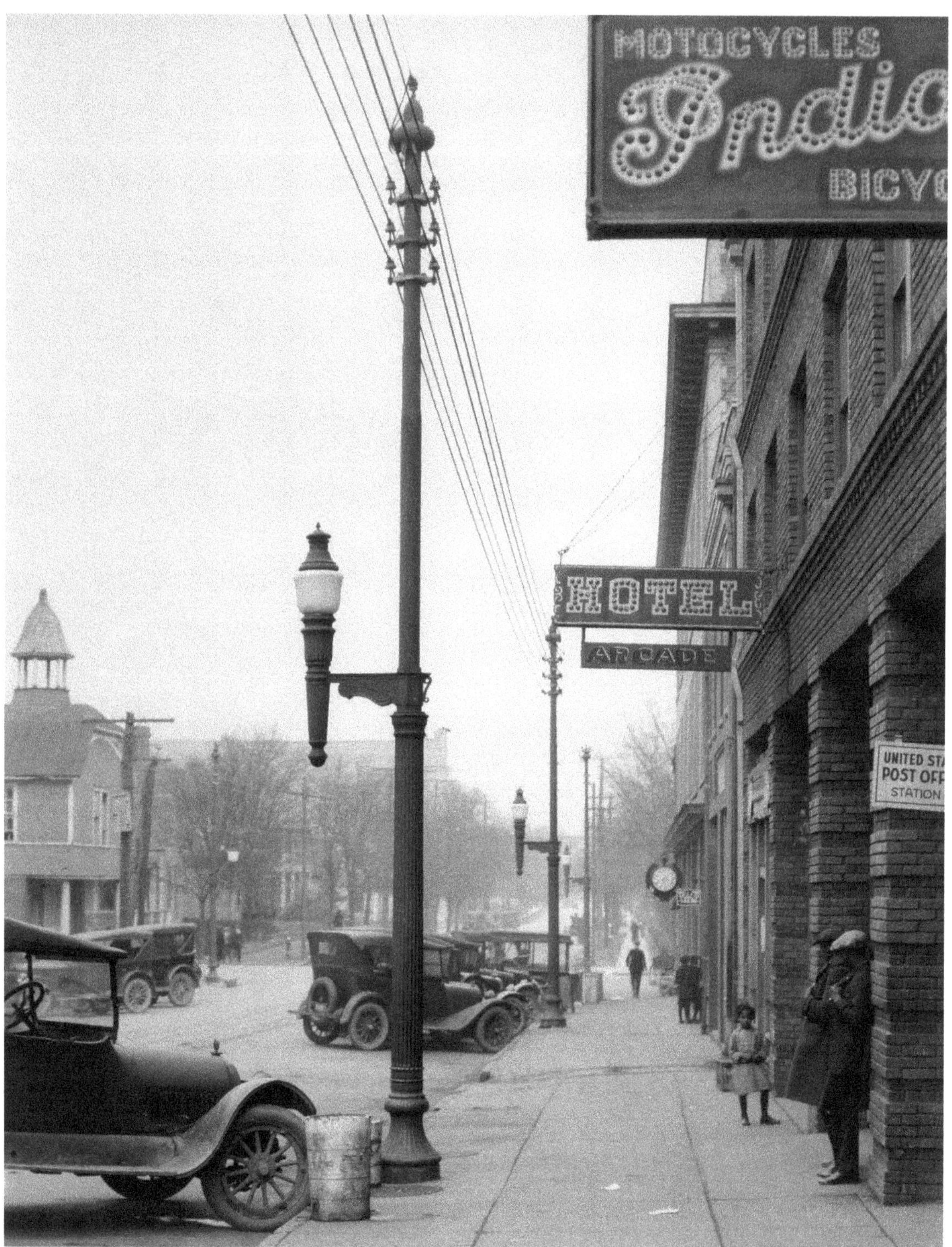

By the 1920s, East Hargett Street in Raleigh had become a thriving business district for the city's African American community. The hotel sign in this image hung from the Lightner Arcade, a business enterprise opened by Calvin Lightner in 1924. The arcade provided offices for several black-owned businesses and operated a hotel for African Americans, at the time a rarity in the segregated South.

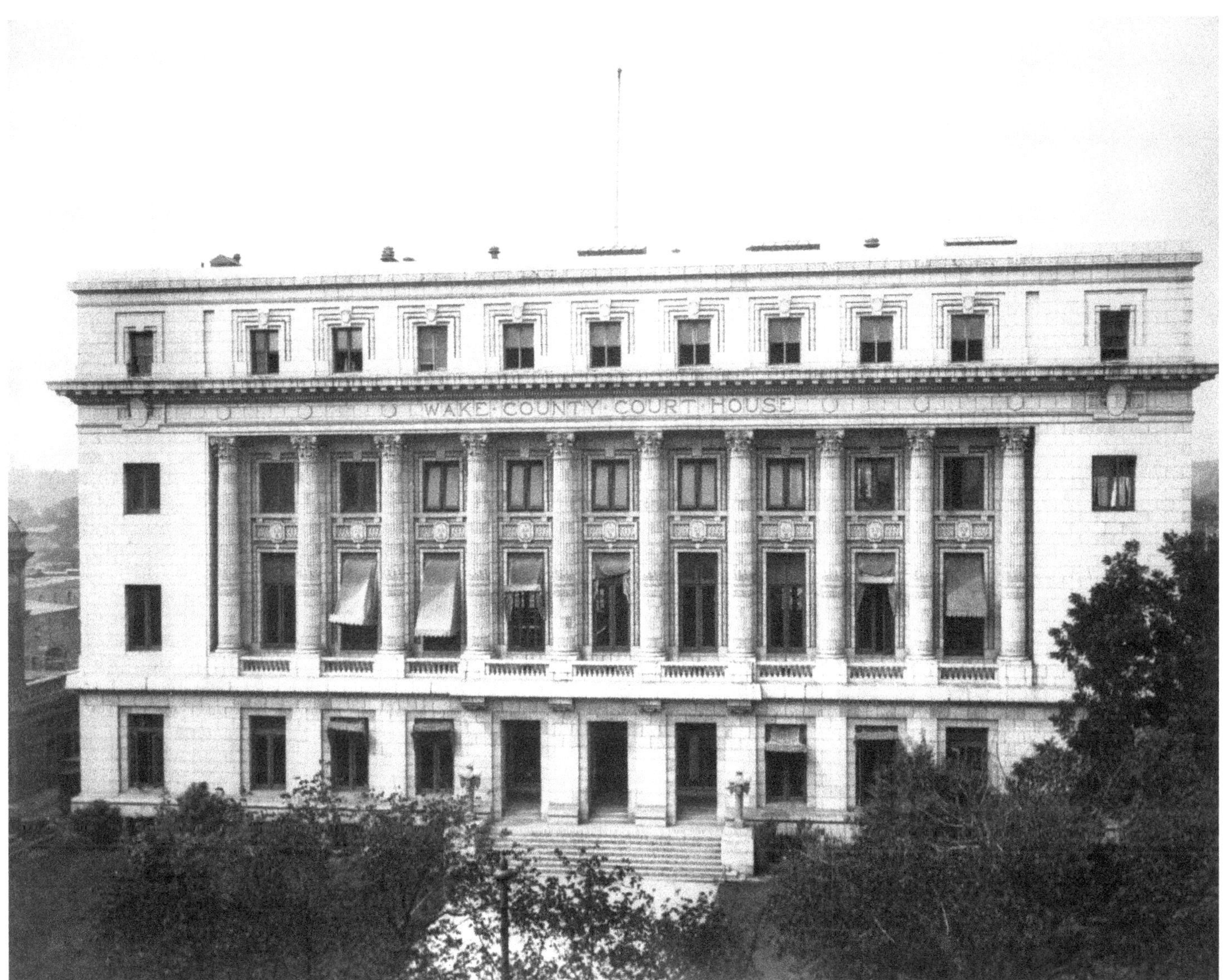

The First Wake County Courthouse predated Raleigh by nearly twenty years. The Second Wake County Courthouse, opened in 1794 on the 300-block of Fayetteville Street, was the first to stand in the new capital city. It was succeeded in the 1830s by the Third Wake County Courthouse. The structure pictured here was the Fourth Wake County Courthouse, built in 1915. It stood until the 1960s, when it was replaced with the current county facility.

Angus W. McLean served as the governor of North Carolina from 1925 to 1929. A Robeson County native, he poses here with his wife in front of the Executive Mansion in Raleigh.

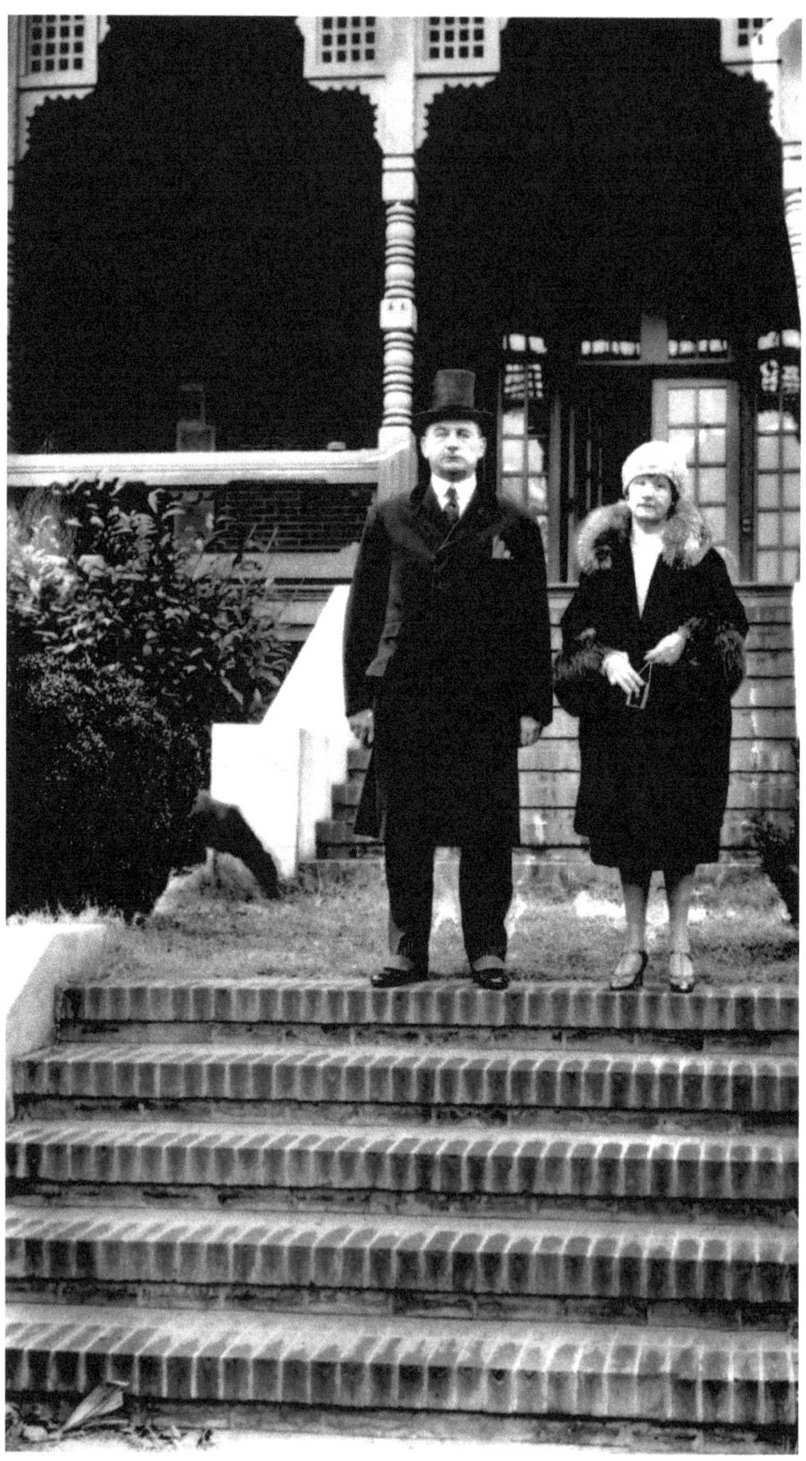

Arnold Taylor draws a crowd as he competes in a national tree-sitting contest. Taylor sat in the tree in front of Denise's Gas Station at the corner of Broad and Markham streets in Durham for six to seven weeks.

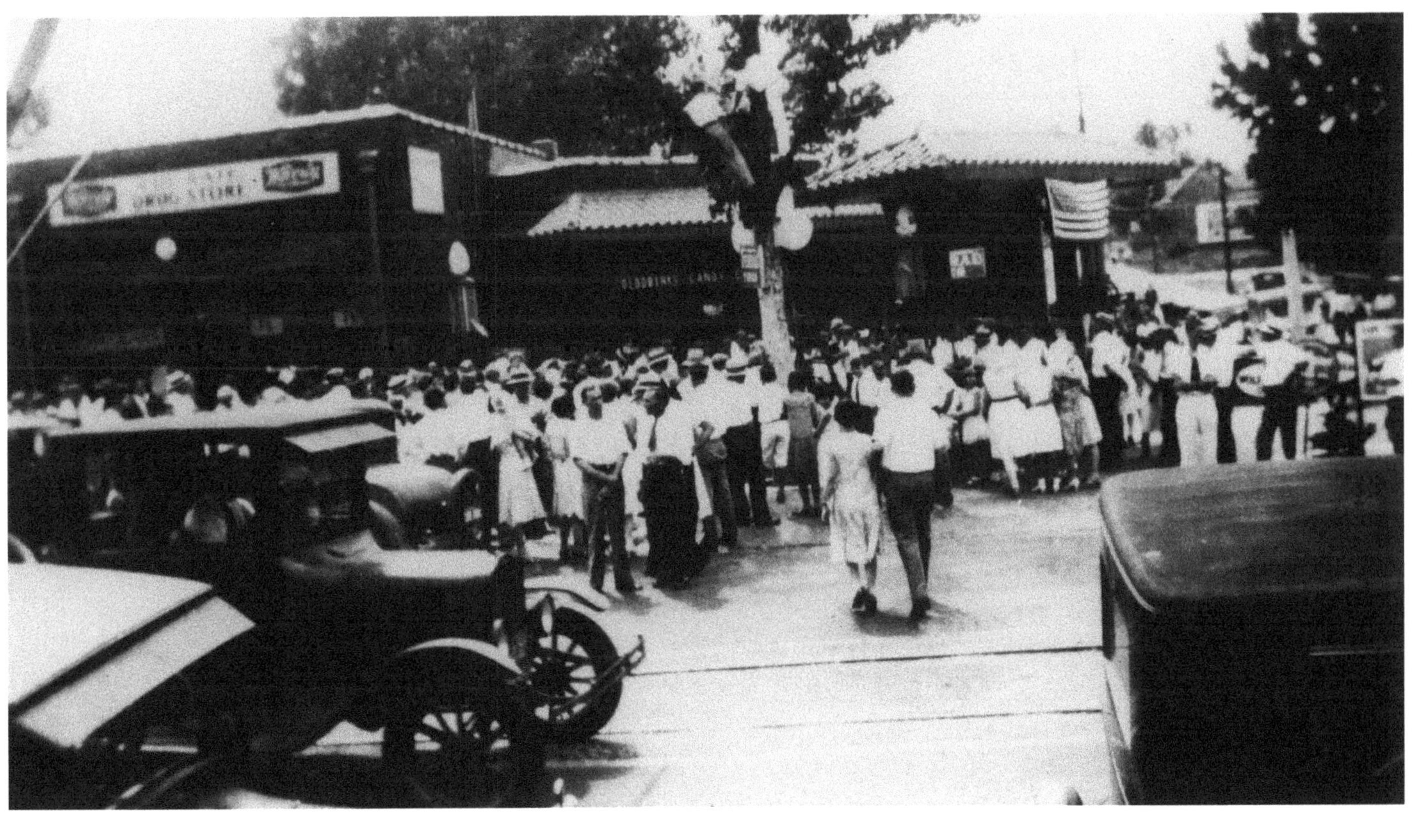

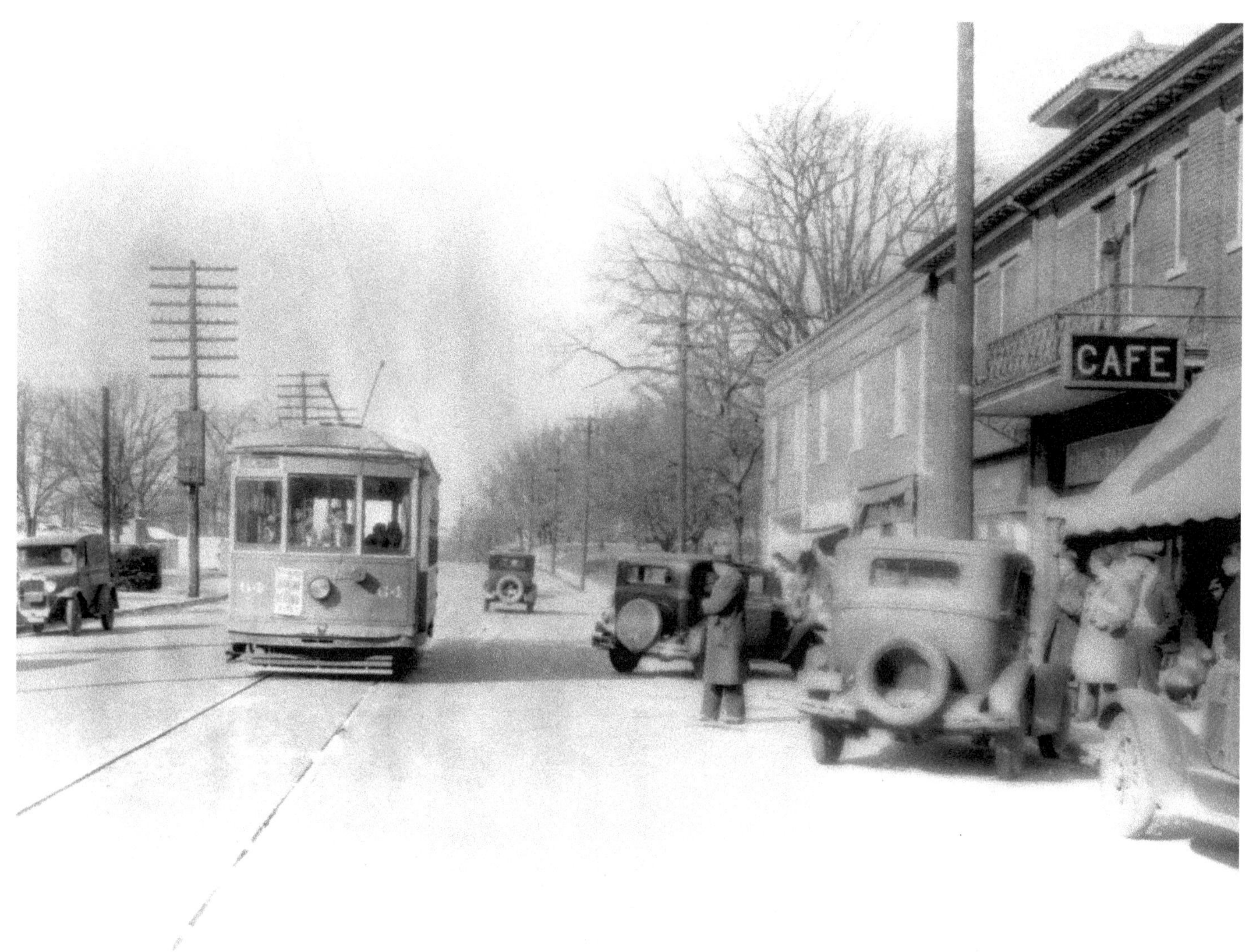

A Carolina Power & Light Company trolley car clanks along Hillsborough Street in West Raleigh, ca. 1927. The still-incomplete North Carolina State University Bell Tower is just visible in the distance, on the left.

A crowd gathers at the corner of Fayetteville and Hargett streets outside the Raleigh Banking & Trust Company offices. Although it has been suggested that this image depicts a 1929 run on the bank, the behavior and attire of the crowd implies an event less onerous.

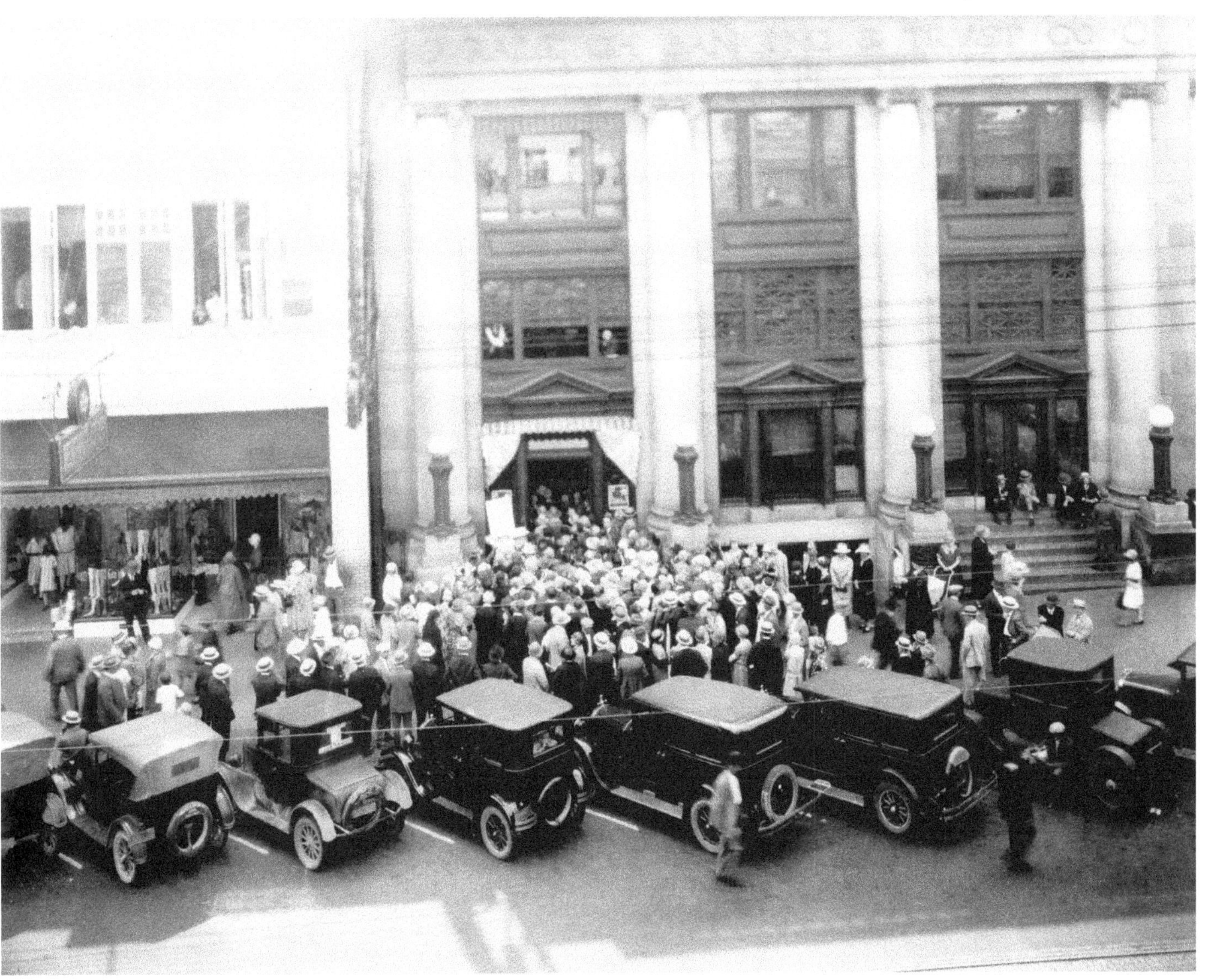

The North Carolina State Capitol at night.

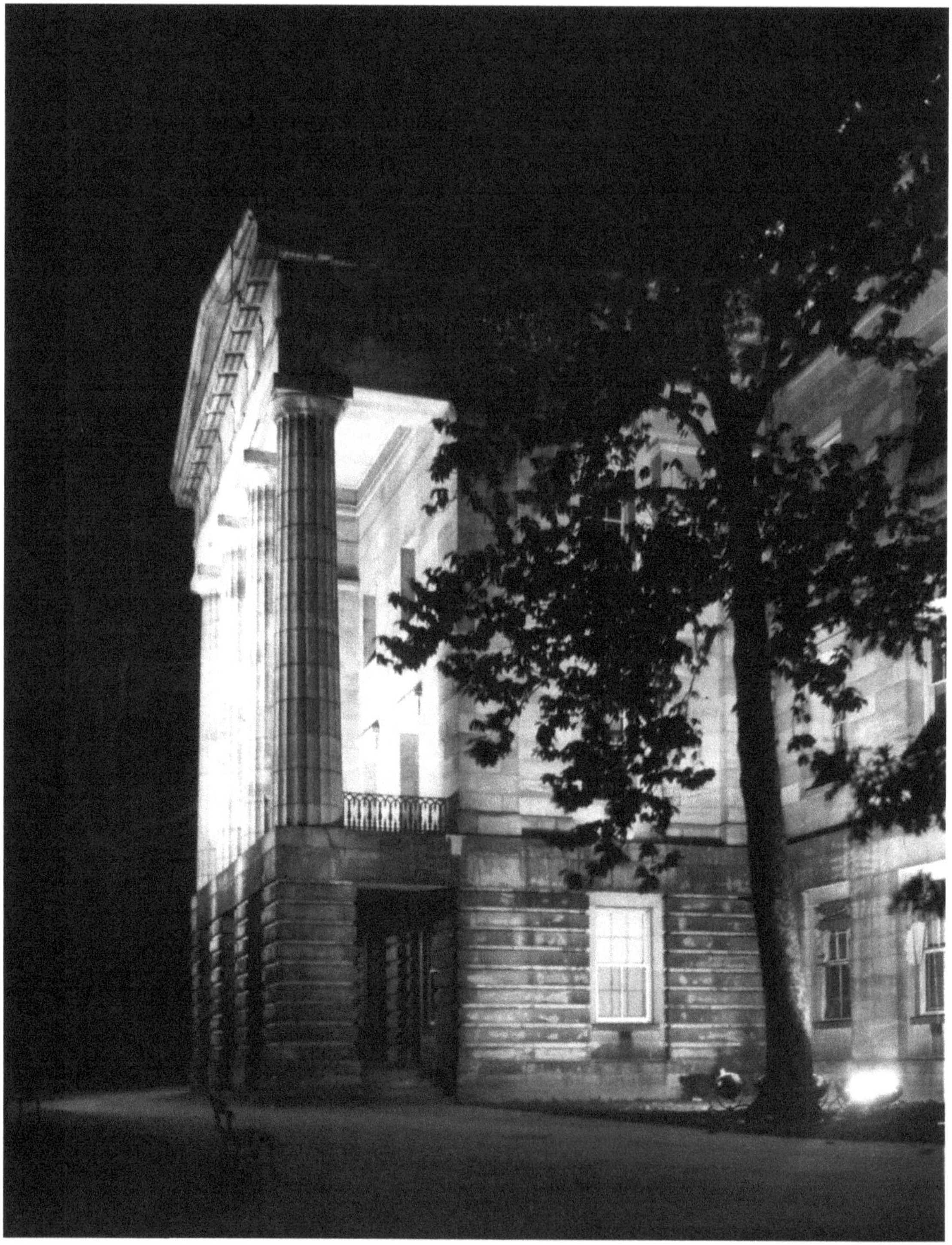

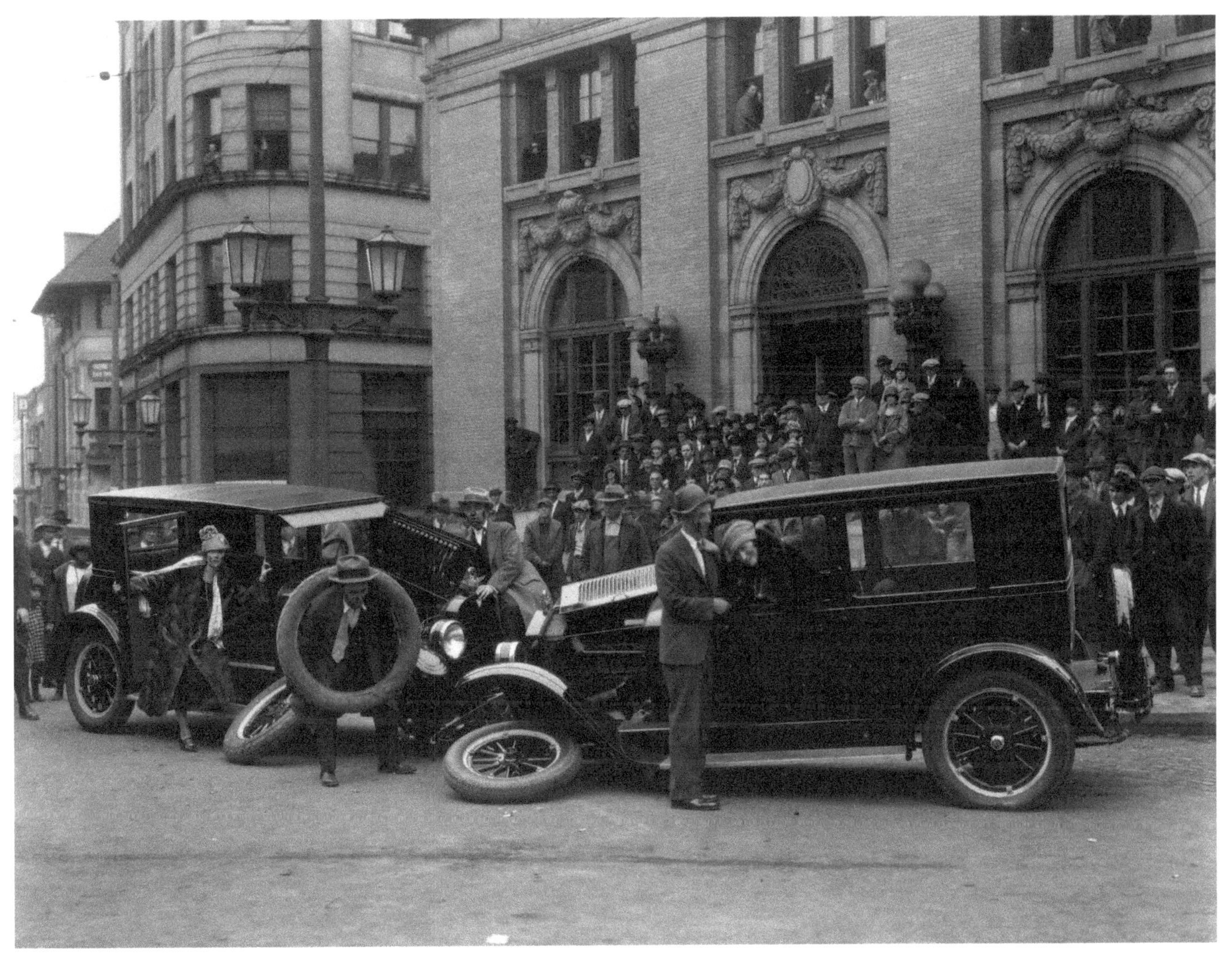

Moviemakers stage a car wreck in front of the Durham Post Office in what appears to be a comedy, ca. 1930.

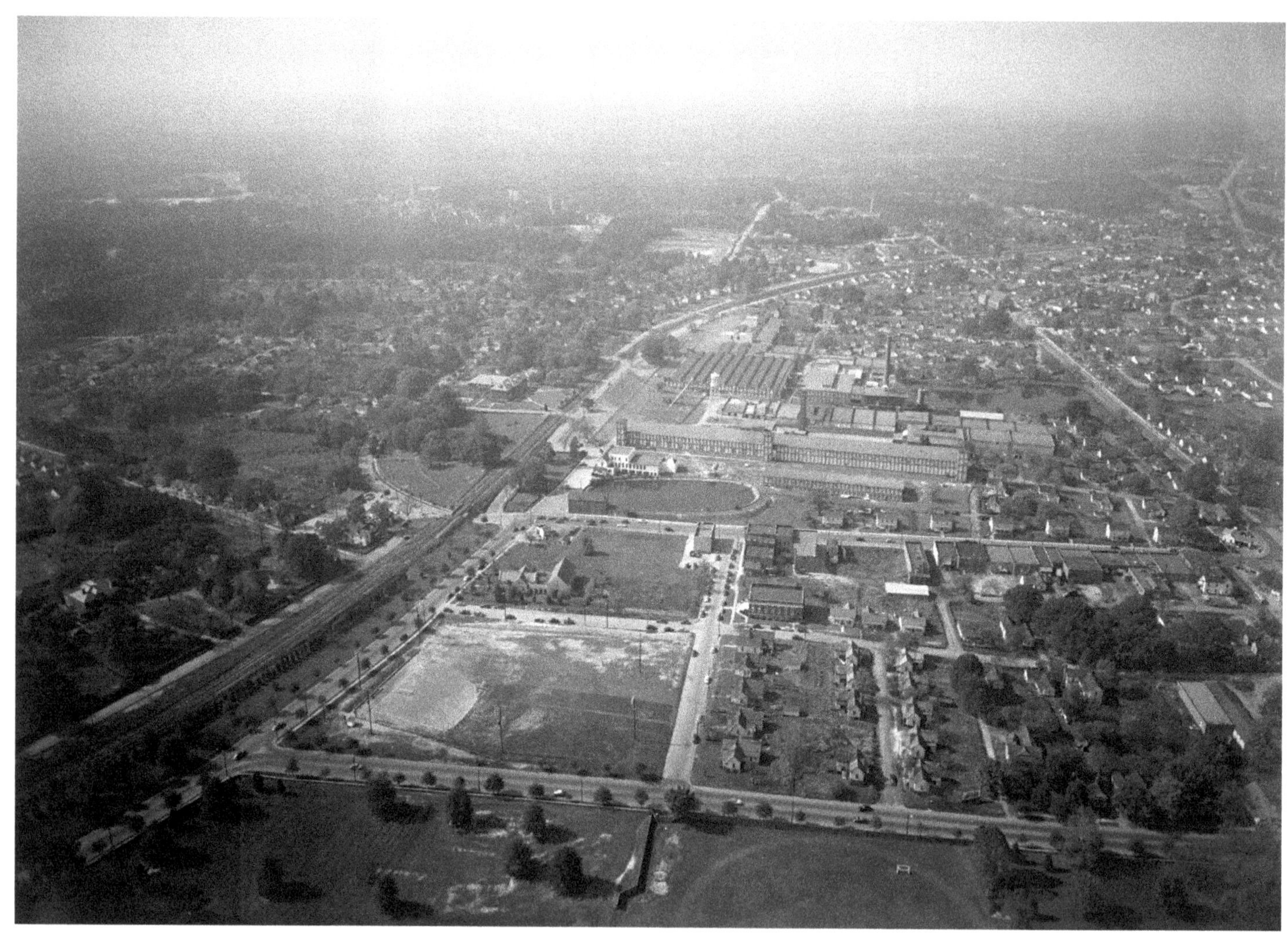

An aerial view of West Durham, ca. 1930, from above the intersection of Main and Broad streets. Ninth Street, Erwin Mills, and Erwin Auditorium are visible at center, and Duke Chapel is in the distance to the left.

S. E. Rochelle (left) and others look on as a young man shows off his motorcycle in front of West Side Pharmacy in Durham, ca. 1930.

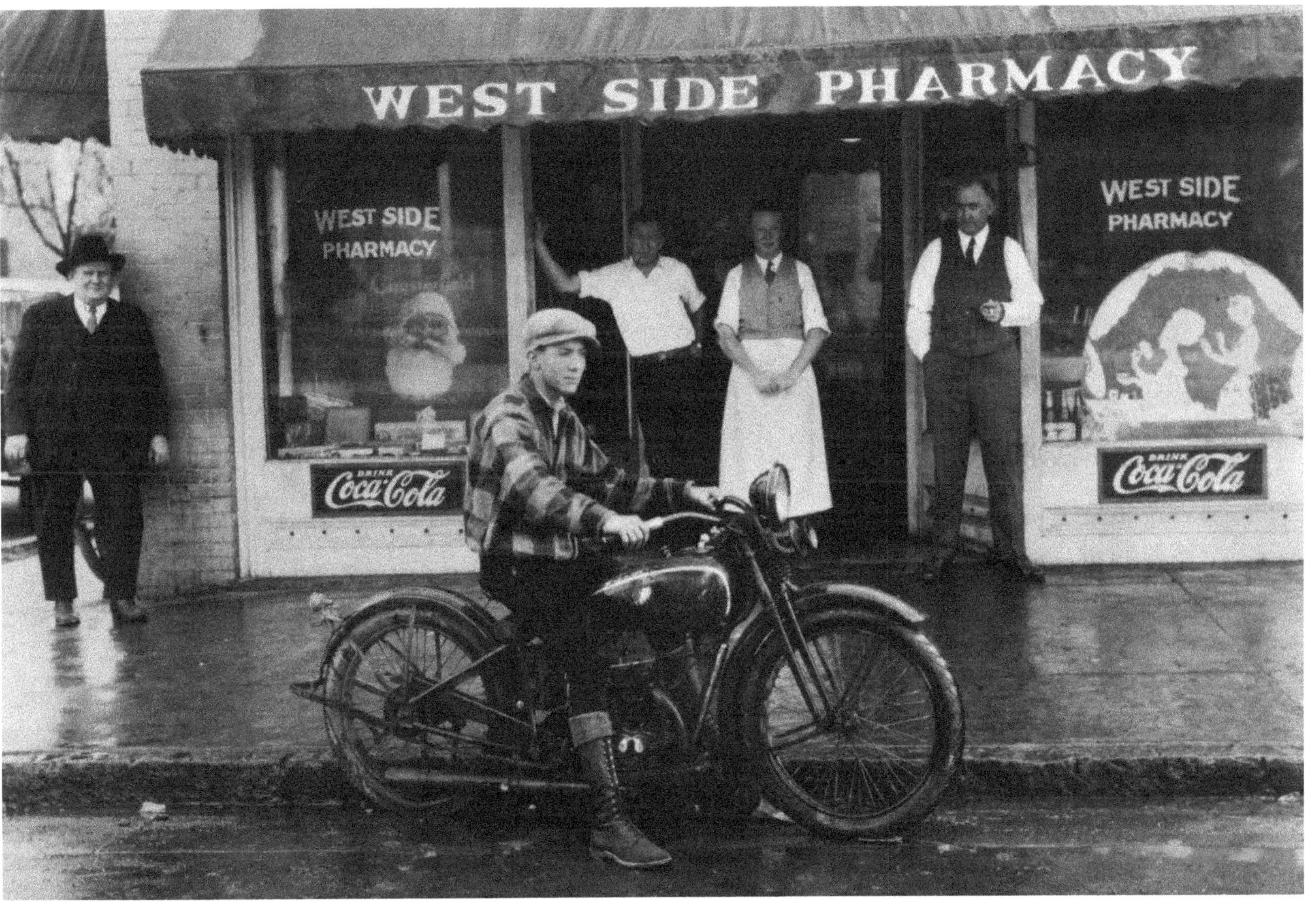

Students and teachers gather outside a Durham County school to pose for a class portrait.

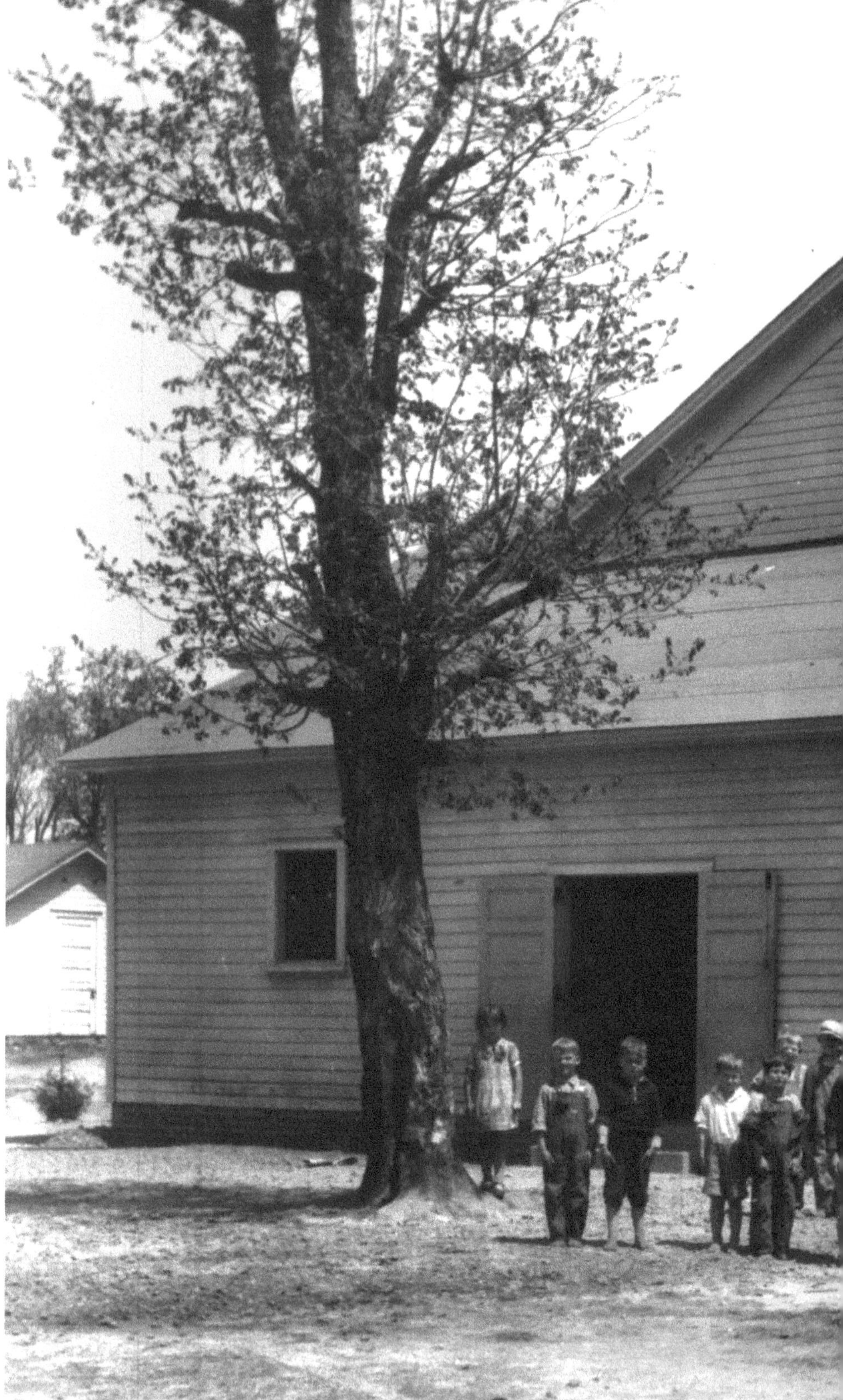

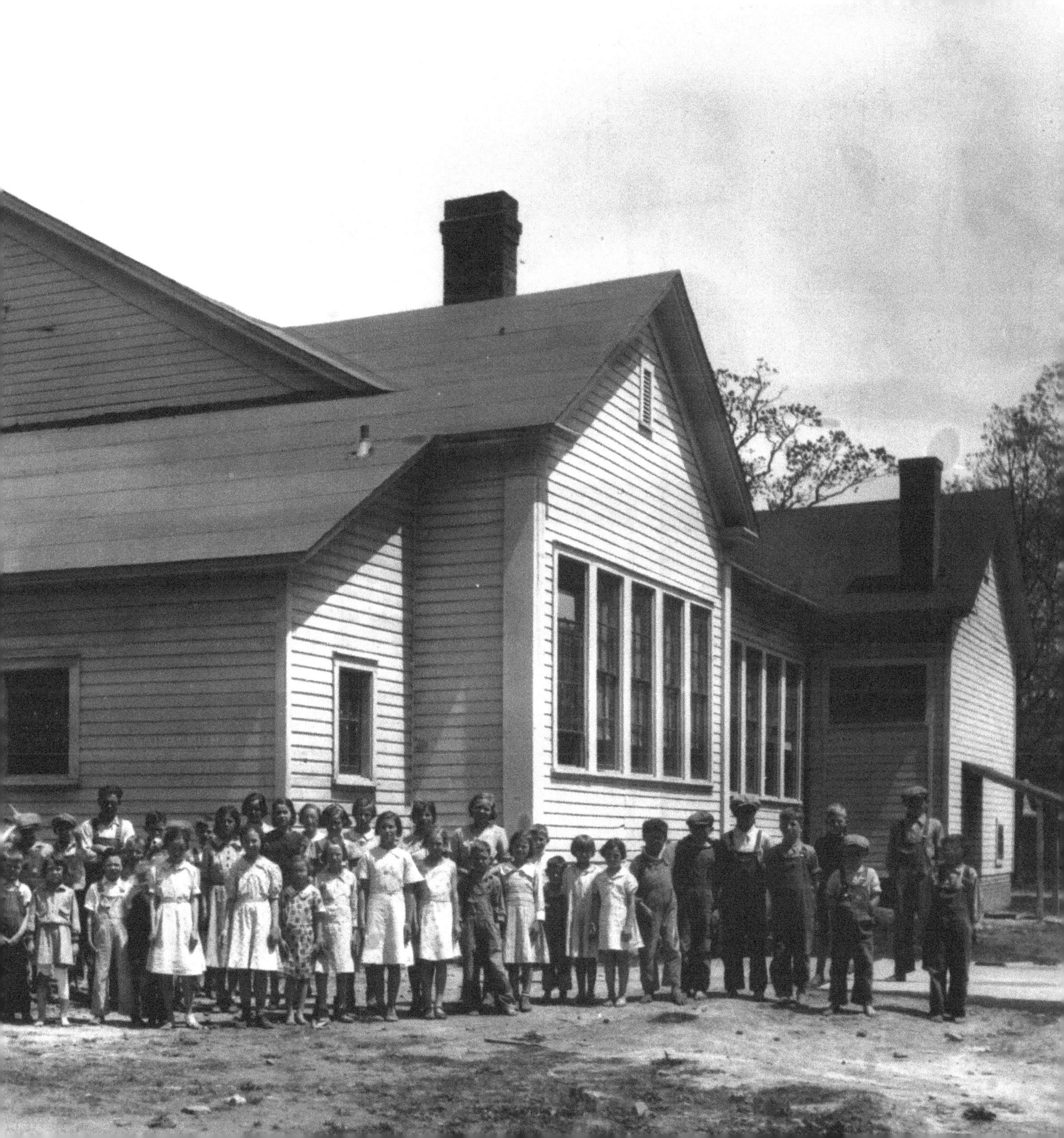

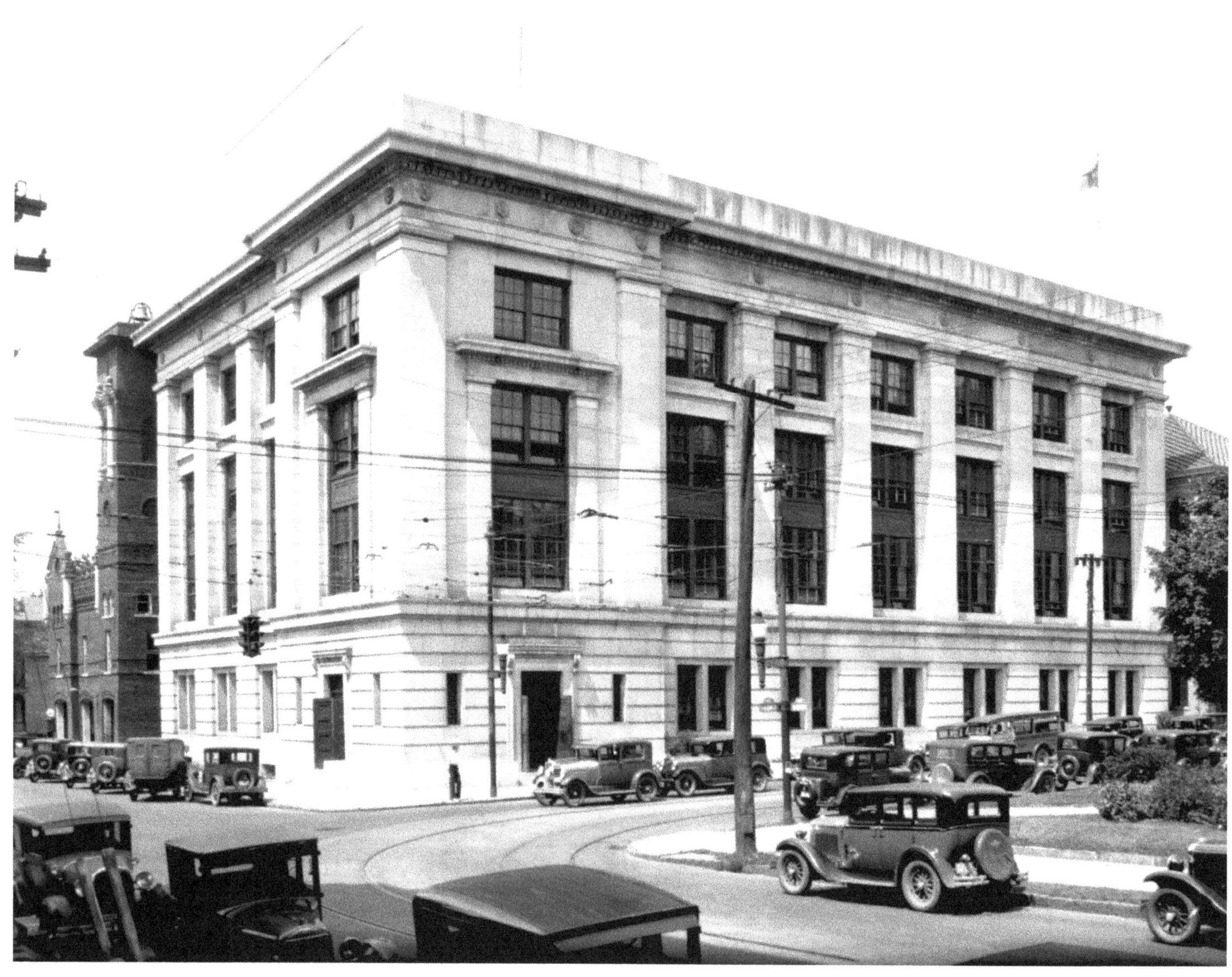

The North Carolina Revenue Building at 2 South Salisbury Street in Raleigh, ca. 1930.

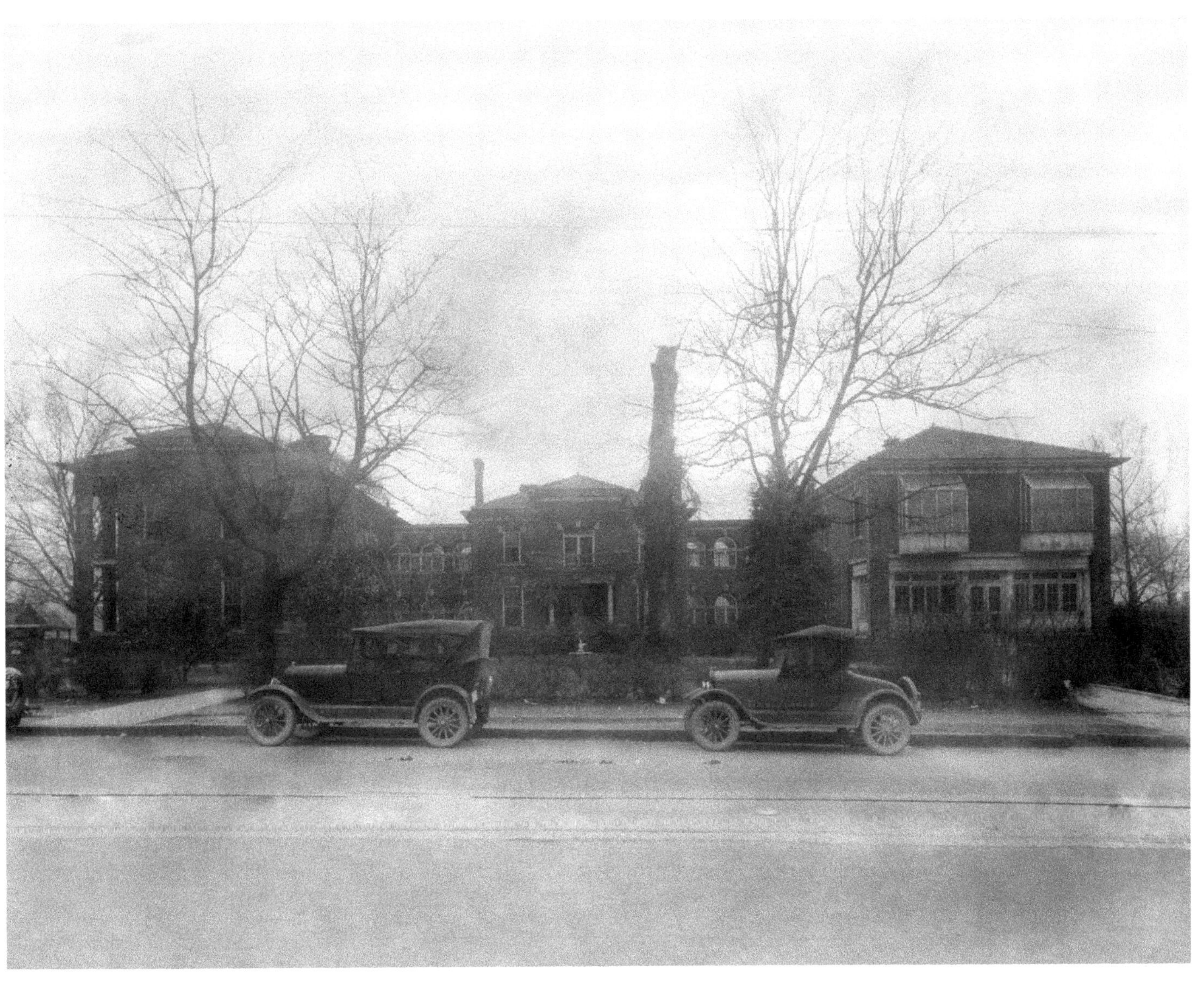

When he died in 1839, Raleigh merchant John Rex left a legacy to the city—a bequest that could be used for the establishment of a hospital. His funds were not utilized until 1894, when St. John's Hospital on South Street was purchased and renamed Rex Hospital. It is seen here in the 1930s before the hospital moved to a larger location on St. Mary's Street.

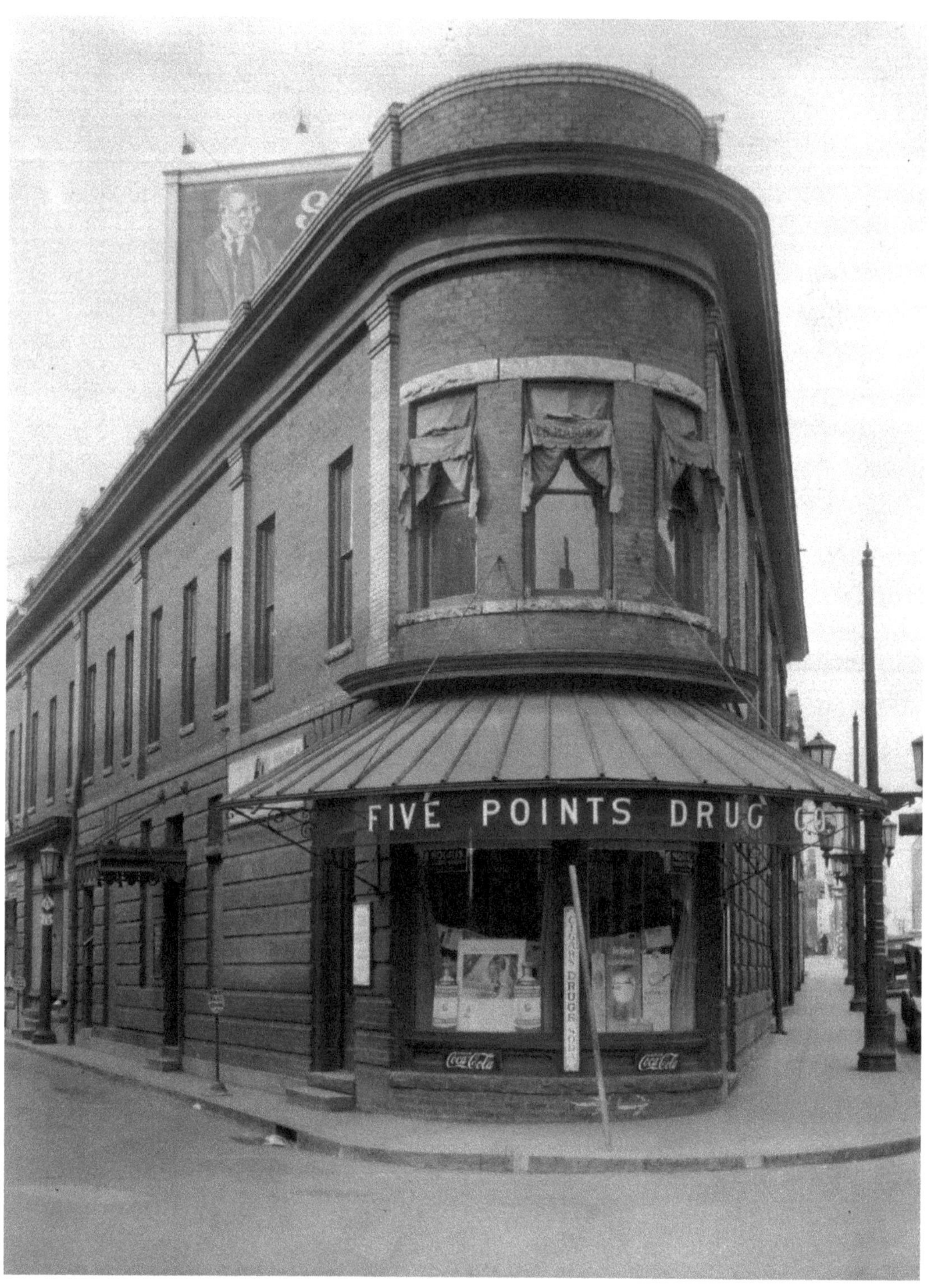

Five Points Drugstore, located in the heart of downtown Durham, 1933.

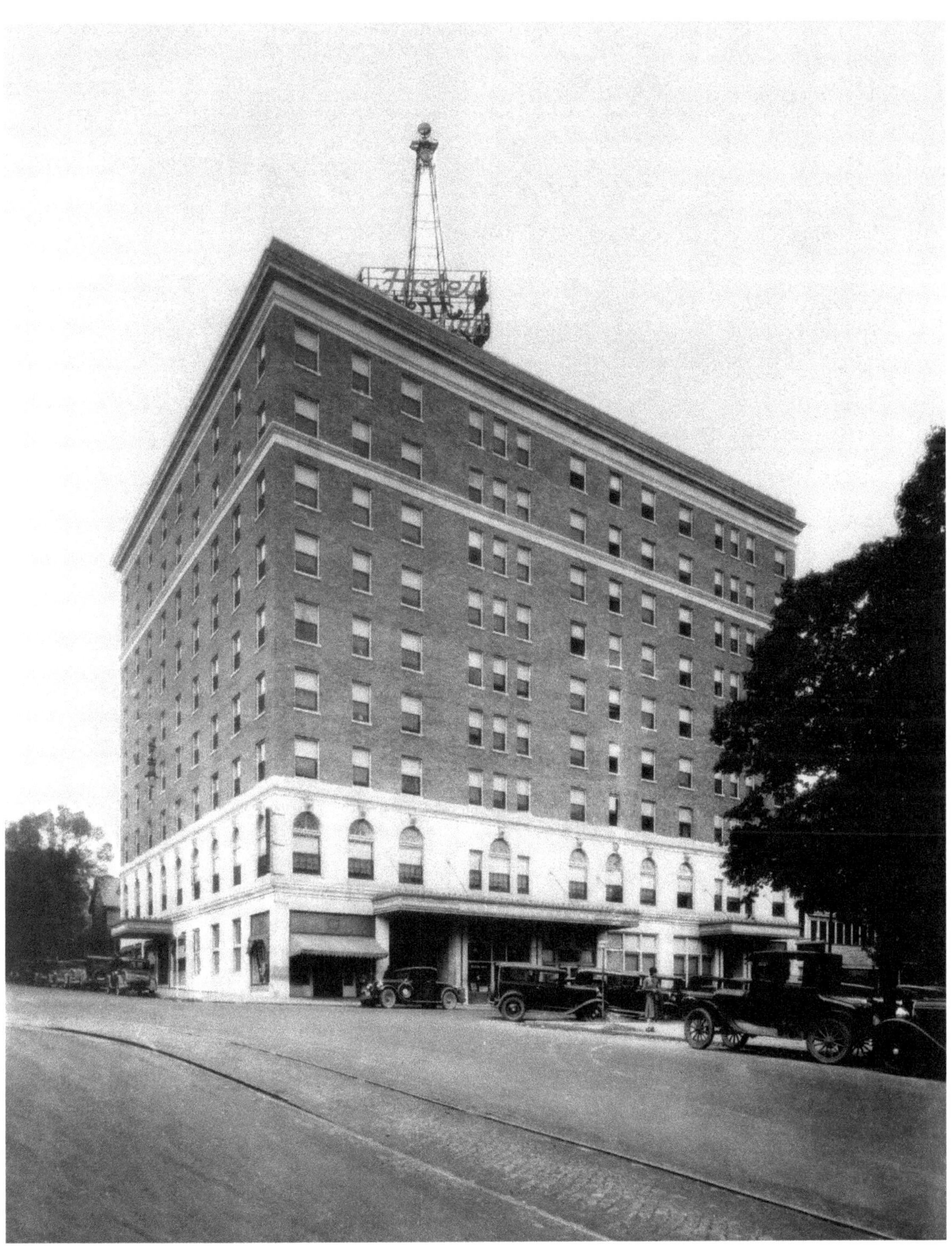

The Hotel Carolina stood on the northeast corner of Hargett and Dawson streets in Raleigh for much of the twentieth century. This location, adjacent Nash Square, placed it within walking distance of the Union Passenger Railroad Station.

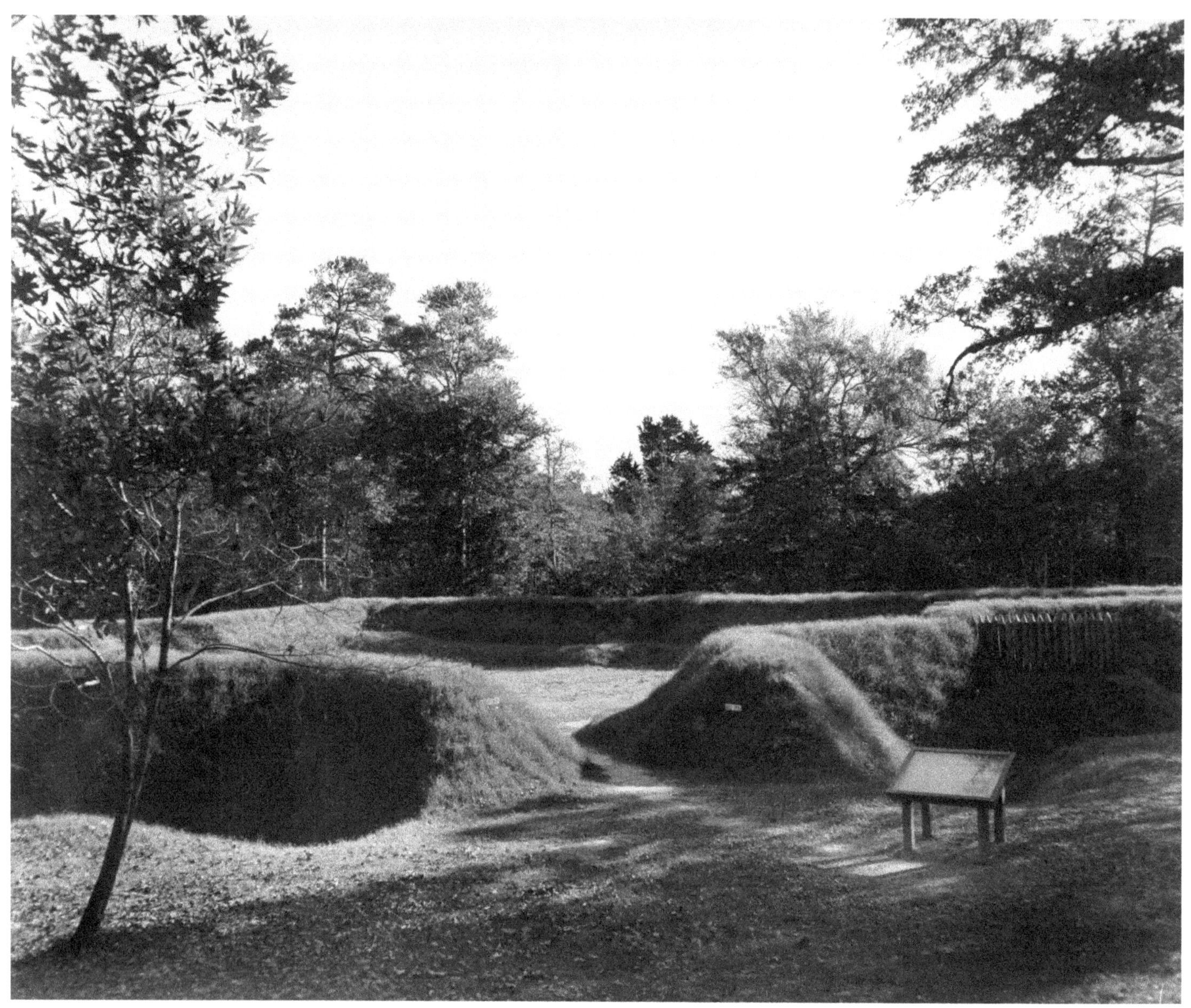

In view here are the reconstructed walls of Fort Raleigh at Manteo. In 1587 John White, appointed governor of the settlement, left for England to restock the colony's supplies. Political complications prevented his return until 1590, whereupon he found that all of the English colonists had vanished. Now known as "the Lost Colony," the settlement's disastrous fate is still a mystery.

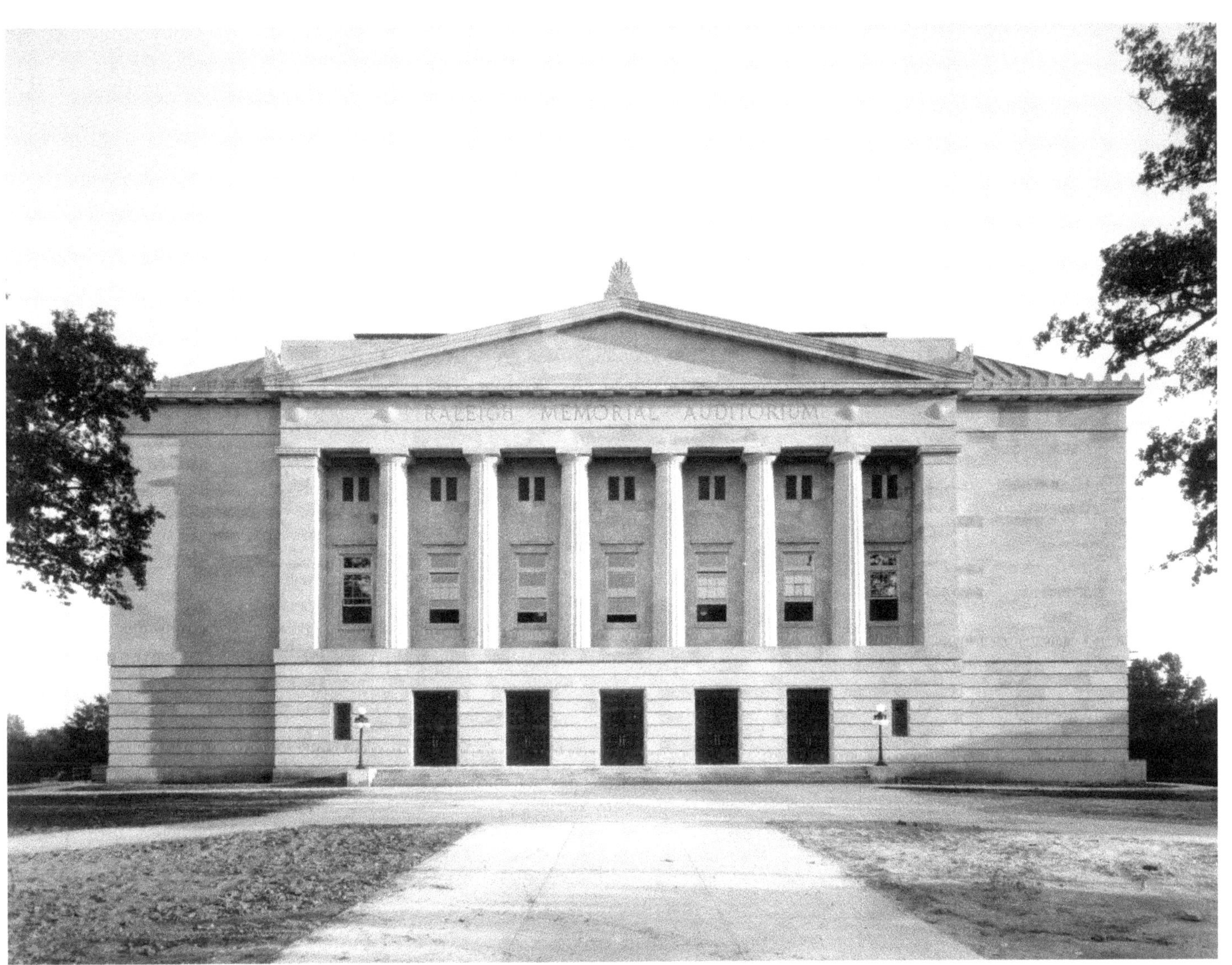

When the Raleigh Civic Auditorium burned to the ground in 1930, the city wasted no time replacing it. Just two years later, Memorial Auditorium opened on South Street on the site of an early governor's mansion.

The Raleigh Municipal Building opened at 333 Fayetteville Street in 1911. When the adjacent auditorium complex burned in 1930, the structure was saved by firemen and continued on as City Hall for another thirty years.

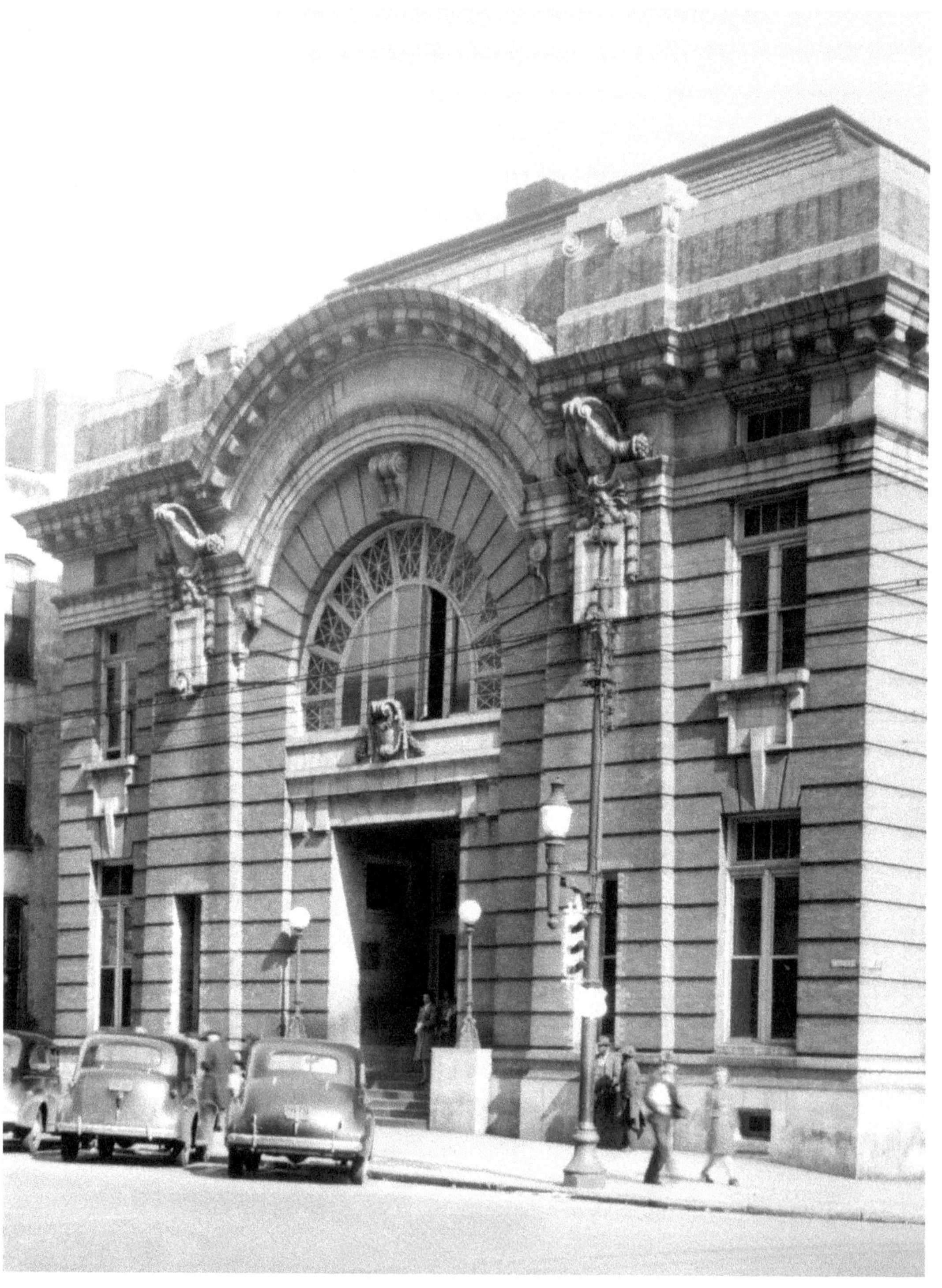

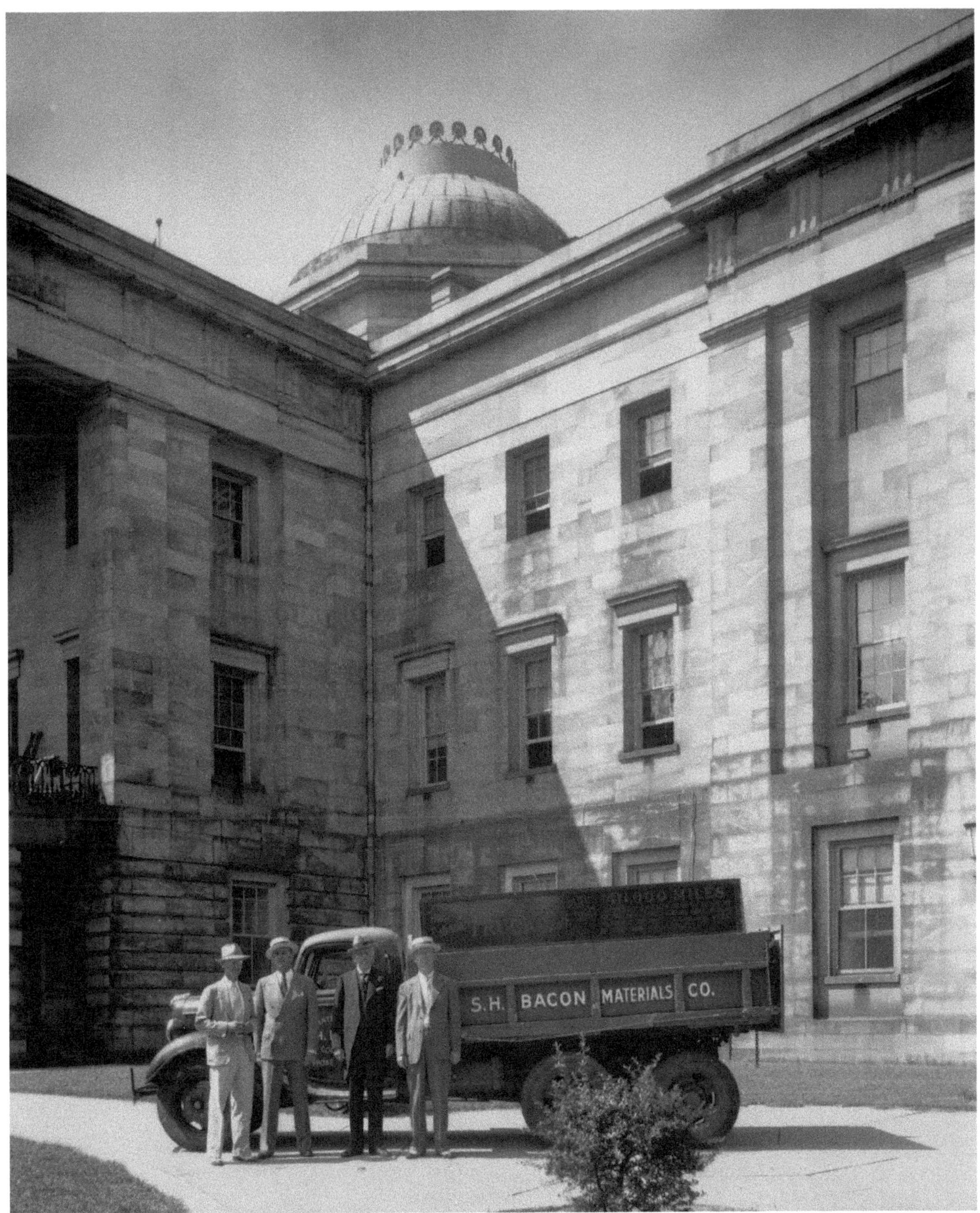

North Carolina governor Clyde R. Hoey poses outside the State Capitol in Raleigh with unidentified men and an S. H. Bacon Materials Company truck in 1939.

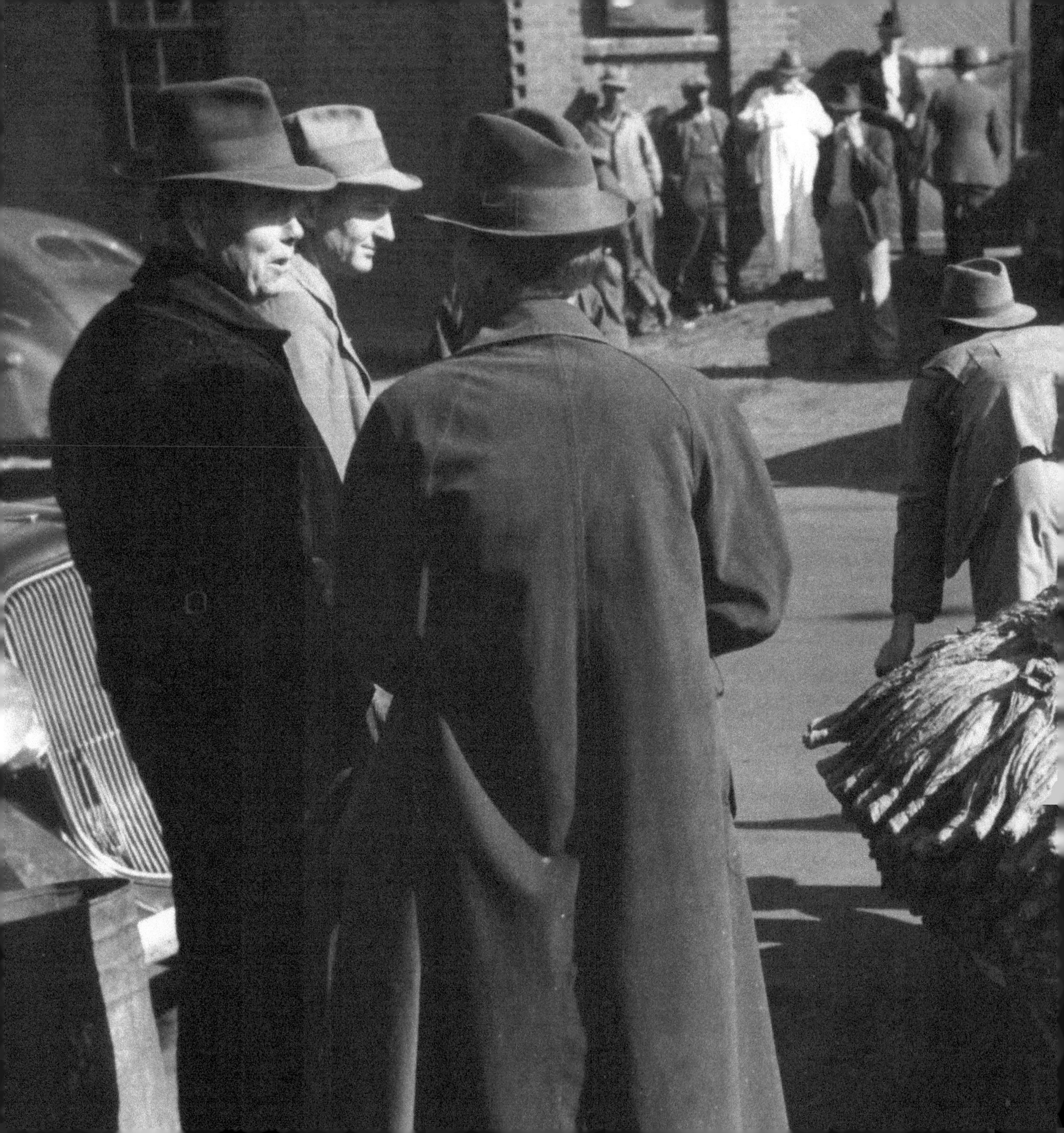

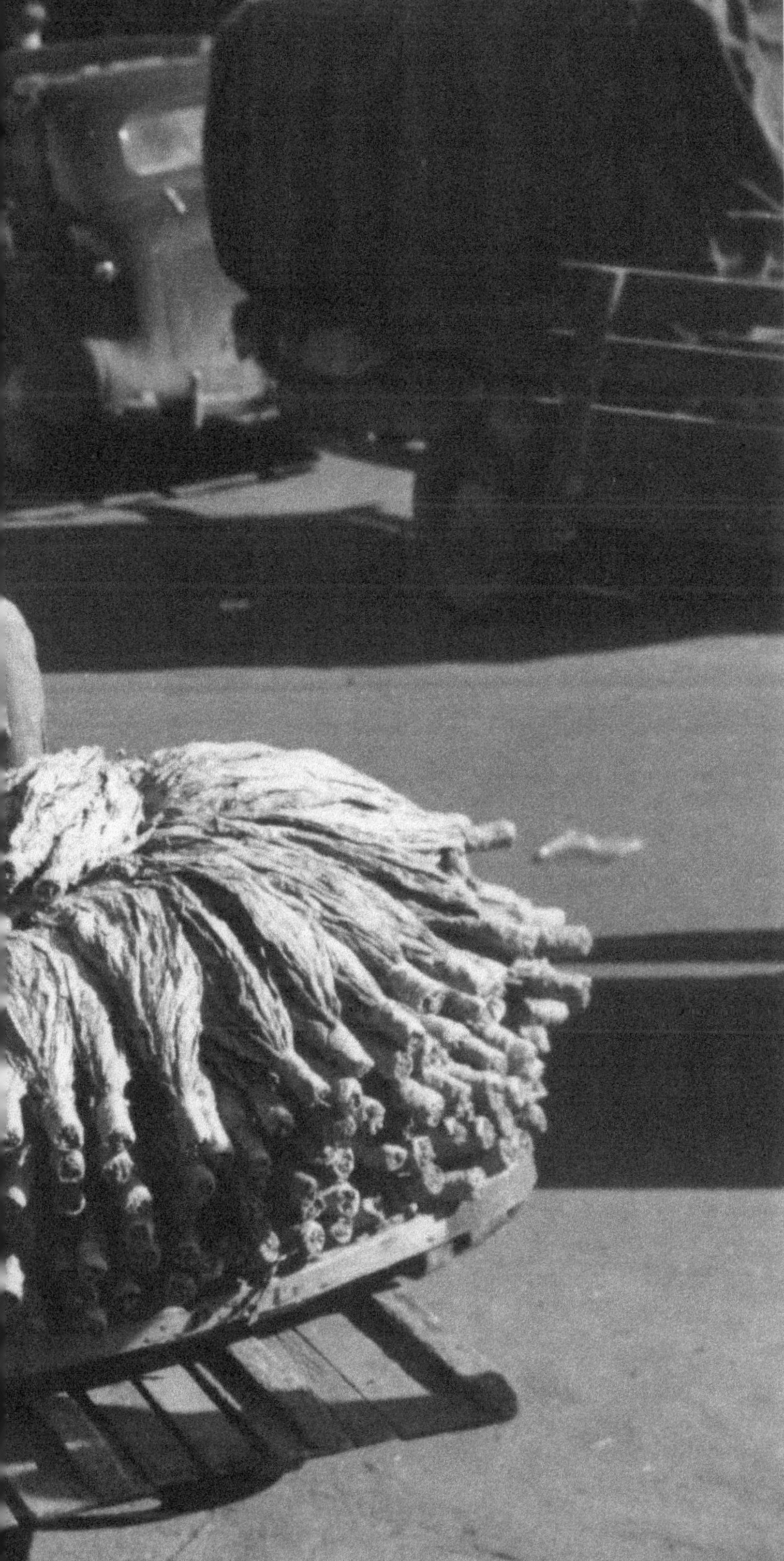

Graded tobacco is moved by hand truck to a Durham warehouse in order to be sold at auction.

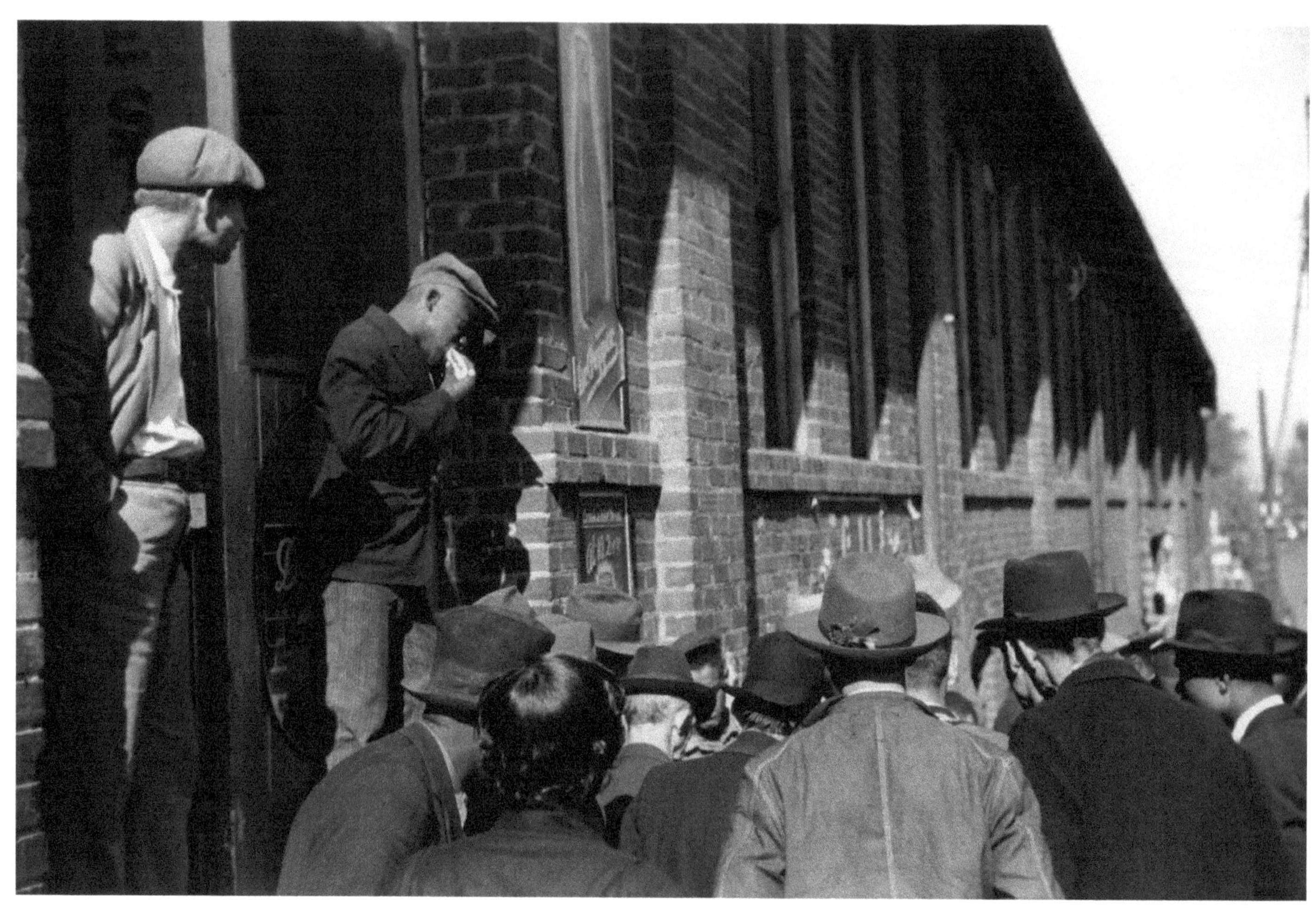

A group of men stand outside a Durham tobacco warehouse in this undated image.

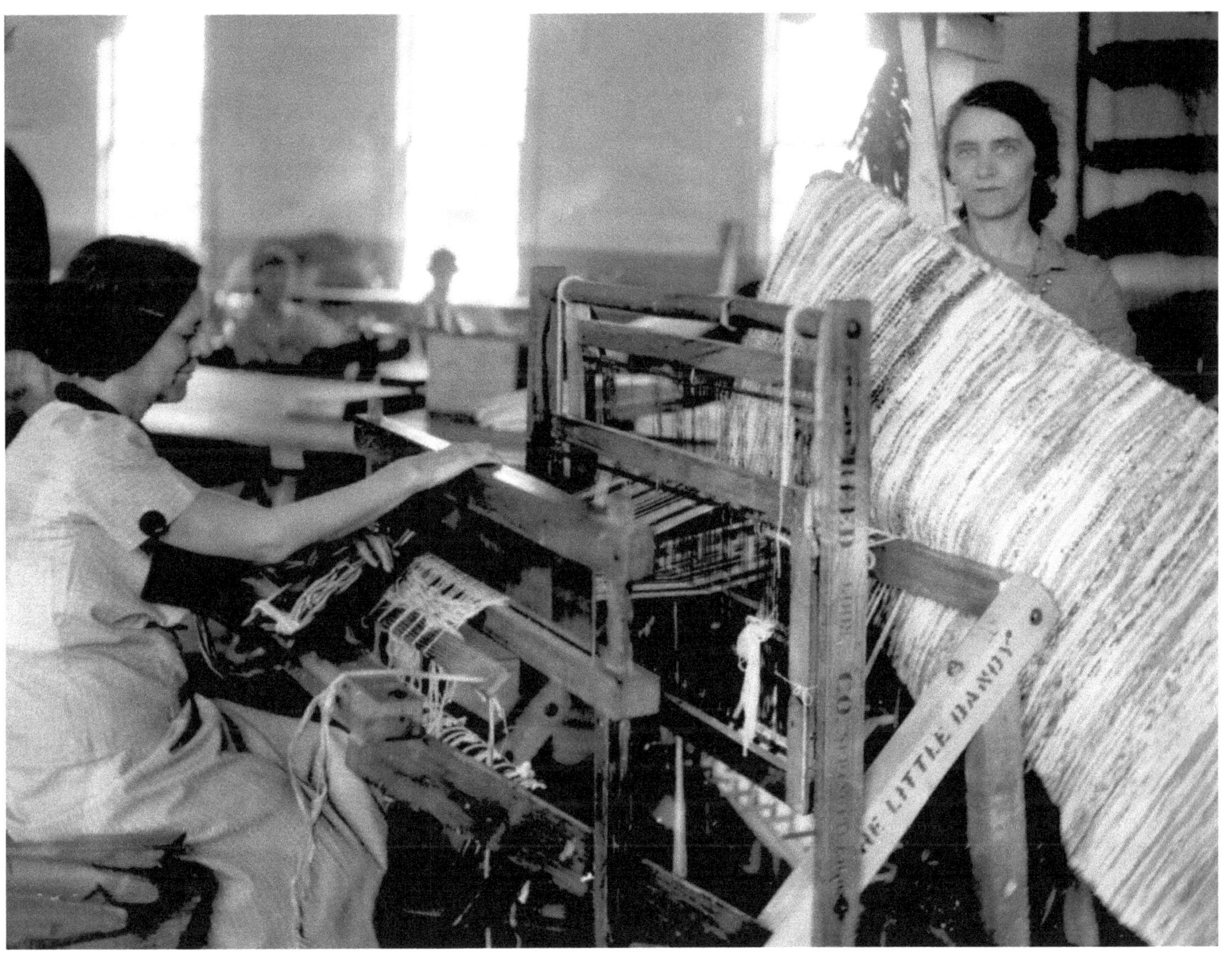

During the Great Depression, the Works Progress Administration was created by the federal government to provide jobs to unemployed workers affected by the economic crisis. In this photograph, women weave rugs at a Durham County women's work center.

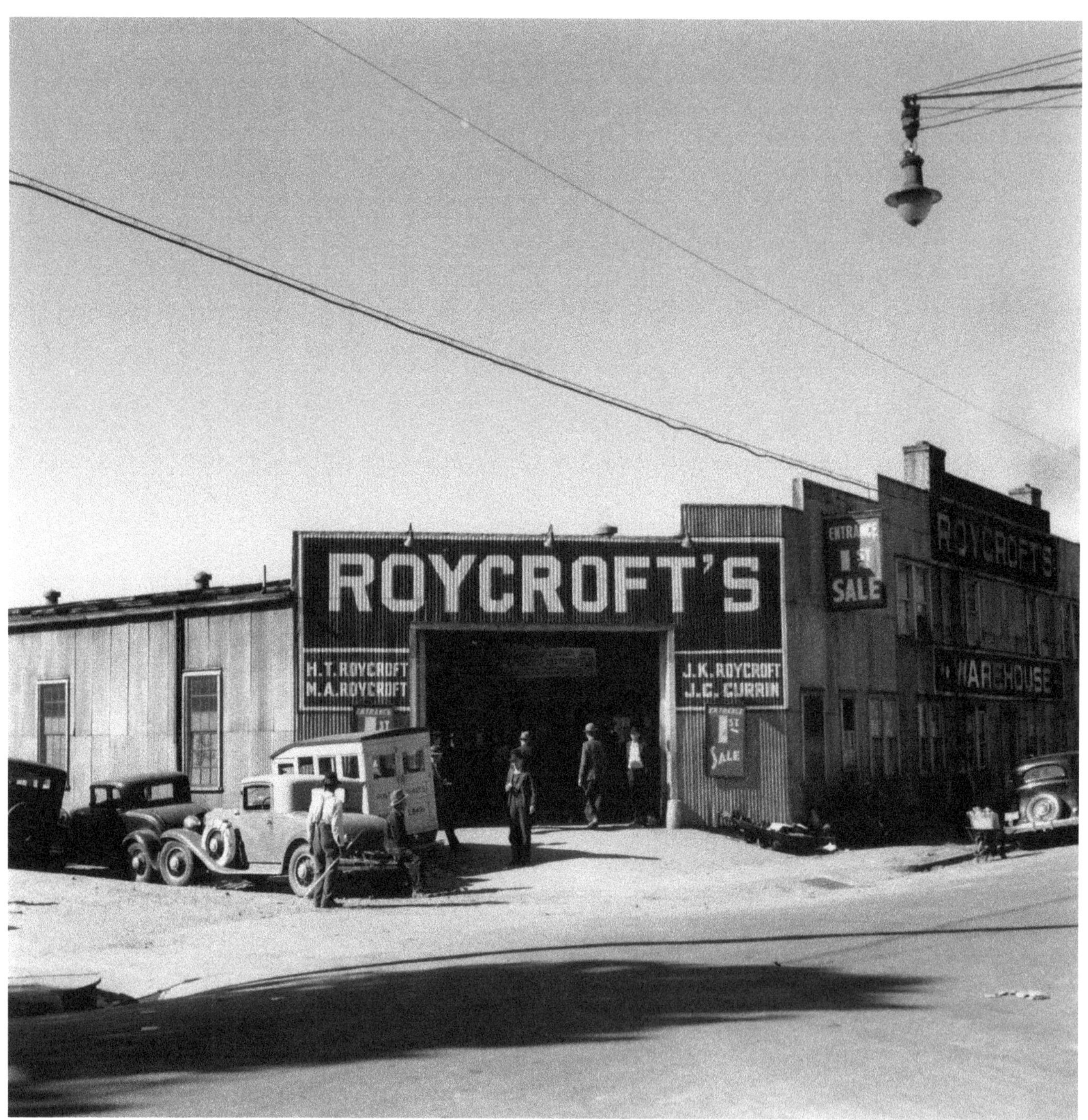

Roycroft's Tobacco Warehouse near downtown Durham.

An itinerant preacher shares his message outside a Durham tobacco warehouse during an auction.

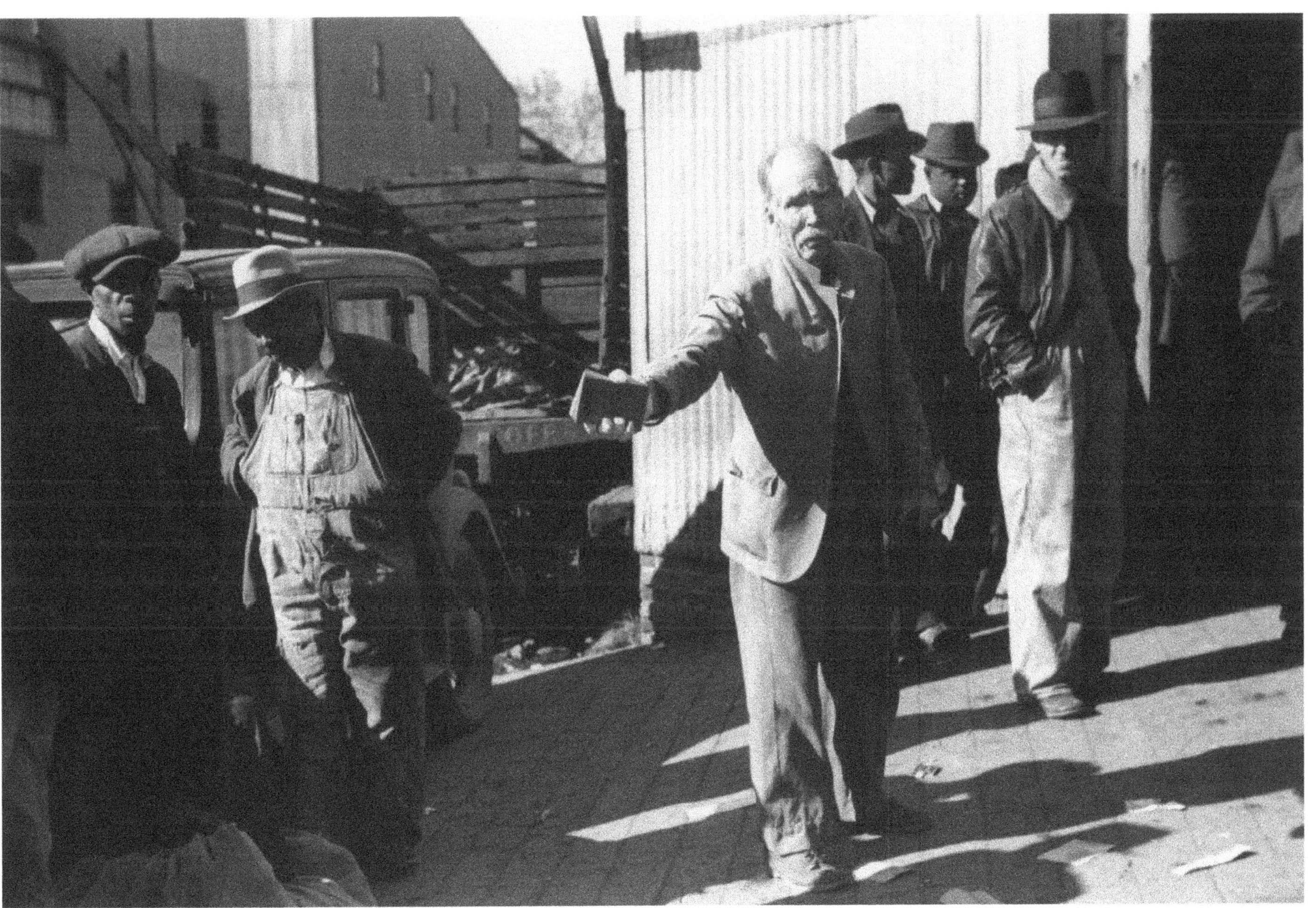

This aerial view shows the old Catholic Orphanage in Raleigh. Established in 1899 by Father Thomas F. Price, the complex stood in the Nazareth neighborhood south of present-day Western Boulevard. After its closing, part of the site was used by the Tammy Lynn Center in the early 1970s. By the late 1980s much of the land had been purchased by North Carolina State University for its Centennial Campus.

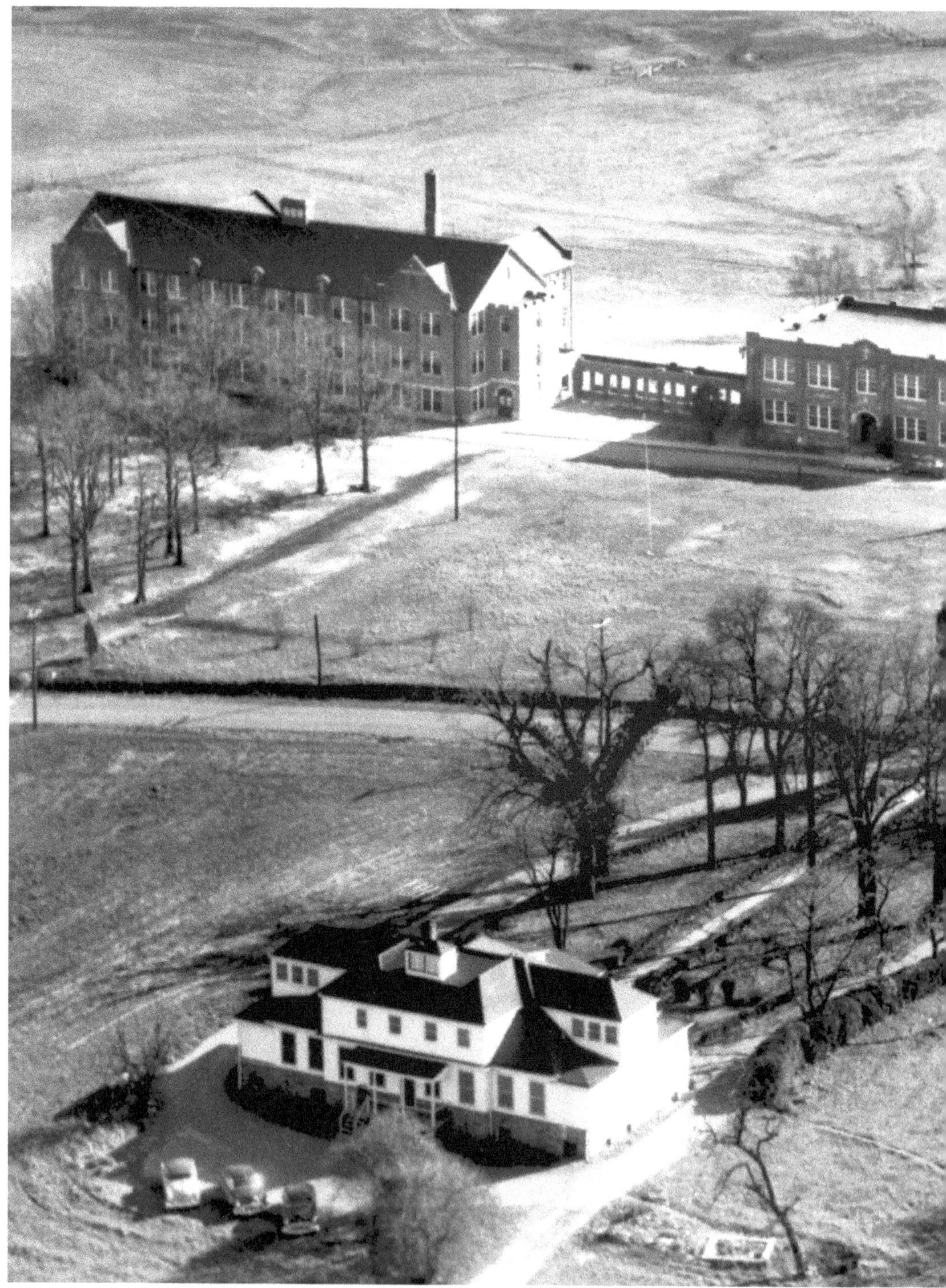

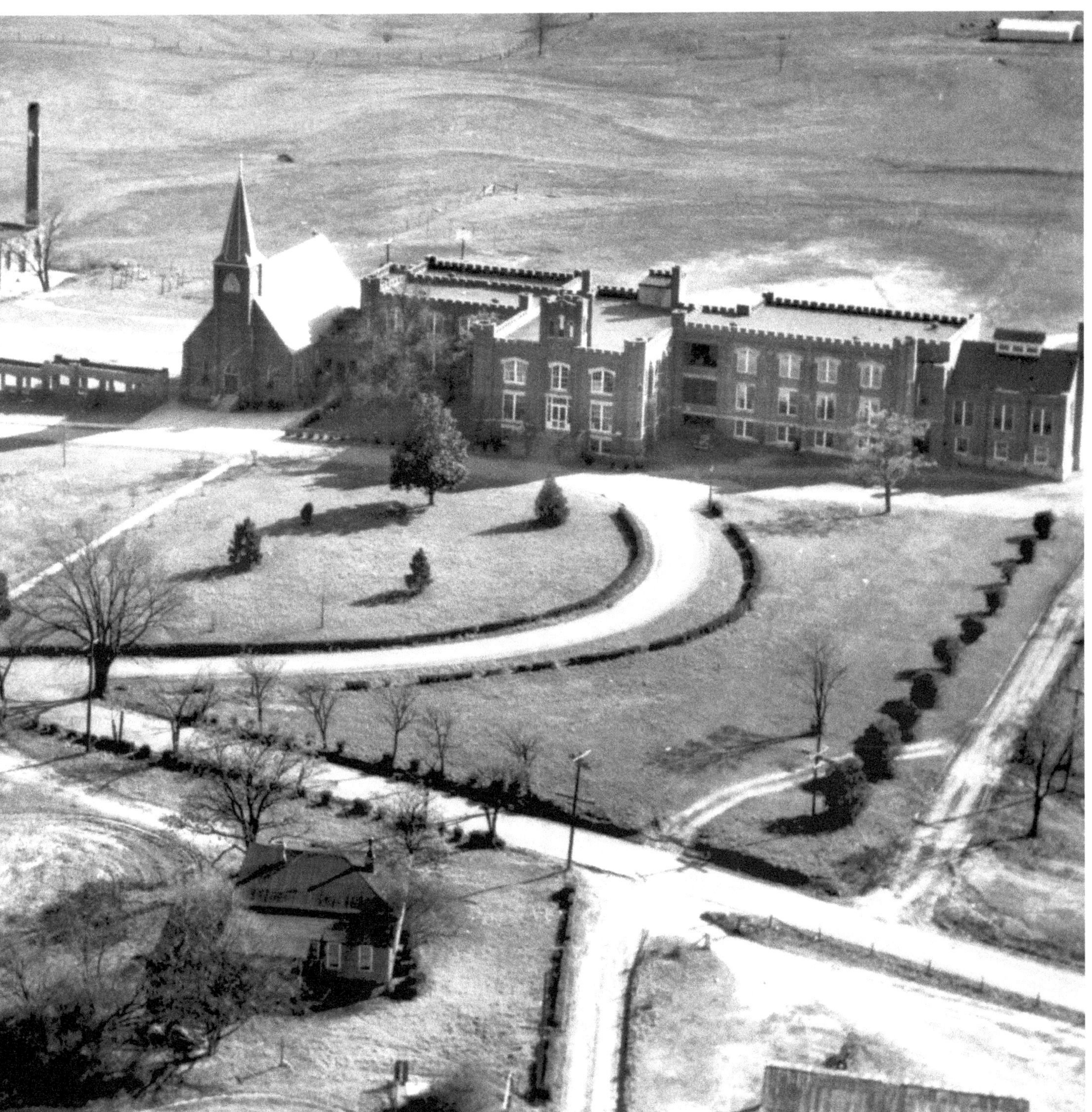

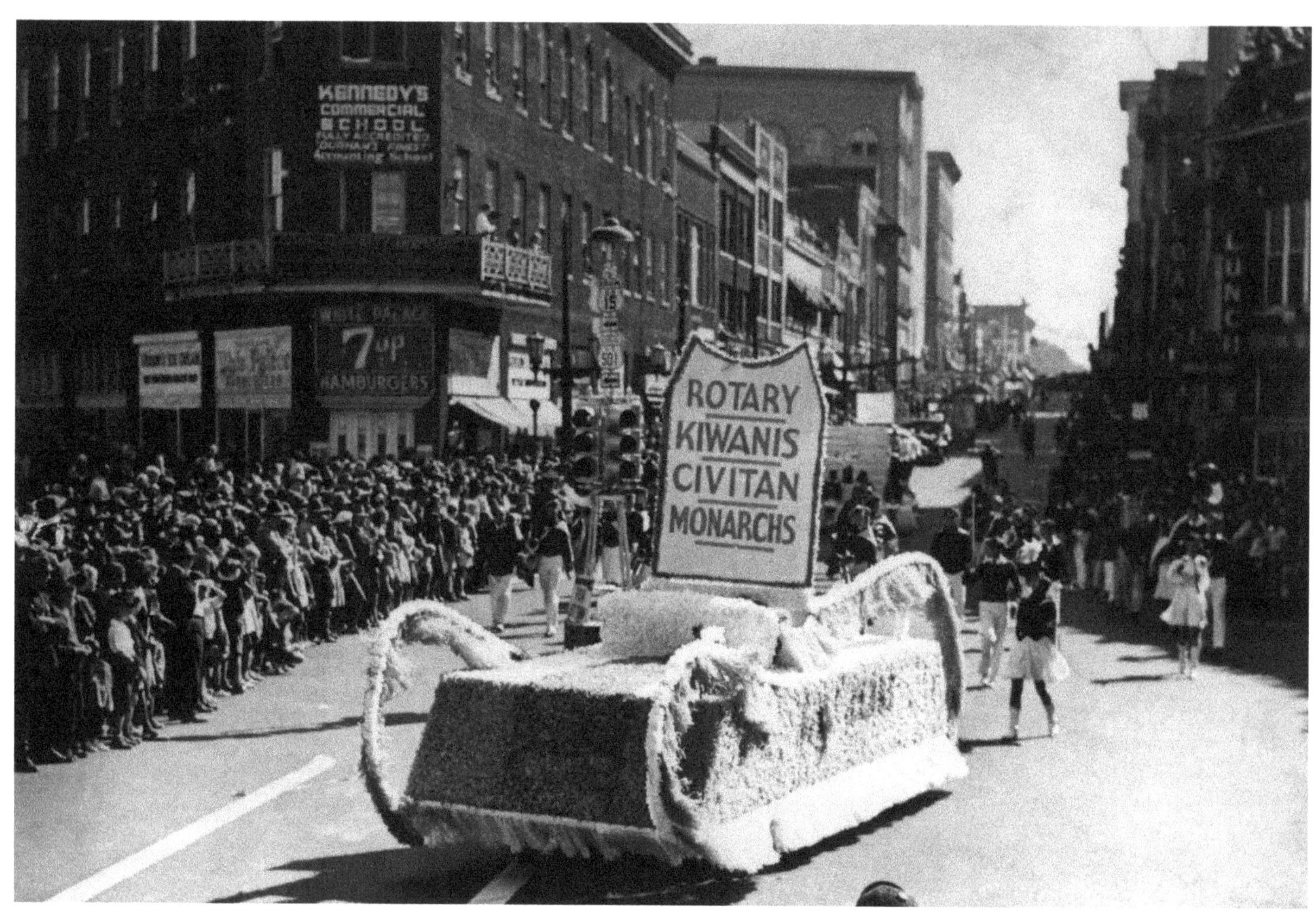

A large crowd watches a float sponsored by local civic clubs pass through Durham's Five Points during a 1936 parade.

Bandleader Kay Kyser helps a UNC cheerleader fire up the crowd during the 1939 Duke-Carolina football game at Duke Stadium.

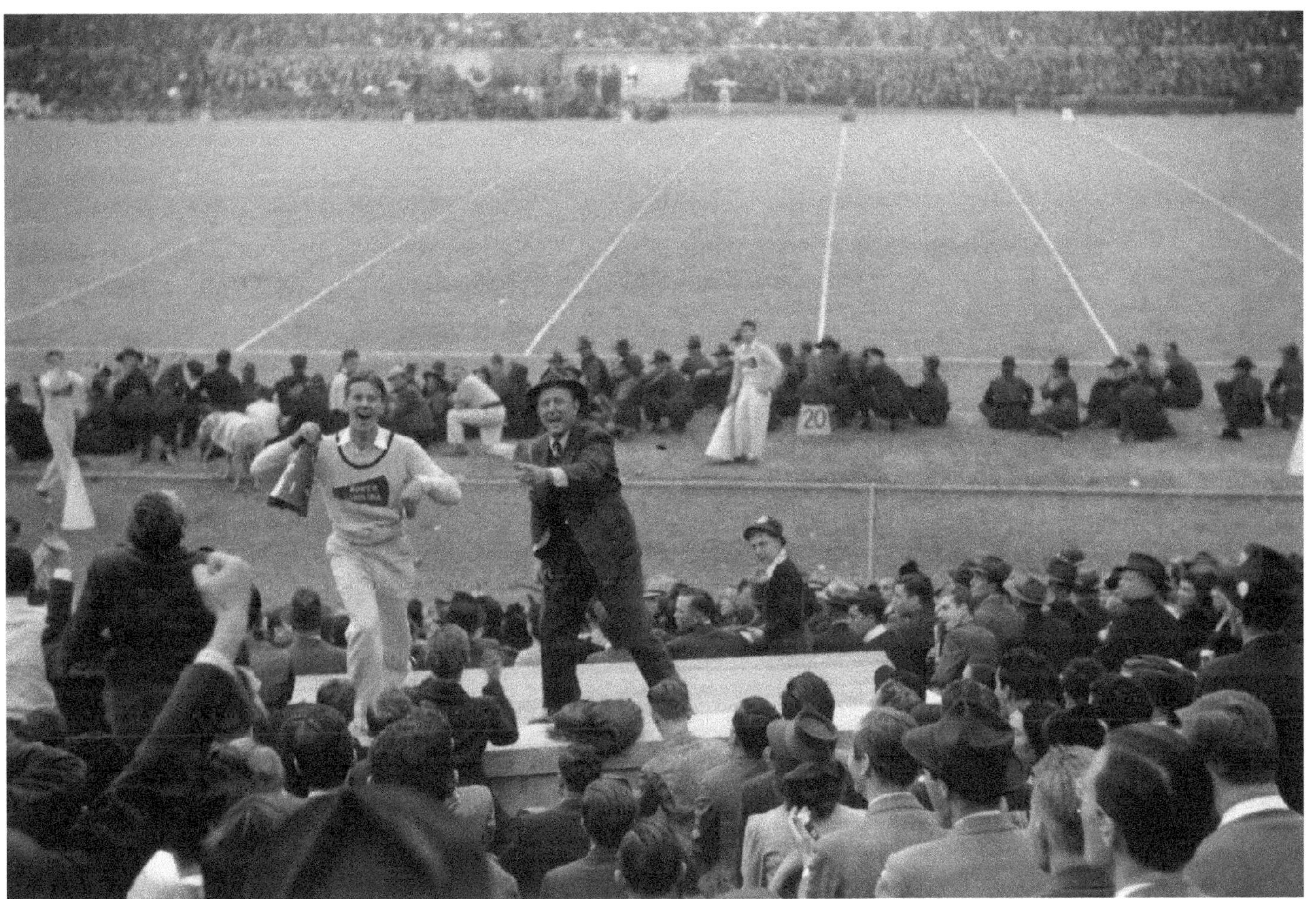

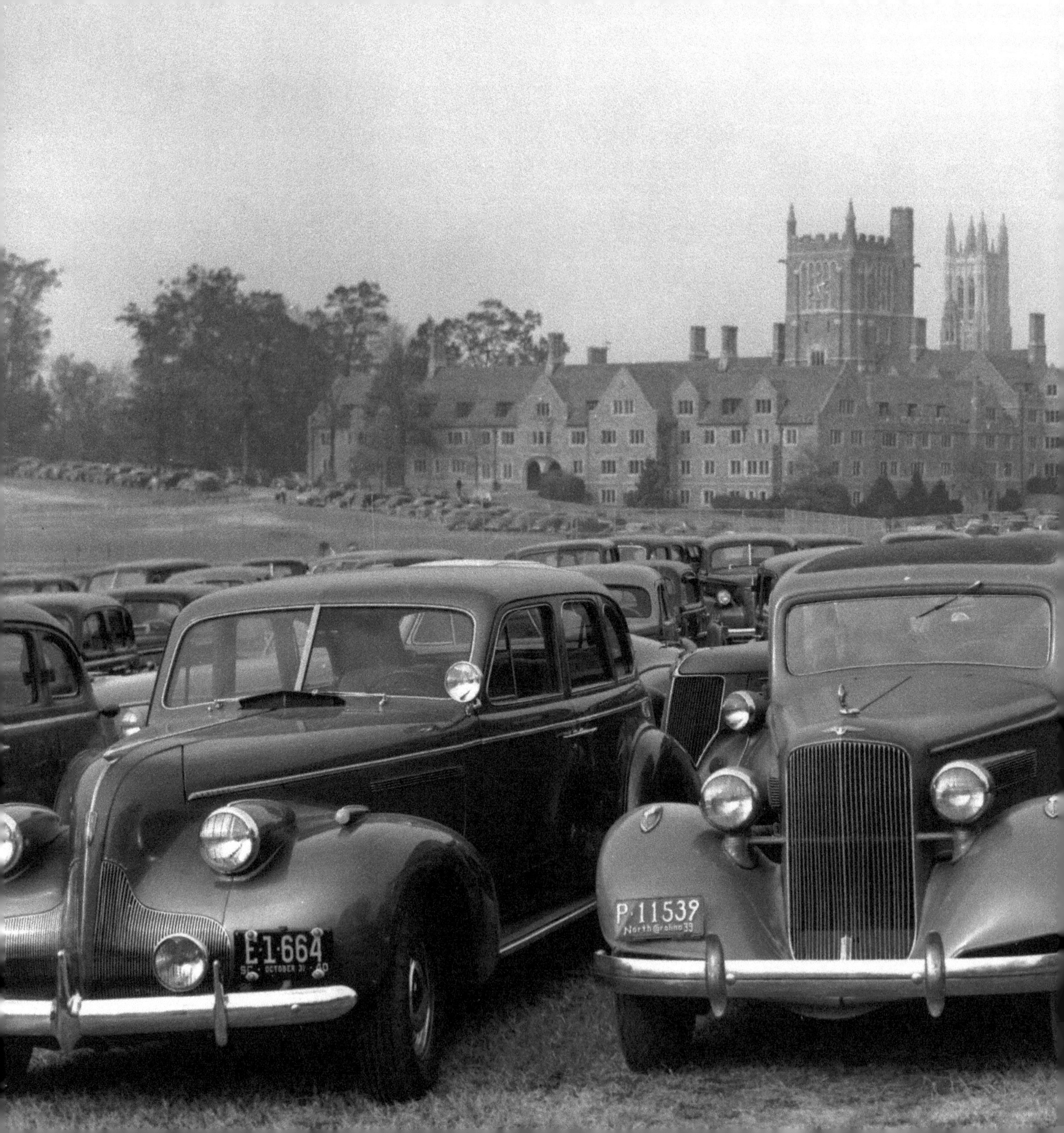
E·1·664
SC · OCTOBER 31 · 40
P·11539
North Carolina 33

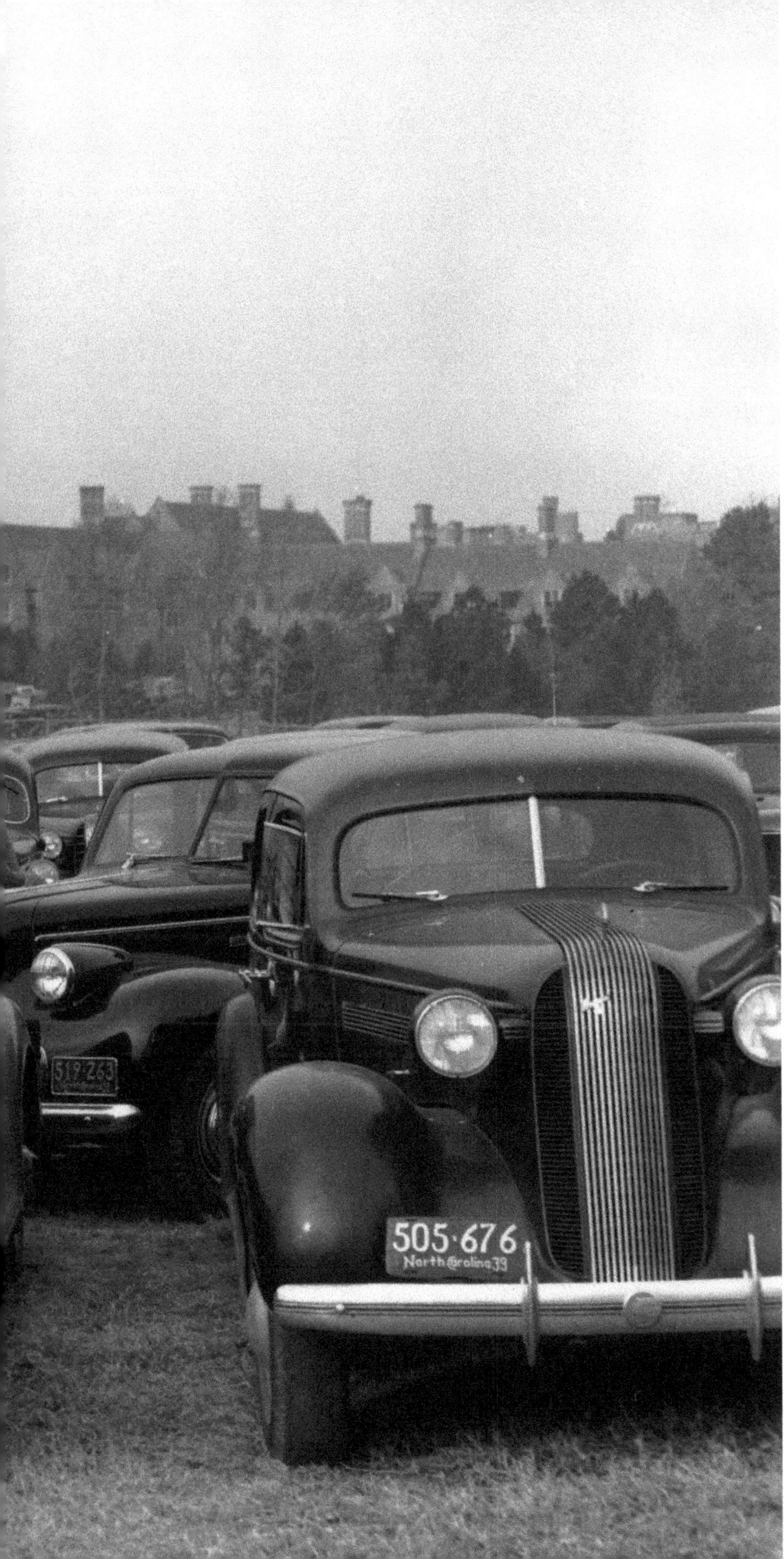

Cars are parked in a field as a crowd of 51,000 packs Duke Stadium in 1939 to see an undefeated (but tied) University of North Carolina team play once-defeated Duke. Duke won the game 13-3.

Named for a Raleigh business leader who was also a strong advocate for public education, Needham Broughton High School opened in 1929 on St. Mary's Street. The school is now the oldest continuously operating public high school in Raleigh, with an enrollment of more than 2,100 students.

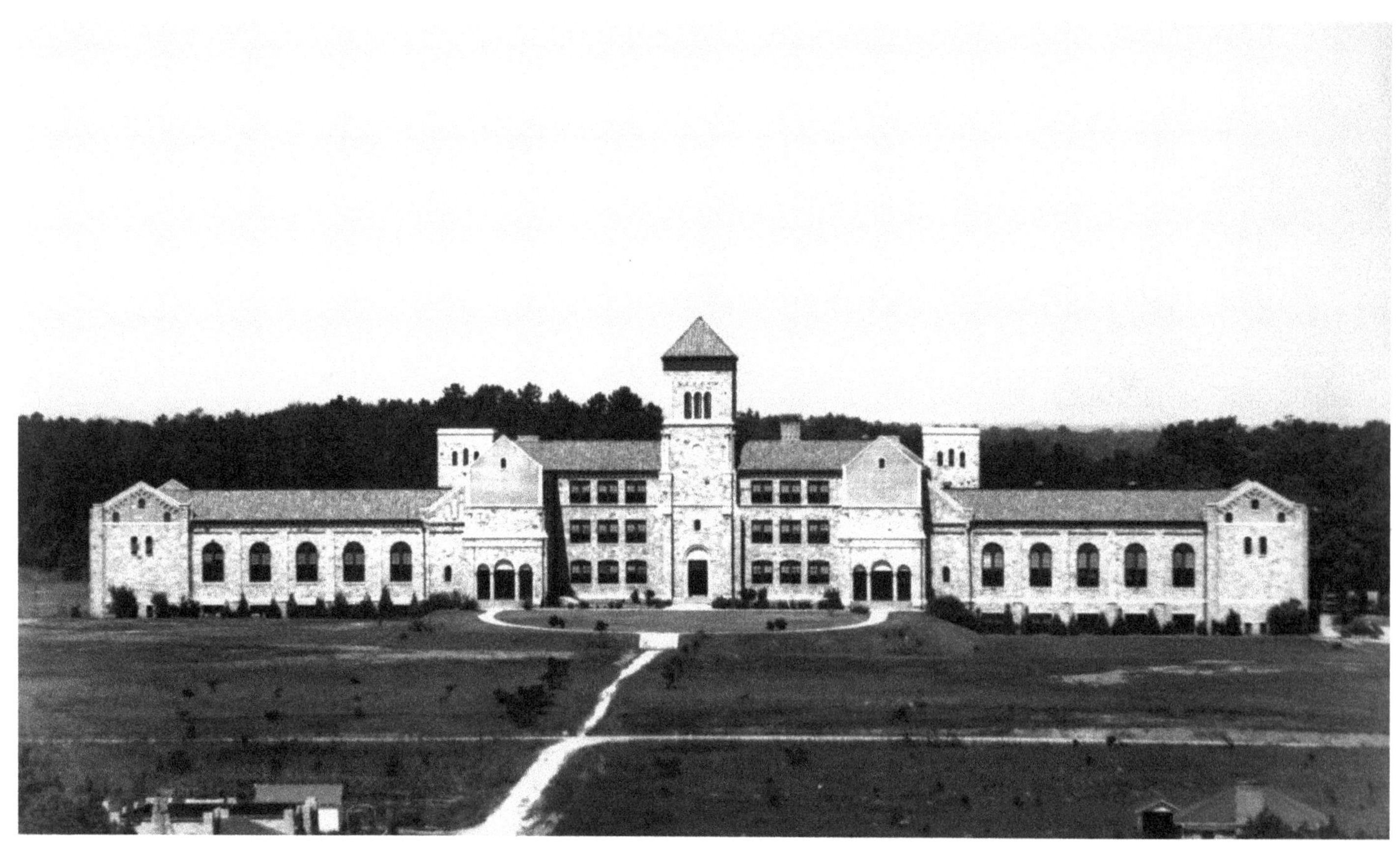

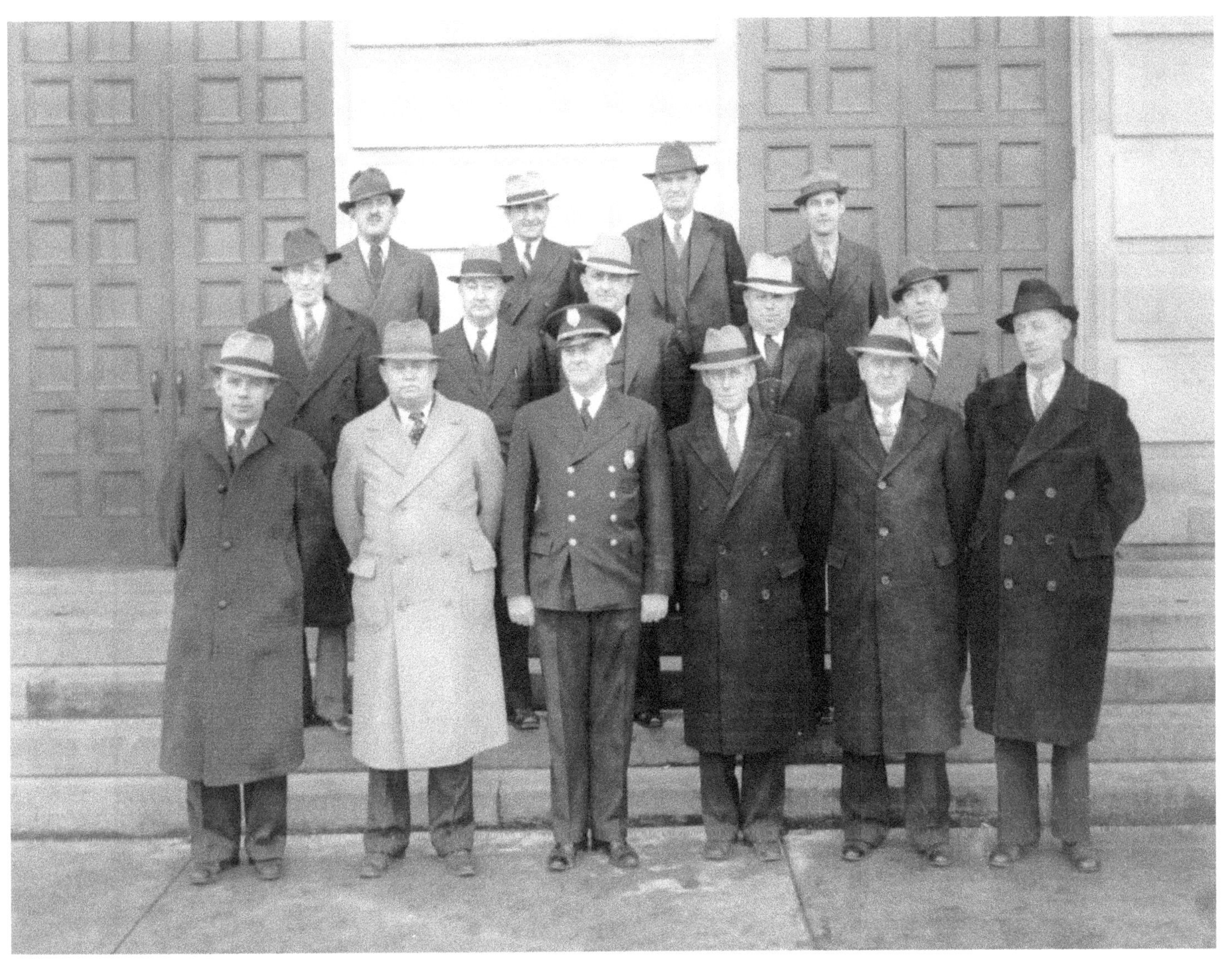

The Detective Division of the Raleigh Police Department stand for a formal portrait in 1938.

In view here is a Raleigh gas station and tire sales company.

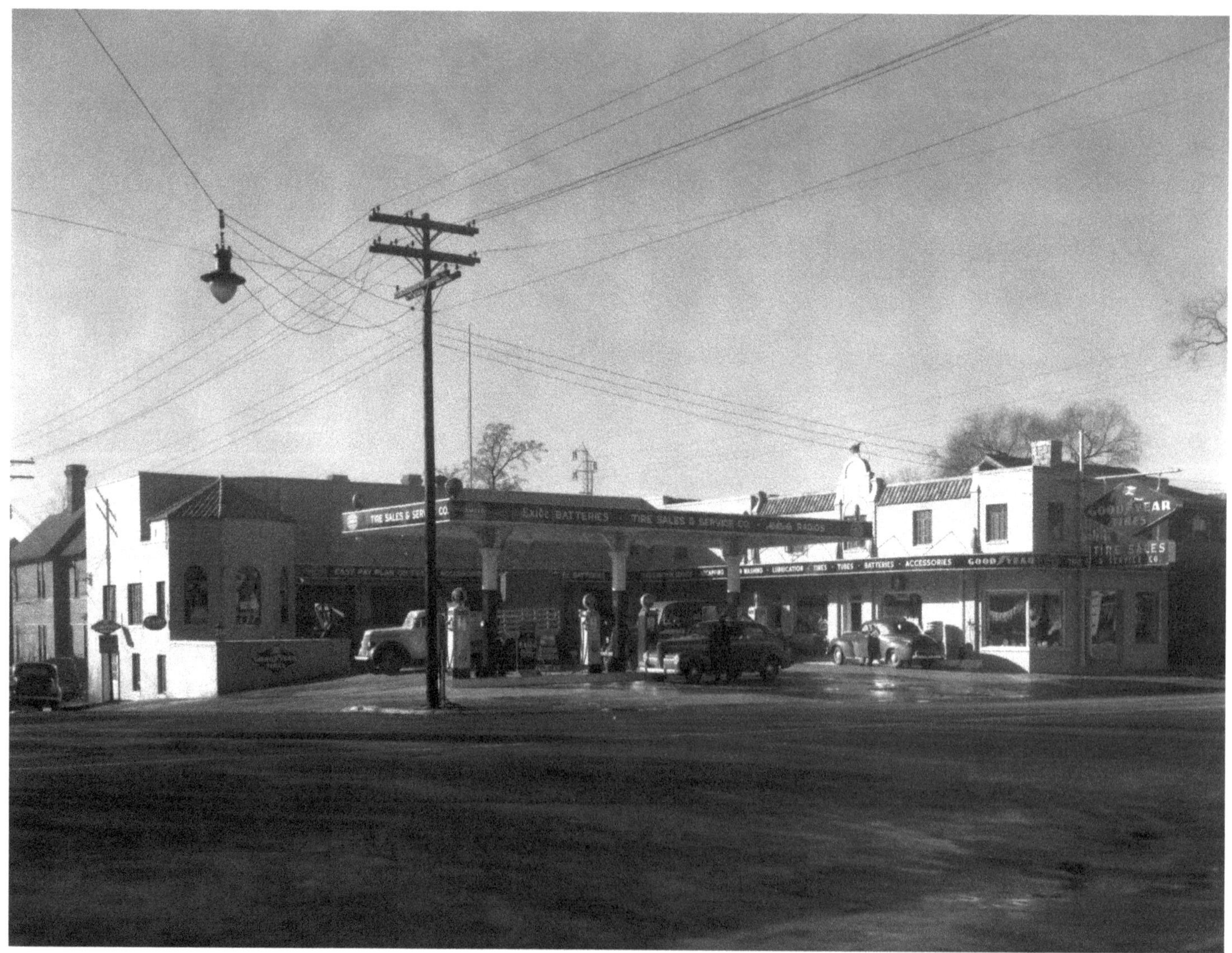

Samuel Harris founded the Harris Barber College in 1930 in Raleigh's Lightner Arcade on East Hargett Street. Established to teach skills to African American men during the era of segregation in the South, the college moved to its current location on South Blount Street in 1942. The Class of 1939 is depicted here.

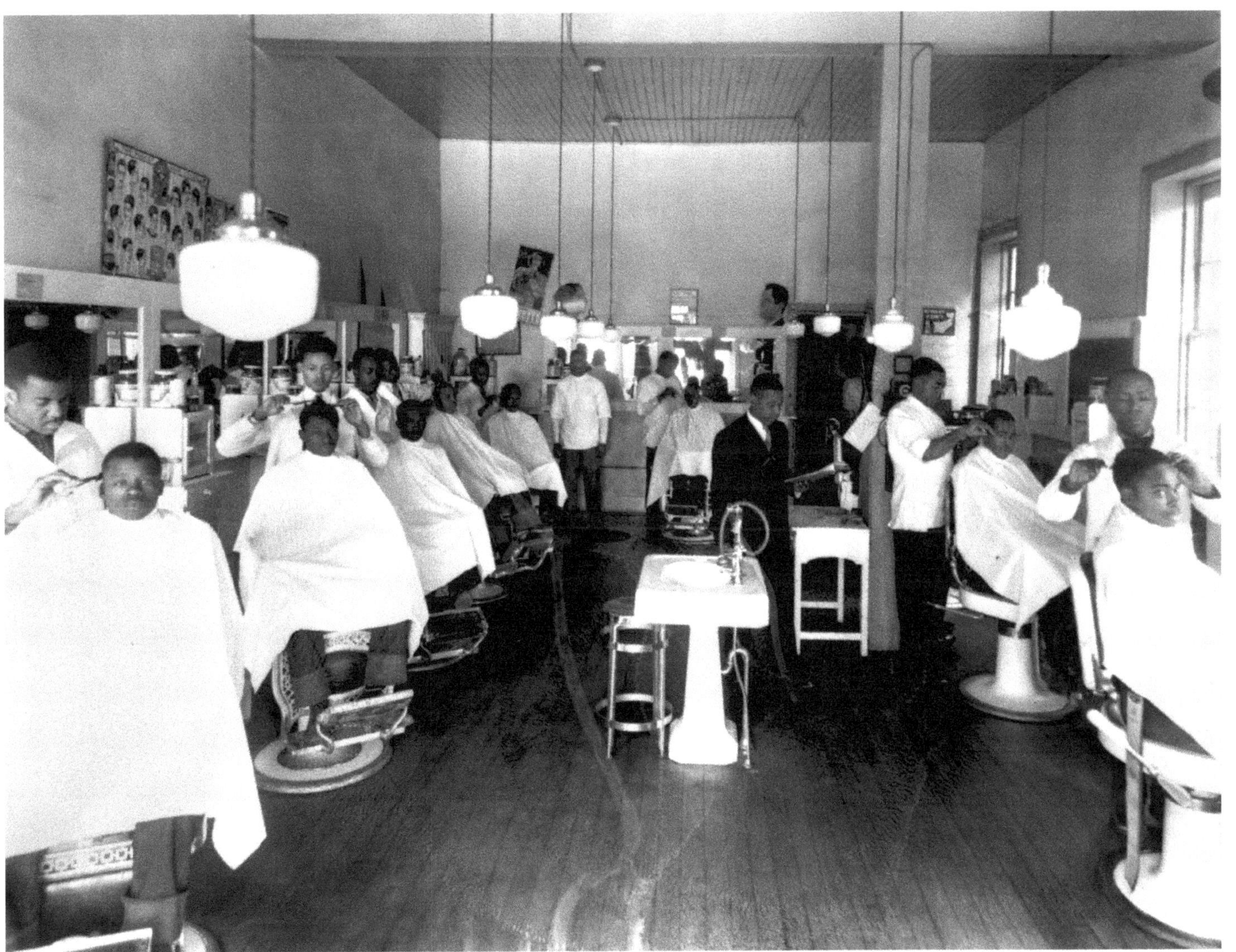

By the 1920s Raleigh's Fayetteville Street supported no fewer than seven drugstores along its four main blocks. One of the most popular was the Boon-Iseley Drug Store on the 100-block.

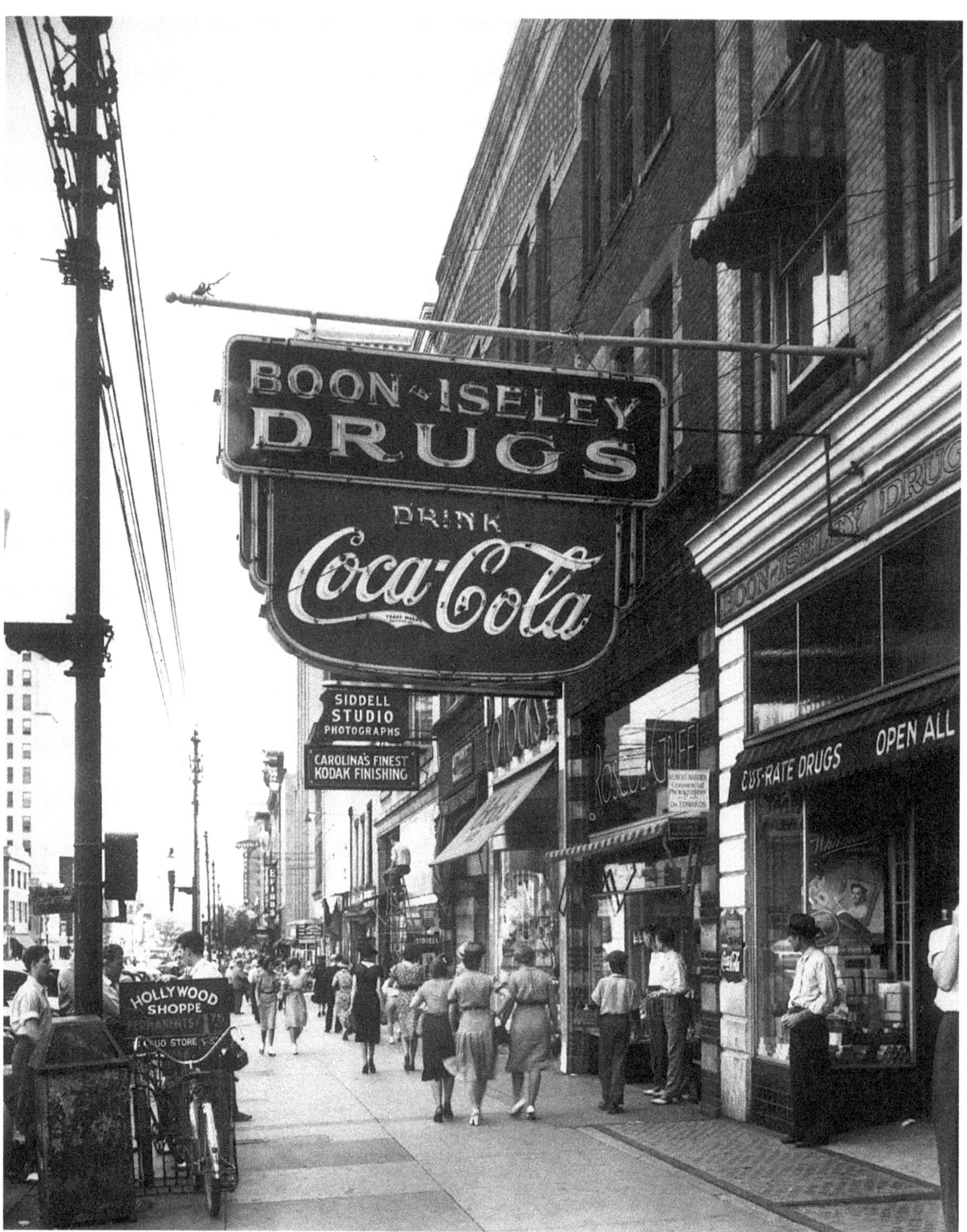

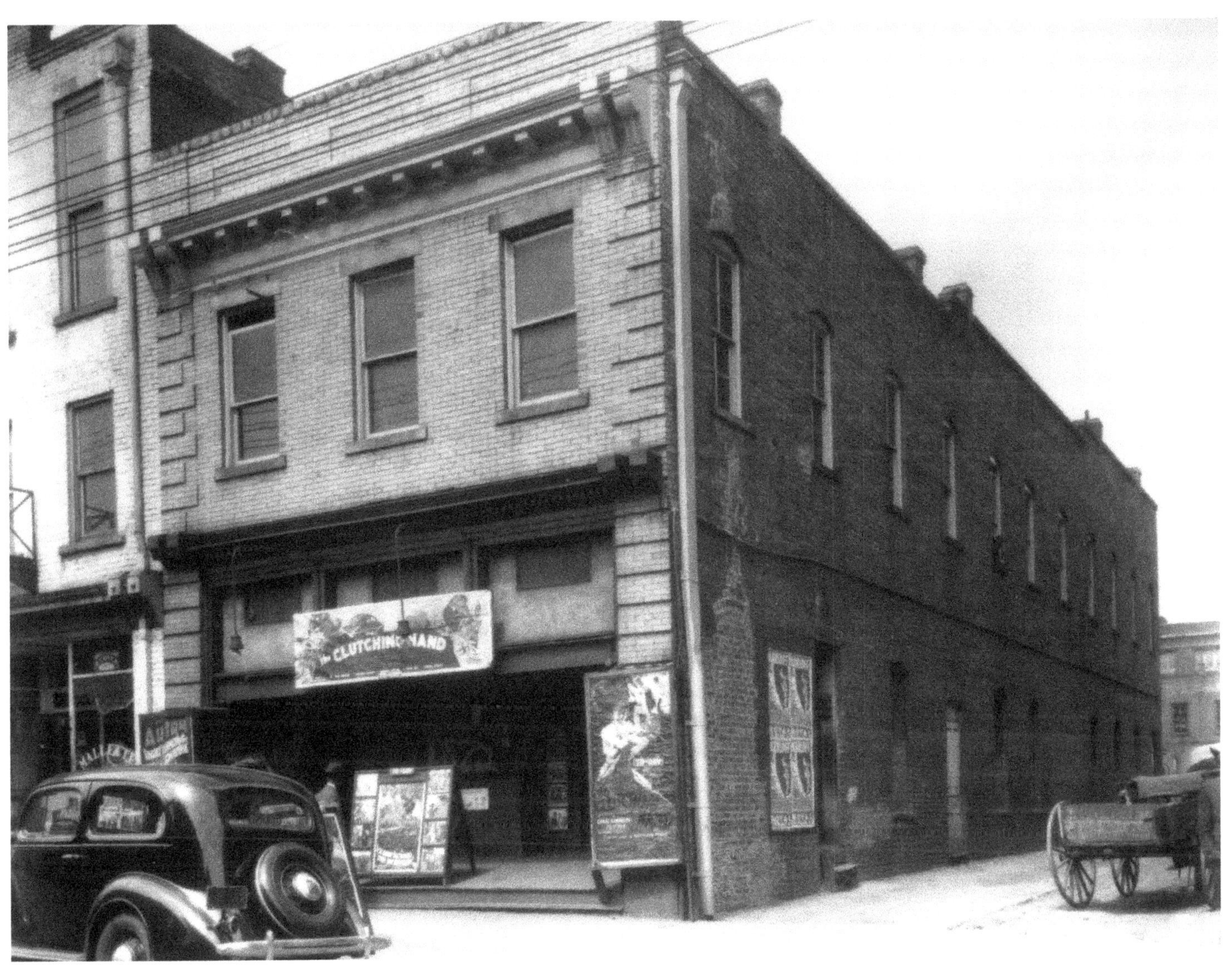

The Royal Theater, located on East Hargett Street in Raleigh, was one of two movie houses operated for black patrons during the first half of the twentieth century.

Raleigh's Fayetteville Street is festooned with Christmas decorations in this 1938 holiday photograph.

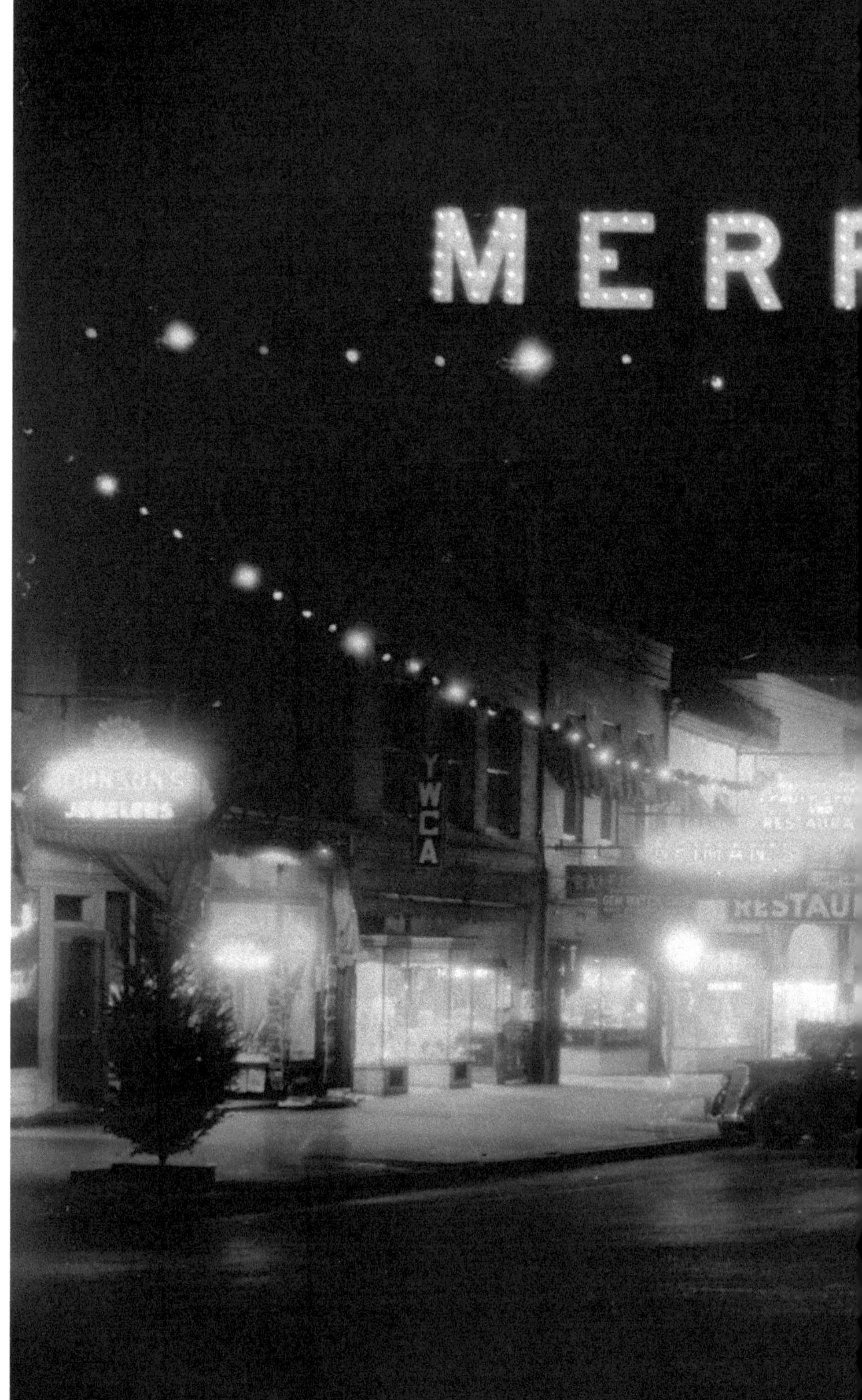

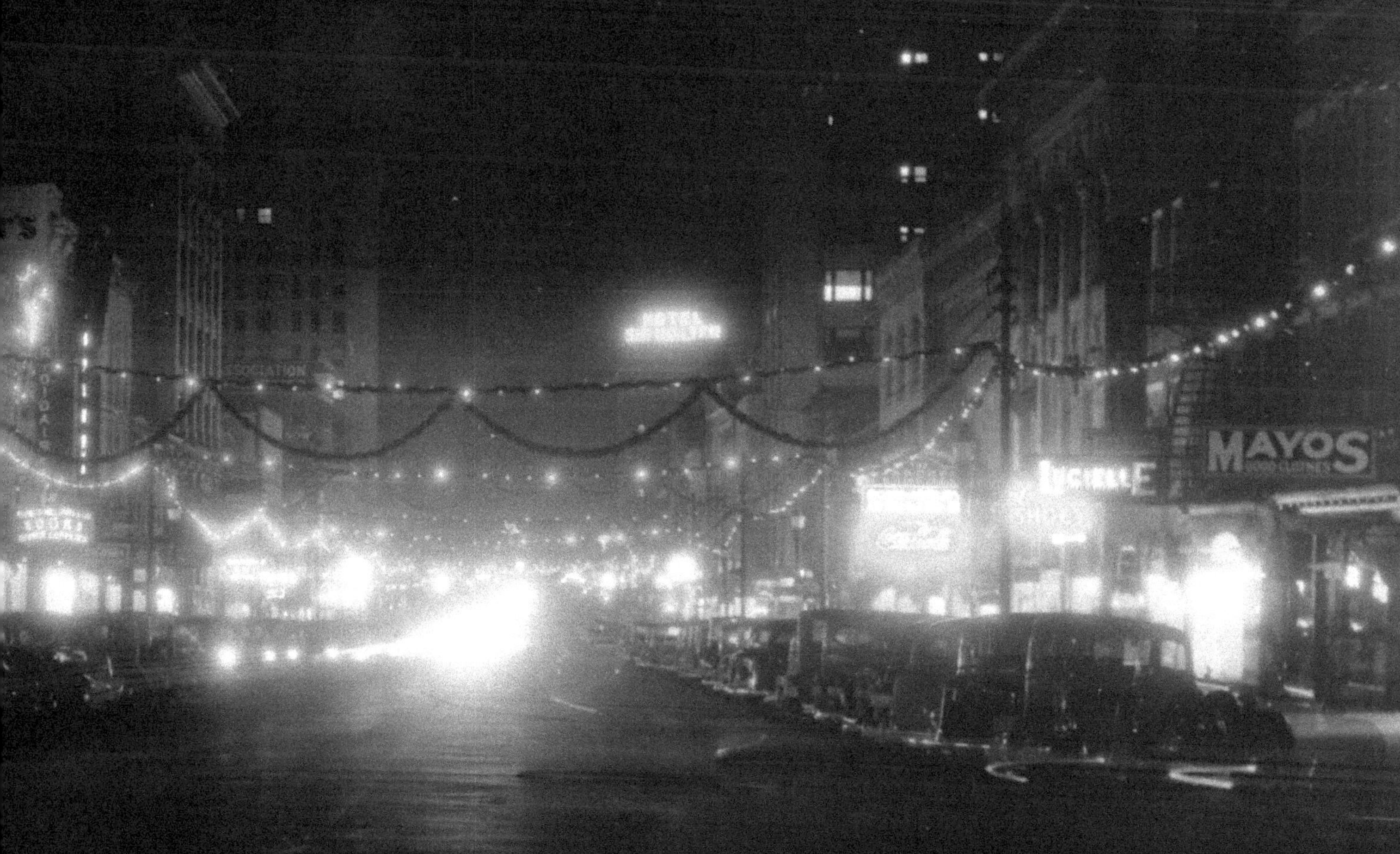
CHRISTMAS
MAYOS

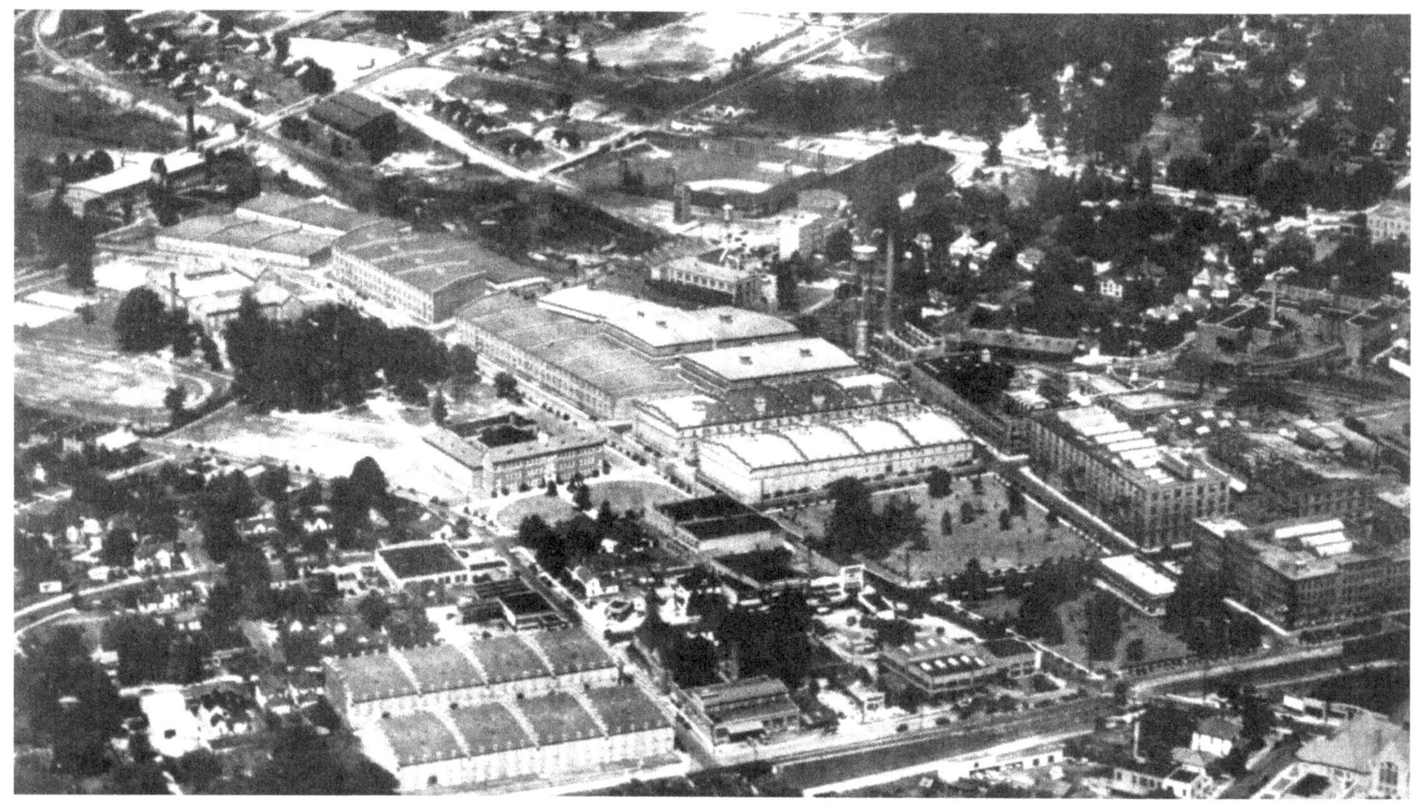

This 1939 aerial image of the Liggett-Myers Chesterfield cigarette plant in Durham includes Central Junior High School and Durham High School (left of center), both now a part of the Durham School of the Arts. The Durham Athletic Park is seen at top-center.

Let Freedom Ring Along Tobacco Road (1940–1965)

It would take a second great conflict—World War II—to bring closure to the Great Depression. With victory won in 1945, veterans returned to a nation in need of housing, automobiles, and virtually every other commodity left unmade during the war effort. Their return fueled a period of economic growth, which would create a level of comfort and convenience never before seen by generations past.

Durham was transformed during the war years. With the opening of Camp Butner in August 1942, as many as four thousand off-duty soldiers could be found in the city on any given day. As the center of off-base activity, Durham's chief war responsibility was to entertain and offer recreation to the troops.

After decades of segregation, African Americans were joined by whites across the nation to protest "separate but equal" public accommodation, creating the Civil Rights Movement of the 1950s and 1960s. In April 1960 one of Raleigh's historically black colleges, Shaw University, hosted a national meeting of student civil rights leaders. Their conference resulted in the formation of the Student Non-violent Coordinating Committee, a leading advocate for civil rights during the decade. The civil rights movement was active in Durham as well. The City Council had its first black member in 1956, and several schools were integrated in 1959.

The traditional downtown retail districts for both Raleigh and Durham began to decline in the 1960s as merchants moved to shopping centers in fast-growing suburbs. Cameron Village, developed in Raleigh in 1949, was the first shopping center erected between Washington, D.C., and Atlanta. It would be followed by Forest Hills Shopping Center in Durham (1955) and Raleigh's North Hills Mall (1967). The creation of the Research Triangle Park between the two cities in 1959—and IBM's relocation there in 1965—further stimulated the rapid suburbanization of both communities.

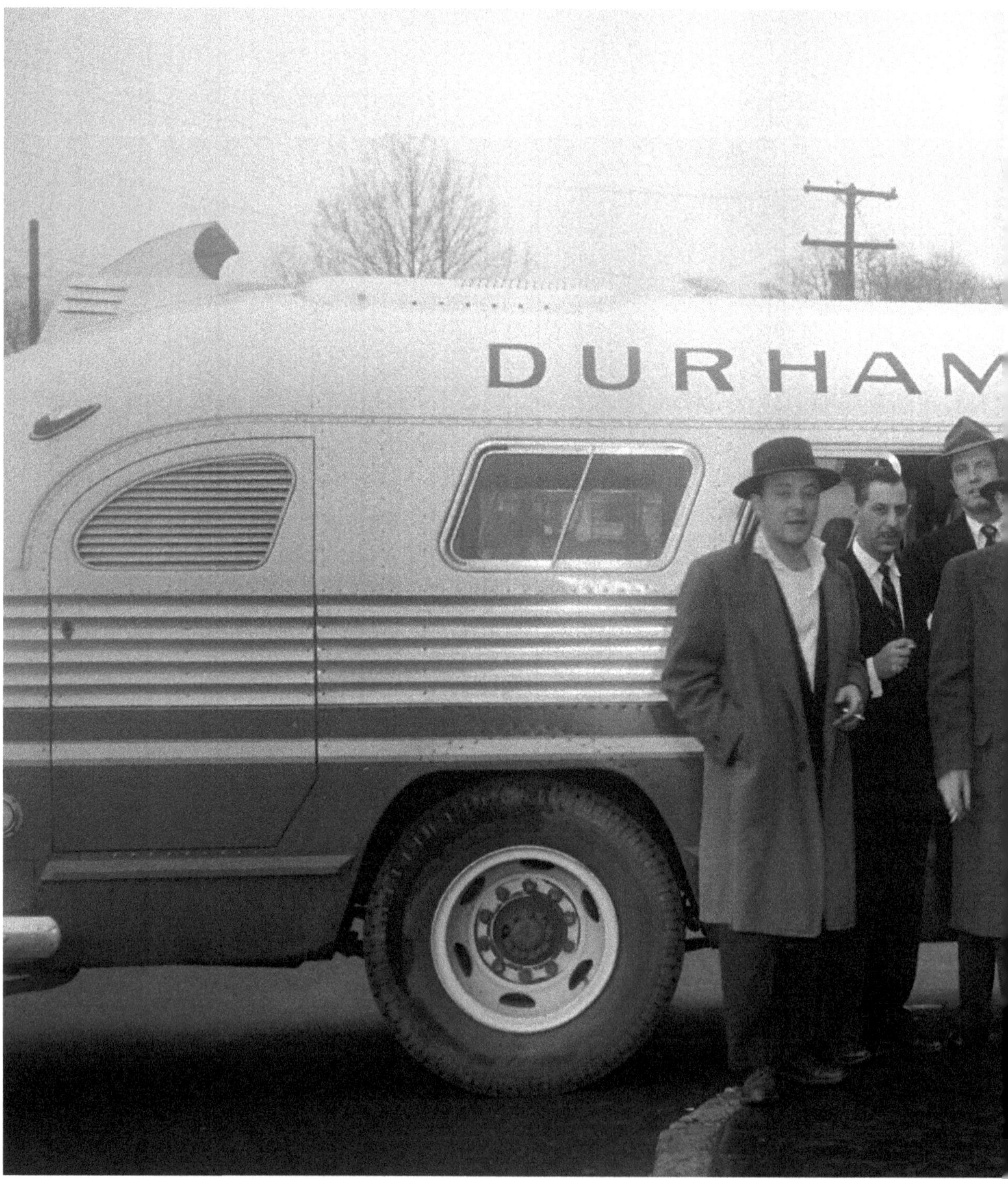

A group of passengers gather in front of a Durham-Dunn bus, ca. 1940s. Established by Louis M. Wade, Sr., and his wife, Katie Mann Wade, the Durham-Dunn Bus Line began service in 1942 at the height of World War II as a commuter service for factory workers. The company quickly expanded, becoming the Southern Coach Company in the 1950s. It still operates today as a Durham-based business.

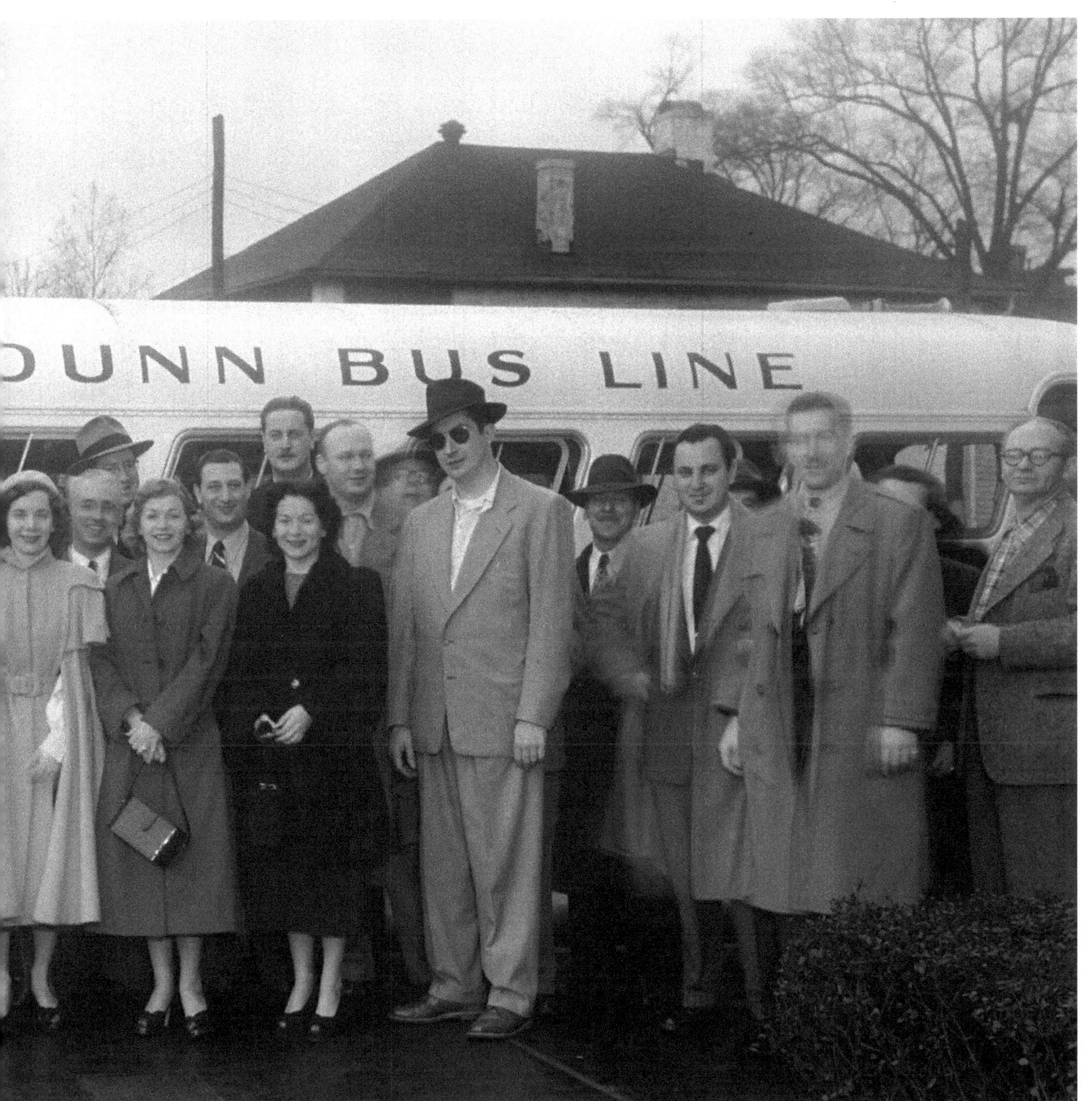
DUNN BUS LINE

A Durham policeman stands across the street from the Farmer's Cafe and Pool Room near the tobacco warehouses, ca. 1940.

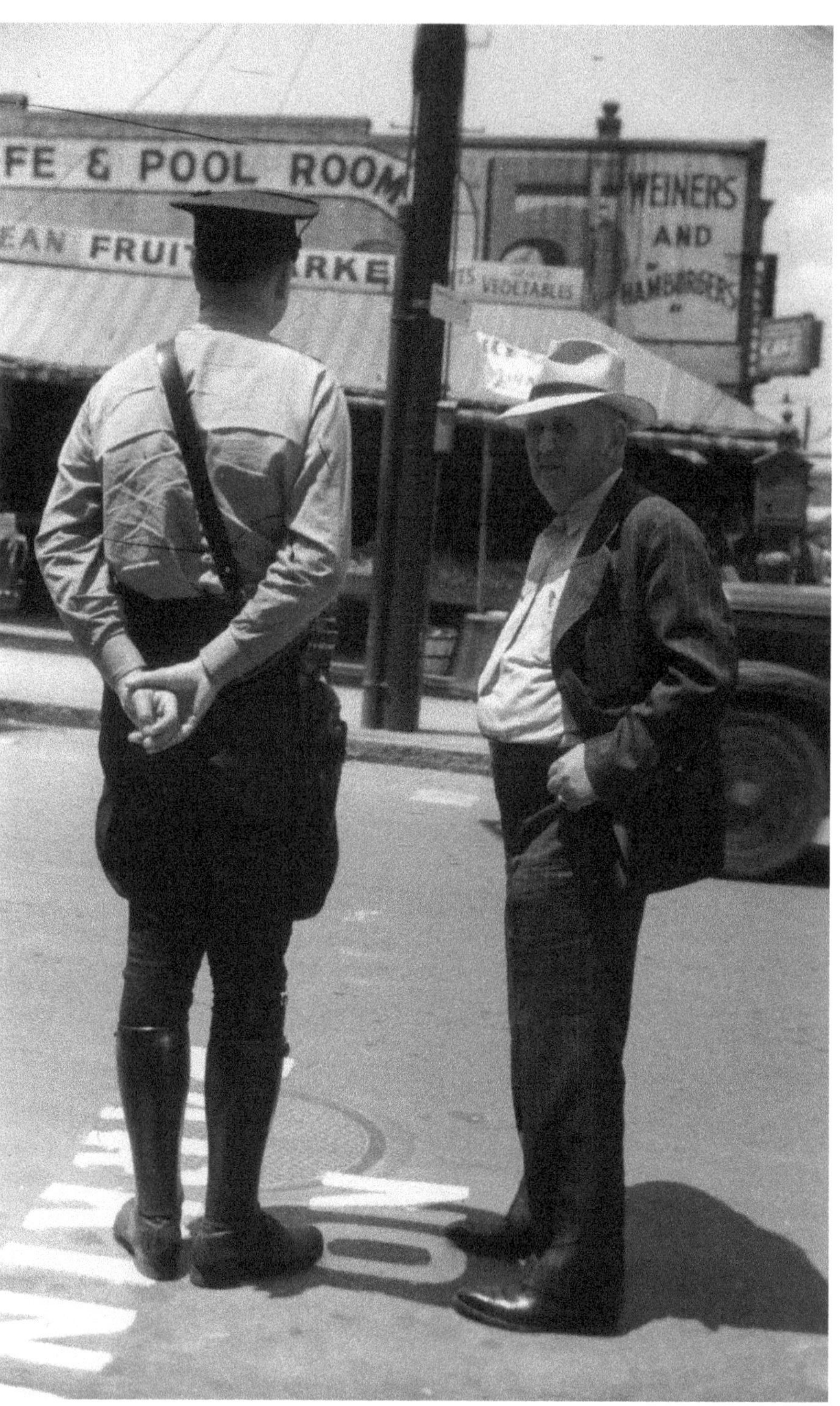

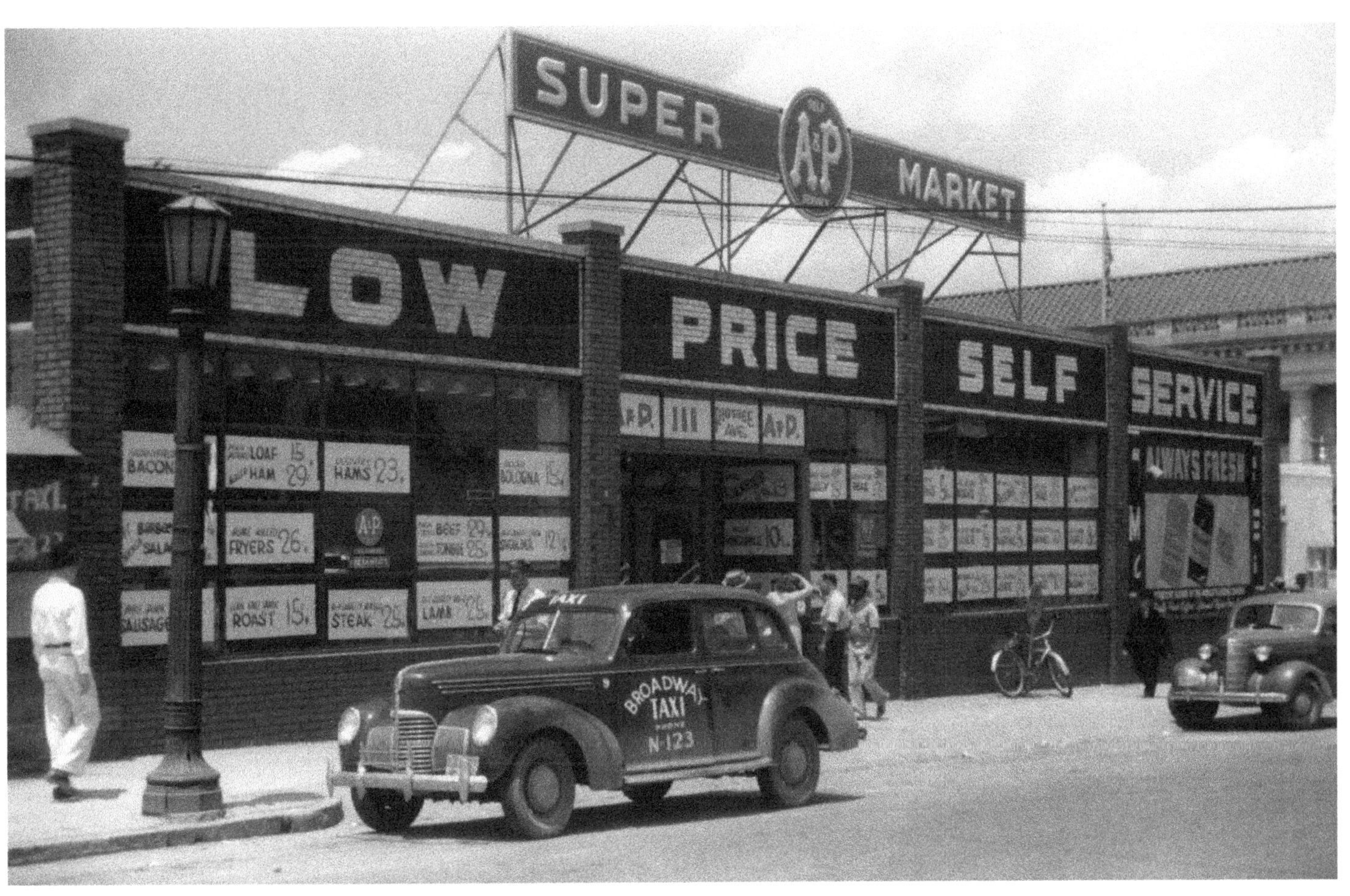

A&P Super Market is open for business near the tobacco warehouses in Durham, ca. 1940.

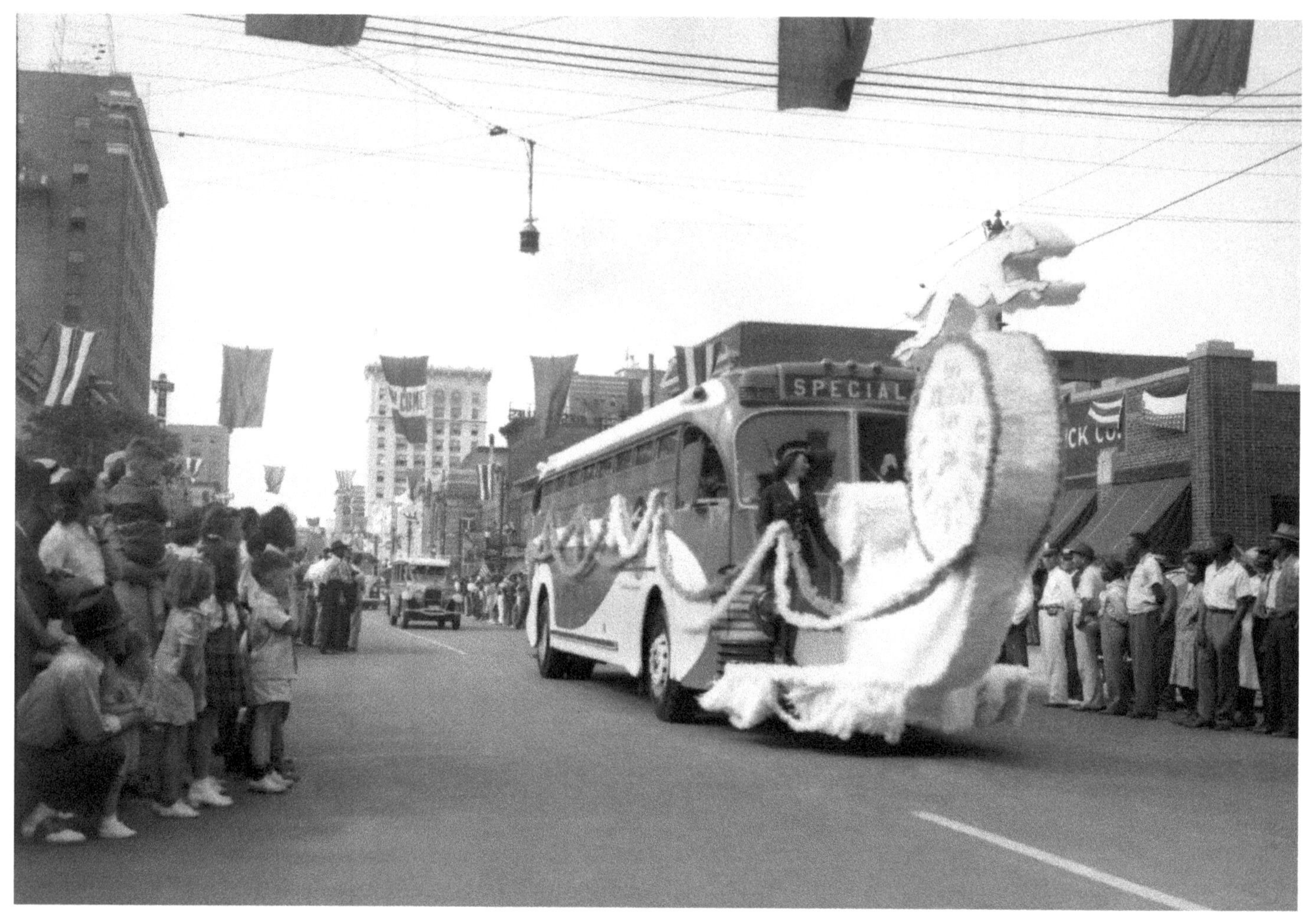

On May 20, 1940, a Raleigh parade celebrates the centennial of the 1840 North Carolina State Capitol.

The intersection of Hargett and Salisbury streets in downtown Raleigh, ca. 1940. Standing on the southeast corner is the eleven-story Odd Fellows Building, constructed in 1924.

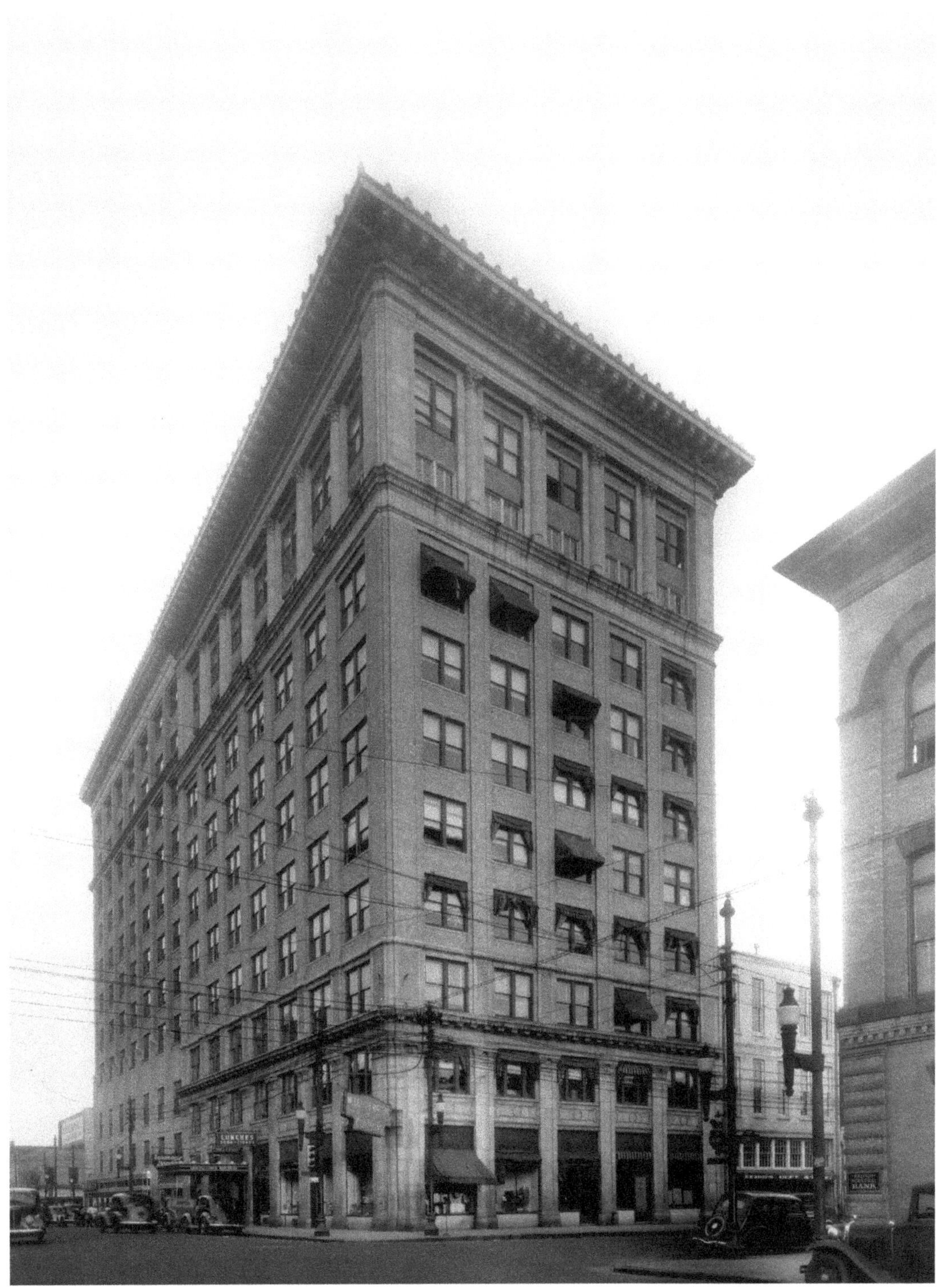

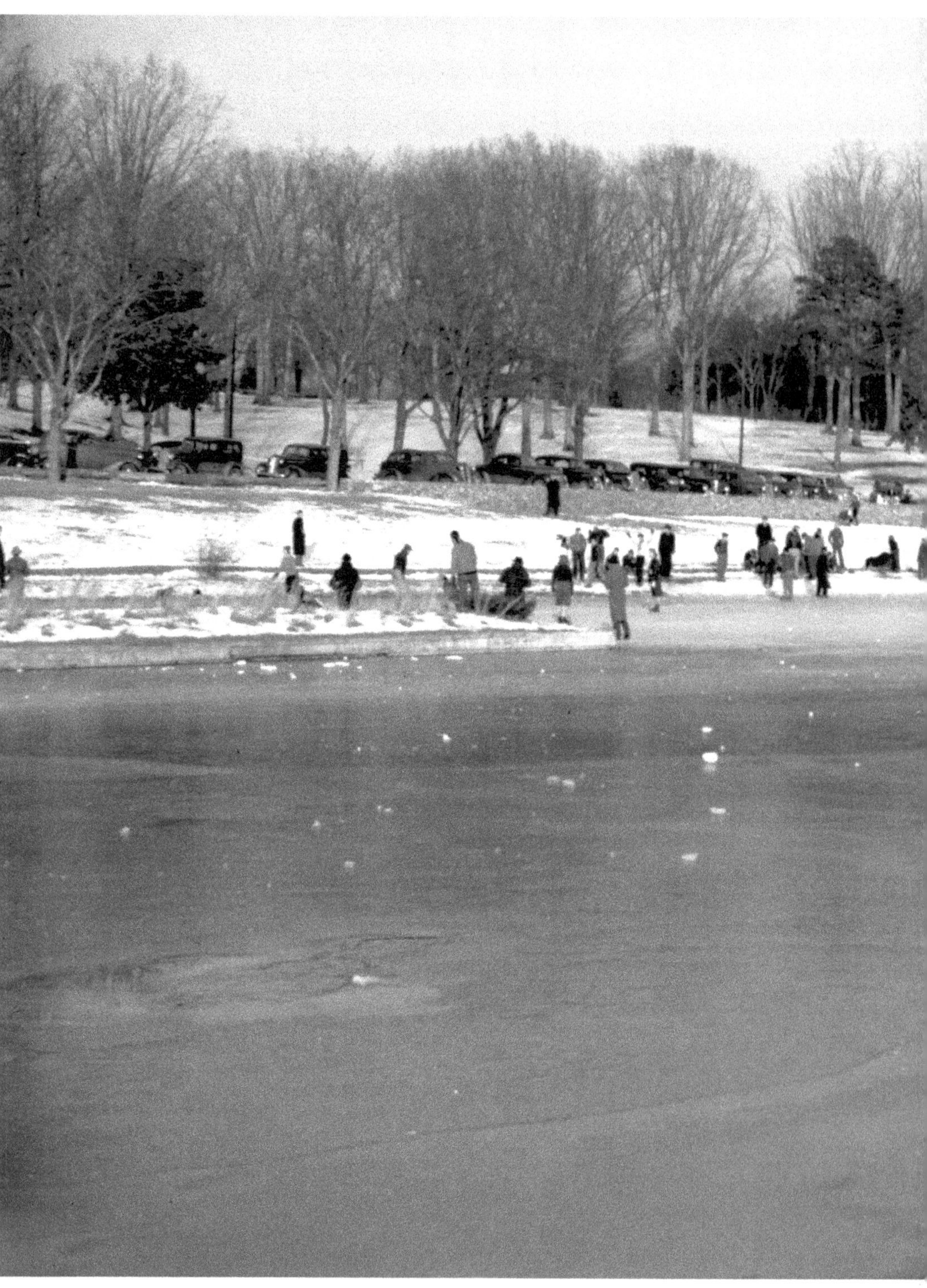

Created on land donated by Richard Stanhope Pullen in 1887, Raleigh's Pullen Park was North Carolina's first public park. In this photograph dated January 28, 1940, ice skaters enjoy a winter afternoon on the park's Lake Howell.

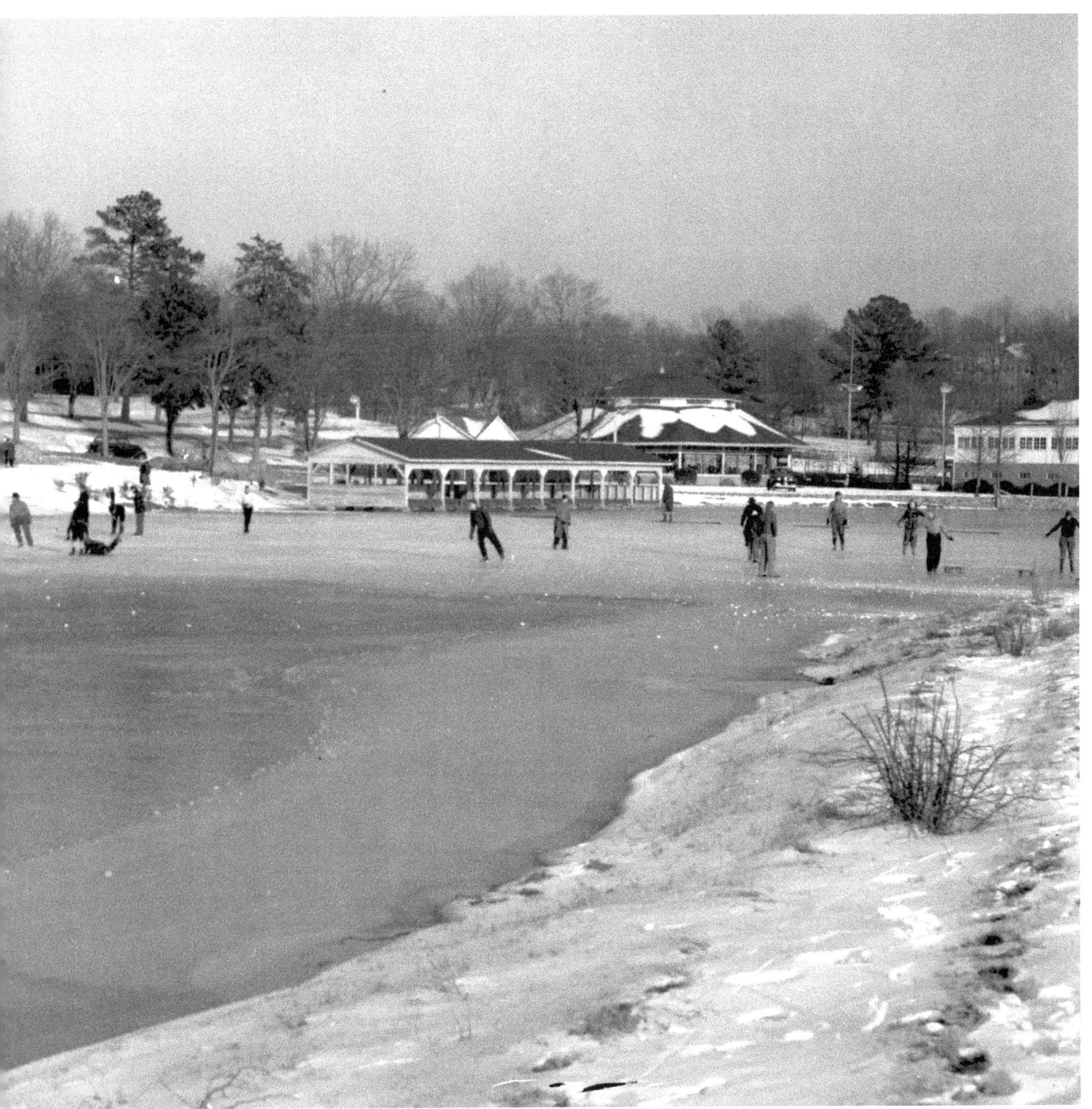

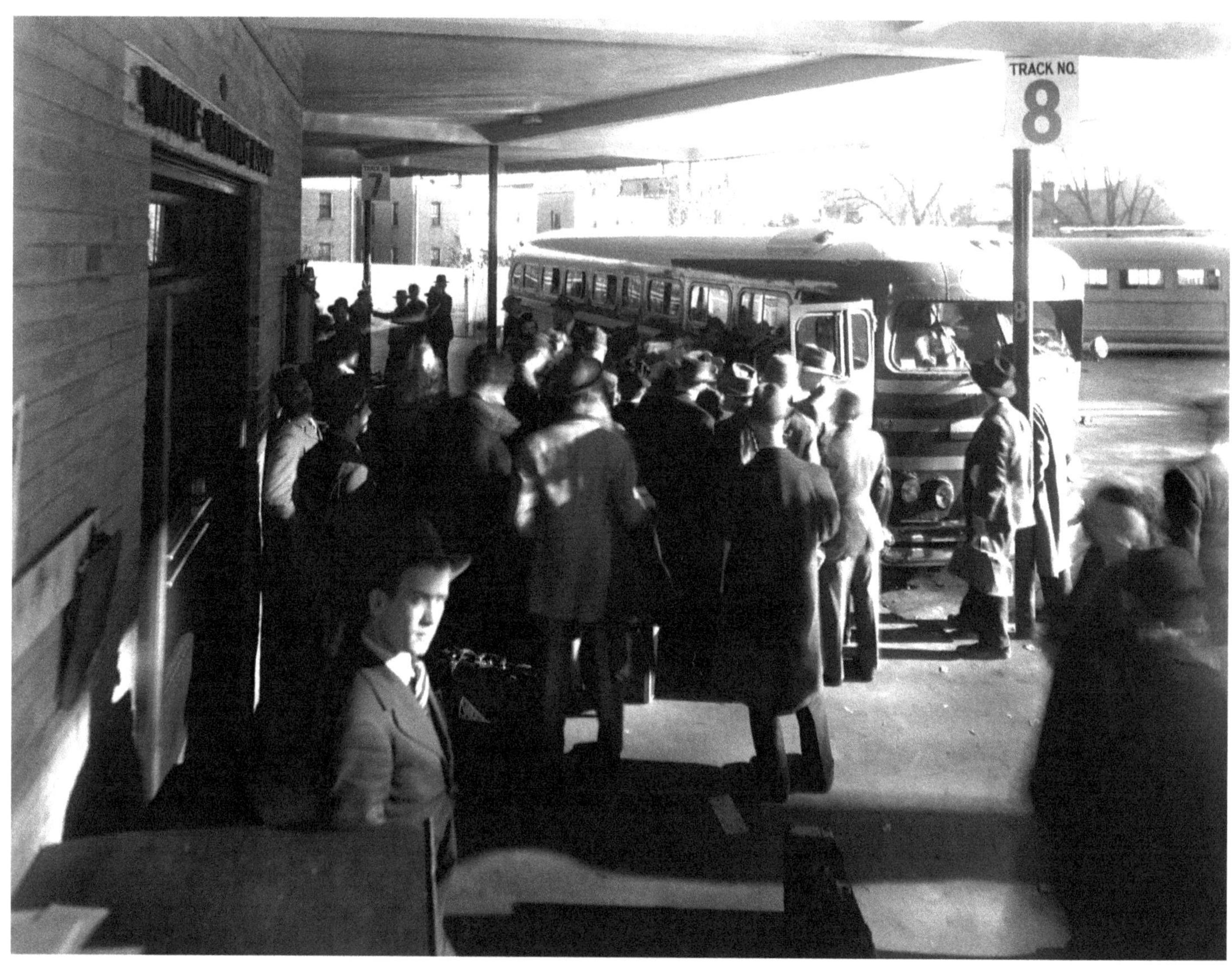

Raleigh's largest bus depot, Union Bus Station, was located on West Morgan Street near downtown. A large group of passengers is boarding a motor coach at the depot in 1942.

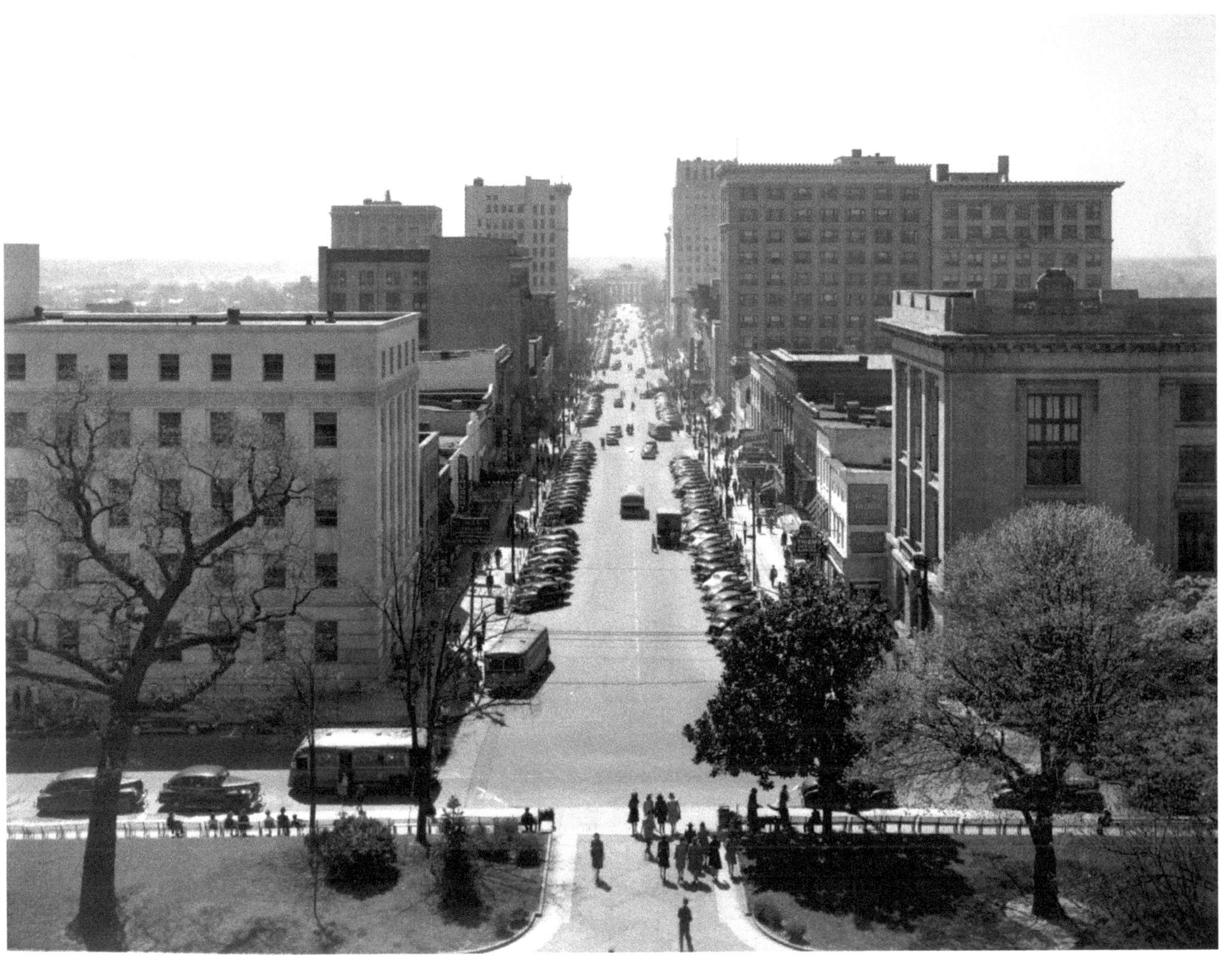

Looking south at Raleigh's Fayetteville Street from the North Carolina State Capitol, 1941. The height of commercial and retail activity along Fayetteville Street occurred in the 1940s preceding the development of the city's first suburban shopping center—Cameron Village—in 1949.

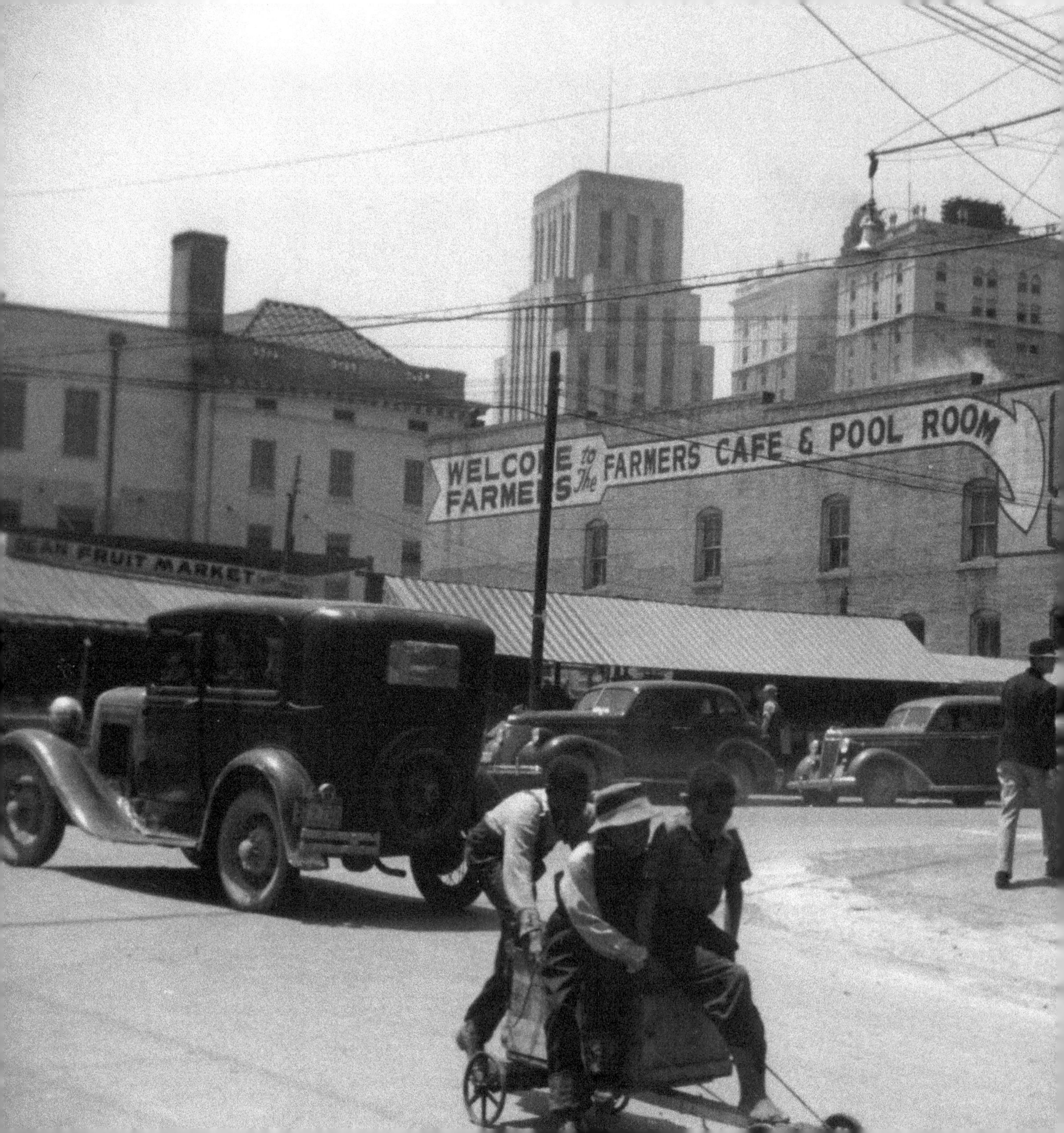
WELCOME to The FARMERS
FARMERS CAFE & POOL ROOM
FRUIT MARKET

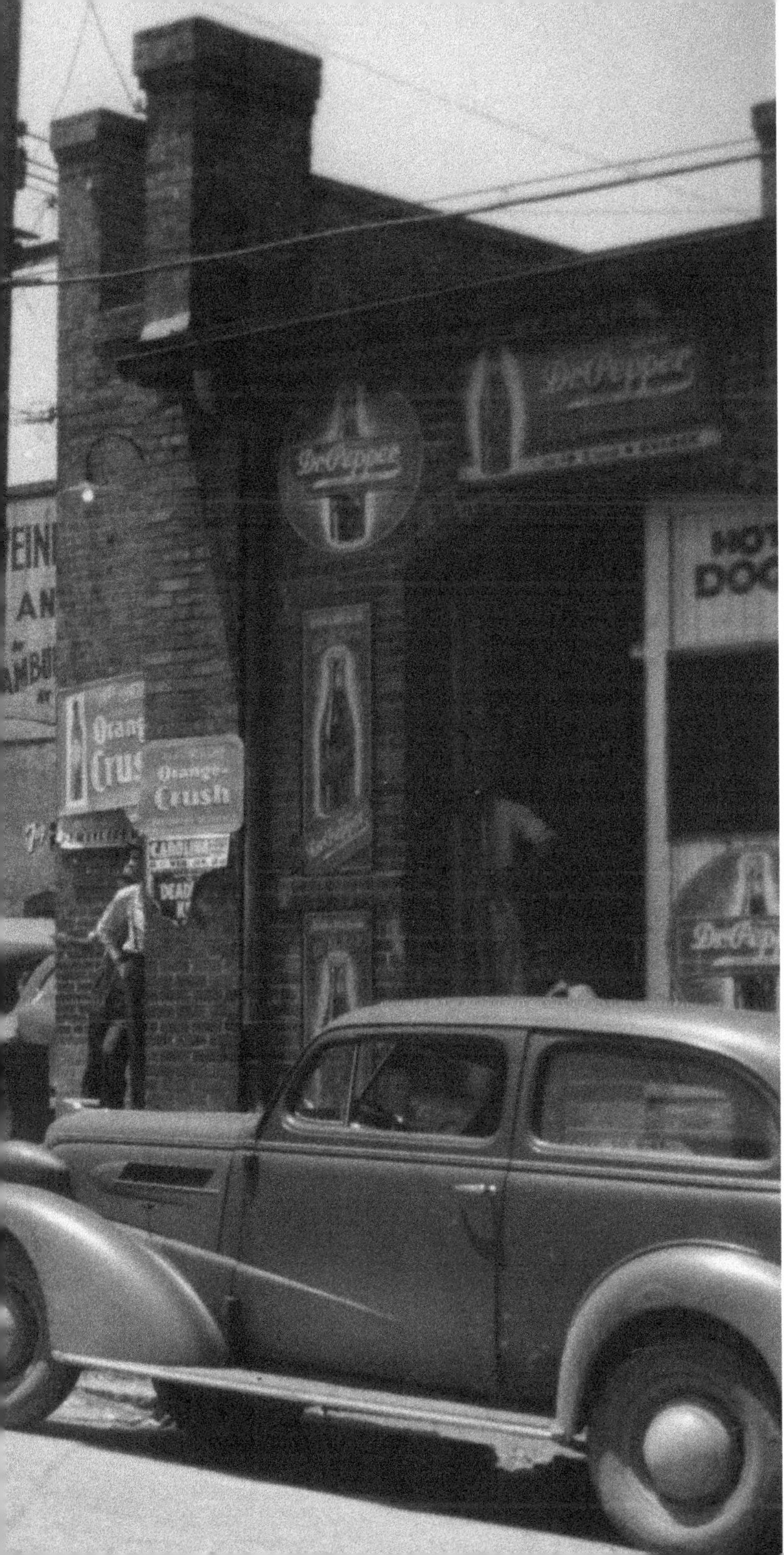

Young boys take a test run in their go-cart near the tobacco warehouses in downtown Durham, ca. 1940.

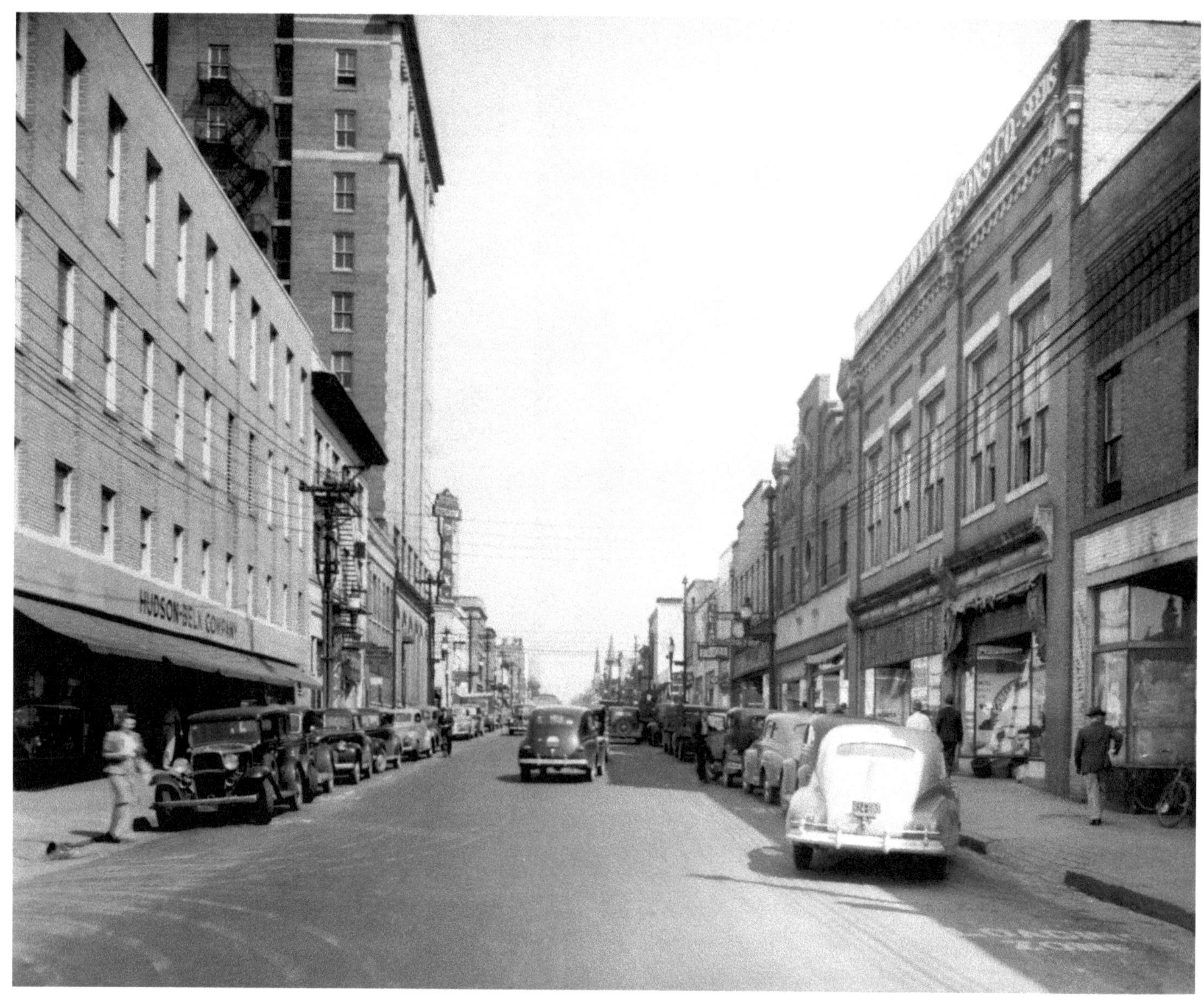

The 300-block of Wilmington Street in Raleigh, facing north from Davie Street, in 1943. The rear entrance to the Hudson-Belk Department Store is visible at far-left.

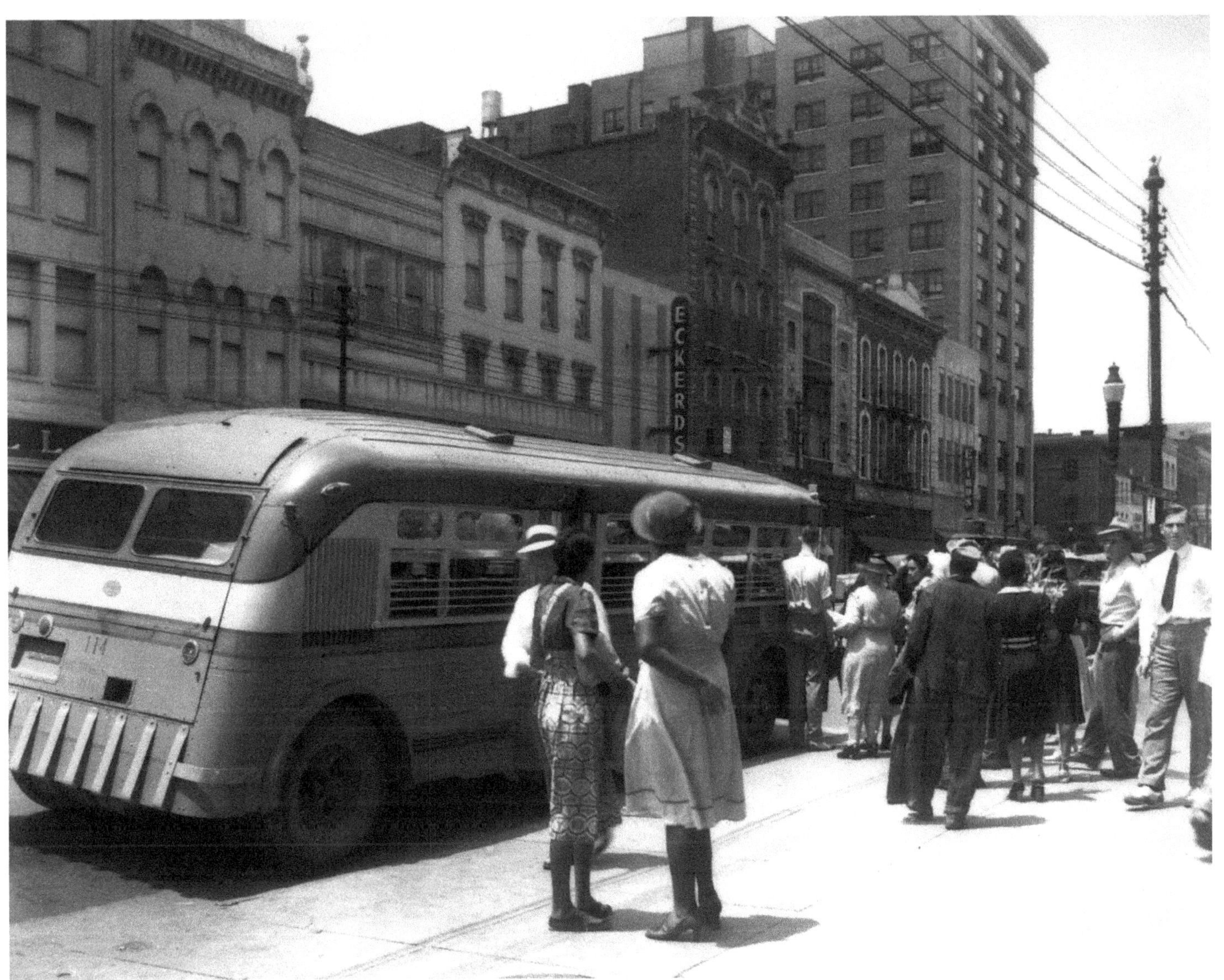

Passengers board a city bus in 1941 at the intersection of Martin and Fayetteville streets in Raleigh. Motorized coaches had replaced the city's electric streetcars by 1933. Behind the Eckerd's sign, at center, is the 1874 Briggs Hardware Building.

A young flower vendor waits for a customer outside Depositors National Bank in Durham, ca. 1940.

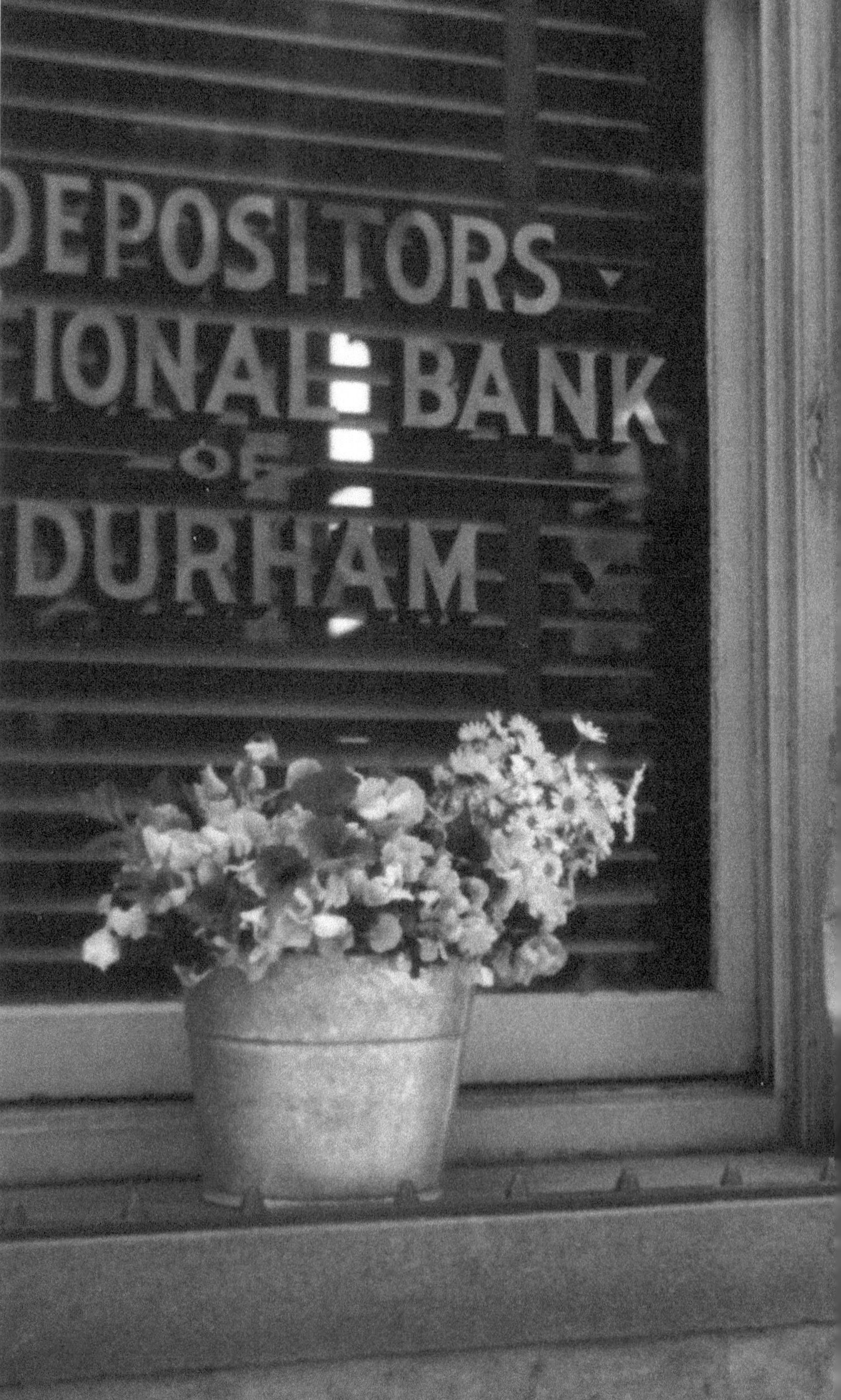

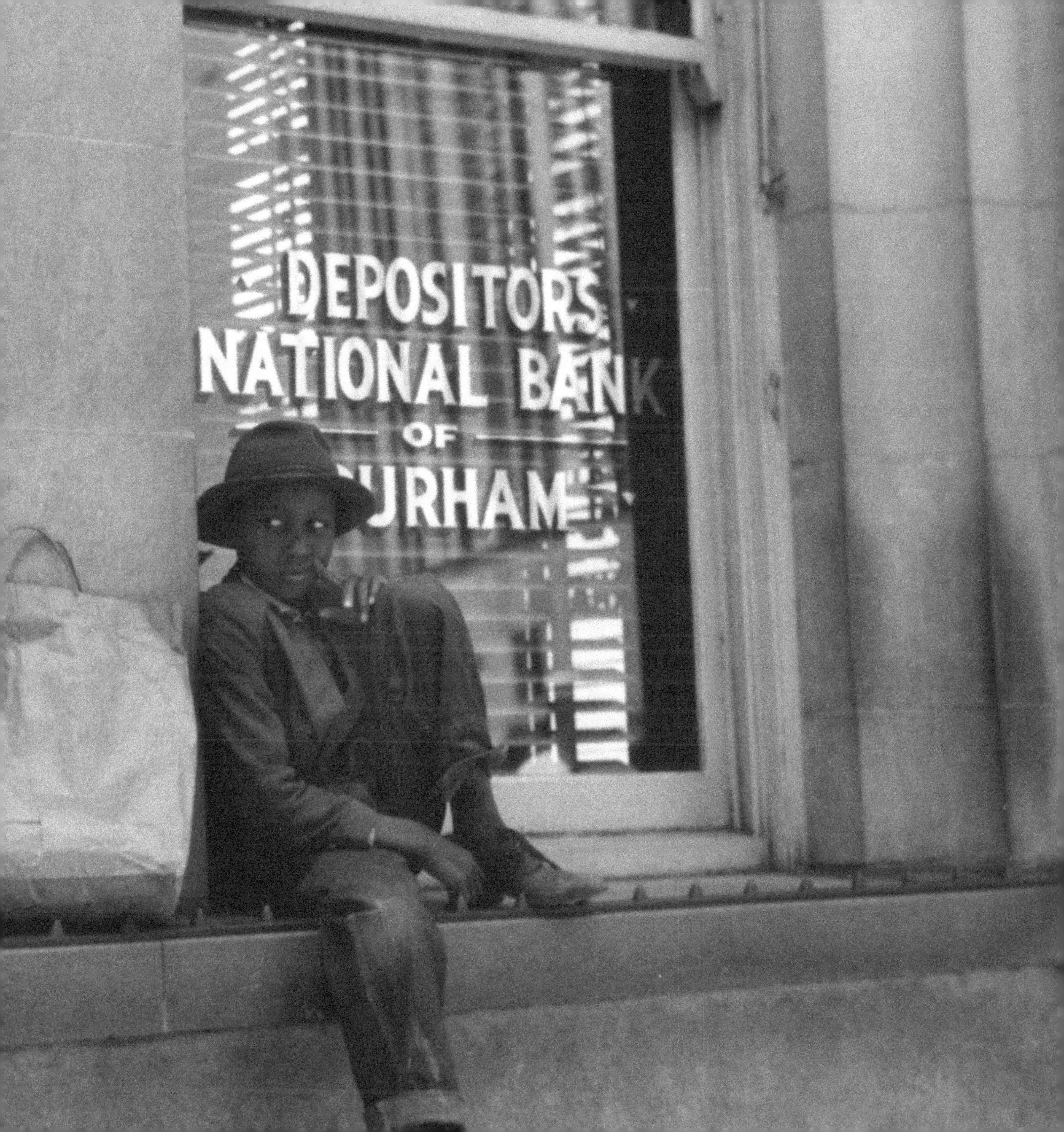

DEPOSITORS
NATIONAL BANK
OF
URHAM

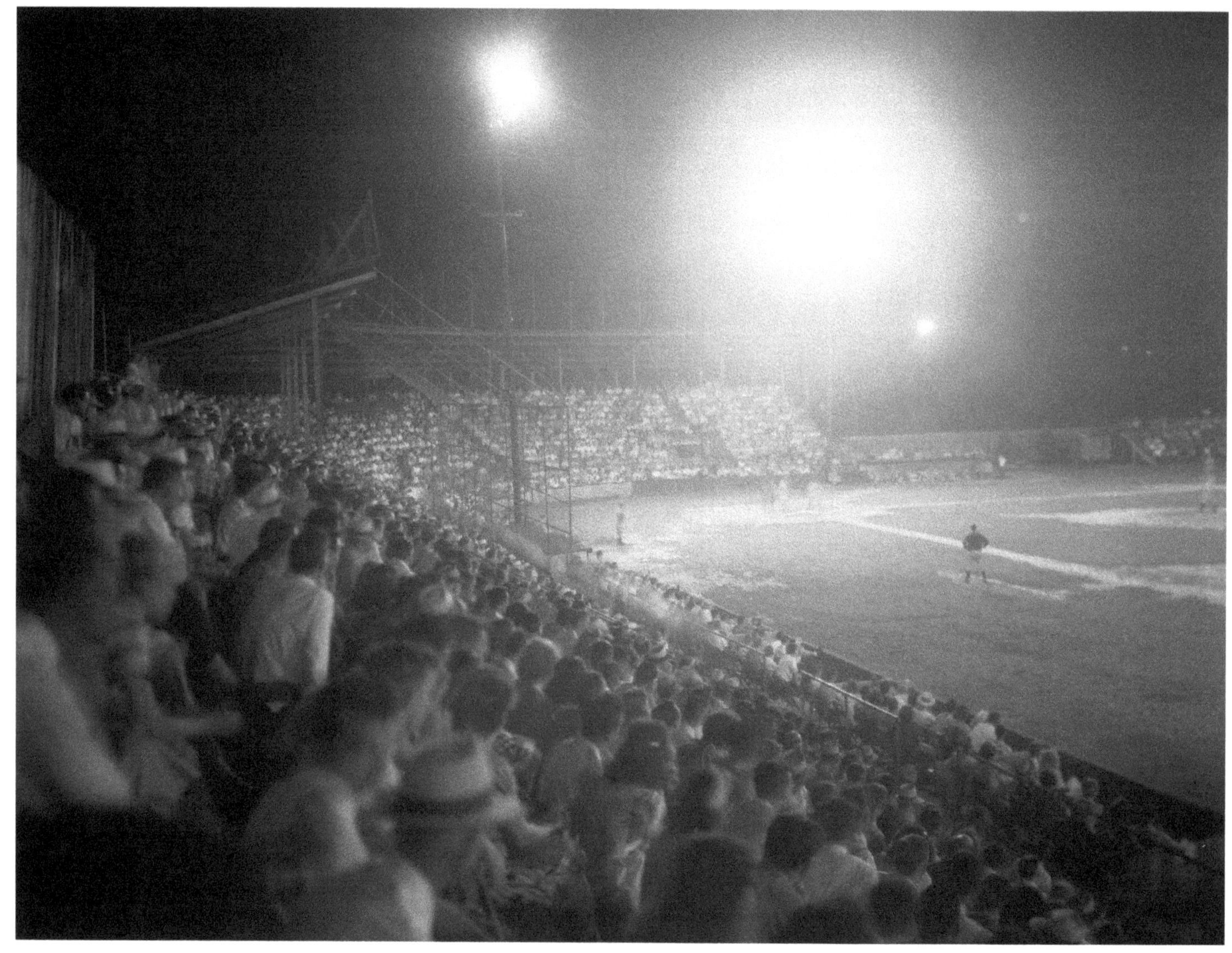

Devereux Meadow Baseball Park was built in Raleigh in the late 1930s as a Works Progress Administration project. It was home to the Raleigh Capitals minor-league baseball team for many seasons. For some time it was the only lighted athletic field in the city. The park was demolished in the late 1970s.

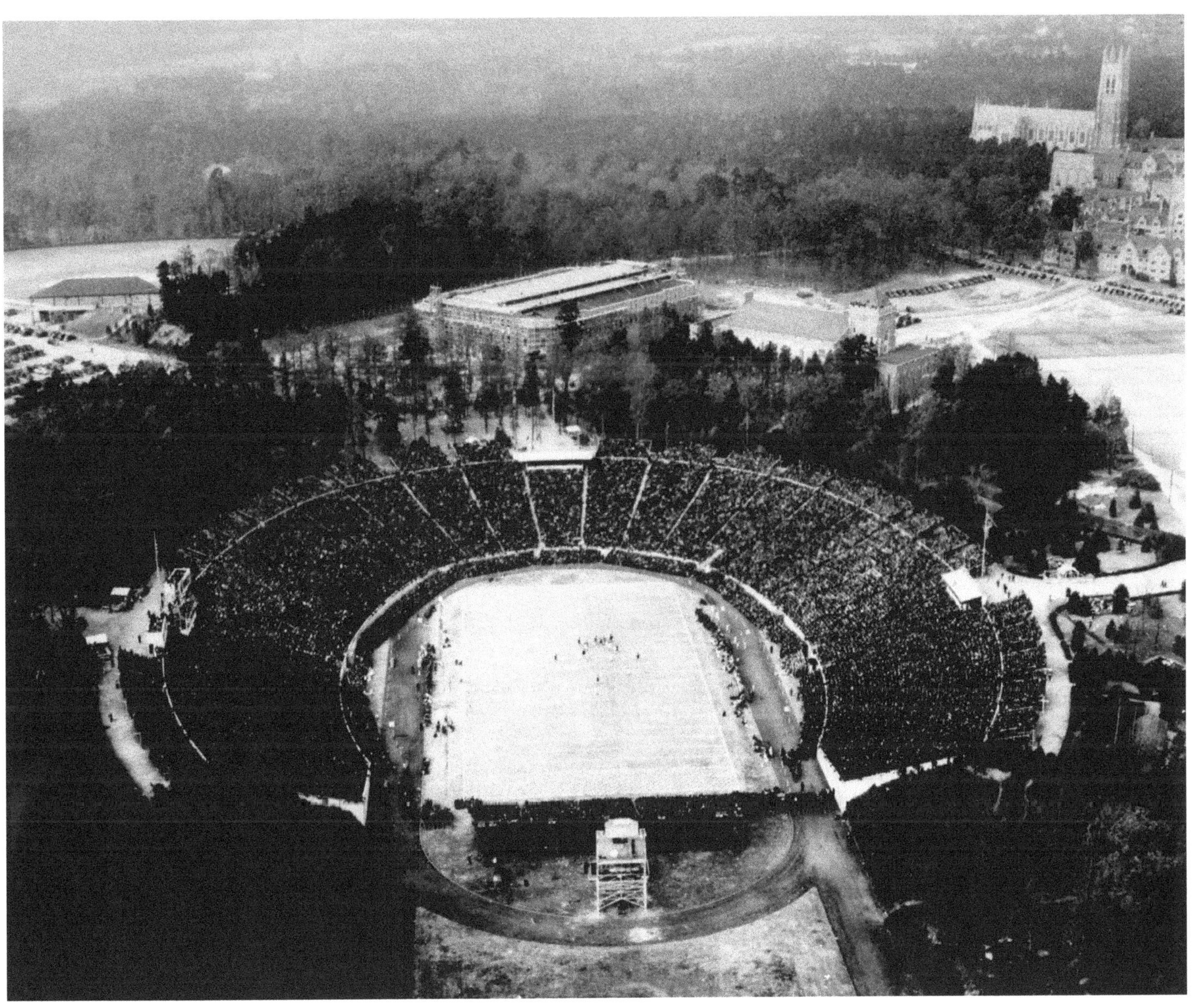

A capacity crowd attends a football game at Duke Stadium, ca. 1941-42. The field, now known as Wallace Wade Stadium, was the site of the 1942 Rose Bowl, the only Rose Bowl held away from Pasadena, California. In that year, a heavily favored Duke squad was beaten by Oregon State, 20-16.

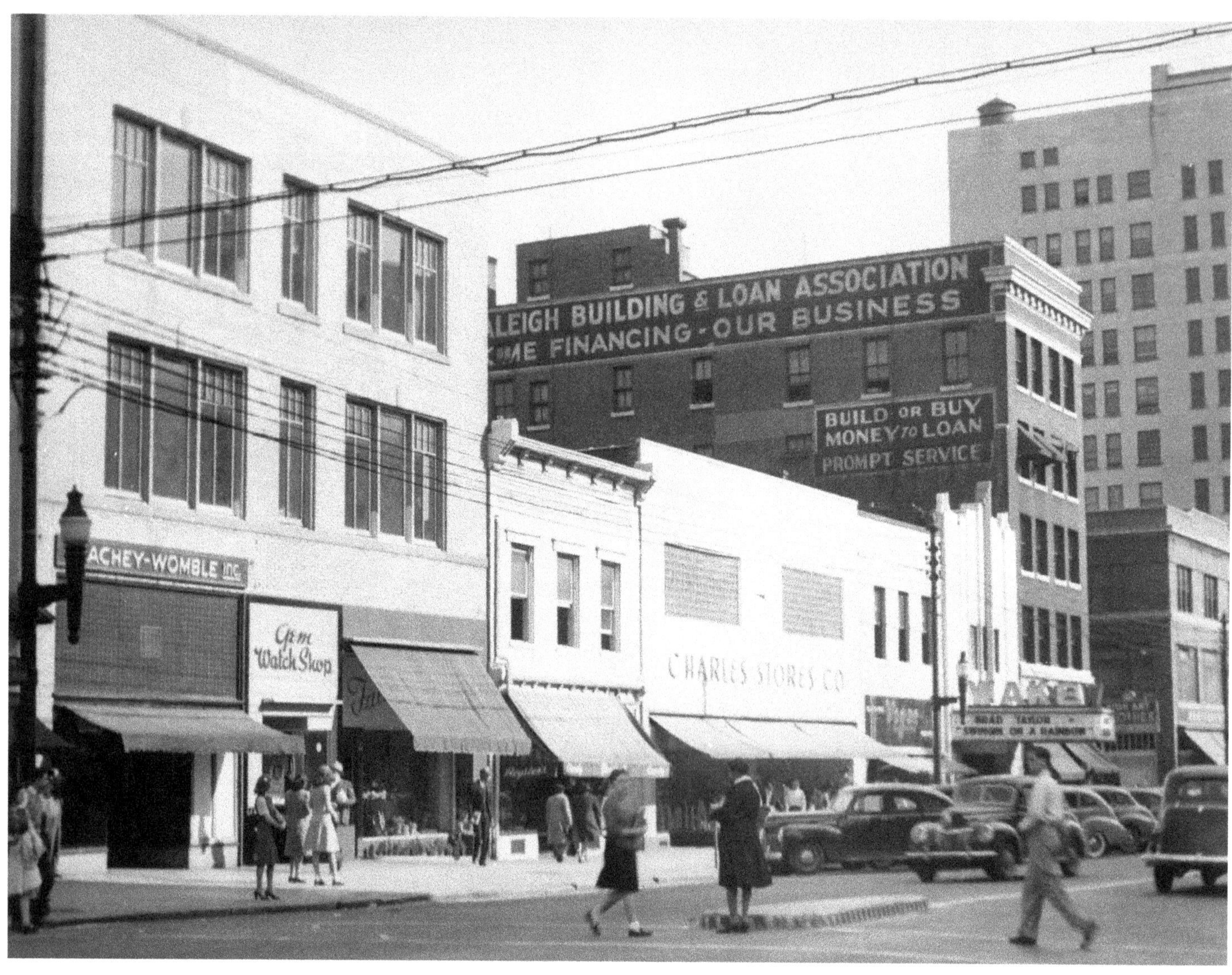

The east side of the 200-block of Fayetteville Street in Raleigh, 1945. At the Wake Theater, Brad Taylor is starring in *Swingin' on a Rainbow.*

This monument is inscribed "James Buchanan Duke, December 23, 1856–October 10, 1925, Industrialist, Philanthropist, Founder of the Duke Endowment." The 8'4" likeness of Duke standing atop a 25-ton granite pedestal was sculptured by Charles Keck. The statue was dedicated in front of Duke Chapel in 1935.

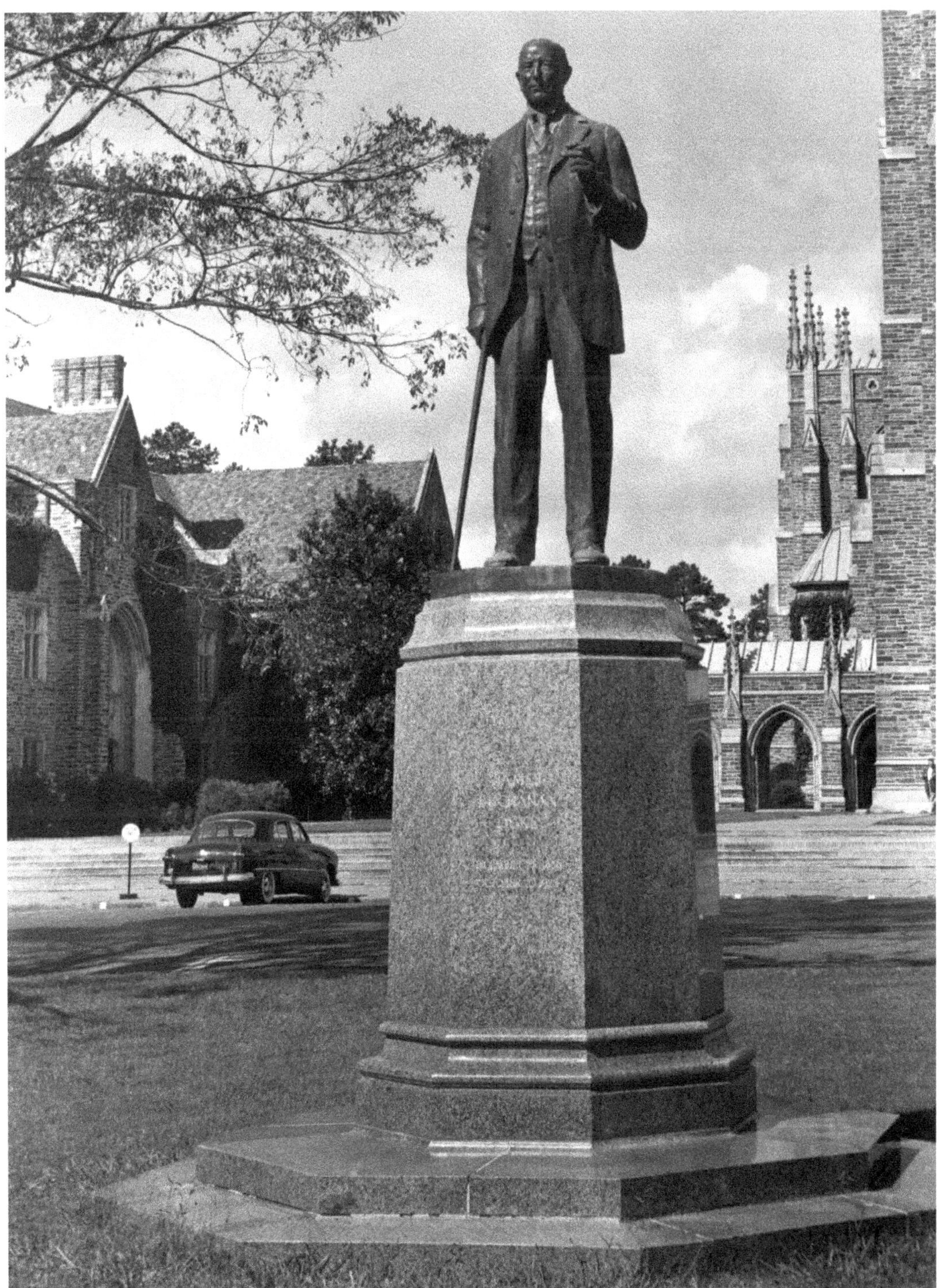

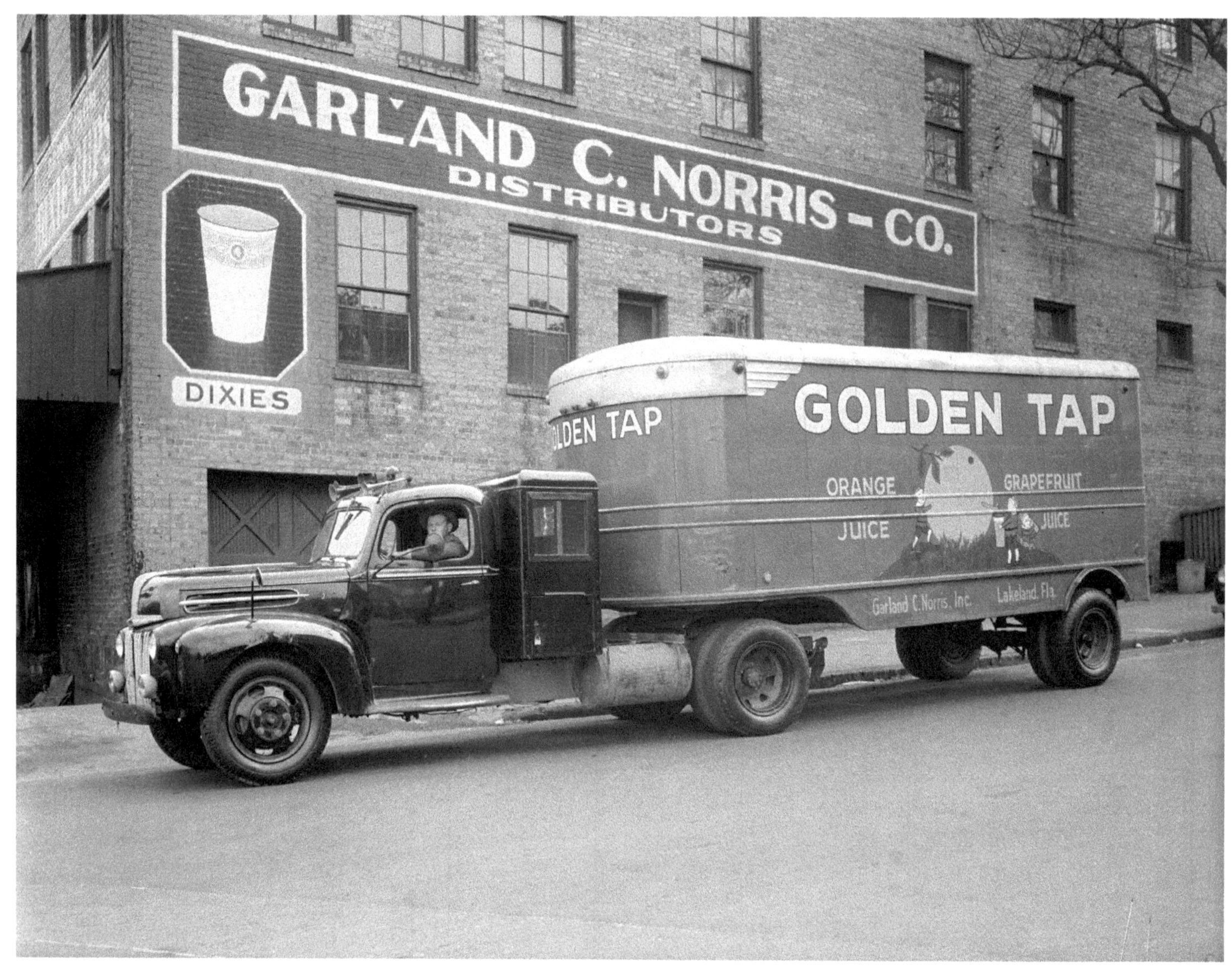

A Golden Tap orange juice truck idles in front of the Garland C. Norris Company building in Raleigh in 1946.

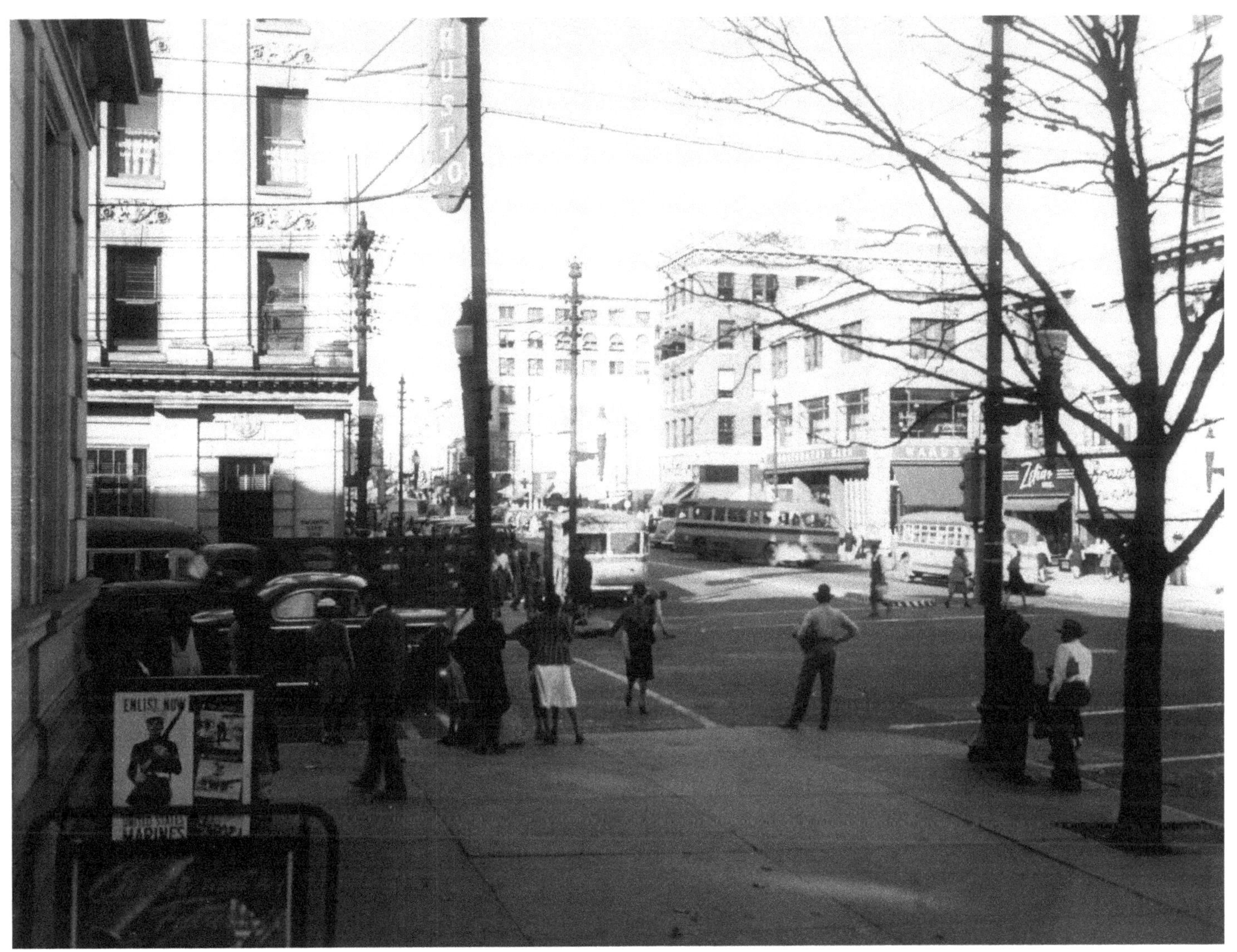

Fayetteville Street in downtown Raleigh, ca. 1942. At left, a recruitment poster for the Marines advertises for enlistees.

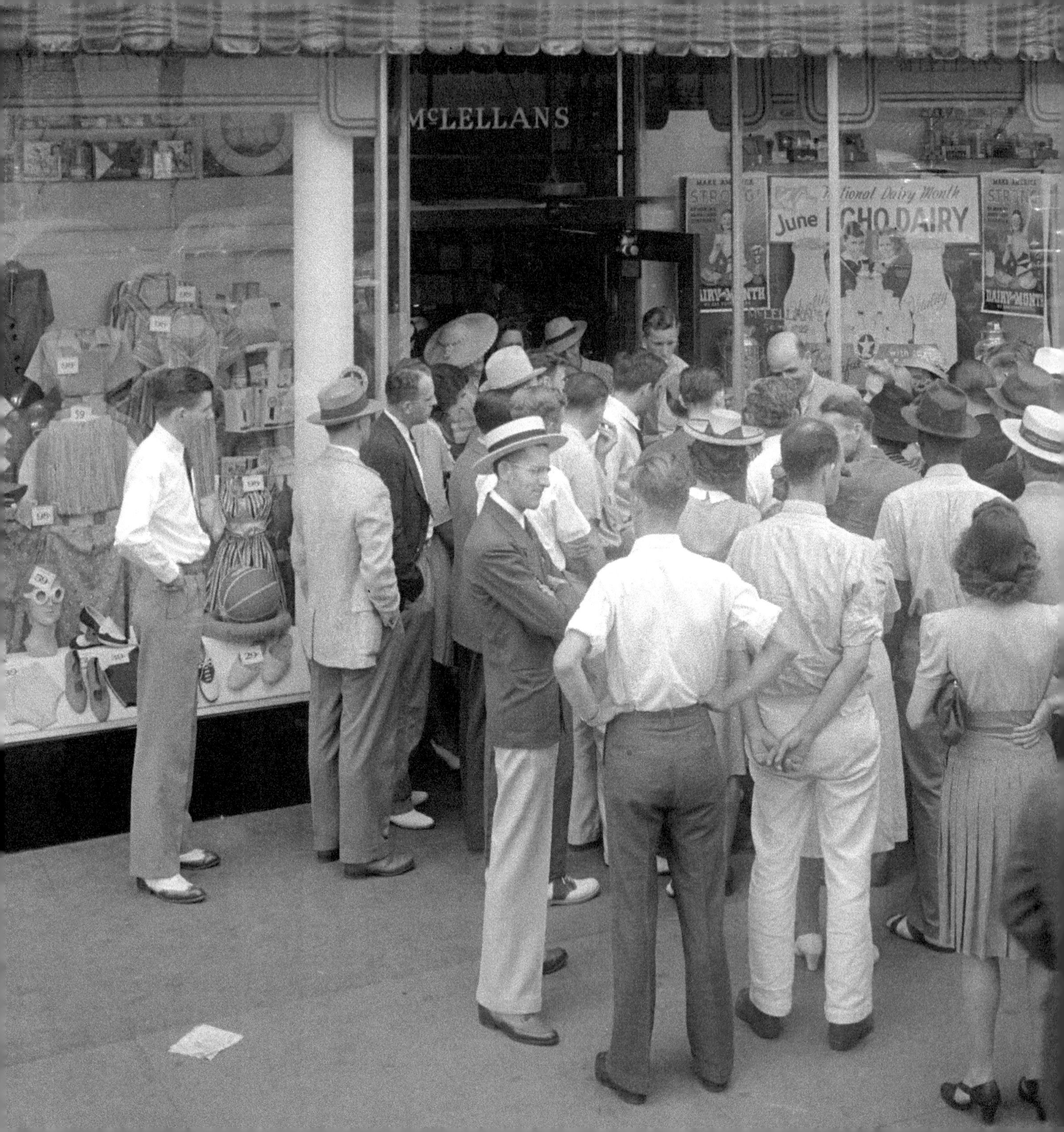
McLELLANS
MAKE AMERICA
National Dairy Month
June
DAIRY
DAIRY MONTH

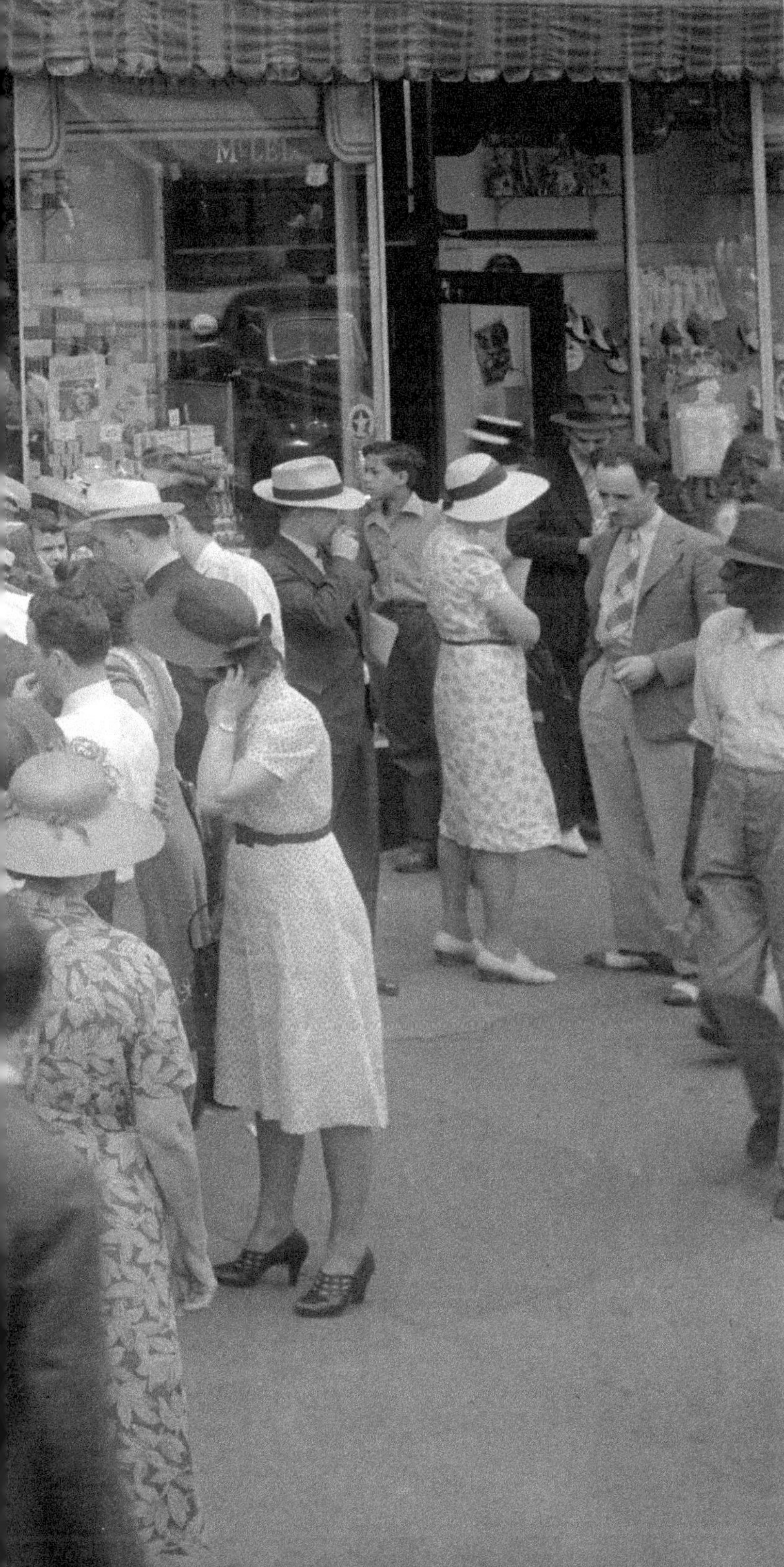

In 1941, a group of spectators in downtown Raleigh watches a spelling bee sponsored by radio station WRAL. Behind the proceedings, posters inside the display windows of McLellans advertise National Dairy Month, Your Hit Parade, and various products sold by the store.

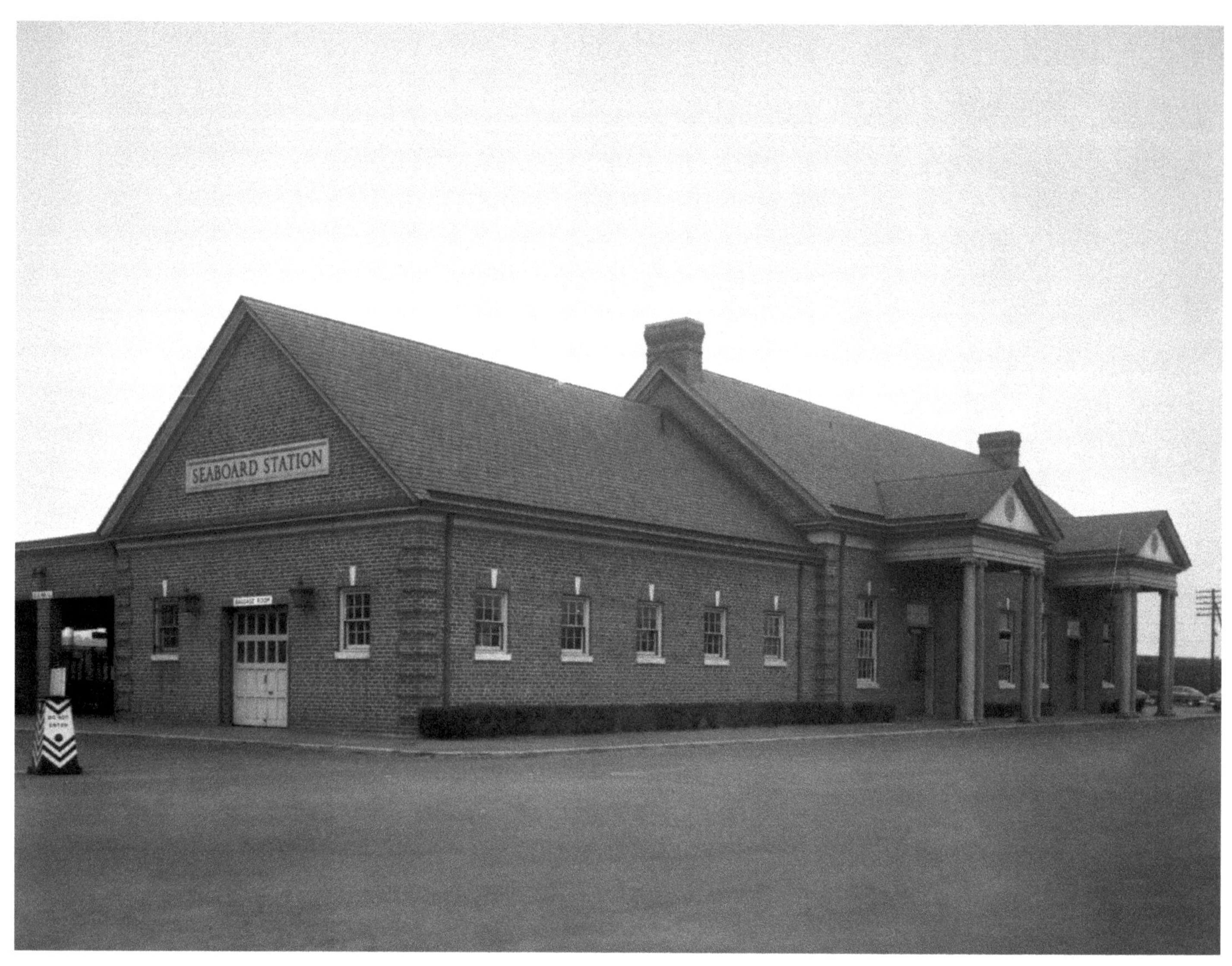

Raleigh's main depot for the Seaboard Air Line Railroad as it appeared in 1950.

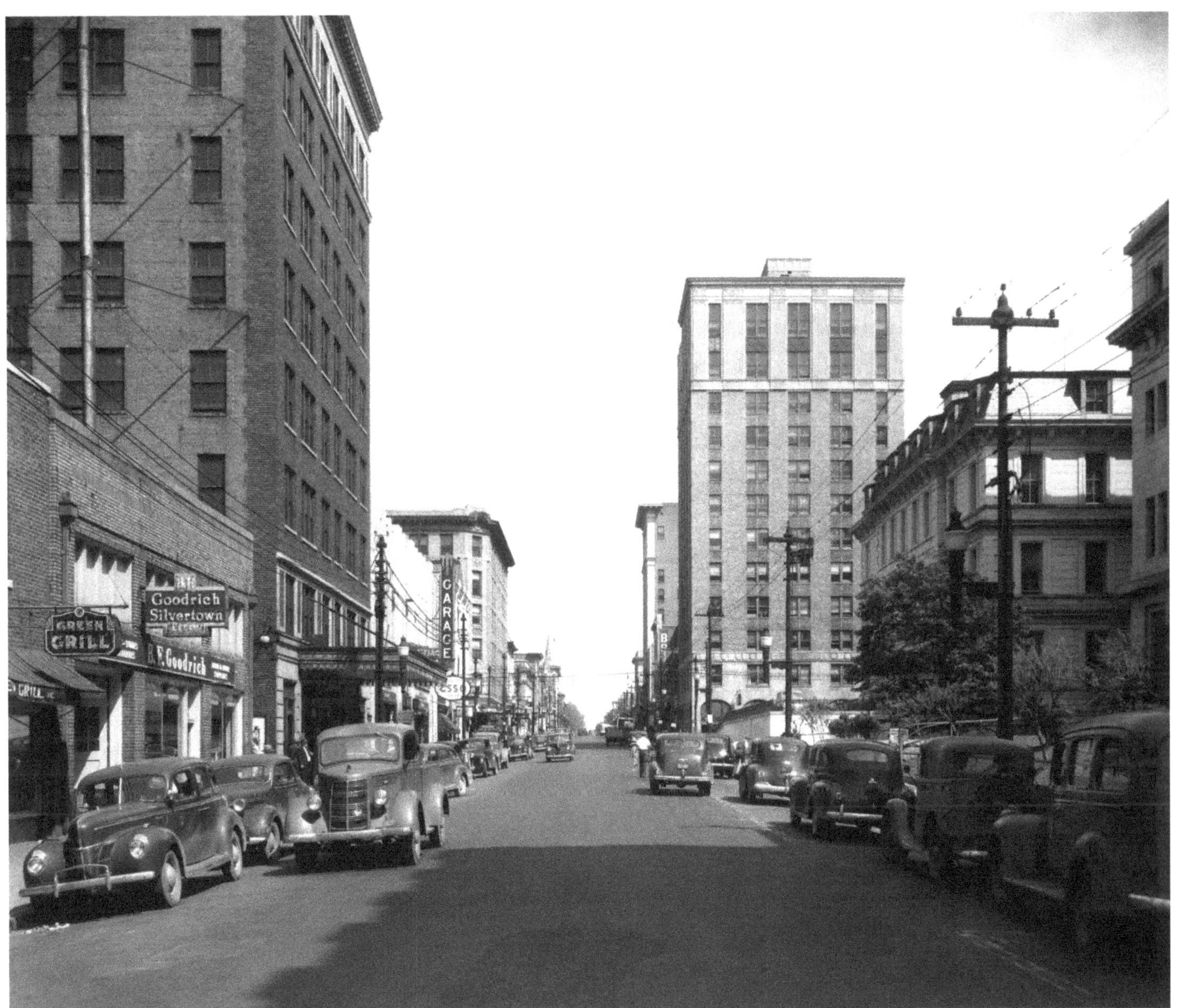

The 300-block of Salisbury Street in Raleigh, facing north, ca. 1943. To the left are the Green Grill, the State Theatre, and other businesses. Century Post Office and Wake County Courthouse are visible on the far right.

At the conclusion of World War II, Raleigh's Fayetteville Street hosted a joyous parade to honor veterans who were returning from the conflict.

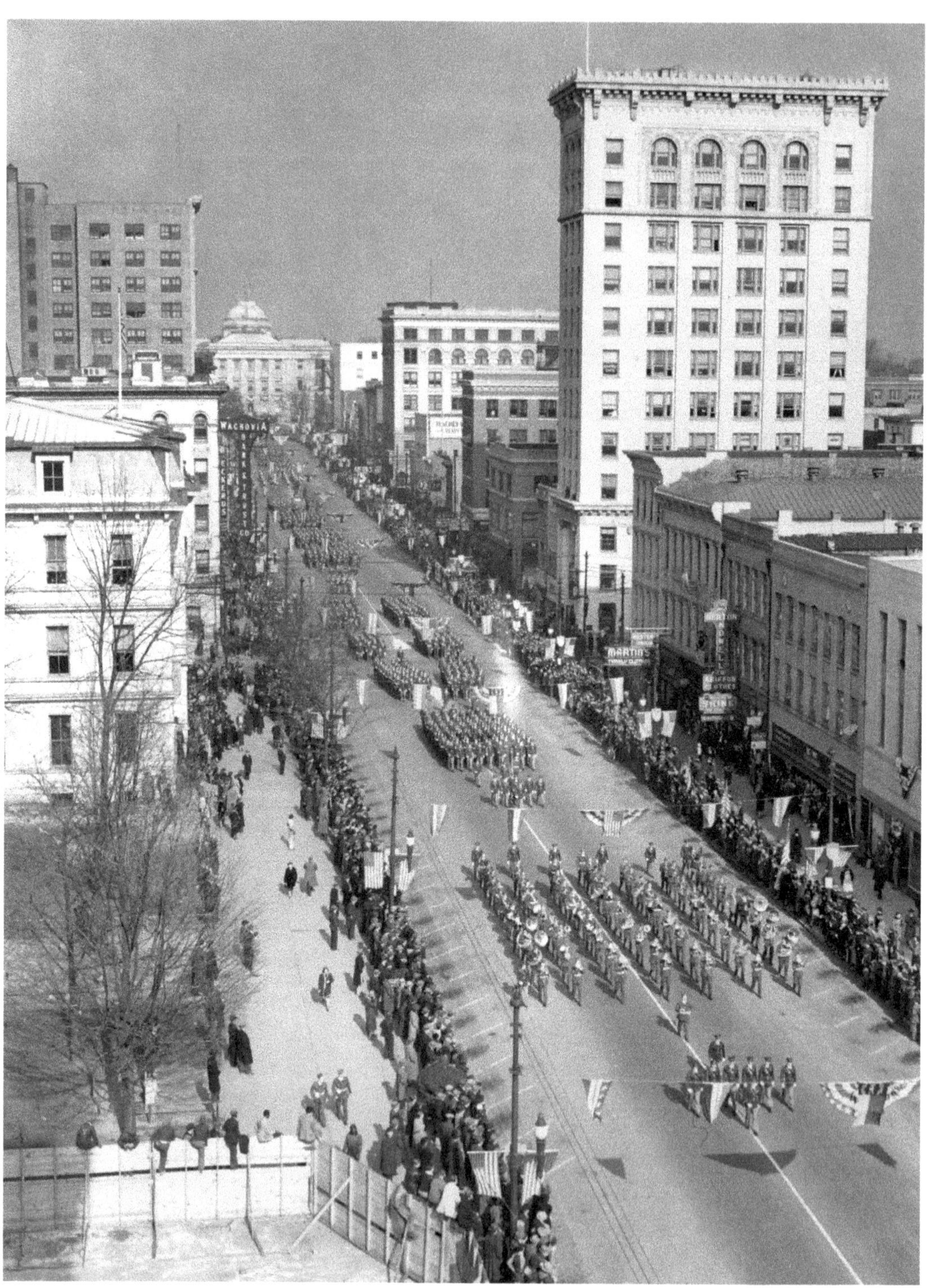

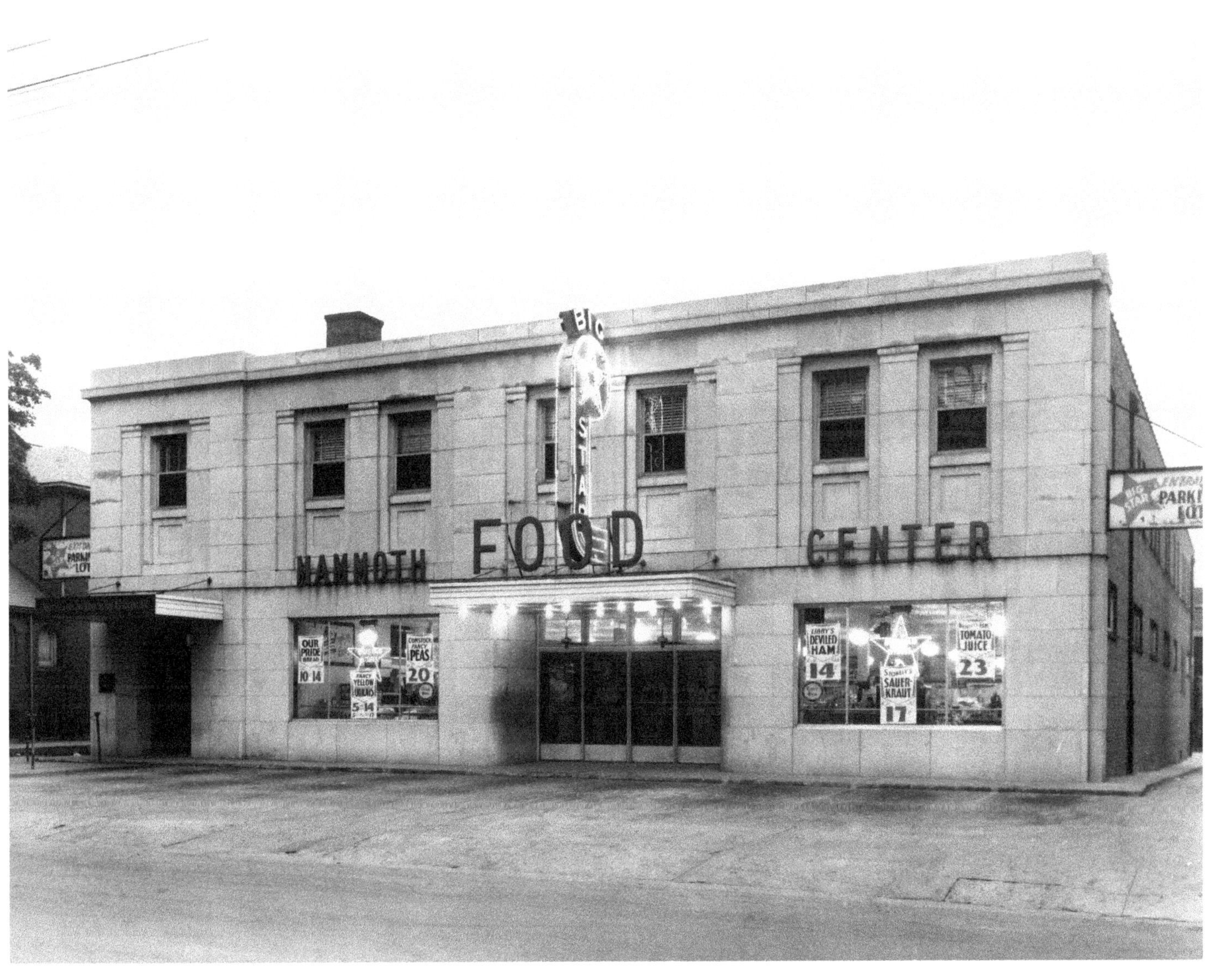

Under the neon star at Raleigh's Big Star Mammoth Food Center in 1946, a no. 2 can of fancy peas is selling for 20 cents and a jar of sauerkraut for 17 cents.

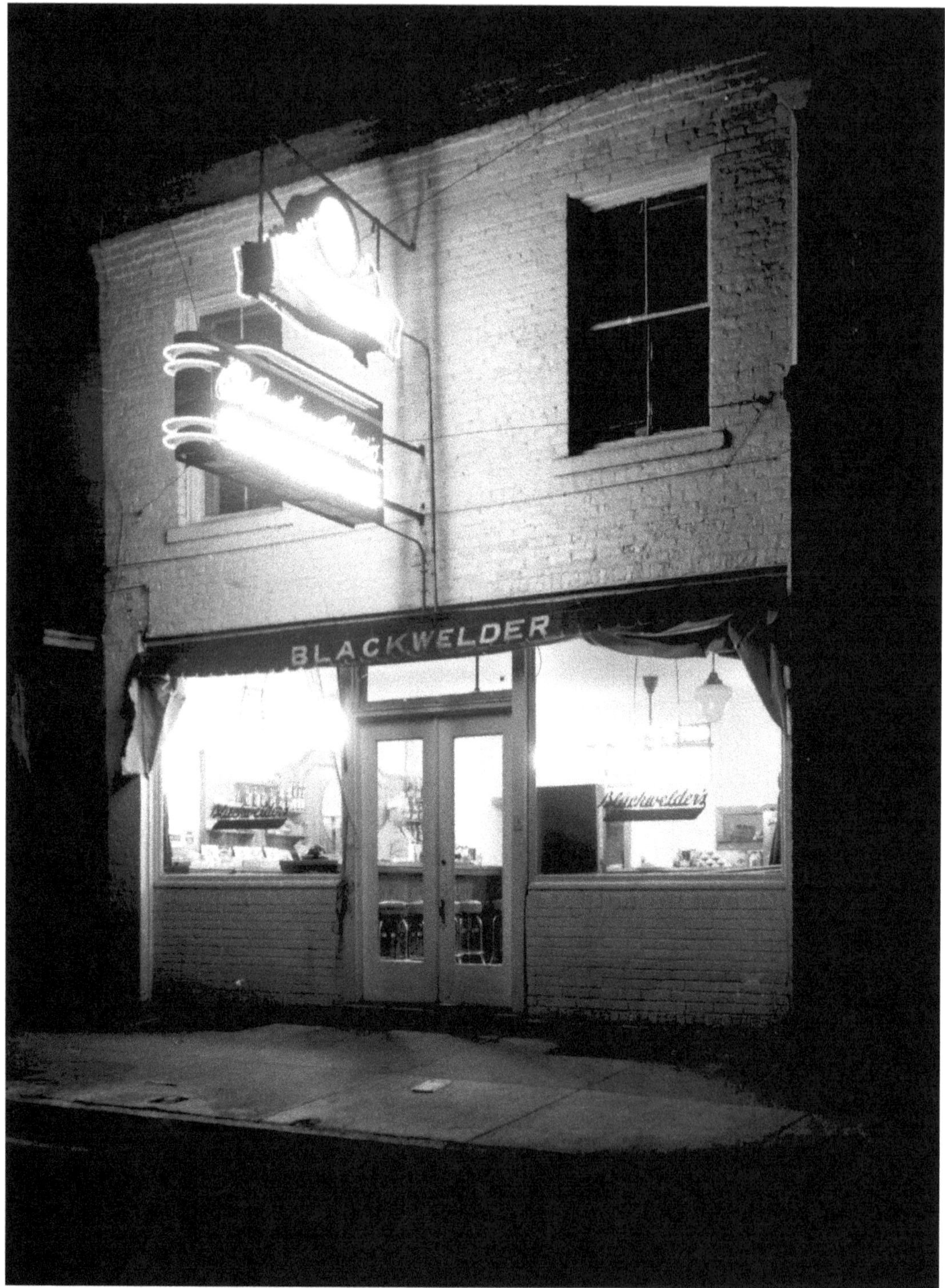

A neon sign invites patrons into Blackwelders, in Raleigh, ca. 1940.

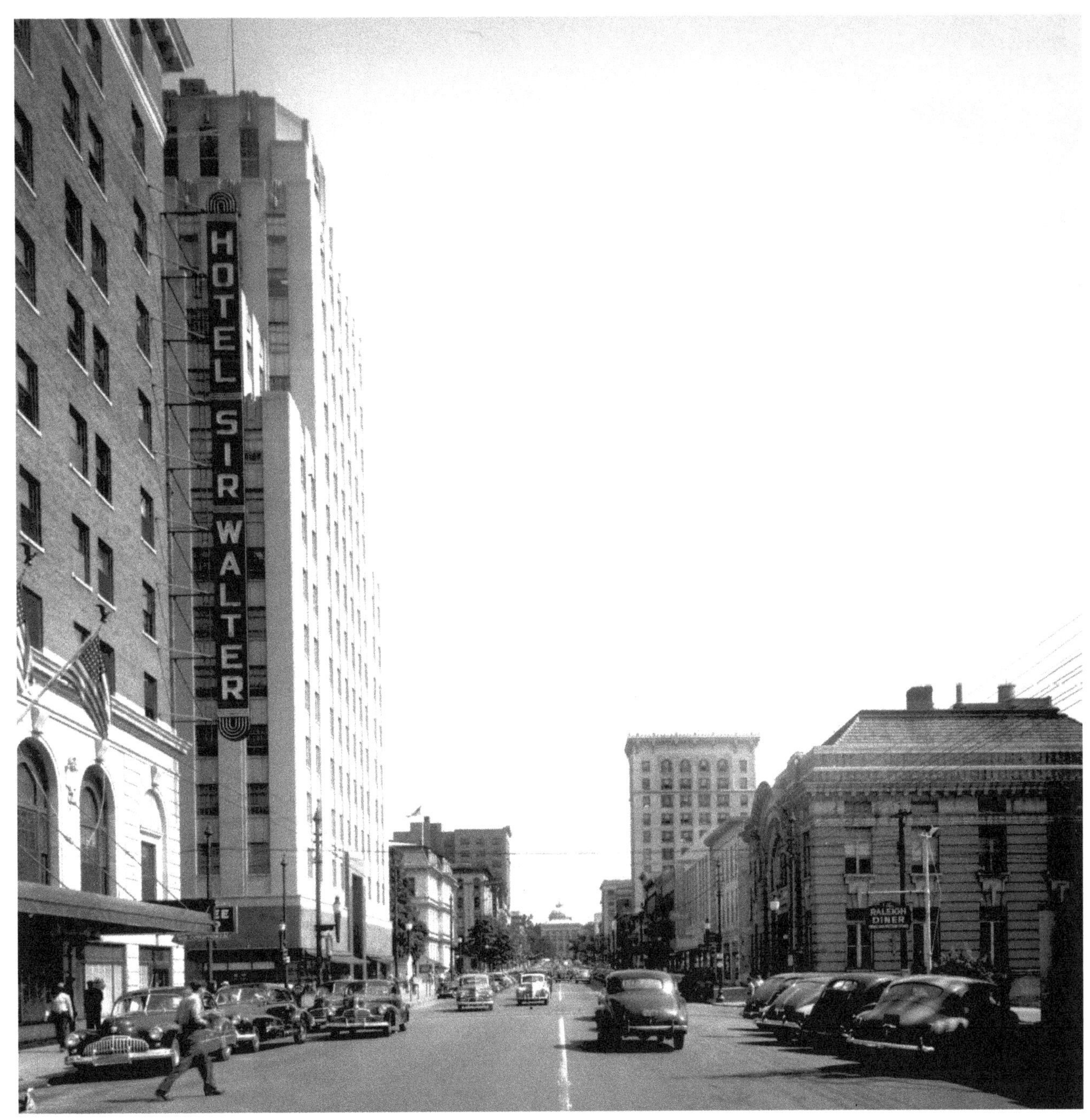

Raleigh's Fayetteville Street in 1947. To the left is the neon sign for the Hotel Sir Walter. On the right is the hipped roof of the old Raleigh City Hall.

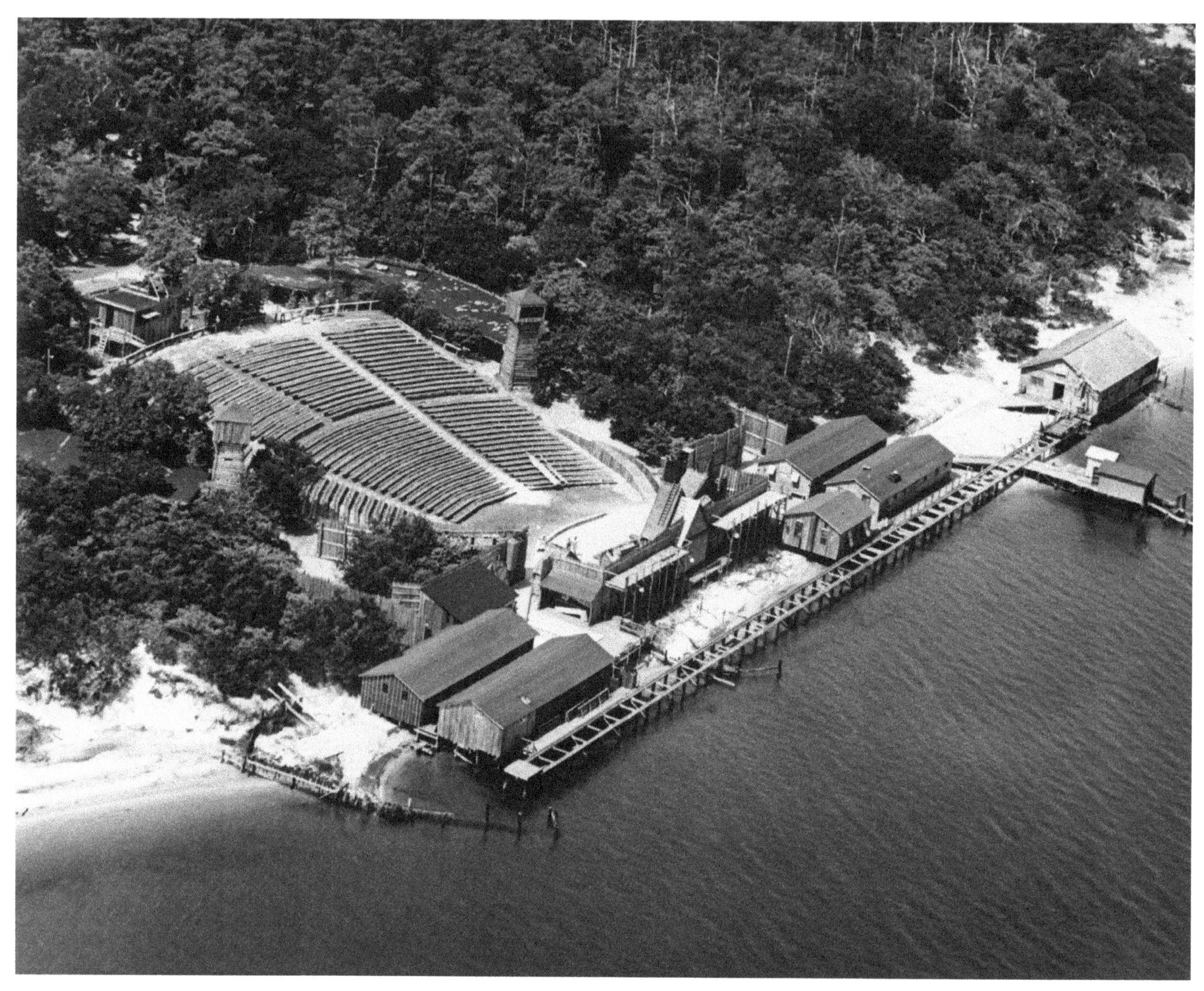

An attraction at Fort Raleigh is the outdoor drama "The Lost Colony," performed in this amphitheater. Written by Paul Green, the theatrical production has been enacted each summer since 1937.

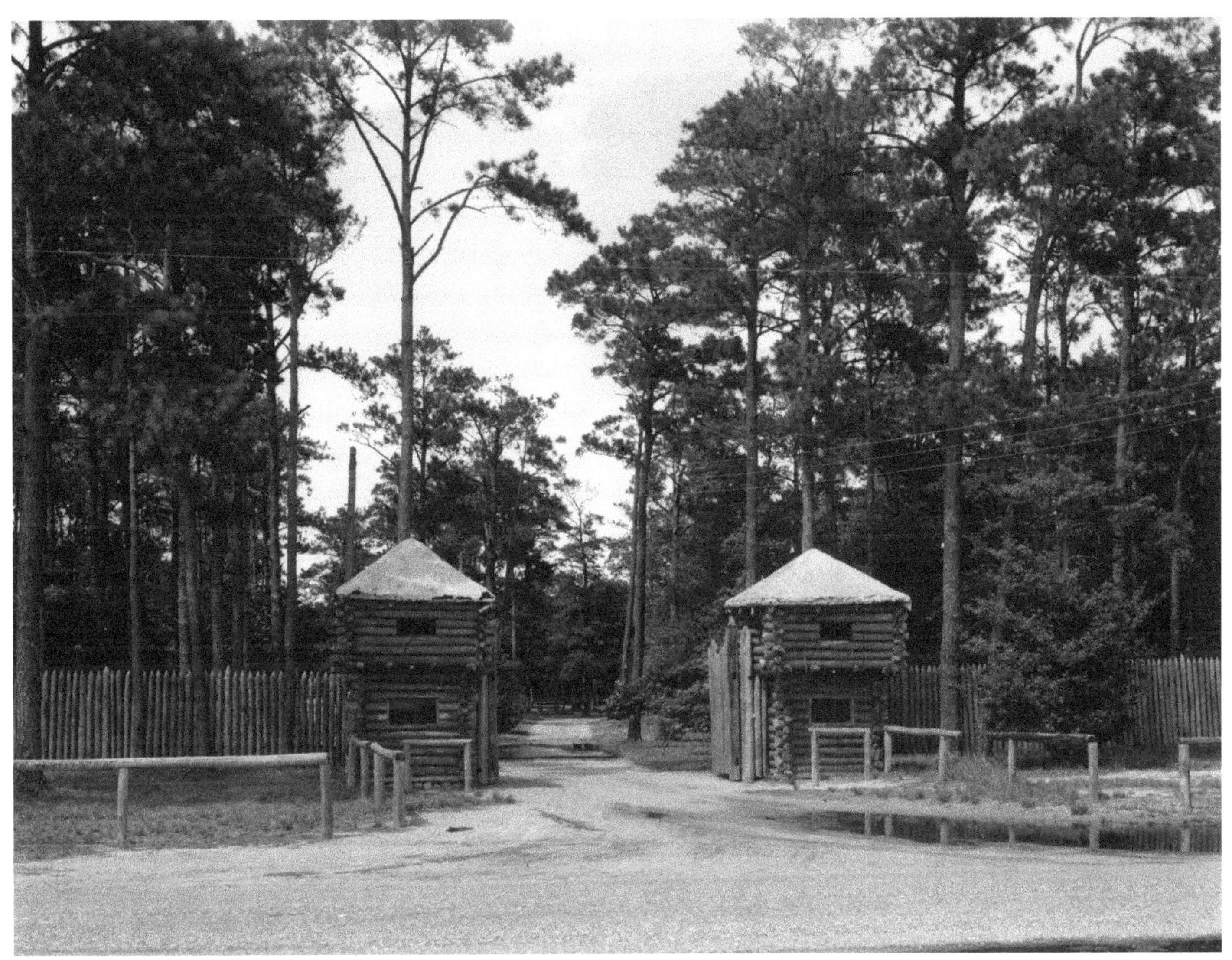

The city of Raleigh isn't the first settlement in North Carolina bearing that name. From 1584 to 1587 England's Sir Walter Raleigh financed and supplied an expedition from England that landed on the Outer Banks of present-day North Carolina. This endeavor, the first English settlement in the New World, was named Fort Raleigh after the colony's benefactor. In 1950 a re-creation of the fort was built by the National Park Service at Manteo.

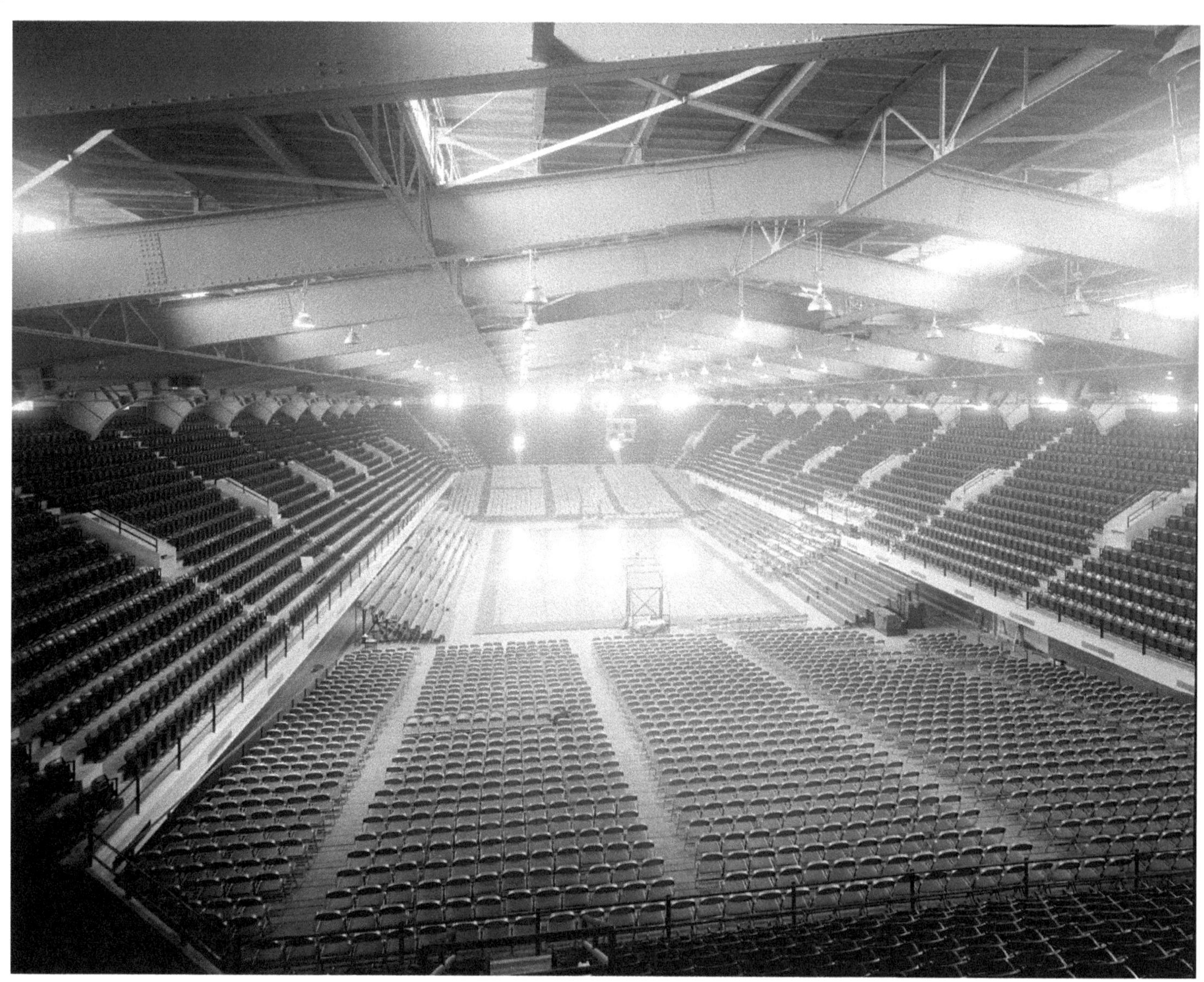

"The House That Case Built," Reynolds Coliseum opened on the campus of North Carolina State University in 1949. It became the home court for NCSU's powerhouse basketball squads of the 1950s, coached by the legendary Everett Case.

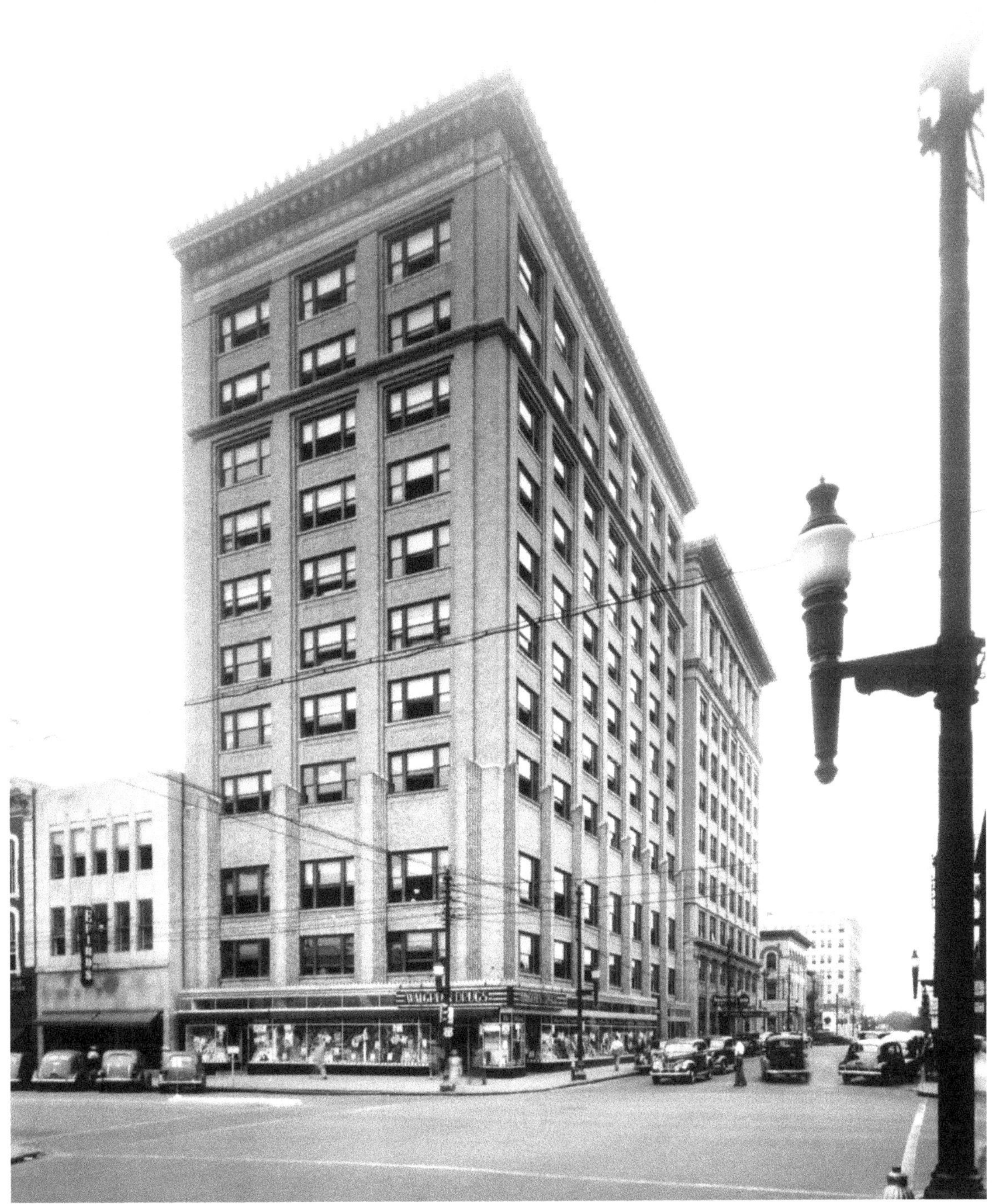

Fayetteville and Hargett streets in Raleigh, 1947. At center (left to right) are the Raleigh Building and the Odd Fellows Building.

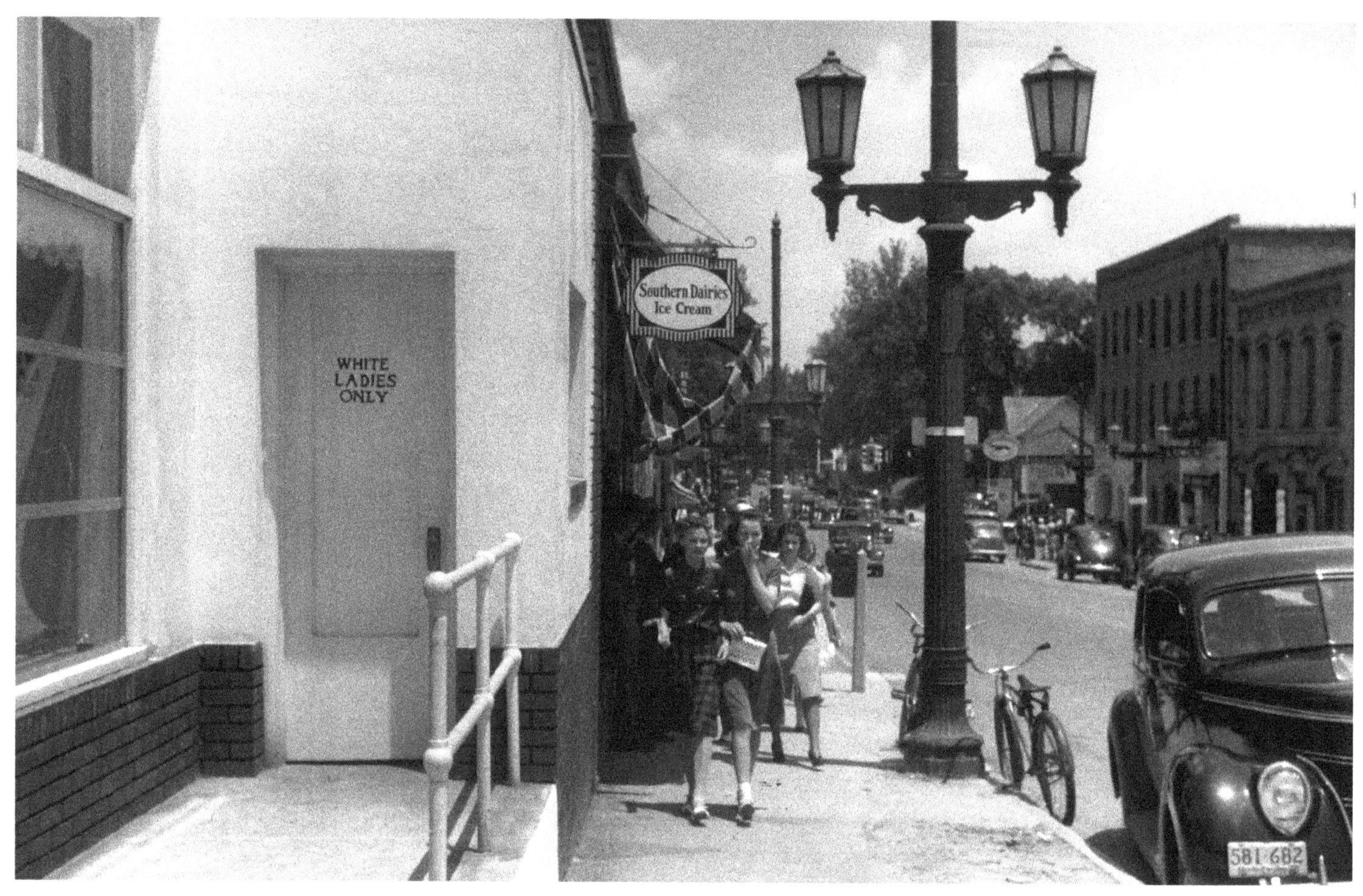

Near the Durham Bus Station ca. 1940, a sign calls attention to the era of segregation.

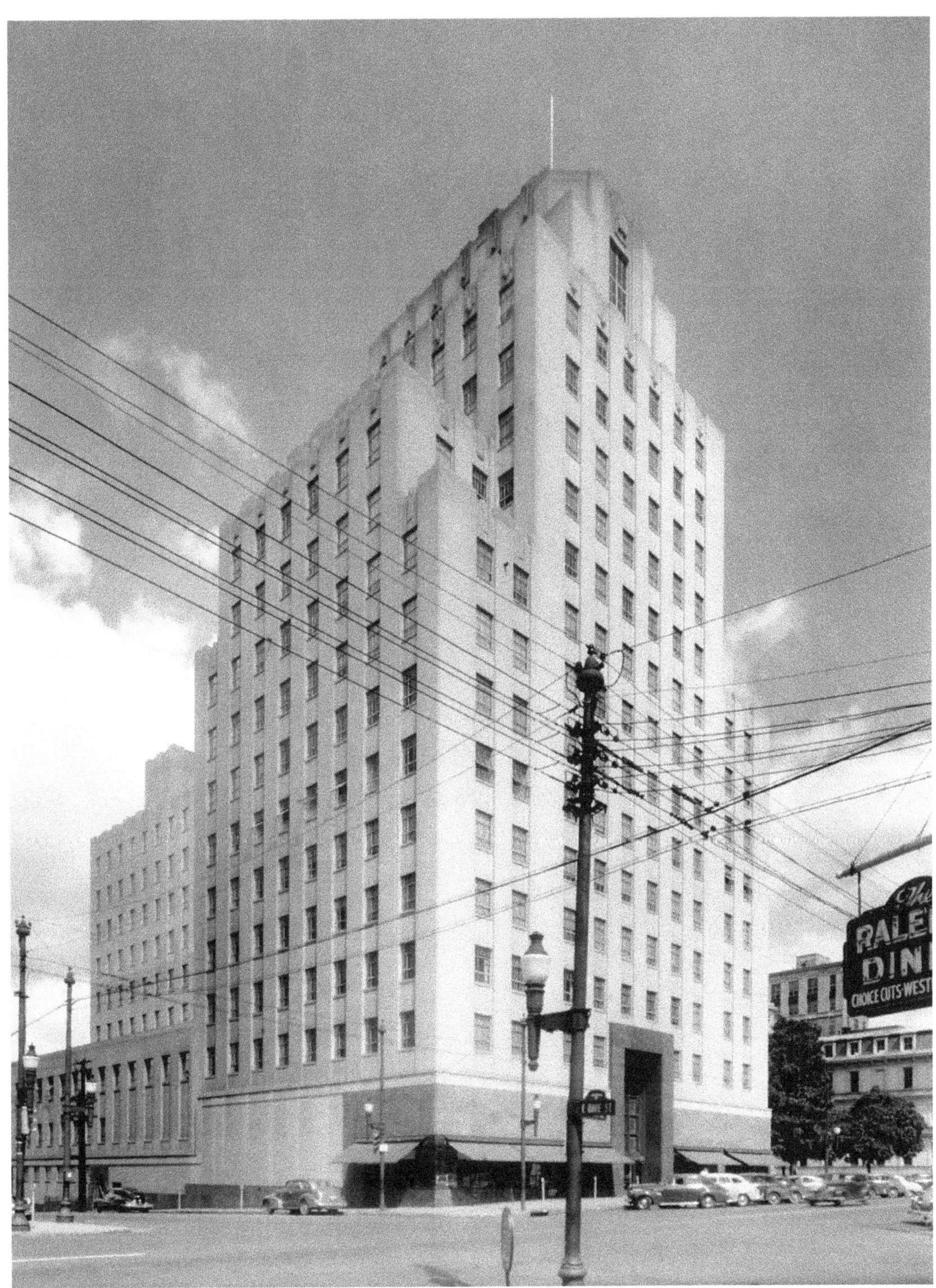

Erected in the early 1940s on the northwest corner of Fayetteville and Davie streets, the Durham Life Insurance Building was briefly Raleigh's tallest structure. Its first floor was home to the S&W Cafeteria, a popular downtown eatery. A neon sign at far-right advertises the Raleigh Diner.

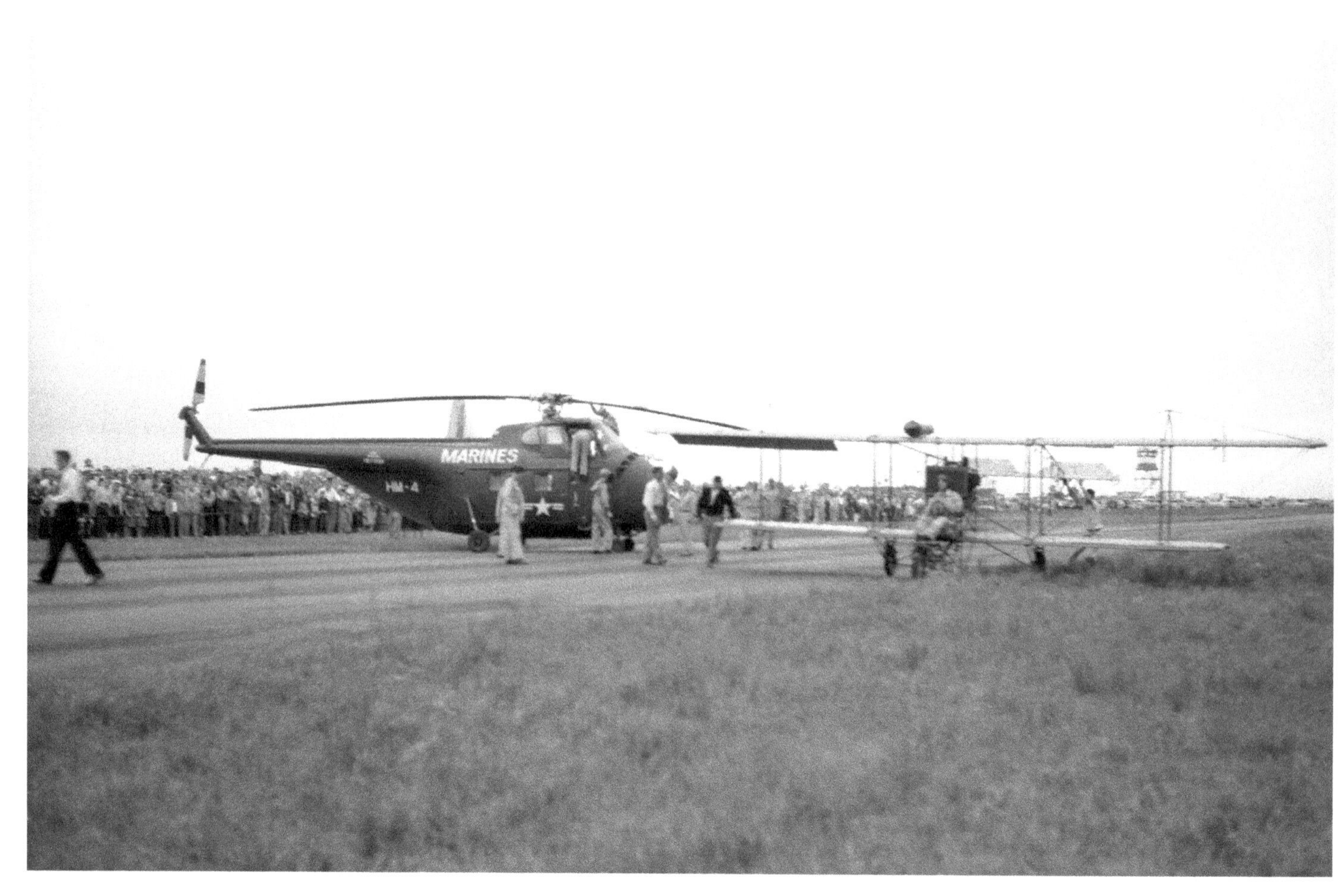

An aircraft exhibition at Raleigh-Durham Airport ca. 1950 brings old and new together as a Marine helicopter rests beside a Wright Brothers–style biplane.

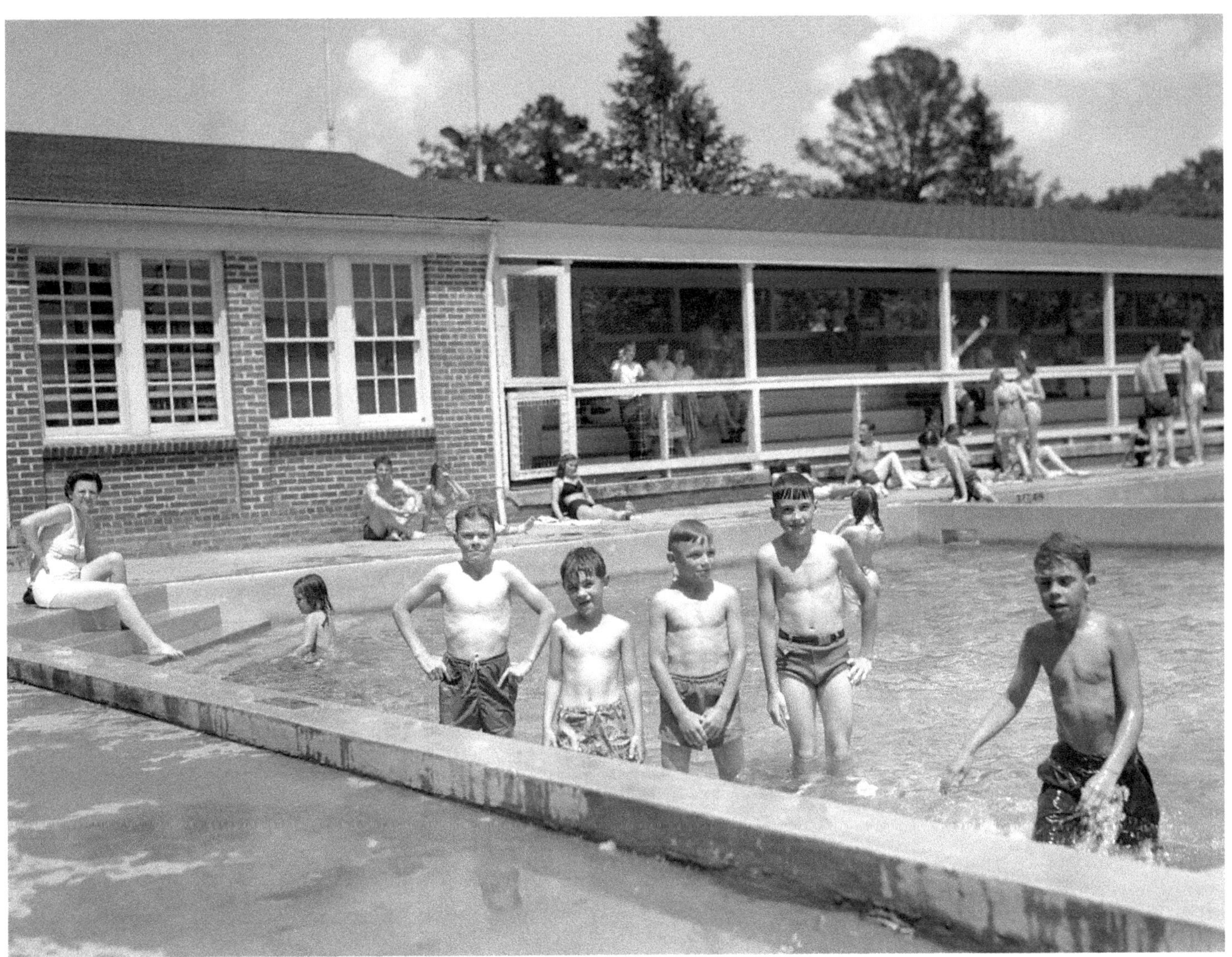

The first swimming pool opened in Raleigh's Pullen Park in 1891. At the time, only male patrons were admitted. By the 1940s, the park boasted a modern pool, a popular destination for kids wanting to cool off on a hot summer day.

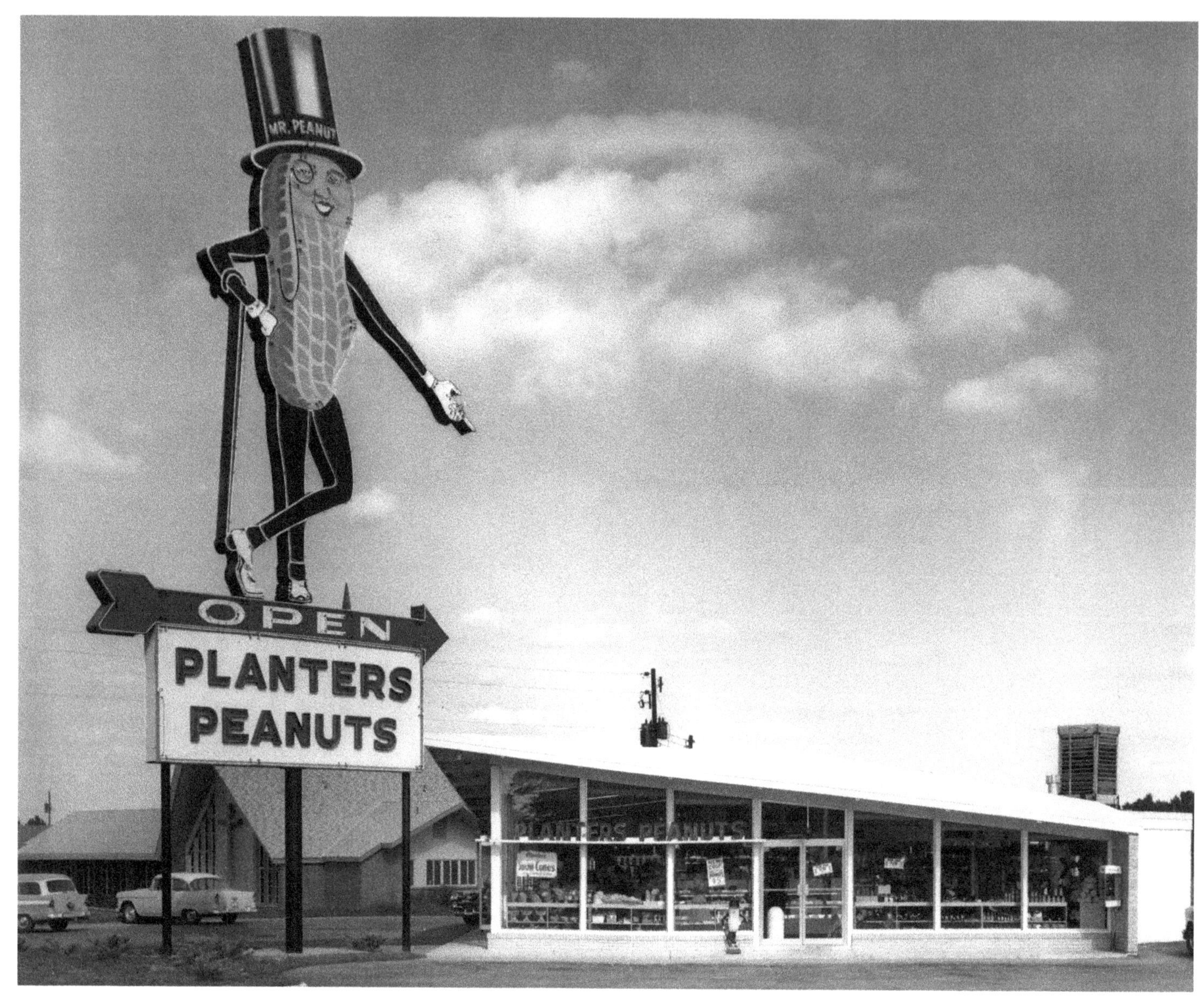

Mr. Peanut presides over the scene at Planters Peanuts on Raleigh's South Wilmington Street, ca. 1950s.

Visible here are the Raleigh Memorial Auditorium in the distance, a historical marker to President Andrew Johnson at lower-left, and various businesses. By the end of the 1960s many of Fayetteville Street's retail merchants would abandon downtown Raleigh for new suburban shopping centers and malls.

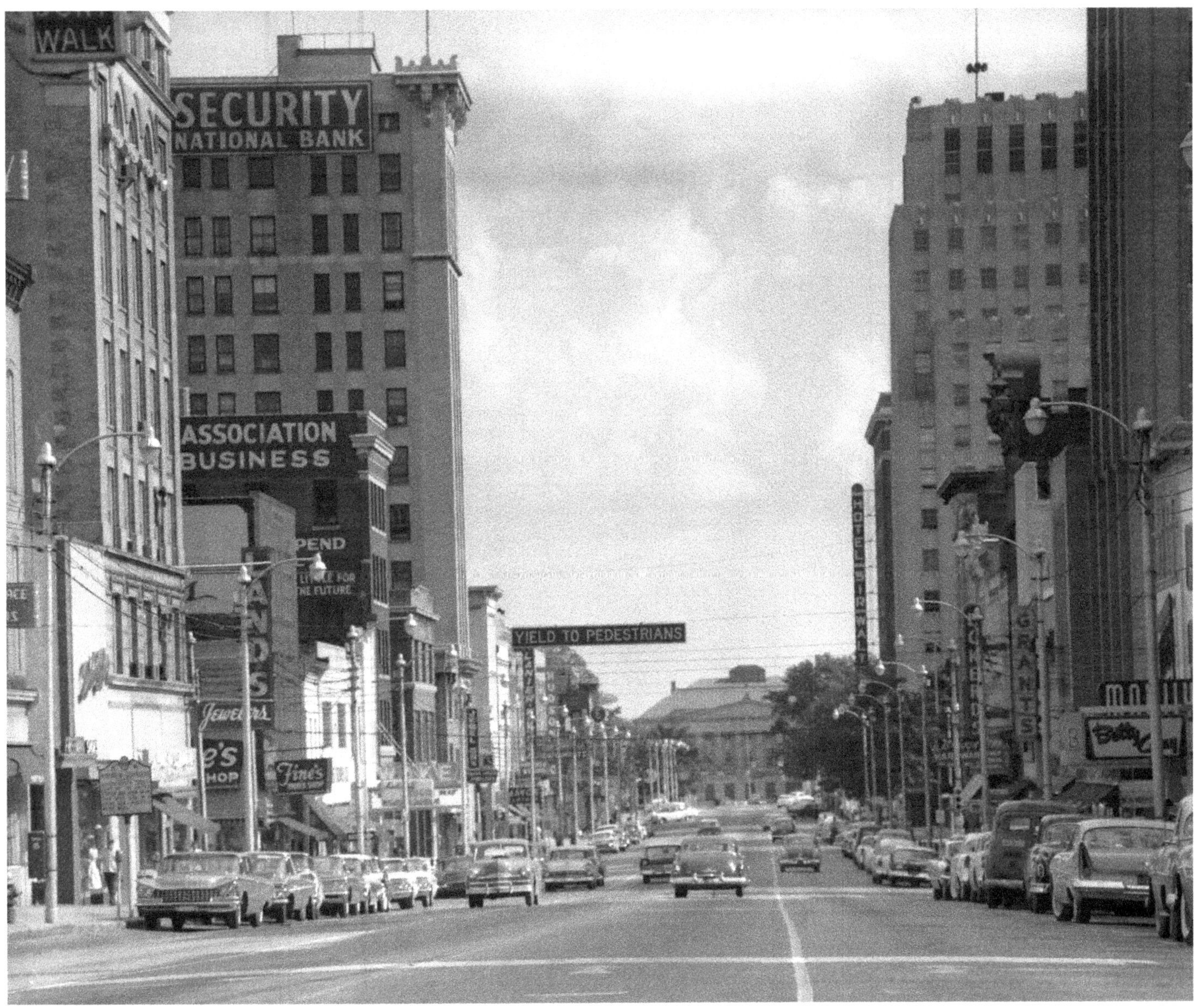

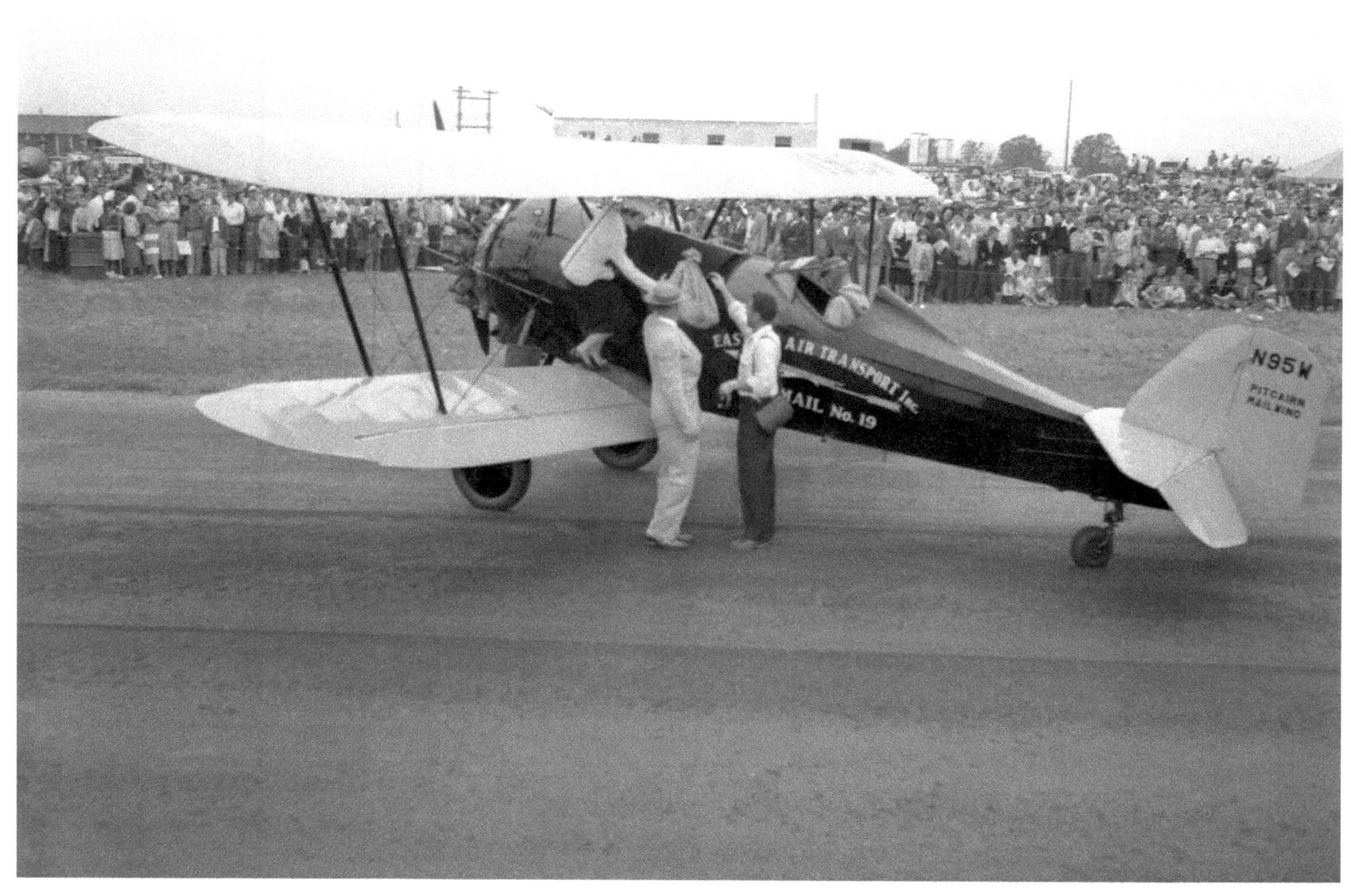

A large crowd watches a re-enactment at the Raleigh-Durham Airport in 1950. A mailbag is being loaded onto this 1930s version of an airmail transport plane.

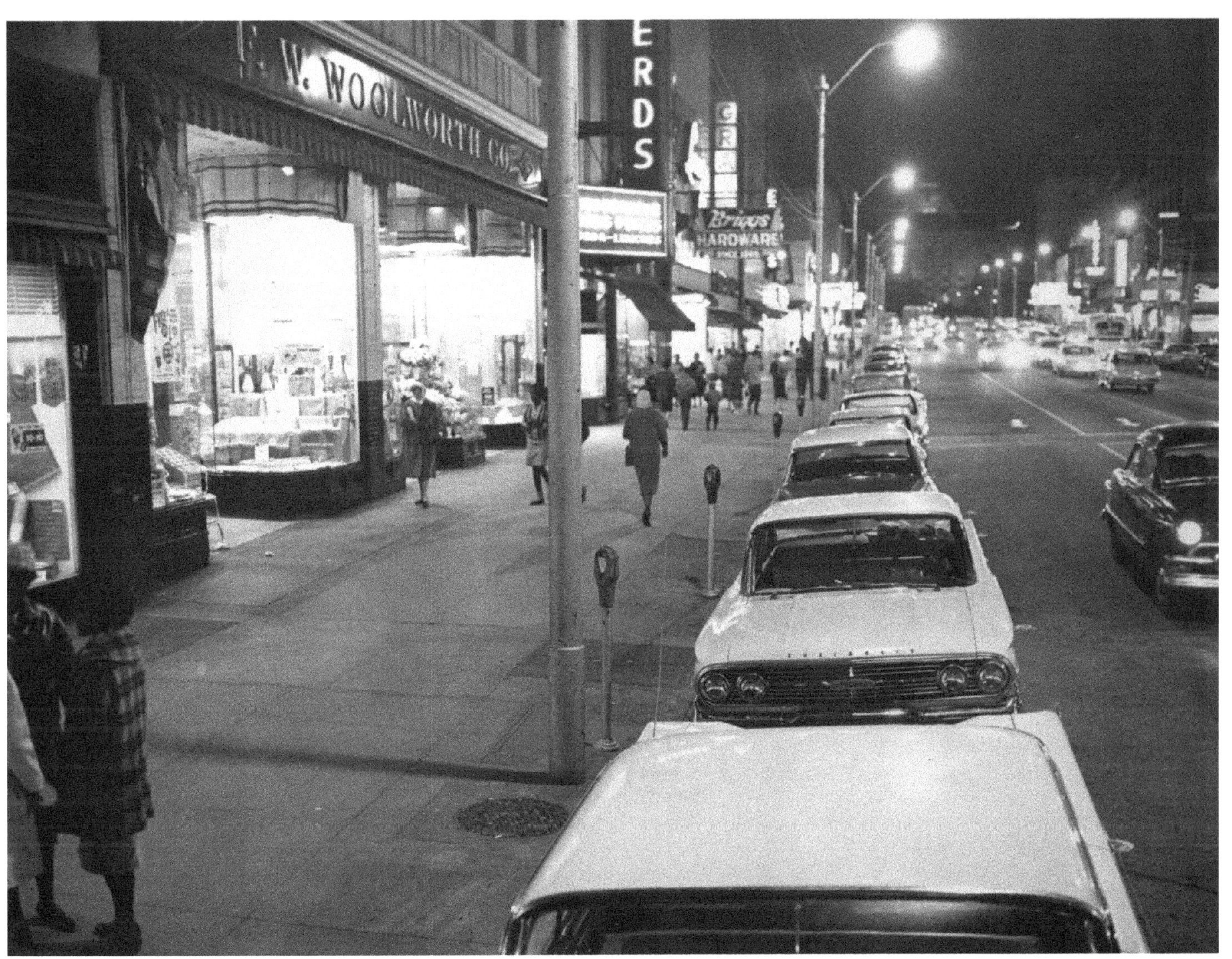

In 1962, downtown Raleigh was still the place for a stroll during evening hours.

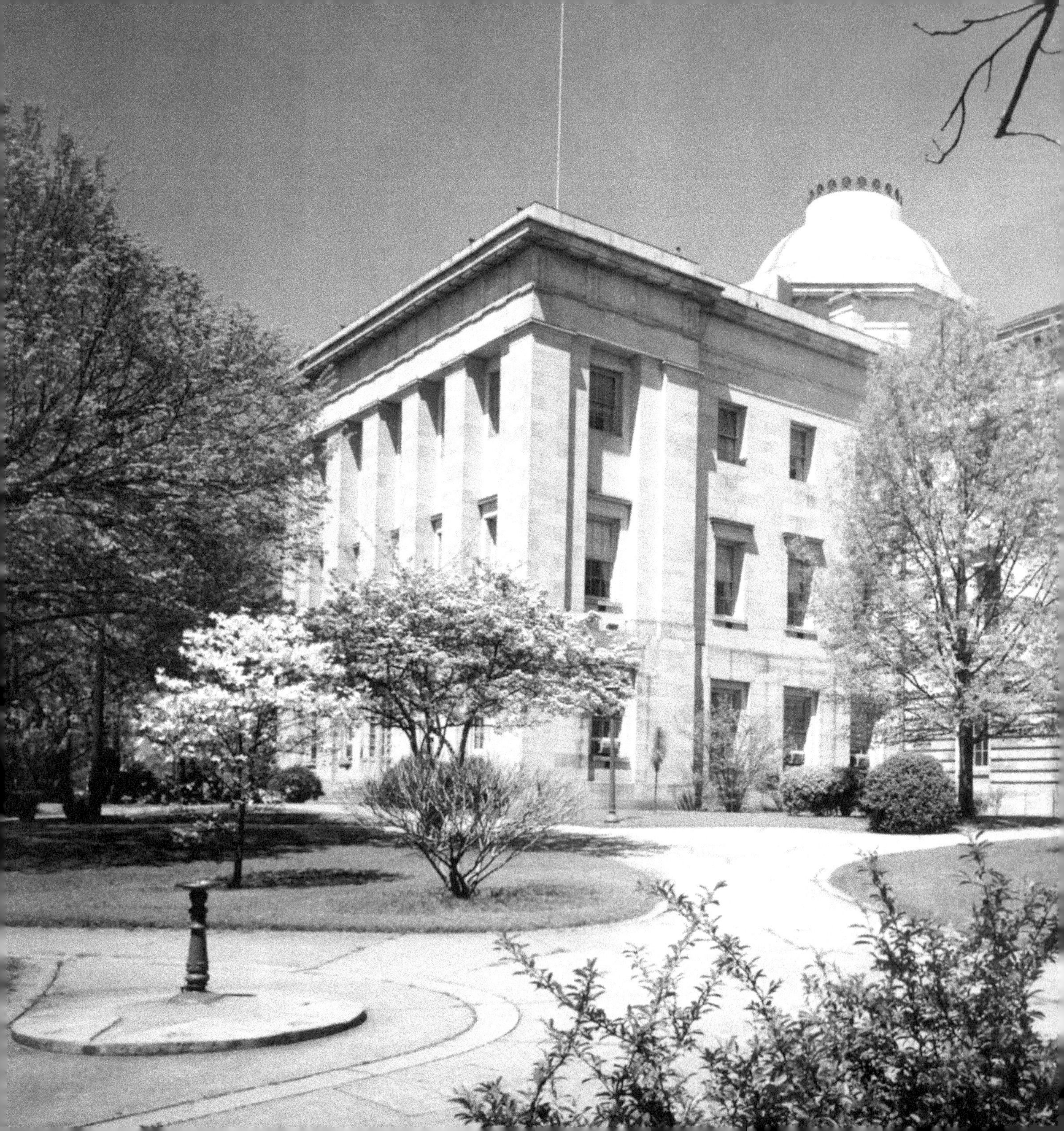

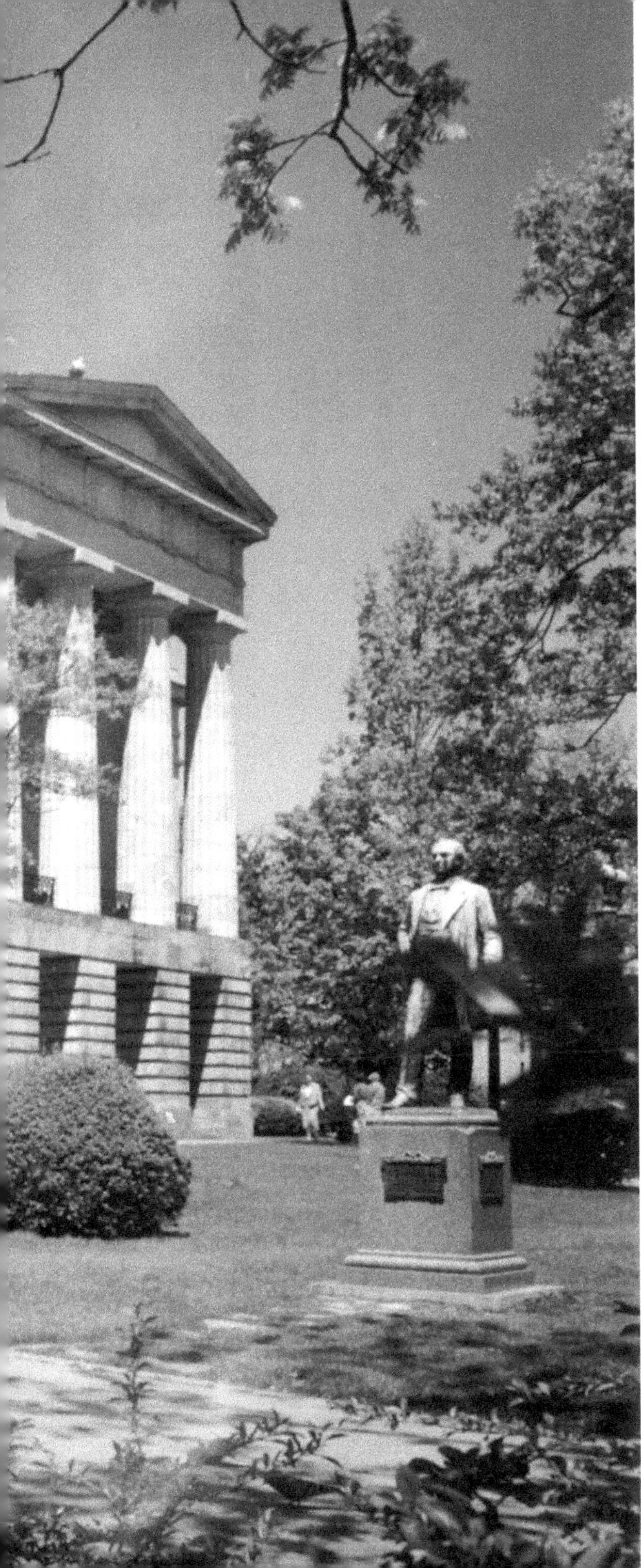

The grounds of the North Carolina State Capitol as they appeared in 1958. The General Assembly moved out of the building in 1962 when the State Legislative Building was completed, but the governor of North Carolina retains an office here. The building's legislative galleries have been restored and are open to the public.

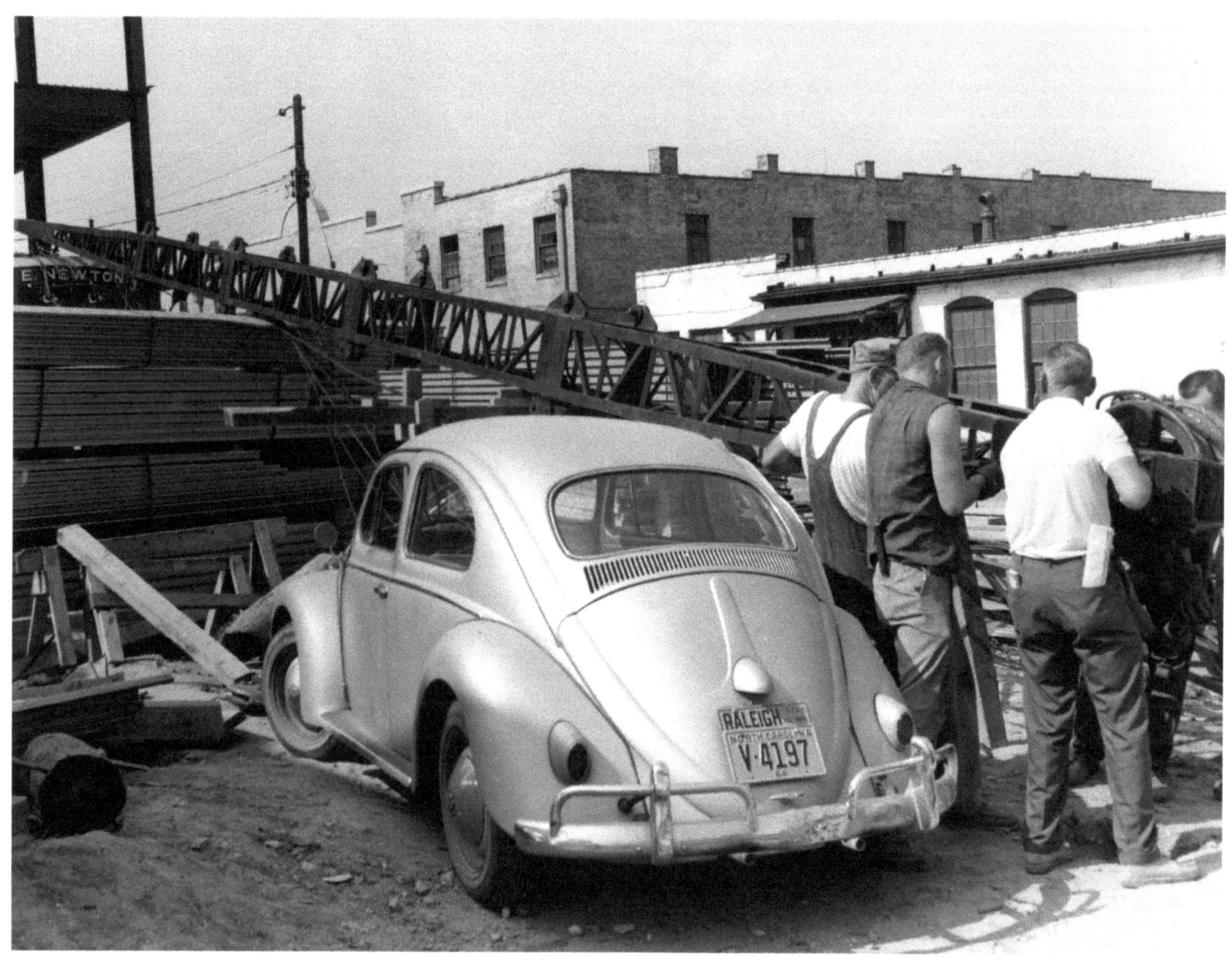

Men are at work on East Davie Street in Raleigh, ca. 1964.

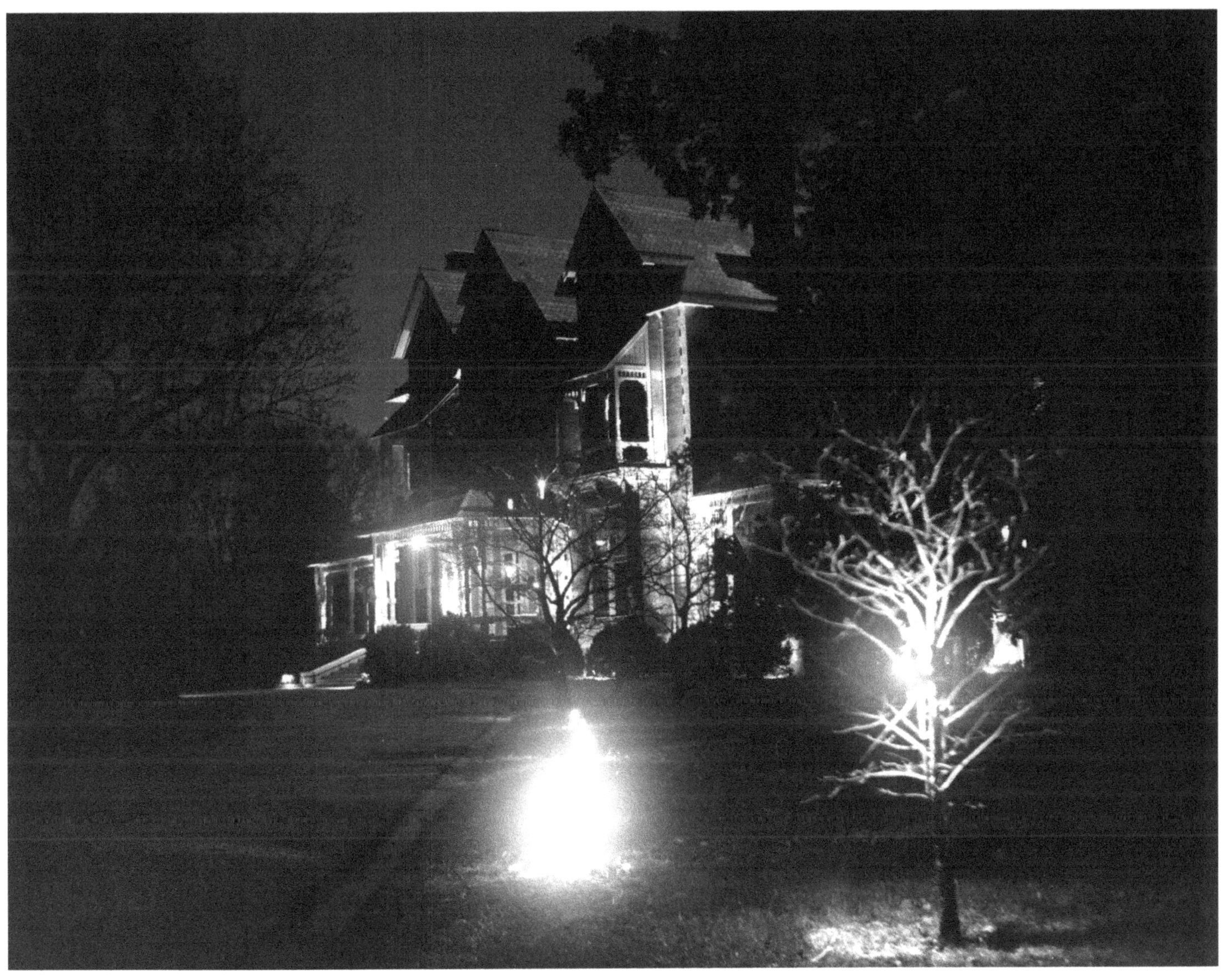

Designed by architects Samuel Sloan and A. G. Bauer, the North Carolina Executive Mansion was completed in 1891 on the former Burke Square in Raleigh. The official home for the state's governor and family, the residence is an outstanding example of Queen Anne–style Victorian architecture popular at the end of the nineteenth century.

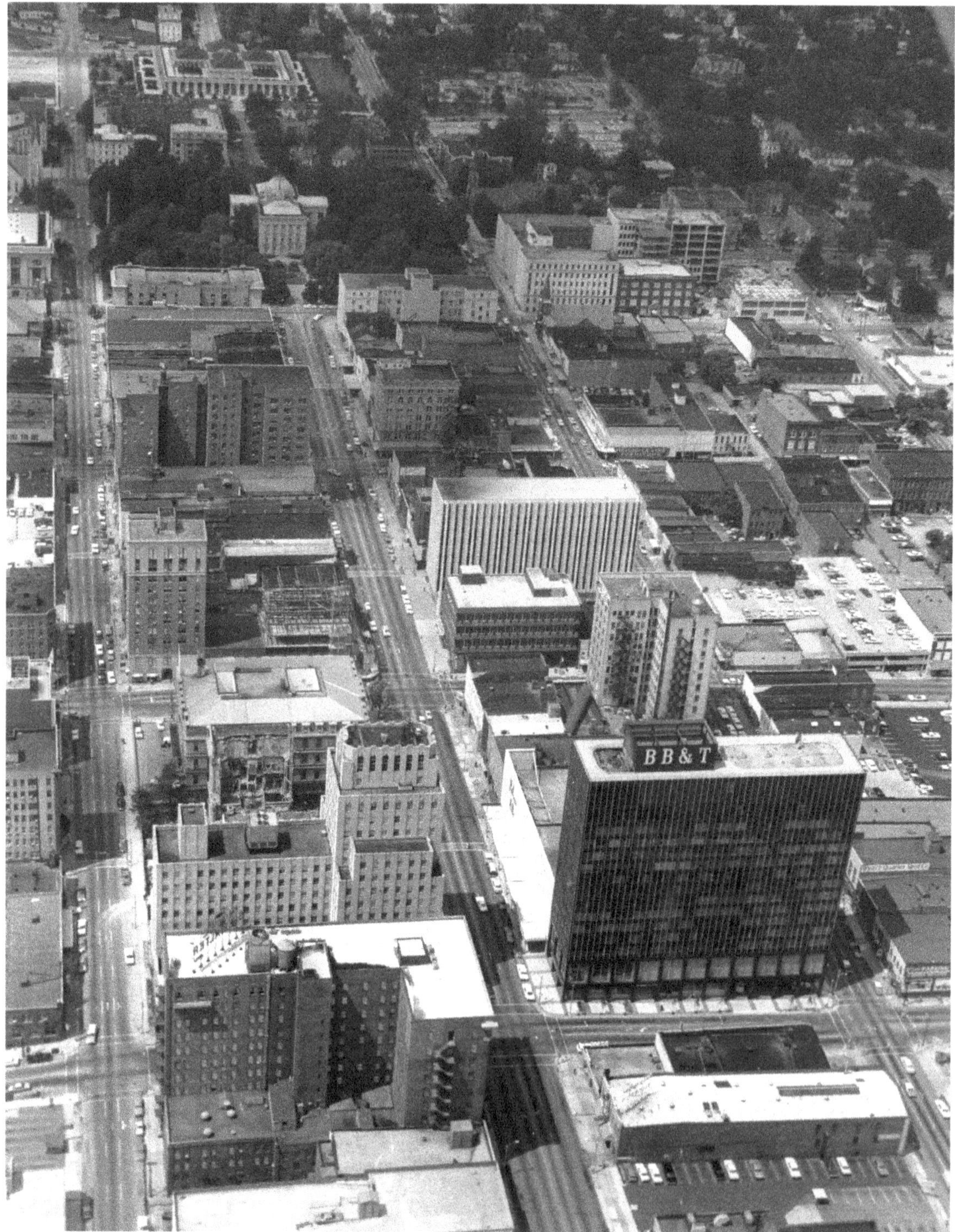

An aerial view of downtown Raleigh, ca. late 1960s. Running up the center of the image is Fayetteville Street, with the North Carolina State Capitol at its northern terminus and the State Legislative Building just beyond and at the top of the photo.

Notes on the Photographs

These notes, listed by page number, attempt to include all aspects known of the photographs. Each of the photographs is identified by the page number, photograph's title or description, photographer and collection, archive, and call or box number when applicable. Although every attempt was made to collect all available data, in some cases complete data was unavailable due to the age and condition of some of the photographs and records.

II **Trinity College**
North Carolina State Archives
N.64.7.22

VI **Streetcars**
North Carolina State Archives
N.53.15.8932

X **Street Scene**
North Carolina State Archives
lc-usf33-020526-m3

2 **E. Bessem's Tailor Shop**
North Carolina State Archives
N.74.12.483

3 **Seaboard Building**
North Carolina State Archives
N.77.10.511

4 **Day and Meadows Store**
Durham County Library
A036

5 **Parade**
North Carolina State Archives
N.75.5.448

6 **Marshals of Trinity College**
Durham County Library
A009

7 **State Capitol**
North Carolina State Archives
N.55.10.16

8 **Raleigh Light Infantry**
North Carolina State Archives
N.79.5.137

9 **Briggs Building**
North Carolina State Archives
N.75.8.354

10 **Yarborough House Hotel**
North Carolina State Archives
N.85.11.17

12 **Michaels Pharmacy**
Durham County Library
A002

13 **S. R. Carrington's Bar**
Durham County Library
A035

14 **North Carolina State Capitol**
North Carolina State Archives
N.53.15.353

15 **Fayetteville Street after Great Blizzard of 1899**
North Carolina State Archives
N.94.12.36

16 **Dig Out**
North Carolina State Archives
N.63.9.9

18 **Mrs. B. N. Duke and Children**
Durham County Library
B048

19 **Duke Homestead**
Durham County Library
B028

20 **Home of Washington Duke**
North Carolina State Archives
N.73.10.287

22 **Tobacco Factory of Washington Duke**
North Carolina State Archives
N.73.10.284

23 **Textile Mill Interior**
Durham County Library
B077

24 **Durham Fire Dept. hose wagon**
Durham County Library
C067

25 **Devereux House**
North Carolina State Archives
N.53.15.299

26 **Fairview**
Durham County Library
A038

27 **Brantley's Drug Store**
North Carolina State Archives
N.2000.4.25

28 **Duke Tobacco Co. Works**
North Carolina State Archives
N.75.3.2

30 **Eno Station**
Durham County Library
B074

31 **Greenhouse at Duke Farms**
North Carolina State Archives
N.74.4.165

32 **Meredith College**
North Carolina State Archives
N.75.5.396

34 **Nash Square**
North Carolina State Archives
CP&L, f.120

35 **Trinity College**
North Carolina State Archives
N.64.7.16

36 **Trinity College**
Durham County Library
C017

37 **W. Duke, Sons & Co.**
Durham County Library
C025

38 **Hotel Carrolina**
Durham County Library
OC003

40 **N.C. Mutual Insurance**
Durham County Library
C050

41 **Alspaugh Hall**
Durham County Library
C014

42 **The Bennett Place**
Library of Congress
lc-usz62-108506

44 **Teddy Roosevelt at Trinity College**
Durham County Library
C024

45 **N.C. Mutual Life Ins. Co.**
North Carolina State Archives
N.77.12.67

46 **Aunt Betty**
North Carolina State Archives
N.77.7.68

47 **Statue of Washington Duke**
North Carolina State Archives
N.73.10.288

48 **Fayetteville Street**
North Carolina State Archives
N.69.8.19

49 **Paving Lane Street 6 June 1906**
North Carolina State Archives
Ph.C.68 CP&L Raleigh f.188

50 **Trinity Baseball Club**
Durham County Library
C063

51 **Stagg Pavilion**
Durham County Library
C007

52 **A Circus Parade**
North Carolina State Archives
N.74.6.565

53 **Durham Traction Co. Trolley Car**
Durham County Library
D198

54 **Citizens National Bank**
North Carolina State Archives
N.53.15.7936

55 **Welcome**
North Carolina State Archives
N.64.8.155

56 **Streetcars**
North Carolina State Archives
CP&L f.98

57 **NCSU Football Team**
North Carolina State Archives
N.53.17.239

58 **Century Post Office**
North Carolina State Archives
CP&L f.99

59 **Horse-drawn Buggy**
North Carolina State Archives
N.70.9.117

60 **Holiday Hall**
North Carolina State Archives
CP&L f.179

61 **Pilot Mills Cotton Band**
North Carolina State Archives
N.53.16.2414

62 **Baptist Female University**
North Carolina State Archives
CP&L f.183

64 **State Prison**
North Carolina State Archives
CP&L f.192

66 **Fairview-Durham**
North Carolina State Archives
N.74.4.160

67 **View of the Capitol from Hillsboro Street**
North Carolina State Archives
CP&L f.117

68 **Martin Street**
North Carolina State Archives
CP&L f.119

70 **Union Station**
Durham County Library
D041

71 **Horse-drawn Hose Wagon**
Durham County Library
D078

72 **Booker T. Washington Visits Durham**
Durham County Library
D176

73 **Motordrome Arena**
Durham County Library
D096

74 **Panorama of Downtown**
North Carolina State Archives
CP&L f.100

76 **Burned-out Main Street**
Durham County Library
D064

77 **Horse-drawn Delivery Carts**
North Carolina State Archives
CP&L f.104

78 **Raleigh Banking & Trust**
North Carolina State Archives
CP&L f.175

79 **Fayetteville Street**
North Carolina State Archives
CP&L f.89

80 **Durham Sign**
Durham County Library
D077

81 **The American Tobacco Company**
North Carolina State Archives
N.77.9.19

82 **Downtown**
Durham County Library
CP&L f.103

83 **Martin Street**
North Carolina State Archives
CP&L f.121

84 **Martin Street at Night**
North Carolina State Archives
CP&L f.144

86 **Raleigh-Durham Airport**
Durham County Library
F098

87 **Dedication of Bennett Place**
Durham County Library
OE050

88 **Construction of Duke Chapel**
North Carolina State Archives
N.80.10.36

89 **The Orpheum Theatre at Night**
Durham County Library
E052

90 **Downtown Durham Parade**
Durham County Library
OE046

91 **Andrew Johnson's Birthplace**
North Carolina State Archives
CP&L f.195

92 **Night View**
North Carolina State Archives
CP&L f.134

93 **Raleigh-Durham Highway**
Durham County Library
E076

94 **Carillon Presentation at Duke University**
North Carolina State Archives
N.75.2.248

96 **Al Stewart**
North Carolina State Archives
N.2003.8.31

97 **Sidewalk**
North Carolina State Archives
CP&L f.107

98 **Football Team N.C. A&M-NC State**
North Carolina State Archives
N.53.17.236

99 **Football Team and Coaches NC A&M**
North Carolina State Archives
N.53.17.238

100 **National Highway**
North Carolina State Archives
N.96.11.29

101 **Laying Road Surface**
North Carolina State Archives
N.96.11.32

102 **Stadium at Duke**
North Carolina State Archives
N.53.15.8342

103 **Davidson Street**
North Carolina State Archives
N.53.15.9162

104 **Trinity College Board**
Durham County Library
E078

105 **Masonic Temple**
North Carolina State Archives
N.53.15.7877

106 **Duke Universities East Campus**
North Carolina State Archives
N.75.2.249

107 **Boy in Cockpit**
North Carolina State Archives
N.2003.8.26

108 **Curtis Travel Air and Waco Planes**
North Carolina State Archives
N.2003.8.23

110 **Academy of Music**
North Carolina State Archives
N.53.16.1525

111 **Bloomsbury Park Trolley**
North Carolina State Archives
CP&L f.197

112 **East Hargett Street**
North Carolina State Archives
CP&L f.112

113 **Wake County Courthouse**
North Carolina State Archives
CP&L f.194

114 **Governor and Mrs. McLeon**
North Carolina State Archives
N53.15.4756

115 **Tree-sitter at Dennis's Gas Station**
Durham County Library
E127

116 **Hillsborough Street**
North Carolina State Archives
N.98.5.170

117 **Fayetteville and Hargett Streets**
North Carolina State Archives
CP&L f.176

118 **State Capitol at Night**
North Carolina State Archives
CP&L f.162

119 **Movie Made in Durham**
Durham County Library
OF017

120 **West Durham**
Durham County Library
OF026

121 **West Side Pharmacy**
Durham County Library
F034

122 **Durham County School**
North Carolina State Archives
N.81.3.14

124 **North Carolina Revenue Building**
North Carolina State Archives
CP&L f.172

125 **Rex Hospital**
North Carolina State Archives
N.53.15.4735

126 **Five Points Drug Store**
North Carolina State Archives
N.87.1.3

127 **Hotel Carolina**
North Carolina State Archives
N.53.15.7848

128 **Earthen Ramparts**
Library of Congress
HABS NC,28-MANT.V,1-C-

129 **Memorial Auditorium**
North Carolina State Archives
CP&L f.193

130 **Raleigh Municipal Building**
North Carolina State Archives
CP&L Ph.C. f.185

131 **Governor Clyde R. Hoey in Front of the State Capitol**
North Carolina State Archives
N.53.15.6508

132 **Tobacco Tote**
Library of Congress
lc-usf33-030670-M2

134 **Crowds Outside Tobacco Warehouse**
Library of Congress
lc-usf33-030669-M2

135 **Durham County Women's Work Center**
North Carolina State Archives
N.84.12.6

136 **Roycroft's Tobacco Warehouse**
Library of Congress
lc-usf34-005506-E

137 **Preacher**
Library of Congress
lc-usf33-030740-M5

138 **Old Catholic Orphanage**
North Carolina State Archives
N.71.6.568

140 **Downtown Parade**
Durham County Library
F068

141 **Kay Kyser**
Library of Congress
lc-usf33-030683-M3

142 **Cars in Field**
Library of Congress
lc-usf34-052651-D

144 **Broughton High School**
North Carolina State Archives
CP&L f.187

145 **Detective Division**
North Carolina State Archives
N.97.12.5

146 **Gas Station**
North Carolina State Archives
N.53.15.6924

147 **Harris Barber College**
North Carolina State Archives
N.53.15.4580

148 **Boon-Iseley Drug Store**
North Carolina State Archives
N.53.15.7198

149 **The Royal Theater**
North Carolina State Archives
N.53.15.7203

150 **Merry Christmas**
North Carolina State Archives
N.53.15.4534

152 **Liggett-Myers Chesterfield Cigarette Plant**
North Carolina State Archives
N.74.7.679

154 **Durham-Dunn Bus Line**
Durham County Library
G116

156 **A Durham Policeman**
Library of Congress
lc-usf33-020526-M5

157 **Super Market**
Library of Congress
lc-usf33-020523-M1

158 **Raleigh Centennial Parade**
North Carolina State Archives
N.53.16.3807

159 **Odd Fellows Building**
North Carolina State Archives
CP&L f.156

160 **Pullen Park**
North Carolina State Archives
No.40.1.11-21

162 **Raleigh Bus Station**
North Carolina State Archives
N.53.15.5903

163 **Fayetteville Street from the North Carolina State Capitol**
North Carolina State Archives
CP&L f.96

164 **Outside the Tobacco Warehouses**
Library of Congress
lc-usf33-020527-M4

166 **300-block**
North Carolina State Archives
CP&L ph.c. f.131

167 **Passengers Board a City Bus**
North Carolina State Archives
N.53.16.3378

168 **Young Flower Vendor**
Library of Congress
lc-usf33-020514-M2

170 **Devereux Meadow**
North Carolina State Archives
N.53.16.3819

171 **Duke University Football Stadium**
Durham County Library
F036

172 200-block
North Carolina State Archives
CP&L f.110

173 Statue of James B. Duke
North Carolina State Archives
N.75.2.251

174 Golden Tap Orange Drink
North Carolina State Archives
N.53.15.2414

175 Fayetteville Street in Downtown Raleigh
North Carolina State Archives
CP&L f.155

176 Spelling Bee
North Carolina State Archives
N.53.16.2341

178 Seaboard Air Line Railroad
North Carolina State Archives
N.53.15.9615

179 300-block of Salisbury Street in Raleigh
North Carolina State Archives
CP&L f.124

180 World War II Parade
North Carolina State Archives
N.2004.4.1

181 Big Star Mammoth Food Center
North Carolina State Archives
N.53.15.9838

182 Blackwelders
North Carolina State Archives
N.53.15.6929

183 Fayetteville Street
North Carolina State Archives
CP&L f.111

184 An Attraction at Fort Raleigh
Library of Congress
nc0400

185 Fort Raleigh
Library of Congress
Habs nc,28-mant.v,1-d-

186 Reynolds Coliseum
North Carolina State Archives
N.53.15.3636

187 Fayetteville and Hargett Streets
North Carolina State Archives
CP&L f.116

188 Street Scene
Library of Congress
lc-usf33-020522-M5

189 Durham Life Insurance Building
North Carolina State Archives
CP&L f.170

190 Aircraft Exhibition
North Carolina State Archives
NO.53.9.1

191 Swimming Pool at Pullen Park
North Carolina State Archives
N.53.16.3832

192 Mr. Peanut
North Carolina State Archives
Ph.C.14,Box11,#78

193 Street Scene
North Carolina State Archives
N.76.9.2509

194 Raleigh-Durham Airport
Durham County Library
H013

195 Downtown Raleigh
North Carolina State Archives
CP&L F.142

196 Grounds of the North Carolina State Capitol
North Carolina State Archives
CP&L F.165

198 Men at Work
North Carolina State Archives
CP&L F.159

199 North Carolina Executive Mansion
North Carolina State Archives
CP&L F.167

200 Aerial View of Downtown
North Carolina State Archives
CP&L F.151

HISTORIC PHOTOS OF RALEIGH-DURHAM

By the late nineteenth century, the city of Raleigh-Durham was a vibrant cultural center of the East. Through changing fortunes, Raleigh-Durham has continued to grow and prosper by overcoming adversity and maintaining the strong, independent culture of its citizens.

Historic Photos of Raleigh-Durham captures this journey through still photography selected from the finest archives. From the first tobacco factory to the retail district along Fayetteville Street, the construction of Duke University to the opening of Camp Butner, *Historic Photos of Raleigh-Durham* follows life, government, education, and events throughout the city's history.

This volume captures unique and rare scenes through the lens of hundreds of historic photographs. Published in striking black and white, these images communicate historic events and everyday life of two centuries of people building a unique and prosperous city.

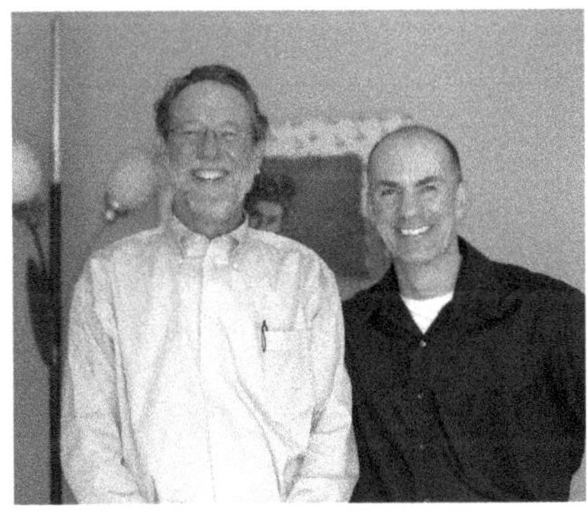

Dusty Wescott (left) has lived most of his life in the Raleigh-Durham area. He is a twenty-three-year museum professional serving in both a natural science museum as an exhibit designer and fabricator and in a local history museum as curator. He is currently working as a freelance designer and fabricator with the North Carolina Museum of History. He holds a bachelor of science degree in biology from Appalachian State University and lives in Durham with his wife and two children.

Kenneth E. Peters (right) is an educator, historian, and visual artist. He earned a bachelors degree in art history and studio arts from the University of Maryland and a master of arts in legal and ethical studies from the University of Baltimore. Moving to Raleigh in 1999, Peters served as the Director of Education and Outreach at the Raleigh City Museum until 2006. He now serves as an educational interpreter at Historic Oak View County Park.

WWW.TURNERPUBLISHING.COM

www.ingramcontent.com/pod-product-compliance
Lightning Source LLC
LaVergne TN
LVHW060606110826
845154LV00003B/47
9781683369523